THE MODERN TREASURY OF CHRISTMAS PLAYS

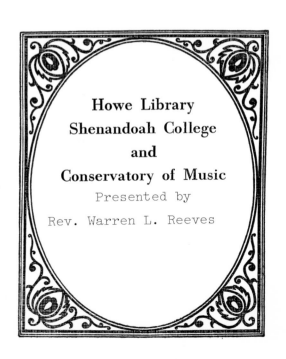

The Modern Treasury of Christmas Plays

A COLLECTION OF ONE-ACT PLAYS FOR CHURCH AND SCHOOL

Edited and Compiled

by

LAWRENCE M. BRINGS, M.A.

Formerly professor of speech at Northwestern Lutheran Theological Seminary, Luther Theological Seminary, and the University of Minnesota.

Selected and adapted for production by teenagers and adults for the inspiration of audiences and participants.

Publishers

T. S. DENISON & COMPANY

Minneapolis

PRODUCTION RIGHTS

All the plays included in this book are available in separate pamphlet form at 50c a copy. Amateurs may produce any of these plays without payment of a royalty fee, provided that the required number of copies as specified in each instance are purchased.

Other Books by Lawrence M. Brings

Prize Winning Orations for High School Contests

The Christmas Entertainment Book

Choice Comedies for Junior High Schools

The Golden Book of Church Plays

Clever Introductions for Chairmen

Humorous Introductions for Emcees

The Master Stunt Book

PREFACE

If a survey were to be made, no doubt the resulting statistics would show that more plays and pageants are presented during the Christmas season by more groups than at any other period during the year. It is significant that this medium should be used to recreate the spirit of Christmas in the hearts and minds of men. The emotional impact of the dramatic form has been proved to be a universal vehicle for observing the birth of Christ.

Although there are literally thousands of plays written around the Christmas theme, producers many times find it difficult to find a suitable play patterned to their needs.

In this volume, I have endeavored to assemble a wide variety of plays and pageants that treat the Christmas theme with solemnity, dignity, and sincerity. I believe that the story of the Nativity deserves such an approach and that most groups desire to concentrate their efforts on plays of this type. However, I have included a few plays that follow a more modern treatment.

In this volume you will find a careful selection of plays. The settings in most instances are simple and easy; the casts vary from five to ten players, with provision for choir participation and extra players. The playing time varies from twenty-five minutes to one hour.

I have directed many plays for church and school groups and it has been my experience that finding a suitable play tailor-made for a specific group or situation was always a primary problem. I hope that this compilation will provide an easy way for directors to examine a group of plays under the covers of one volume and help to alleviate the stress and strain of a last-minute search for an appropriate play. If this book accomplished this purpose, then my effort in assembling this material will not have been in vain.

—Lawrence M. Brings.

CONTENTS

9

10

THE
SHEPHERD OF BETHLEHEM

A ONE-ACT CHRISTMAS PLAY

By

JANET KNOX

PRODUCTION RIGHTS

THE SHEPHERD OF BETHLEHEM
For eight boys and eight girls

CHARACTERS
(In order of their first appearance)

CARMI ....*A shepherd of Bethlehem*
MERAB ....*His wife*
ABIGAIL ⎫
MICHAL ⎬...........................*Their daughters*
JUDITH ⎭
THREE ANGELS.............*Heralds of the newborn king*
ASAPH ....*An aged shepherd*
CASPAR ⎫
MELCHIOR ⎬................*Two wise men of the East*
JOEL ⎫
EPHRAIM ⎬.................*Other Bethlehem shepherds*
ABIHU ⎭
MARY ....*The mother of Jesus*
JOSEPH ....*Her husband*
TWO ROMAN SOLDIERS...........*In King Herod's service*

NOTE.—*The parts of the wise men and the Roman soldiers should be doubled.*

PLACE—*The home of a shepherd on the outskirts of Bethlehem.*

TIME—*The night of the nativity of Christ, and an afternoon some weeks later.*

TIME OF PLAYING—*About thirty-five minutes.*

12

COSTUMES AND CHARACTERISTICS

Carmi is a man of thirty-six or -seven. He is unlearned and rough, but fundamentally kind, and a leader among the shepherds. His apparent ill temper in the latter part of the play is due more to a troubled state of mind than to a morose nature. He wears a short brown or grey tunic and a cloak of sheepskin or leather, with sandals on his feet.

Merab is a good-looking woman in her early thirties. She is both gentle and spirited, and in spite of her humble surroundings shows much racial pride. She wears a close-fitting tunic of dark red with a short veil and a girdle of a lighter shade.

Abigail, aged twelve, is a gentle, dreamy girl, but accustomed to assume considerable responsibility about the house. She wears a tunic of any becoming color, and when she goes out, a mantle in a contrasting color. Her hair is bound about the forehead with a band matching her tunic.

MICHAL, aged eight, in contrast to her sister is quick of speech and action, mischievous, and somewhat of a tomboy. She wears garments similar to Abigail's.

Judith, aged four, is sweet and shy, and except when playing with her sisters, stays close to Merab. Her garments are like those of the other children. This part may be taken by a small child older than four years.

The three angels wear long white robes with flowing sleeves. If desired, they may have silver or tinsel headbands.

Caspar and Melchior are bronze-faced, bearded men. They wear rich-looking robes and cloaks, and headdresses resembling a bishop's miter, all ornamented with gold and silver embroidery. Their legs, above their sandals, are bound with leather leggings.

Asaph, Joel, Ephraim, and Abihu, the four shepherds, are simple, good-hearted men, under their rough appearance. They all wear clothing similar to Carmi's, except that Asaph's appears older and more worn than that of the other men. Joel is the youngest of the shepherds, being little more than a boy, and is of a visionary nature.

Mary is a beautiful girl in her early twenties. Her recent motherhood has given her a kind of gentle dignity, and she is collected and unafraid in the midst of danger. She wears a robe of bright blue, with a long veil of white or light blue and a girdle to match.

Joseph is a man nearing forty, with a kindly face and dark hair and beard. His manner is preoccupied because of his concern for Mary and her child. He wears a yellow tunic with dark brown mantle and headdress, and appears ready for a long journey. His clothes are of better quality than those of the shepherds.

The two Roman soldiers, while doing their duty in a soldierly fashion, show no signs of cruelty. They wear tunics to the knee, and over these the armor of a light-armed foot soldier, with helmet, shield, and sword. Descriptions of armor may be found in almost any book of Roman history. If the armor is difficult to obtain, it may be successfully imitated with light weight bristol board which has been silvered.

PROPERTIES

Rude table
Two wooden benches
Wooden chest
Two low beds (mattresses or pads, with bedding, laid on the floor)
Water jar
Gourd dipper
Wooden strip with row of pegs
Several cloaks or mantles
Shepherd's crook
Lamp
Five or six smooth stones
Leather scraps
Cord
Leather scrip or bag

Earthenware bowl	Wicker basket
Wooden spoon	Money pouch in chest
Cruse of oil	Small amount of whole grain
Small stone mortar	Small amount of straw

For Carmi, shepherd's sling, awl. For Merab, distaff and spindle with wool, small cloth-wrapped package supposedly containing food, needle and thread, child's garment to sew. For Asaph, a staff. For Melchior, pouch containing coins.

The beds are made by laying mattresses or pads on the floor and spreading bedding over them. A shallow vessel with oil and wick will serve for the lamp. If a stone mortar is not available, a round block of wood, hollowed out so that the upper stone will fit into it, may be used. Merab's distaff is a pointed stick of wood on one end of which the wool is loosely bound. It is held under the left arm, in spinning, and the thread twirled with the fingers of the left hand. The spindle is a shorter stick around which the spun thread is twisted with the right hand. Ordinary white yarn may be wound on the spindle and attached to the distaff under the wool, and twirled lightly between the fingers to simulate spinning.

MUSIC NOTE.—The old carol, *"Hark! What Mean Those Holy Voices?"* suggested for the angels' song, is presumably familiar to most persons. If not, however, it may be found is "Denison's Christmas Songs and Carols," which may be obtained from the publishers for the price of 50 cents, postpaid.

PUBLISHERS' NOTE.—For the sake of dramatic effect, it has been necessary in this play to compress into a short space of time events which probably occurred over a much longer period. The author has tried to accomplish this without doing violence to the spirit of the biblical narrative.

THE SHEPHERD OF BETHLEHEM

SCENE: *The humble one-room home of* CARMI, *a shepherd, on the hills near Bethlehem. There are two doors: one up center, opening out of doors, and one at left, leading to an inner storeroom. There is a window in the right wall. The room is meagerly furnished. At center is a rude table on which are a lamp (a wick thrust in a vessel of oil), a shepherd's scrip or leather bag, a handful of leather scraps and pieces of stout cord, and a small pile of round smooth stones such as can be hurled from a sling. A wooden bench is behind the table, up stage, and another bench is under the window at right. A plain, stout chest is up center, left of door, and near it, leaning against the wall, is a shepherd's crook. Against the left wall, up stage from the storeroom door, stands a large water jar, with a gourd dipper or similar drinking vessel hanging above it. Down left is a row of pegs on which are hanging several cloaks and mantles of dark colors and coarse materials. In the upper right corner are two low beds, one along the right wall, the other along the back wall. It is late at night, time for the night watch to go on duty over the flocks pastured on the hillsides nearby.*

At rise of curtain, MICHAL *and* JUDITH *are asleep in the bed near the back wall.* ABIGAIL *is sleeping in the bed at right. The outer clothes of the three children are folded in three piles on the bench at right.* CARMI, *about to join the watch, is sitting on the bench at center, mending his shepherd's sling.* MERAB *is standing near him, twirling her spindle.*

MERAB. Mend it stout and strong, Carmi. I have a feeling thou'lt need it to-night.

16

CARMI.. Why? Hast thou heard the wolves howling already?

MERAB. Nay, it is only a strange feeling I've had all day—

CARMI (*looking up*). Of ill to come?

MERAB. I know not. Only I wish thou wert not with the night watch. I would have thee at home to-night.

CARMI (*working a piece of leather in his fingers*). Peace to thy forebodings, wife. Thou'rt but excited by the crowds coming in to the enrolling. Yet we are far enough from the town that there is naught to fright thee.

MERAB. Hast thou been in yet to pay thy tax?

CARMI (*piercing the leather of his sling with an awl, and passing a string through the hole*). Nay. Not until to-morrow. It is a grievous burden, that tax of Caesar's. What with Judith's illness and the loss of so many sheep these last few months, it lieth heavily upon me.

MERAB (*twirling her spindle thoughtfully*). When the King of the Jews comes we shall be delivered from all that.

CARMI (*tying firm knots in his strings*). Nay, count not upon that, wife. We have looked for him long, and he hath not come. We shall not see him in our day, I think. The best we can hope for is that one will arise in the place of Herod, who is not so cruel and so harsh as he.

MERAB (*with spirit*). If ye men of Israel would arise as in the old days, ye could drive out Herod as David drove out the Philistines, and have whom ye would for king!

CARMI. Nay, Merab. Thou knowest we are sore scattered and there is none to lead us. All Rome is behind Herod. Nay, the time of our deliverance is not yet ripe. When it is, the God of our fathers will raise up a warrior and a king for his people. Until then we must wait.

MERAB. Yea, and old Simeon, who dwelleth hard by the Temple in Jerusalem, saith we have not long now to wait. I talked with him but the last time we were in the city. It hath been revealed to him by the Spirit that his eyes shall not see death before the King is come.

CARMI (*fitting a stone into the sling and testing it carefully*). Simeon is an old man, and a dreamer of dreams.

17

MERAB (*smiling*). Thou'rt ever cautious about these feelings for the future, my Carmi, whether thy wife's or another's.

CARMI (*pushing back the bench and rising*). I must be off now. Get thee to bed with the little ones, and let thy feelings rest. (*He puts several of the rocks in the leather scrip and fastens the scrip and sling to his girdle.*)

(MERAB *lays her spinning on the table, goes to the pegs down left, and brings him his cloak. While he is wrapping it about his shoulders, she goes into the grain room at left, returning immediately with a small packet of food which she hands to* CARMI.)

MERAB. Here is thy midnight bread. And I put in a bite for old Asaph. He is so old and so poor.

CARMI (*moving up center toward door*). That is like thee, my Merab. If thou hadst but one loaf of bread, thou wouldst give half of it to him who had none.

MERAB. Peace go with thee, husband. It is a beautiful night on the hills.

CARMI. Yea. A bright and a chilly one. (*Smiles at* MERAB.) Thy roaring wolves will be abroad surely.

MERAB. See then that Michal's lamb with the crooked leg stray not far from the flock.

(CARMI *lays the packet of food on chest up center, goes to water jar, dips gourd dipper in, and drinks. He takes his shepherd's crook from near door up center, goes to* MERAB *and kisses her on both cheeks.*)

CARMI. Forget thy fears, and sleep soundly. Peace be upon thee and upon our house. (*Exit, up center.*)

(MERAB *moves quietly about, clearing the table. She carries the remaining stones into the storeroom at left, then gathers up the leather scraps on the table and goes to the chest up center left, with them. She sees the packet of food which* CARMI *has forgotten. Hastily catching it up and dropping the leather scraps into the chest, she runs to the door and opens it.*)

MERAB (*calling*). Carmi! Carmi! (*There is no answer.* MERAB *looks about the room an instant, then goes to pegs down left and takes down a cloak which she carries to* ABIGAIL'S *bed, up right. She leans over* ABIGAIL *and shakes her shoulder gently.*) Abigail! Abigail!

(ABIGAIL *slowly opens her eyes, sits up, and looks about her in a dazed way.*)

ABIGAIL. Didst call me, mother?
MERAB. Yea, daughter. I called thee. Thy father hath forgotten his midnight bread. 'Twill be a long night on the hills with naught to stay his hunger. (*Picks up* ABIGAIL'S *outer tunic and sandals from bench below window at right, and hands them to her.*) Here are thy dress and sandals. (ABIGAIL, *still half asleep, puts on the garments.* MERAB *gives her the cloak.*) Put this cloak about thee and run quickly to thy father and give the packet into his hand.

(MICHAL *sits up suddenly in bed, watching* MERAB *and* ABIGAIL.)

ABIGAIL (*takes the packet and goes to door up center*). Yea, mother, I will do as thou sayest. Is there aught else to tell him?
MICHAL. Mother, where is Abigail going? I would go, too!
MERAB (*to* MICHAL). Hush thee, Michal. Lie down, little one, lest thy sister get cold. (*To* ABIGAIL.) Nay, naught else. But see thou return home straightway. Ask thy father to send one of the dogs back to guard thee. Or perhaps young Joel will walk with thee.
MICHAL. Mother, pray thee, let me go with Abigail. I want to run out to father and see the sheep, too. (*She puts a foot out of bed.* ABIGAIL *goes out up center.*)
MERAB. Nay, child. Thou'rt too little to be running out in the night. I like it not that Abigail must go. (JUDITH *stirs and whimpers.*) See, thou'rt waking thy sister.
MICHAL. I want to see my lamb with the crooked leg!
JUDITH (*sitting up sleepily*). I want my lamb!

MERAB (*to* MICHAL). Naughty one! See what thou hast done! (*To* JUDITH.) Lie down, little lamb, and go to sleep.

JUDITH (*continuing to whimper*). Take me!

MICHAL. Sing to us, then, mother. Sing us to sleep again.

MERAB *takes* JUDITH *up from the bed, wraps her in a garment which she picks up from the bench at right, and comes down to bench near table, where she sits, cuddling* JUDITH *in her arms.* MICHAL *slips out of bed, wraps herself in a garment she takes from bench at right, and perches herself beside* MERAB, *drawing her feet up under her and nestling close to* MERAB'S *side.*

MERAB (*chanting in a low voice*).
The Lord is my shepherd,
I shall not want.
He maketh me to lie down in green pastures.
He leadeth me beside the still waters.

(*The room seems slowly to be filling with light. A white spotlight, turned on gradually from off stage or above center door, may be used. A sound of singing is heard off center above* MERAB'S *voice.* MICHAL *lifts her head and listens.*)

MICHAL. Mother! Listen. What is that?

(MERAB *stops singing, and all listen. Off center, the* THREE ANGELS *sing the third stanza of "Hark! What Mean Those Holy Voices?" If the voices are good enough, they may sing without accompaniment.*)

ANGELS (*singing off up center*).
Peace on earth, good will from heaven,
Reaching far as man is found;
Souls redeemed and sins forgiven!
Lord, our golden harps shall sound.

(*The* ANGELS *continue their song, singing stanzas four*

*and five of "Hark! What Mean Those Holy Voices?" or
any other appropriate Christmas song, repeating as often as
is desired.)*

MERAB. Perhaps some revelers from the village—
MICHAL. It is all light! (*The music swells louder.*)
Mother, open the door and see who it is!

MERAB *rises and goes toward door up center.* MICHAL
*runs ahead and throws open the door. The light streams in
upon them. In the background are seen* THREE ANGELS, *singing.* MICHAL *and* MERAB, *with* JUDITH *still in her arms,
stand at one side of the doorway peering out, and listening in
wonder. As they stand, the light fades, the music dies away,
and the* ANGELS *disappear.*

MICHAL (*in awe*). They were angels!
JUDITH. Angels.
MERAB (*softly*). "Glory to God in the highest." We have
seen a wondrous thing this night, my daughters. The Lord
hath sent us a sign. (*She steps into doorway and peers
out, then comes in and closes the door.*) I would thy sister
were safe home again. (*Turning to* MICHAL *and laying
her hand on* MICHAL'S *head.*) Get thee to bed now, little
one. It is cold.
MICHAL. The angels, will they—?

The door up center bursts suddenly open, and ABIGAIL
comes bounding in, her eyes large with excitement.

ABIGAIL (*speaking rapidly*). Mother! Michal! The
King hath come! The angels of the Lord came down and
told us, just now, out there. (*Points out center door.*)
He is in Bethlehem, and he is wrapped in swaddling clothes
and lying in a manger, and all the shepherds are going in
to see him, save Elim and Jehu. They are keeping the flocks.
And father says I may go with them and see the new King
if I keep close by his side. Oh, mother, thou'lt not say nay?
MERAB. What is this of a new King? Speak slowly,

daughter, and tell me what it is thou hast seen. Did the angels appear to thee also?

ABIGAIL. Yea. First one, then a multitude of them. Oh, mother, they were beautiful! Shining and white. And their song— (*She hears the tramp of feet outside, runs to door up center, and looks out.*) Mother, the men are going by! Thou'lt not forbid me?

MICHAL. Mother, I want to go, too. I want to see the new King!

MERAB (*to* ABIGAIL). Nay. Run on, since thy father hath spoken—though I like not thy going about in the night. (ABIGAIL *starts out door up center.*)

MICHAL (*pulling her mantle tight about her and going over to* ABIGAIL). Me too!

MERAB. Nay, little Michal. Thou'rt much too small. Get thee into bed, and thy sister shall tell thee all when she returneth. (*To* ABIGAIL.) - See thou bring back strict word of all that passeth.

(*Exit* ABIGAIL, *up center.*)

MERAB *closes the door and, pushing* MICHAL *ahead of her, goes over to bed up right, and lays* JUDITH *between the covers. There is a knock at the door up center.* MERAB *goes over and opens it to admit* ASAPH, *who hobbles in slowly, leaning upon his staff.*

ASAPH. Peace be with thee, Merab, daughter of Lemuel.

MERAB. And with thee, Asaph. Is aught wrong that thou hast come back?

ASAPH. Nay; but my legs are too stiff and my joints too old to keep pace with yonder eager ones. Pray let me tarry in thy house until they return from finding the King.

MERAB. Stay, and welcome. (*She pulls the bench at center to left of table and leads* ASAPH *to it.*) Then the King is come, verily? Thou knowest it for truth?

ASAPH (*sitting on the bench*). Nay. I know not surely if he be a king. But the Lord hath sent a sign, and strange things have come to pass on the hills this night.

MERAB. Yea. There were strange happenings here, too, and I would I knew the meaning thereof.

MICHAL (*who has been standing close to* MERAB *during this conversation*). How was it out there, Asaph? Pray tell us.

(MERAB *seats herself on the bench near* ASAPH, *and resumes her spinning.* MICHAL *sits on the floor at her feet drawing her mantle close about her shoulders.*)

ASAPH. It happened thus. We were all sitting on the ground and were half asleep. The sheep were quiet and the dogs all lying down. The night was so still there was no sound at all. Suddenly there was a stirring among the sheep, and thy husband's great dog Ur began to growl in his throat. We all sprang up, and lo, there was a great light shining all about us, so bright that our eyes could not endure it, and we fell to the earth again, and were sore afraid.

MICHAL (*eagerly*). Yea. The light shone upon us, too, and filled the house, brighter than the sun.

MERAB. Hush thee, daughter. Give ear unto Asaph.

ASAPH. When we could look again, behold an angel of the Lord in shining raiment stood in the midst of the light, and his arm was raised on high. He spoke and his words were plain: "Fear not, for behold I bring you good tidings of great joy, which shall be unto all people. For unto you is born this day in the city of David, a savior which is Christ the Lord." And for a sign, he told us that we should find a babe wrapped in swaddling clothes and lying in a manger. Then, even while we looked, there was with him a great host of heavenly beings singing praises in voices never heard on earth—

MERAB (*softly*). We heard it. "Glory to God in the highest—"

ASAPH. Yea. "Glory to God," they sang, "and on earth peace, good will among men." Their singing drove the fear from our hearts, and when they were gone we fell a-wondering what thing had been made known to us. Young Joel leaped up and cried, "Come! Let us be off. We will go

·even unto Bethlehem and see what it is hath come to pass."
We cast lots then to see who should abide with the sheep,
and the lot fell on Jehu and Elim. The rest made haste
toward the village.

MERAB. And Abigail—didst thou see her? Had she come
unto her father?

ASAPH. Yea. When she came or how, I know not. When
the angels were singing I saw her clinging to her father's
hand. She was less afraid than any of the men.

MERAB (*smiling*). That is well. (*Musingly.*) So the
sayings of the prophets have come to pass. The Deliverer
hath come, and in our time.

ASAPH. Be not too sure, daughter. Thy husband Carmi
thinketh not. That the angels meant—

(*There is a loud rapping on the door up center.* MERAB
and MICHAL *start to their feet.*)

MELCHIOR (*calling from outside center door*). Peace be
upon thy house. We be friends, and desire a word with thee.

MERAB *goes up center and opens the door, admitting* MEL-
CHIOR *and* CASPAR.

MERAB. The peace of the God of Israel be with ye. What
would ye of me?

MELCHIOR (*making a deep bow*). Thy pardon for entering thy house at this hour. We be strangers in a strange
land, and would ask of thee if the town of Bethlehem be
near.

MERAB. 'Tis but a few furlongs off. (*Impulsively, as
she notes the strange apparel of the two men.*) But surely
ye are not come for the taxing? Ye are not of the house of
David!

CASPAR. Nay. We be three seekers after truth, from a
far country. One awaits without, beside the camels. We
are in search of one who is to be born King of the Jews.
Know ye aught of such an one?

(MERAB *and* ASAPH *exchange startled glances, but do not*

24

speak. MICHAL *takes a step forward toward and stands gazing at the strangers, fascinated by their appearance.* CASPAR *smiles at her kindly, and she goes up to him and feels of his robe.*)

MELCHIOR. The ancient writings have long foretold his coming, and now, by all the signs, his time is at hand. Even as the astrologers said, his star arose in the east—

ASAPH (*who has been leaning forward on his staff and listening intently*). What? Hath he a star in the sky also? We have seen no new star.

MELCHIOR. Yea. It hath been our guide these many weeks of our journey, though at times its light hath been obscured. Here it hath seemed about to rest. At Jerusalem we inquired of Herod the King, but he knew naught of any new King, and was very wroth to learn of it. Only the wise men of thy people had heard of him, and they told us the saying of their prophets that the King was to be born in Bethlehem of Judea. But of the time they knew naught. The star hath led us hither, and we have hastened lest we be too late to present our gifts. But one of the camels hath suddenly gone lame, and unless we be very near we must tarry until morning.

MERAB. Nay. It is not far, and the road lieth straight over yonder hill. (*Points right.*) But—

ASAPH (*springing up and speaking tensely*). Verily the Lord of Hosts hath sent ye! His hand is upon us, and he hath showed forth his wonders to his children. His angels have descended and walked among men. They sang in the heavens and declared his glory, even the birth of Christ the Deliverer. This night is fulfilled what was spoken by the prophets in olden time.

MERAB (*earnestly*). It is true what the old man saith. We have seen strange things, and the shepherds have left their flocks and gone into Bethlehem to learn what they may mean.

MELCHIOR. Then we may not tarry, but must press on, since the journey is so near its end. (*He draws a pouch*

from his bosom and takes from it a coin which he hands to
MERAB.) This for thy kindness.

MERAB (*drawing back*). Nay. I cannot take thy gold.
Keep it for the King!

(MELCHIOR *restores the coin to the pouch, but in putting
the pouch into his clothing it slips to the floor and lies there
unnoticed.*)

MELCHIOR. Then may the blessings of thy God be upon
thee and thy house.

CASPAR (*to* ASAPH). And upon thee, old man.

(*They start toward door up center.*)

MICHAL (*plucking at* MERAB'S *skirt*). Mother, tell them
he is in the manger.

MERAB (*smiling*). The word of the angel was, "Thou
shalt find him wrapped in swaddling clothes and lying in a
manger."

CASPAR. A strange cradle for a king!

MELCHIOR (*opening the door and looking out*). The star
standeth still in the heavens. By its light we shall find him.
Our peace we leave with you.

MERAB. The Lord be·with you and bring you to the King.

(*Exeunt* MELCHIOR *and* CASPAR, *center.* MERAB *closes
door and comes down to bench at center.* ASAPH *is still gazing after the strangers.*)

ASAPH. Now, indeed, have we seen a wonderful thing.
They are no common men who have been here, but belike
kings themselves.

MERAB. Yea. Their garments were costly, and such as
are not seen in this country, even in Jerusalem.

(MICHAL *suddenly springs forward and picks up the
pouch from the floor, running with it to* MERAB.)

MICHAL. Mother! Look! The stranger hath lost his

gift for the King. (*She runs to the door quickly, and before* MERAB *can protest, is gone.*)

MERAB (*looking after her*). I like not her running out into the night that way. She is too little for such errands.

ASAPH. Nay, chide her not. There is naught can harm her. The strangers cannot have gone far, and the men will soon be returning.

MERAB. And she was sore hurt not to go with her sister to see the child.

ASAPH (*shaking his head and musing aloud*). Yea.. Michal is too young, and I am too old. Our eyes may not see the King. But we have seen the glory of his coming and we have heard the promise of his heralds. And little Michal will see his kingdom set up in Israel, the kingdom that hath no end.

MERAB (*seating herself on the bench*). I know not what to make of these strangers. How came they who are not Jews to know of the birth of a king to our people? They have known it many months, else they could not have prepared him gifts and made so long a journey. And yet to us it is revealed but to-night!

ASAPH. Nay! Had we known how to read the scrolls aright, we too would have been looking for him. These are wise men who are learned in many tongues and know the sayings of the prophets of many lands. Moreover, what is written in the stars is an open scroll to them. His coming hath long been foretold there.

MERAB. But our own wise men—they too can read the stars, and surely they know the prophets.

ASAPH (*scornfully*). Nay. Time was in Israel when we lacked not wise men to interpret the hidden things to us. But now no longer. Those who pretend wisdom in this day but quibble over vain questions. The ancient writings and the stars alike are sealed to them. The Lord God hath turned his face from them and revealed his wonders unto strangers.

MERAB. Perhaps, Asaph, He did it that these kings, seeing the Great King, shall be moved to go home and raise armies against the day of his declaring himself.

ASAPH. It may be true. The ways of the Lord— (*The noise of tramping feet and muffled voices is heard off center.*) Harken! The men are returning!

ABIHU (*off up center*). Nay, Carmi. I tell thee, thou'rt wrong. Thou didst not see— (*The rest of his sentence is lost in the confusion of entering.*)

MERAB *goes swiftly to the door up center and flings it open to admit* EPHRAIM, ABIHU, JOEL, ABIGAIL, *and* CARMI, *who has* MICHAL *by the hand.* MICHAL *is struggling to restrain her tears.*

EPHRAIM. Peace be unto you, daughter of Lemuel.

MERAB. Enter, all of ye, and tell us quickly what things ye have seen.

JOEL. We have seen such a wonder as hath never been seen in Israel before!

MERAB. Did you find the King?

ABIGAIL (*excitedly*). Oh, mother, he is only a baby, and he hath no look of a king at all. But his mother is more beautiful than the angels who sang in the sky!

CARMI (*not unkindly*). Hush thee, daughter. Let thy elders do the speaking.

(MICHAL *breaks away from* CARMI *and runs to hide her face in* MERAB'S *mantle.*)

MICHAL (*sobbing*). I did not see the King! Father made me come back with him as soon as I had given the stranger his pouch and gone with him but a little way along the road. And I didn't see the King!

(MERAB *motions the men to seat themselves. They all sit on the floor, grouped about the bench down center.* MERAB *sits on the bench beside* ASAPH, *takes* MICHAL *on her lap, and comforts her while the men talk.*)

ASAPH (*to* MICHAL, *as the men are settling themselves*). Fret not thyself, little one. Thou hast long to live, and wilt surely see the King in all his glory.

28

JOEL (*thoughtfully*). 'Tis indeed a humble beginning for a great king.

MERAB. But how found you the babe?

ABIHU. We went first to the inn to inquire for a newborn child. The place was so full of those come for the enrolling that the very courtyard swarmed with sleeping beasts and men. The landlord was half distraught, and knew nothing of any child. But at length came up a man-servant who said that about the first hour a man from the north had come seeking lodging, if not for himself, for his wife who was ill. There was no room, but the servant had compassion on them and led them to the stable.

MERAB. The King of Israel, born in a stable!

JOEL. As we came nigh, lo, a great star hung over the stable and filled the yard with its light.

EPHRAIM. We entered, past the oxen and asses which stood all wide awake, and went back to where a lantern hung upon a beam. There we found the family. The husband was Joseph, a carpenter of Nazareth, a goodly man. And in the shadows lay his wife—

JOEL (*with enthusiasm*). She was comely to behold, and full of a kind of strength, though she spoke not a word.

MERAB. But the child—?

EPHRAIM. Yea. The child had been wrapped in swaddling clothes and laid in the hay of the manger. And though he was but a newborn babe, a strange power was about him insomuch that we all fell to our knees and worshiped him.

JOEL. And there was in the place a light that came not from the lantern nor yet from the stars without, but was surely the glory of God.

CARMI. Thou art a dreamer, young Joel, and hast seen more than was there to see. The stable had no light save what came from the lantern. Nor did I feel any strange power come forth from the child.

ABIHU. But thou wert not properly in the stable, Carmi.

CARMI. True. The place was small and there were many beasts. I tarried near the door. Yet had there been aught

I would have seen and felt it. I saw but a man child newly born, and his father and mother.

EPHRAIM (*sternly*). Thou sawest the King of Israel who shall sit upon the throne of David and rule all peoples! Jehovah himself hath said.

JOEL. Already the throne of Herod is in danger, so hated is he among the people. Now that we are assured of a leader in a few years, the men of Israel and of Judah can band together once more. When the King is old enough to lead forth his army it will be ready for him, if we but work carefully and diligently.

CARMI (*with some heat*). Thou speakest with the words of an infant! I tell thee, these many years I have pondered diligently the sayings of the prophets—and the time for the Deliverer is not yet. Nor when he comes will he be born in a stable. Is it not written: "Kings shall be thy nursing fathers and queens thy nursing mothers"? He will come of warrior stock, not carpenter's!

ABIGAIL (*protesting*). But father, the angels—the word of the Lord—!

CARMI. Hold thy peace, child. I deny not that we have seen a wonder from the Lord, and that this child which is born is sent to be a prophet and a teacher. But the King he is not.

MERAB (*gently*). How is it then, husband, that the strangers from the East knew of his birth and came bringing gifts?

ASAPH. Yea, and return to their own far country to raise up armies for his aid?

CARMI (*impatiently*). Let me hear no more of armies and conspiracies! That is but the vain imagining of rash youth and old age!

EPHRAIM. Wouldst have us submit forever to the yoke of Caesar and Herod his underling?

CARMI. Wouldst put all our heads into Caesar's noose with thy untimely talk of rebellion? All that remaineth to us is to obey the laws of Caesar and submit unto Herod until such time as Jehovah sends us a conqueror who shall follow in the footsteps of Saul and of David.

JOEL (*muttering, half to himself*). In my heart I know this is he.

ABIGAIL (*moving near to* JOEL). I, too, am sure.

MERAB. Surely God doth not send his angels to announce a common prophet, nor lead wise men from far countries to the birthplace of one less than a king.

CARMI (*springing up, his temper aroused at having his word disputed*). I say, let there be no more talk of a new king in my house!

(*The men draw back from him, as he stands in threatening attitude.* ABIGAIL *clings to* MERAB *as if for protection.*)

(*The curtain is lowered for a few minutes to denote the lapse of several weeks' time. When it is raised, the lamp has been removed from the table, and in its place is a large earthen bowl of meal, a cruse of oil, and a wooden spoon. The bench at center has been pulled over to the right, forming an angle with the table. On the floor down left is a small stone mortar for grinding grain, and in front of it a cradle-shaped basket, large enough to lay a baby in, supposed to contain grain. As it is mid-afternoon and a warm day, the door up center stands open.*)

(*At rise of curtain,* MERAB *is sitting on the bench at right of table, sewing on a garment for* JUDITH, *who is asleep on the bed up right.* MICHAL *is sitting on the floor down left, grinding grain in the mortar. She now and then pours a few grains with her hands from the basket into the mortar.* ABIGAIL *is standing at left end of table mixing meal cakes in the earthen bowl.*)

ABIGAIL (*draining the last drop of oil from the cruse into her bowl.*) That is the last drop of oil, mother, and it will not finish the meal cakes for supper.

MERAB. The jar is empty, I know, but there is still a

cruse in the grain room. (ABIGAIL *starts toward left door.*) It is on the floor near the great jar.

(ABIGAIL *goes out, left, and returns immediately, empty-handed.*)

ABIGAIL. Nay. There is none. There is only an old sheaf of unthreshed grain beside the great jar. Dost thou not remember? Father bade thee give the cruse to old blind Anna when she came by the other day.

MERAB. I did not think it was the last. Go thou into the village, then, and buy a bit in the market, until we can fill the jar. (*Rising and going to chest up center left.*) I'll give thee a penny. (*She opens chest, takes out a money pouch, and reaches into it for a coin. She exclaims in surprise.*) The pouch is empty! Thy father hath forgotten to leave so much as a penny.

ABIGAIL. Then how can I buy oil, with no money?

MERAB (*sighing*). Look for thy father along the road or in the village and ask him for the penny. But see thou ask him gently and anger him not.

ABIGAIL. Mother, what hath come over father, that he groweth angry so quickly? He hath never spoken shortly to me in my life before, but now sometimes he scoldeth me for naught.

MICHAL (*looking up suddenly from her grinding*). He is cross to me, too. Yesterday he would not let me go with him to play with my lamb with the crooked leg.

MERAB. I know. He is strange and unlike himself.

ABIGAIL. Yea, ever since the night the angels sang on the hills.

MERAB (*returning to the bench and picking up her sewing*). What time he is not out with the flocks he is in the village. Thy uncle Benjamin saith he is often in the synagogue talking with the priest. I think he is troubled over the new King.

ABIGAIL. The men have noticed it, too. Yesterday, young Joel did fill my pitcher at the well, and he told me that father keepeth much to himself, and he singeth not, as he used to do, nor joineth in the story-telling at night. He said some of the men declare that he is a friend of Herod and no true son of Israel, because he saith the baby in the manger is not the new King.

MERAB (*with spirit*). Nay; that is not true, and they know it is not. I know not what troubleth him, but he is no traitor! (*Calmly.*) But go now, daughter, and fetch the oil, lest we have no cakes for supper.

ABIGAIL. Yea, I go, mother, and I shall be very gentle with father when I find him.

She starts to door up center, but before she can go out, there is a knock at the door, and MARY *stands in the doorway, her baby son in her arms. She looks pale and weary.* ABIGAIL *gives a cry of joy and runs to her.*

ABIGAIL. The mother of the King—and the baby! Oh. mother, come!

(MERAB *comes quickly up center, and* MICHAL *jumps up, spilling her grain, and joins her.*)

MARY. The peace of God upon thy house.

MERAB. And upon thee and thy son. Welcome art thou. Wilt thou come in and rest thyself under our poor roof?

MARY. Yea, if I may. I have been walking in the sun upon the hills, and I am more weary than I thought. I would sit for a moment in a cool place.

MERAB. Michal, do thou bring a drink of water. (*She leads* MARY *to bench beneath window at right. To* MARY.) Rest thee here, and I would I had a softer couch to offer thee.

(MARY *seats herself, throws back her veil, and loosens the wrappings from around the child.*)

ABIGAIL (*who has followed* MARY *across the room and is standing near her, gazing raptly*). The baby King in our very house!

(MICHAL *brings the dipper of water and shyly offers it to* MARY, *who takes it and drinks.*)

MARY (*returning the dipper to* MICHAL). I thank thee, little one. I am much refreshed.

(MICHAL *runs over left to replace the dipper on the wall, and returns immediately to stand close to* MARY.)

ABIGAIL (*still gazing at the child*). Is he not beautiful, mother, as I said?

MERAB (*looking down at the baby*). Never have mine eyes beheld a babe more perfect.

(MARY *smiles her appreciation of the praise, then turns to* ABIGAIL.)

MARY. Thou hast seen him before?

ABIGAIL. Yea. The night of his birth I went with my father and the other shepherds to the stable. Once I stood so close to the manger I could touch his clothes with my finger.

MARY. Thou art the child, then. It was a beautiful thing for thee to do, and for the shepherds. Long will I remember it.   .

MERAB (*to* ABIGAIL). Hast forgotten thine errand, daughter?

ABIGAIL (*reluctantly*). Nay. I will run now.

(*With a backward glance at* MARY *and the baby, she goes out up center.*)

MARY. These are thy daughters, then?

MERAB. Yea, these two, and the little Judith, asleep in her bed. (*She points to the bed in upper right corner.*) Their father is Carmi, son of Nathan, and I am Merab, his wife.

MARY. Thou hast sons also?

MERAB (*sadly*). Nay. One son I had, betwixt Michal and Judith. He died when he was no older than thy son is now.

MARY (*seeing the longing expression in* MERAB'S *eyes*). Wouldst hold the babe a few moments? I have carried him far, and mine arms are weary.

MERAB (*taking him and holding him against her breast*). It is good to hold a man child in my arms again.

MARY. Mayhap the Lord will yet bless thee with a son of thine own. (*She draws* MICHAL *over to her, and takes the child's face in both her hands.*) How is it, little one? Wouldst like to have a baby brother to care for?

MICHAL. Yea, if he were like thy baby, I would.

(JUDITH *suddenly wakens, and crawling out of her bed, runs over to* MERAB, *holding up her arms to be taken.* MERAB *lays the baby back in* MARY'S *arms, sits on the bench, and picks up* JUDITH.)

MERAB (*stroking* JUDITH'S *head*). Thou art grown a great girl, little Judith, and thy mother hath no longer a baby.

MICHAL (*who has stood as close as possible to* MARY). Is he truly a king? Where is his crown?

MARY (*smiling, but with a far-away look in her eyes*). He is of a line of kings. But he hath no crown—yet.

MICHAL. I wanted to go to see him, too, the night the angels sang, but my father bade me turn back, because I am too little.

MARY. Then thou shalt look thy fill upon him now.

MICHAL. If thy arms are tired, wouldst—wouldst let me hold him?

MERAB (*shaking her head*). Nay—

MARY (*to* MERAB). She will be careful, I know. (*She places the baby in* MICHAL'S *arms.* MICHAL'S *eyes shine with pleasure.* MARY *speaks to her gently.*) Mayhap if thou wouldst sit in the sun and rock him to and fro a little, thou couldst put him to sleep.

(MICHAL, *holding the child very carefully, goes over and sits on the floor near her grain basket, down left.* MERAB *watches her anxously, but* MARY *is serene and without fear.*)

MERAB. Art thou not afraid to trust him with so young a child?

MARY. Nay. Little girls are already mothers in their

hearts. She loveth the babe and cannot be otherwise than gentle with him. See what happiness it giveth her.

(JUDITH *slips down from* MERAB'S *lap and joins* MICHAL. *The two little girls croon over the baby.*)

MERAB. How callest thou the child?

MARY. We have called his name Jesus, for so it was ordained by the prophet before he was born. (*She leans back against the wall for a moment and closes her eyes.*)

MERAB (*rising*). Thou art overtired. Wilt not lie down upon the bed?

MARY. Nay, I thank thee. In a moment I shall be rested. I love thy warm Judean hills and the sunlight upon them. So I walked upon them farther than I knew. It hath made me weary and athirst.

MERAB (*starting left toward the water jar*). I would we had wine to offer thee.

(*Meantime, the child has fallen asleep in* MICHAL'S *arms, as she has been sitting rocking him back and forth.*)

MICHAL (*to* JUDITH, *in a low voice*). Sister, the baby hath gone to sleep. Do thou bring a mantle to lay him on, and I will make him a cradle in the basket. (JUDITH *goes to the hooks down left, and pulls down a mantle which she brings to* MICHAL.) Spread it smoothly in the basket.

(JUDITH *arranges the mantle in the basket, and* MICHAL *lays the sleeping child upon it, drawing the folds together so as nearly to cover the baby's form.*)

JUDITH (*clapping her hands softly*). Now he is little Moses in the bulrushes!

MICHAL (*with enthusiasm*). Yea. And thou shalt be his sister who hides him, and I will be Pharaoh's daughter and come and find him. Thou canst hide under the table. Be much afraid, for Pharaoh's soldiers are like to come at any moment, and they would put the child to death. (JUDITH *creeps under the table and* MICHAL *tiptoes up center, stands*

*still a moment, then comes down again and pretends to dis-
cover the basket. She speaks to her imaginary maidens.*)
What can this basket be? (*She stoops down to examine it,
and* JUDITH *comes out from under the table.*) A baby! He
will drown if we leave him here. (*She starts to pull the
basket gently toward the left door.*)

While this play has been going on, MERAB *has filled the
dipper with water from the jar up left, and carried it to*
MARY. MARY *has sipped the water slowly, and both women
have been silently watching the children. As* MARY *hands
the dipper back to* MERAB, *a knock is heard on the door
jamb, up center, and* JOSEPH *appears.* MICHAL *and* JUDITH
*jump up, frightened at sight of him, and hover close over
the basket.*

JOSEPH. May the God of our fathers give thee peace.

MERAB (*setting the dipper on the table and going up to
the door*). And thee, also. What wouldst thou?

MARY. Joseph! Husband! What dost thou here?

JOSEPH (*going right, followed by* MERAB). I have been
searching for thee for upwards of an hour. A shepherd I
met on the road said he saw a woman with a young child
walking in this direction.

MARY. I grew weary, and this good woman (*laying her
hand on* MERAB'S *arm*) hath given me rest and drink.

JOSEPH (*to* MERAB). The blessing of God upon thee.
(*Turning to* MARY.) Make haste, wife, and bring the child.
Where is he?

MARY (*smiling and pointing to the basket*). Asleep yonder in the bulrushes. I think he is about to be rescued from
Pharaoh's army.

JOSEPH (*drawing* MARY *down right, as* MERAB *goes over
to window at right*). Bring him and come quickly. All is
ready for our departure from Bethlehem, and there is need
for more haste than we thought. I heard even now in the
village that Herod is sending out soldiers to search for the
new King to slay him.

MARY (*indignantly*). Slay a little child? Oh, the wicked one!

JOSEPH. I have an ass without for thee. I will bring it to the door, and be thou ready.

(*He goes out up center and* MARY *takes a step down left toward the basket when—*)

ABIGAIL *bursts excitedly in through the open door at center.*

ABIGAIL (*out of breath*). Mother! The soldiers— Herod's soldiers! They are in the village. I saw them in the street.

MERAB (*turning from the window*). Herod's soldiers?

ABIGAIL. They are seeking out all the babies to put them to death! Two of them are coming this way with father. Oh, mother, let them not find the little King. Hide him, quick!

MERAB (*looking out the window, then turning back in consternation*). The child is right. They approach even now—and my husband with them. (*She seizes* ABIGAIL *by the shoulder.*) Carmi is not— Thy father is not giving them aid?

ABIGAIL (*almost in tears*). Nay, I think not. I know not Oh, mother, hide the baby!

MERAB *and* ABIGAIL *look about quickly for a hiding place, but there is not a nook in the room which cannot easily be seen.* MARY *clasps her hands on her breast and looks up for a moment, as if in prayer. Before any of them can make a move,* CARMI *strides in through the door. The* TWO ROMAN SOLDIERS *halt in the doorway, behind him. At sight of them,* MICHAL *jumps up in terror, standing before the basket so as to shield it from their sight.* JUDITH *huddles close to her.*

CARMI. Thou lookest frightened, wife. There is naught to fear—for us.

MERAB (*regaining her composure*). I did not expect strangers with thee, husband. Their coming startled me.

(*To* MICHAL, *in a calm voice.*) Daughter, there are guests in the house. Carry thy corn into the grain room. (*She points significantly to the basket.*)

MICHAL (*to* ABIGAIL). Help me, sister.

(ABIGAIL *runs down left and takes one end of the basket, keeping her back turned toward the door so that the men cannot see the contents of the basket.* MICHAL *lifts the other end, and they carry the basket carefully off by the left door.*)

ABIGAIL (*under her breath, as they go out*). Pray God naught wakens him!

JUDITH *begins to tug at the mortar,. which is too heavy for her.* ABIGAIL *returns immediately and helps her. They carry it off left.*

(*In the meantime,* MARY *has gone over to the bench at right.* *During the ensuing dialogue, she sits as serenely as though the discussion did not concern her. From time to time, she glances out the window, and once makes a signal to* JOSEPH, *whose face momentarily appears outside it, not to approach the door. His face at once disappears.*)

CARMI. Wife, these be two soldiers from Jerusalem who are come by the order of Herod to search our house.

(*The soldiers step into the room.*)

MERAB. What think they they will find in our humble house to interest King Herod?

ABIGAIL *and* JUDITH *enter at left.*

FIRST SOLDIER. Naught, good woman, thy husband hath assured us. Nevertheless, we are commanded to search every house round about Bethlehem for children under two years old.

(JUDITH *breaks away from* ABIGAIL *and runs to* MERAB, *hiding in her skirts.*)

FIRST SOLDIER (*looking away from* MERAB'S *steady gaze*) It is Herod's command that they be put to death.

MERAB (*with scorn*). Brave soldiers ye are in truth, to stalk about the country slaughtering babes at their mothers' breasts!

CARMI (*sharply*). Peace, wife! Let them accomplish their task quickly and be gone.

(*The* SECOND SOLDIER *has kept his eyes upon* MARY *since his entrance. She returns his gaze steadfastly, more of pity than of fear in her look.*)

SECOND SOLDIER (*in a softened voice*). Think not that it is a pleasure to us to put innocent babes to the sword and bring their parents to grief. But a soldier does as he is commanded.

CARMI. Already have I told them that our children be three daughters, and the youngest is past four years. (*To the soldiers.*) These are they. Come hither, daughters. (ABIGAIL *goes obediently up right and stands near her father.*) This is the eldest. (*He swings* JUDITH *up in his arms.*) And this is the baby. Ye can see for yourselves whether she be more than two years.

FIRST SOLDIER. That is plain enough.

(JUDITH *squirms out of* CARMI'S *arms and runs back to* MERAB.)

CARMI. Where is Michal?

MERAB. At some task in the grain room, I think.

CARMI (*calling*). Michal! Come forth!

Enter MICHAL *from left. Bits of straw and chaff are sticking to her clothing, and her face is flushed.*

MICHAL (*coming center to table*). What wouldst thou, father?

CARMI. Only to show the soldiers of Herod that thou hast more than two years on thy head.

MICHAL (*saucily*). That they can see! (*She goes over right and stands near* ABIGAIL.)

CARMI (*to the soldiers*). These three be our children, and before the God of Abraham, of Isaac, and of Jacob, I swear that there is none other beneath our roof.

FIRST SOLDIER (*to* MERAB). What sayest thou, woman?

MERAB (*in a clear voice*). My husband sweareth truly. My oath I take with his.

FIRST SOLDIER (*pointing to* MARY). What of her? Is she of thy household?

MERAB. Nay. She is but a wayfarer, stopped to rest herself and drink a cup of water as she passed by.

SECOND SOLDIER. I believe thy word. Yet must we search, according to our orders.

(*He goes to beds in upper right corner, runs his hands over them, lifts the covers, looks under the bench on which* MARY *is sitting, and goes over to table at center. Meanwhile the* FIRST SOLDIER *has lifted the lid of the chest up center left, looked into the water jar, moved the clothing on the hooks down left, and has moved toward the left door.* MERAB *grows tense, clasping her hands tightly together.* ABIGAIL *shudders and turns away.* MARY *alone seems fearless and unconcerned.* CARMI, *up right, seems to have forgotten the soldiers, and stands watching* MARY *as though trying to recall some memory of her. As the* FIRST SOLDIER *pushes open the left door,* MICHAL *runs a few steps toward him.* MERAB *puts out a hand to stop her, but drops it to her side.*)

MICHAL. Pray thee, good soldier, step softly in there, and do not shake dust upon the floor. I have but just swept it!

(*The* FIRST SOLDIER *thrusts his head through the left doorway, but does not go out. After a moment he turns about, half a smile on his face.*)

FIRST SOLDIER. I am satisfied there is no child here. I see naught save the usual oil and grain jars, and a basket full of wheat unthreshed. We will go and leave ye in peace.

(SECOND SOLDIER *joins him and they go out at center.* ABIGAIL *tiptoes to the door and looks after them, making sure they are gone. The others stand in silence.*)

ABIGAIL (*turning to* MERAB). Mother! Oh, mother, they found him not!

JOSEPH *enters suddenly at center, brushing past* ABIGAIL, *and going straight to* MARY.

JOSEPH. Mary, wife! Where is thy son? Is he safe?
MARY (*smiling confidently*). Yea. He is safe. (CARMI *stares at* MARY *and* JOSEPH *in amazement.*)

MERAB *crosses quietly to left, goes out left door, and returns immediately carrying the basket with the sleeping infant. Straw and grain are in the folds of the mantle covering him. She sets the basket on the bench at center, lifts the baby out, and going over to* MARY, *lays him gently in her arms.*

MERAB (*almost tearful in her relief*). Behold thy son, unharmed!
CARMI (*angrily*). What is this? Am I made a liar in mine own house and by mine own wife?
MERAB (*gently*). Yea. Thou and I also. And the Lord judge whether I am guilty in his sight! (*Coming over to* CARMI *and putting her hands on his shoulders.*) Carmi, say truly: Thou wouldst not have delivered the little one up to be slain. Think if it had been thine own son!
CARMI (*a little ashamed*). Nay. Perhaps I would not. Yet we sware in the presence of Jehovah, and are liars in his sight.
MARY. Is not the life of one of his children greater in his sight than truth told in an evil cause?

(CARMI *looks at* MARY, *and as he looks, the anger fades from his face.*)

MERAB. Knowest thou not what child it is, husband? Verily, it is the babe of the stable, the little King.

CARMI. So. I have not believed in him, yet he hath been saved from death in my house, as by a miracle. Now do I understand why ye were all in such deathly fright at sight of the soldiers of Herod. (*Looking at* MARY.) Woman, how was it thou couldst sit calmly and see cruel soldiers seek out thy son to slay him with the sword, and not cry out? What power hast thou beyond others that thou knowest not fear and hast the look of being among angels?

MARY (*rising, the baby in her arms, and speaking raptly*). Know this, Carmi. Before my son was born, the angel of the Lord spake unto me and told me of him, saying: "He shall be called the Son of the Highest, and the Lord God shall give unto him the throne of his father David, and of his kingdom there shall be no end." There is set for him a greater task than ever yet a man hath had, though I know not what it will be. How then shall I fear for his life? Will not Jehovah protect his Son until his time is come? But that it was by the hands of thy wife and thy daughters he was saved, I thank thee.

CARMI (*looking at* MARY *and the babe humbly*). These many weeks have I been wrong, swearing that thy son is not the promised King of Israel, and chiding those who believed, because it hath seemed to me that the prophecies were not rightly fulfilled. In this hour hath the Lord revealed my folly and my blindness. Behold, I worship at the feet of the King—I and my house with me.

(*He falls to his knees and bows his head, and* MERAB, ABIGAIL, MICHAL, *and* JUDITH *do likewise*. MARY, *with* JOSEPH *beside her, smiles gently upon them.*)

MARY. May Jehovah bless thee and give thee all good things!

CURTAIN

THE
CANDLE IN THE WINDOW

A ONE-ACT CHRISTMAS PLAY

By

CLARA CHILDS

PRODUCTION RIGHTS

THE CANDLE IN THE WINDOW

For five boys and six girls

CHARACTERS

(In the order in which they first speak)

MARY McMASTER......................*A young believer*
JOHN McMASTER.............*Her brother, also a believer*
KATE McMASTER......................*Her sister, ditto*
AMY WHITE ⎫
SARAH GRAHAM ⎬............*Their guests, all believers*
PAUL WHITE ⎪
JAMES SEYMOUR ⎭
FANNY SEYMOUR...............*James' sister, the doubter*
HARRY MORGAN..............*Another guest and believer*
MISS ANGELICA FREEM ....
...................*The children's Sunday school teacher*
LITTLE BOY......................*The mysterious stranger*

TIME—*About eight o'clock on Christmas Eve.*

PLACE—*Living room of the McMaster home.*

TIME OF PLAYING—*Thirty minutes.*

COSTUMES AND CHARACTERISTICS

Mary is a pretty, ethereal-looking little girl of thirteen, John a studious-looking boy of twelve with large spectacles, and Kate a small, bright-eyed girl of eleven. Amy, Sarah, Paul, James, Fanny, and Harry are bright and lively children between the ages of ten and thirteen. All are dressed in their Sunday best, but not too elaborately. Miss Angelica is a beautiful young woman, with a spiritual expression. She is dressed with simple elegance, wearing a dark winter coat over a plain, modish dress, with a becoming hat, removing her wraps at her entrance. The Little Boy is a handsome child of six or seven, with big, serious eyes and a delicate, wistful face, very gentle, and wise beyond his years. The part should be played by a somewhat older boy of small stature. He wears a ragged suit, and his head and feet are bare.

PROPERTIES

For Mary, vanity case. For John, compass in a case. For Kate, pair of bracelets. For Amy, a ring. For Sarah, a scarf. For Paul, a stick pin. For James, a watch. For Fanny, a few garnets. For Harry, a gold medal. For Miss Angelica, a locket with a gold heart. For Little Boy, eleven small holly wreaths.

MUSIC OF THE PLAY

The complete words and music of the carols suggested for use in the play may be found in "Denison's Christmas Songs and Carols," which may be obtained from the publishers for the price of 50 cents, postpaid.

STAGE DIRECTIONS

Up stage means away from footlights; *down stage,* near footlights. In the use of *right* and *left,* the actor is supposed to be facing the audience.

THE CANDLE IN THE WINDOW

SCENE: *The living room of the McMaster home, about eight o'clock on Christmas Eve. It is large and well furnished and is handsomely decorated with Christmas greens. It has one door at left, opening into a hallway, which in turn leads to the rest of the rooms and to the outdoors. In the back drop are three windows, up center, up left center, and up right center respectively, the middle window being somewhat higher than the other two. These two have their shades lowered, while the one in the middle has its shade up, revealing an expanse of starry sky. This effect is produced by having exterior backing in the form of a blue curtain pricked with tiny star-shaped holes, through which yellow bunch lights are allowed to shine on the darkened space between the curtain and the back drop. All three windows have narrow silken draperies, drawn well away from the windowpanes. In the corner up right is a piano with scarf and bench, and on the piano a pile of music and a large bowl of red carnations. In the corner up left is a small decorated Christmas tree, unlighted and with no gifts hung on it. In the center of the right wall is a fireplace, with a brass fender in front of the grate, and a mantelshelf above, on which are appropriate ornaments, including a clock whose face is not clearly visible to the audience, and a candle in a handsome silver candlestick. Facing the fireplace is a fire seat or bench, while two upholstered armchairs stand close together on the upstage side of the grate, making a kind of semicircle with the fire seat around the fireplace. A footstool is near one of the armchairs. A little down left center is a table, on which are a scarf, a large poinsettia or some other seasonal plant, a small smoking stand with matches, and a table lamp with a*

*fancy shade.   There is a straight-backed chair behind the
table, and another is at left of it.   A handsome portrait hangs
above the mantelshelf, and other pictures adorn the walls,
while rich rugs are on the floor.   In each window hangs a
holly wreath, and over each picture is a festoon of holly or
evergreen.   Holly wreaths decorate the front and ends of the
mantelpiece, and a vase of poinsettias stands on the mantelshelf.   The room has two floor lamps with fancy shades, one
between the armchairs at right and the other on the left side
of the piano and close to it.   The room is well lighted by
these two lamps, the table lamp, and the red glow from the
fireplace, where red electric bulbs concealed under an artificial log simulate a blazing fire.   The footlights are also on,
though rather subdued.   Amber bunch lights are just off
left above left door, giving hall light effect.   This lighting
prevails throughout the play, except for the few minutes that
the stage is darkened at the exit of the* LITTLE BOY.   *Just
before the curtain rises, "Silent Night, Holy Night" is softly
played off stage, while some sweet-toned chimes are still more
softly rung in time to the music.*

*At rise of curtain, the three McMaster children are dis-
covered sitting around the fireplace,* MARY *on the long bench
with her profile to the audience,* JOHN *in one of the armchairs, and* KATE *on the footstool, the two latter with their
faces toward the audience.* JOHN *looks a little uncomfortable
in his best suit, but very important and serious, as he gazes
owlishly at his sisters through his spectacles.   All three appear weighed down by the importance of some tremendous
event impending, and are a little formal and unusually earnest
in their speech.   When the curtain is well up, the music and
chimes off stage die away.*

MARY.   Mother was pretty to-night in her new dress.
Silk is so soft and shimmery, and that gold color just suits
her.

JOHN.   I think mother is the most beautiful woman in the
whole world.   I love the way she smiles.   It's sort of—
(*Pauses helplessly.*)

KATE. I know! Thrilling! And mother smiles nearly all the time. But I can always tell when she's not quite happy.

JOHN. Kitsy has turned mind reader. How?

KATE (*gayly*). Oh, it's easy. When she's altogether glad, she smiles with both her lips and her eyes. But when she's the least bit uncertain or puzzled, she smiles with her lips, and her eyes look far away and misty.

MARY. Why, that was just the way she smiled when I told her about what we were going to do to-night. You know, I don't think she believes it will happen.

JOHN (*very wisely*). Did she say she didn't believe? It's hard, sometimes, to tell what grown-up people are thinking. They are not like us children: all of one piece, straight out and simple.

MARY. How you talk, John! But grown-ups are funny! That's why they look queer sometimes. Now, there's mother. You should have seen her look when I told her about the meeting we were going to have, the carol singing, and the legend.

KATE. What did she say?

MARY. "How wonderful!" That's what she said. "I wish I could be with you. It's a beautiful thing to do, singing His praises and waiting to welcome Him, even if nothing comes of it. It is a beautiful thing to believe."

JOHN. Mother's a trump, and she loves us. But she doesn't believe that the Christ child will pay us a visit on Christmas Eve if we put a candle in the window. You're right, Mary. That's what made her sad. But that doesn't shake me. I do believe. Don't you believe, Mary? You, Kate?

KATE. I should say I do.

MARY. Yes, I believe with all my heart that He will come. Miss Angelica believes, too. She understands things. Dear mumsie! I suppose she can't help it—not believing. Sometimes I wish never, never to grow up.

KATE. Oh, I do. I should like to be a grown-up.

JOHN. A grown-up is a person who has finished growing.

Nearly always they grow fat and smoke cigars and play golf, and they are always in a hurry.

KATE. Why, dad's a perfect grown-up. That's dad to the life!

MARY. Isn't that rather disrespectful, John?

JOHN. No, of course not. Father is a perfect grown-up. Mother isn't quite. She has one foot over on their side, but she hasn't left us altogether. Now, Miss Angelica is hardly a grown-up at all. I would like to save mother, but I suppose it's hopeless, father having the pull with her he has. (*With sudden excitement.*) Say, what did father explode when you told him?

MARY. I didn't tell him. Mother did. He said— Oh, you know what he said.

JOHN. I can guess just about. But what really? What did he say?

MARY (*quoting scornfully*). "Superstitious rot!" Then he said something about mesmerism and hypnotism and things like that. Everything was "bosh" or "rot" or "idiotic nonsense." "What I believe in," he said, "is that two and two make four." Dear old dad! He really did get excited. He's so practical. And he asked mother if she were trying to work up an excuse for not going to the dance to-night.

JOHN. Oh, father didn't mean all he said. But of course no one expected him to believe in a miracle.

MARY. A miracle! Well, I should say not. He really is provoked about our doing this. Said it was the kind of stuff pulled off in the Dark Ages. But mother smoothed him down.

JOHN. Well, they've gone.

KATE. They'll have a long drive under the stars. Mother really couldn't miss this dance, you know.

MARY. Oh, of course, she had to go on father's account. Business is business, as he says, and then there was the dress, made especially for this occasion. How beautiful she was! And didn't father look nice and important? They really are parents you have to be proud of—

KATE (*interrupting*). And love.

MARY. Yes, and love.

JOHN (*who has been deep in thought*). It must have been like that the first Christmas Eve: Everybody believing that two and two make four, business is business, dances, pretty dresses. No one expecting the King. Nobody sitting up, eager to welcome Him. All the earth busy or sleeping. Even the shepherds, counting their sheep, were taken by surprise, were frightened when the angel told them Jesus was born. They didn't believe in miracles. But why shouldn't Jesus come back to earth on His birthday and be on this one night what He once was—a human being? I believe He can. I believe in miracles.

KATE. So do I, John.

MARY (*thoughtfully*). Have you ever thought, John, you and Kate, how different that night was in heaven from what it was on earth? I've thought about it a lot. I like to think of the excitement that was up there among the angels, and God himself all anxious and tense. Can't you see them waiting for the news that the Son of God had been born on earth a simple little child, just like us? Think of the songs that broke that night from the happy angels!

KATE. Oh, Mary, that's wonderful! It sounds like a book. The angels couldn't stand it, could they, looking down and seeing that on earth there was no rejoicing?

MARY. No, they couldn't stand it. They flew over the walls of heaven, and, singing, they came to earth to rouse men from their sleep, singing, "Glory to God in the highest, and on earth peace, good will toward men."

JOHN. I couldn't have thought it all out any better myself. I'm sure that's just the way it was. That's what is called inspiration—seeing things like that. Maybe you'll be a Sunday school teacher like Miss Angelica, Mary. She has inspiration.

MARY. She's precious.

KATE. Her face shines softly like a candle flame.

MARY. Wasn't she coming early? She's the one to light the candle. I'm so glad mother lent us the silver candlestick. (*Goes up to the mantelshelf, lifts the candlestick as she speaks, and looks at the clock.*) Why, it's time they all were coming. You don't suppose they are not coming? (*Sets candlestick back in place.*)

KATE. Of course they're coming.

JOHN. I bet Fanny Seymour doesn't show up. She doesn't believe a miracle can happen.

(*The doorbell rings, off left, and loud voices are heard.*)

MARY. There's the bell. (*Rises and starts left.*)

KATE (*jumps up and runs after* MARY). My, what a rumpus! They all must have come at once.

(MARY *and* KATE *rush off at left.* JOHN *crosses and stands in the doorway, looking after them. A babble of voices comes from off left.*)

MARY, KATE, *and* OTHER CHILDREN (*in confused chorus, off left*). Hello! How are you? Take off your wraps. Let me take 'em. Hang it there. There's a place!

KATE (*in loud, clear tones, off left*). Come in by the fire.

HARRY (*off left*). How cold it is outside!

SARAH (*off left*). You should see the stars.

MARY (*off left*). We've been waiting for you; just wondering if you were coming.

Enter KATE *and* MARY *at left, followed by* AMY, SARAH, PAUL, JAMES, FANNY, *and* HARRY.

KATE. Come and get warm. I know you are just frozen. (*Crosses to fireplace, while the others straggle along behind her.*)

JOHN. But where is Miss Angelica?

AMY. She picked us all up in her car. When she got to Sarah's house, she decided she wanted to walk the rest of the way here. (*Sits on fire seat.*)

(HARRY, JAMES, *and* FANNY *stand beside the grate, warming their hands.*)

53

JOHN. Has it stopped snowing altogether? (*Goes up to center window and looks out.*)

AMY. Yes. It's clear and still and white. I never saw anything so lovely.

SARAH (*sitting beside* AMY). Anything could happen on a night like this.

PAUL. It sure is wonderful out there. (*Joins* JOHN *at center window.*)

JAMES. Sort of mysterious. And the sky looks enormous.

FANNY (*scornfully*). You and your mystery! Oh, bosh!

AMY. It *is* mysterious. Anyone but you could feel it. It's as if the earth had put on a white robe and stood under a starry tent, hushed and waiting—waiting for something wonderful to happen.

MARY. Waiting, as we are, for the little Jesus.

HARRY (*glancing at the candlestick*). That's a pretty nice holder you have for the candle. Silver.

FANNY. You all make me sick, believing all this nonsense! Pooh! I wouldn't stuff myself with such foolishness.

JAMES. Why did you come then?

FANNY. I came along for the company—there! (*The others look at her, distressed and silent.*) Say, do you really believe that little Jesus is coming to see you? You haven't any more common sense than a bunch of peanuts. (*Laughs.*) One would think you were living in the Dark Ages.

KATE. That sounds like dad, to the life.

FANNY. You nuts read a story—nothing but an old legend, a fable. It tells you to stick a candle in the window Christmas Eve, believing that little Jesus comes back to earth every anniversary of His birthday, and, if He passes your way, He will drop in and pay you a visit. Pooh! I live in the twentieth century, and miracles don't happen!

JOHN. You are an unbeliever. To unbelievers miracles do not happen. But we believe.

ALL THE OTHERS. Yes, we believe.

MARY. It's a very beautiful story, Fanny. Just this once every year God's son becomes a son of man and walks among the children of men. The candle is only a sign to show Him that in the midst of our festivities we remember Him and love Him, who first loved us. Is that so hard to believe?

FANNY (*weakening*). Well, all I say is He must love people a lot to leave heaven and come back to this old earth that treated Him so mean. Catch me coming back, if I were He!

PAUL. Everybody didn't treat Him mean.

AMY. Some were willing to die for Him.

SARAH. It was only some who turned Him down. It would be that way if He came again.

FANNY. I suppose you mean me. Well, maybe I would and maybe I wouldn't. Seeing is believing, with me. I'm like that fellow Thomas. Anyway, I can't see why he'd ever come again. It was rotten the way He was treated, even if a few did stick by Him.

MARY. He loved them. He wasn't thinking about what He could get from them. He only wanted to give to them. That's the way it is when you truly love anyone.

MISS ANGELICA *has softly pushed the left door open. She stands on the threshold, unnoticed for an instant.*

MISS ANGELICA (*interposing*). That's the whole secret, Mary. But only those who love unselfishly can ever understand.

ALL THE CHILDREN (*running to her and crowding about her, speaking in confused chorus*). Oh, Miss Angelica, we're so glad you came! Let me take your things. We've waited for you!

(MISS ANGELICA *smiles happily upon them as she tries to extricate herself, and removes her wraps, which* MARY *takes and carries off at left, returning immediately without them.*)

HARRY. Wasn't it awfully cold walking?

MISS ANGELICA. Oh, no, not a bit too cold. And such a wonderful night! The stars burn like happy faces in the sky—like angel faces.

KATE. You look like an angel yourself, all shiny-like.

There are little bits of melted snow on your hair. See how they glisten! Come to the fire and get warm, for your hands are cold. (*Leads her to armchair beside fireplace.*) Here; sit on this seat and put your toes up on the fender.

(MISS ANGELICA *sits and puts her feet on fender.*)

MISS ANGELICA (*looking around the room with a smile*). I see you have everything decorated for Christmas, and that lovely tree all ready for the Christmas presents. Isn't it wonderful for us all to be here together this blessed night? I wish we could think of something splendid to do for some one who needs us.

JOHN. When He comes, maybe He will show us how we can help.

MISS ANGELICA. If our hearts are right, He will. Come and sit by me, Fanny. I'm so glad you came, after all. After what you said on Sunday, I was afraid you might desert us. We must sing some carols and get the real Christmas spirit bubbling up inside of us.

HARRY. Aren't you going to light the candle?

MISS ANGELICA. Yes, right now. Who has a match?

JAMES. Here's one. (*Takes match from smoking stand on table.*) I'll strike it.

MARY. Let's all be still while Miss Angelica lights the candle.

MISS ANGELICA. Yes, let us be silent.

(JAMES *strikes match and hands it to* MISS ANGELICA, *who lights the candle and sets it in the window up center.*)

KATE. How brightly it shines out into the night!

PAUL. It looks like a little star.

JOHN. From the outside it will look bigger. In the dark even a little light looks big.

AMY. It can be seen, I bet, a long way down the street.

SARAH. I wonder how many people in the town will see our candle.

MARY. If only He sees it! Miss Angelica do you think He will really come?

MISS ANGELICA. Yes, I think He will come, but maybe we shall not all see Him. (*Crosses to piano.*)

FANNY (*thoughtfully*). Maybe we shall not all see Him. Now I wonder— (*Pauses, lost in thought.*)

MISS ANGELICA (*turning the leaves of a music book on piano*). Come close around the piano. We'll sing "Silent Night, Holy Night" first. Sing softly, children, but everyone sing, and try and think of the beautiful words and what they mean. (*She begins to play softly, then she nods for them to join in, and they sing "Silent Night, Holy Night." At close of the song, she smiles on them approvingly.*) That was lovely. Now, let's sing "O Little Town of Bethlehem." (*She plays, and the children sing "O Little Town of Bethlehem," singing the first and third stanzas.*)

FANNY (*at close of song, thoughtfully repeating the last two lines of the third stanza*).

> "Where meek souls will receive Him still,
> The dear Christ enters in."

That means— (*Hesitates.*)

MISS ANGELICA (*turning around on the piano bench and putting an arm around* FANNY). —that Christ comes to us all, but whether we see Him and receive Him depends on our faith. If we believe—

FANNY (*interrupting, with an attempt at defiance*). Well, that lets me out.

MISS ANGELICA (*still holding her and appearing not to have heard*). It also depends on what one is looking for. The Jews believed the Messiah was coming. But they were looking for a great earthly king to lead them out of bondage and make Israel the greatest nation on earth. (*A low knocking is heard off left, but no one notices it.*) When He came as a little child, they did not recognize Him. When He grew to manhood and proclaimed Himself their Lord and Savior, they were angry and jealous. Then they led Him to Calvary and slew Him upon the cross. Earthly kings rule for a little while, but Christ reigns forever in the kingdom of the soul. This is the King whose praises we are singing to-night.

(The knock at door off left is repeated, but none hear it.)

MARY. I wonder if we shall know Him.

KATE. How beautiful He must have been!

JOHN. How strong and fearless!

SARAH. How patient to bear all that suffering and not complain!

PAUL. How loyal and true of heart!

FANNY. How forgiving!

MISS ANGELICA. Forgiving, yes. He saw the good underneath the evil, the beautiful under that which was ugly. And He believed in men.

JOHN. Even if we don't see Him, He'll see us, and He'll know that we are on His side.

HARRY (*startled*). What was that? Did you see that? (*Points toward center window.*)

PAUL (*stares toward center window*). I didn't see anything, but I thought once or twice I heard a knock at the front door.

HARRY. I saw what you mean. A light. It shone in the window.

JOHN. It wasn't. It was a face—right against the pane.

HARRY. It was a light.

KATE. It *was* a light. It moved right across the window.

AMY. Maybe it was a falling star. Did you see it, Miss Angelica?

MISS ANGELICA. Yes, I saw something. For an instant, just before Harry spoke, I thought I saw a light—a beautiful glow. (*Rises and takes a few steps toward windows.*) Then I'm quite sure I saw a face, only for a second.

JOHN (*to* AMY). There. Now maybe you'll believe. I saw it plainly—a little face against the pane.

FANNY. Spooks! The way you all talk sounds nuts to me. Haven't you any common sense? I heard it, too—the noise, the knocking. It was an automobile light, of course. A car coming down the street.

MISS ANGELICA. Fanny, no car light ever shone like that. Are you certain you saw a car?

FANNY. I thought I did. (*Runs to the window and looks out.*) There is no one out there. There are only the empty street and the stars.

JOHN. Some day you will see something.

FANNY (*turning away from window*). Hear the prophet!

MISS ANGELICA. Come, children. Let's sing some more. What shall it be next?

AMY. "What Child Is This?"

(NOTE.—*Any other appropriate Christmas carol may be substituted, if desired.*)

ALL THE OTHERS. Yes. We like that one.

(*All return to the piano.* MISS ANGELICA *plays, and they sing "What Child Is This?"*)

(*There is a sound of knocking off left.*)

FANNY. There's that sound again.

JOHN. The knocking. Why, it's right here at this door. (*Starts left.*)

KATE. Some one has been knocking all this time.

MARY *and* MISS ANGELICA *follow* JOHN *to the left door.* JOHN *opens it. The* LITTLE BOY *stands in the open doorway. His head is bare, and the hall light touches his hair till it shines. He carries over one arm a number of Christmas wreaths. All in the room are taken aback.*

ALL (*except* LITTLE BOY, *in a long-drawn breath of wonder*). Oh! Oh!

JOHN (*awed*). It is the same face.

MISS ANGELICA (*almost reverently*). Yes, the same face.

MARY. How did you get into the house, little boy? Did you come in at the front door?

LITTLE BOY (*sweetly*). Only a thief comes in by the back.

MISS ANGELICA (*putting her hand gently on his head*). Who sent you here, my child? (*Takes his hand and leads him into the room.*)

LITTLE BOY. My Father sent me.

KATE. Those wreaths that you have— You want us to buy some of them?

LITTLE BOY. Don't you want them? I must have help.

MISS ANGELICA. Dear little boy, let me see your wreaths. It's late for a child to be out. Ah, they are made of holly. How the thorns must prick you! (*Takes two or three of the little wreaths off the boy's arm.*)

LITTLE BOY. They did once, but they prick no longer.

MARY. Poor little boy! Who could send such a child out on such a night—barefooted? Oh, your feet are hurt! (*Looks at them.*)

JOHN. Come over by the fire and warm. How did you hurt your feet?

LITTLE BOY. Those are old wounds. When the world turns cold, they bleed again. See! They are better already. It is warm in here.

MISS ANGELICA. And the money you get for your wreaths, child—what do you do with it? What is it for?

LITTLE BOY (*seriously*). For my people.

AMY. Where are your people? (*The* LITTLE BOY *makes a gesture toward off left.*) Are they out there in the cold and dark?

LITTLE BOY. Yes, out there in the cold and dark.

FANNY. They must be poor, indeed, or heartless. They couldn't le: you go so thinly clad. Aren't you freezing?

LITTLE BOY. I do not feel the cold now. My people suffer, too.

JOHN. Are they out there (*pointing off left*) waiting for you?

LITTLE BOY (*slowly and sadly*). Yes, some are waiting, but some have forgotten—those who are eager just for the money. I cannot always bring gold and silver.

MISS ANGELICA. My child, how strangely you talk!

LITTLE BOY (*looking into her face with a deeply serious expression*). Have you ever been forgotten by those you love?

MISS ANGELICA. Dear child, yes. We all have. (*Sees a look of pain on the child's upturned face.*) Ah, your little hands! Those thorns have wounded them. Let me take your wreaths (*lifts the remaining wreaths from off his arm and places them on her own*) and you come closer to the fire. (*Examines the wreaths.*) How pretty they are! They look like little crowns, but they are not easy to carry. They hurt. Children, have you any money with you? I left my pocketbook at home.

ALL THE CHILDREN (*in confused chorus*). I haven't got a penny. I didn't bring any money. I spent all I had. My purse is at home. Not a bit of money.

MARY. And father and mother are away, and we haven't any money, either.

MISS ANGELICA. Child, what are we to do? None of us has any money.

LITTLE BOY (*disappointed*). You mean—you don't want any of these?

MISS ANGELICA. Yes, yes, dear child, we want them; only we have nothing to give you—no money. (*She ponders.*) Oh, children, I tell you what we'll do! We'll each of us give to the little boy the thing we have with us that we love most. Then we can each take a wreath. Child, will that be all right? Will you take what we can give?

LITTLE BOY. How kind you are! I'll gladly take what you have to give. See? My hands don't bleed now.

JAMES. That's a big order. (*Looks at* MISS ANGELICA.) I don't want to be mean, but honestly— (*Looks at the* LITTLE BOY.) Say, I guess you do need it more than I. Here, boy, here's my watch. It's worth several bucks, and it keeps good time, honest.

LITTLE BOY (*smiling sweetly and seriously*). Thank you. (*Looks at it and speaks deliberately.*) A watch measures time, but kindness lasts forever.

Miss Angelica (*takes the locket from around her neck and gives it to him*). And here's my little locket, beautiful child. I give it to you with love.

(Little Boy *smiles sweetly at her.*)

Fanny. Oh, Miss Angelica, not the gold heart Mr. Jerry gave you—the one with his picture inside!
Miss Angelica (*gently reproving*). Remember we said we were to give the thing we loved most.

(Fanny *retires up left near Christmas tree and watches the others during the ensuing scene.*)

Amy. Then here's my ring. (*Takes ring from her finger.*) See how pretty it is! The stone shines like a little sun. It's been the dearest thing to me. (*Gives it to* Little Boy.)
Little Boy. And now it is dear to me.
Mary. I haven't anything but my vanity case. It's a silly thing to give but I love it more than anything else. (*Takes it from her pocket and opens it.*) See? It has a darling little mirror inside. Your mother will like it. (*Gives it to* Little Boy.)
John (*taking compass from his pocket, coming forward and looking at it as it lies in his hand*). I'm going to give you my compass. It has a silver case. Did you ever see a compass, boy? It tells the direction, and when you are lost it helps you to find the way. (*Hands it to* Little Boy.)
Little Boy (*taking the compass and looking at it smiles*). When the way is hard to find, I get my Father to help me.
Kate (*unclasping bracelets from her wrist*). Here, little boy, I give you both my precious bracelets. Don't they look like little gold handcuffs? Take both of them. (*Hands them to him.*)
Sarah. I have only this scarf. My uncle Hardy brought it back from Paris for me. I love pretty things to wear. (*Holds it out hastily to* Little Boy.) There! Please take

it. Put it around your neck, and it will help to keep you warm.

LITTLE BOY (*as* SARAH *puts the scarf about his neck*). Yes, it warms me.

PAUL (*tugging at his necktie*). Jim, I say, Jim! Here, help me get this pin out my tie. (JAMES *runs to help him.*) It's got a safety— Thank you. (*Takes out stick pin.*) Here, boy! That's a diamond in the center. Sho' 'nough. No kidding. I got it for my birthday. (*Turns to* LITTLE BOY.) There! I want you to have it. Honest, I do.

LITTLE BOY (*taking the pin and smiling sweetly up at* PAUL). How hard it is to part with a treasure!

HARRY (*unpinning medal from his coat*). I haven't got a thing but—but this medal. I won it for making a speech. It's gold, all right. See? (*Shows it to* LITTLE BOY.) It has my name written on the back: Harry Morgan. Here, you take it. (*Thrusts it quickly into the* LITTLE BOY'S *hand.*)

LITTLE BOY. You'll win other rewards some day.

FANNY (*crossing down to* LITTLE BOY). Here, little boy, I want you to have my garnets. (*Takes stones from her pocket and holding them out to him.*) I said I wouldn't ever give them away—not for the King of England, but—

LITTLE BOY (*looking at the garnets*). They are like drops of blood. How pretty!

(MISS ANGELICA *gives each child a holly wreath.*)

FANNY. I want you to have them, but don't go thinking I'm good like these others (*motions to the other children*) 'cause I'm not. I don't believe in things I can't see. (*Meditatively.*) But I did like that:

"Where meek souls will receive him still,
The dear Christ enters in."

Do you know that song? (LITTLE BOY *nods.*) You do? I would like you for a friend. You seem to understand things, even if you are so little. I want you to come and see me and my brother Jim over there—that big boy that gave you the watch. Will you come?

LITTLE BOY. Yes, I'll come whenever you want me. I *am* your friend.

MISS ANGELICA. All the wreaths are gone, except for this little one.

MARY (*taking it from* MISS ANGELICA). Why, it looks just like a little crown. And see! It is golden. Here, little boy, let me put it on your head. I believe it will just fit. (*Puts it on the child's head.*) Oh, did the thorns prick? I'll take it off.

LITTLE BOY. No, please. I'll wear it so.

JOHN. How like a little king he looks!

JAMES. And all of us giving him gifts. Say! (*Brightens as if a thought has struck him, but he says nothing more.*)

LITTLE BOY. You've been kind to me—all of you. I shall never forget. Now, I must be going, for my Father who sent me will have need of me. I hope you'll be happy this Christmas. I shall be happy.

(MISS ANGELICA *pats his head and leads him to left door, as the children wave to him.*)

ALL THE CHILDREN (*in concert*). Good-bye, good-bye!

(*As* MISS ANGELICA *escorts the* LITTLE BOY *off at left, the lights are extinguished, and the stage is left in total darkness, long enough for each member of the company to get his gift back from the* LITTLE BOY, *giving up his wreath in exchange. All this should be done silently, so that it will not be detected by the audience. If preferred, the curtain may be lowered for a few moments in order to make the exchange more conveniently, then raised again with the lights on. During this interval, a group of carol singers off stage are heard singing very softly "Come, All Ye Faithful," as if they were far down the street. As the lights gradually come on and the stage resumes its former lighting effect, the singing dies away, and the children are discovered in their former positions, with their offerings to the* LITTLE BOY *each in its accustomed place.* MISS ANGELICA *is still absent.*)

JAMES. What's happened to the lights? They're coming back, now. Funny the way they dimmed!

PAUL. Say, honest, did you see that awful patch on his shirt? I didn't notice it till he turned to go out.

HARRY. Yes, I saw it. It looked like a cross.

JOHN. It was a patch. But at first, just for an instant, it looked like a great shadow—the shadow of a cross. Then I saw it was a piece of dark cloth sewed on. And, of course, there was nothing to make a shadow like that.

PAUL. It made me feel funny; honest, it did.

KATE. Poor little boy! And did you see how ragged his clothes were? He was certainly glad to have us take those wreaths. He had the most beautiful face I ever saw.

FANNY. He had the kindest face, and he seemed to understand everything.

MARY. Yes, such a little fellow, and yet he had a way of talking that made you know he was strangely wise.

KATE. I'd like to have him for a brother.

FANNY. So would I.

SARAH. He was poor, but he didn't talk like a rough person. He wasn't at all afraid. You'd think, all of us being strangers, he might have been afraid.

JAMES. He trusted us, and—and he kind of made us— (*Hesitates.*)

MARY (*finishing* JAMES' *sentence*). —believe in him. Yes, he did.

AMY. He never said a word about his hurts. I never saw a little boy like that before. He seemed to be thinking only of his people.

MISS ANGELICA *enters at left, closing door behind her. She appears radiant. The children crowd around her, eager with questions.*

ALL THE CHILDREN (*in confused chorus*). Has he gone? Wasn't he nice? Did you see the patch? Did you ask him his name?

JOHN. Strange none of us asked him his name!

Miss Angelica. No, I never asked him his name. How stupid!

Paul. I wonder where he lives. We didn't think to ask him that, either. We are dumb; honest, we are.

Fanny. It's funny we never saw him before. Right here in town, and all. Anyone would notice him, for his face is like an angel's.

Mary. And the unusual way he talks, that would make people—

Kate (*interrupting eagerly*). You never saw him before; did you, Miss Angelica?

Miss Angelica (*thoughtfully*). No; no. I'm quite sure I never saw him before. And yet—

John. What did you say?

Miss Angelica. I wonder— I just wonder if— (*Hesitates.*)

James (*confusedly*). You know, I've been thinking— And I— Say, it sounds queer, but you know— Say, you know I had a notion it might be little—

Mary (*interrupting him*). Oh, Miss Angelica, do you think it—it could have been—?

Miss Angelica (*quoting*). "As ye have done it unto the least of these my brethren, ye have done it unto me." (*Puts her hand up to her throat and starts. The children look bewildered, for there around her neck is the gold chain with the gold heart.*) I—I—dear me, my locket!

Kate. Did he give it back?

Fanny. Oh, Miss Angelica!

Miss Angelica (*bewildered*). Dear children, I—I can't imagine how it got back here. No, he did not give it back. Why, I saw it in his little hand as he went away.

John (*whose hand has gone to his pocket*). That's strange! Why, here's—

Fanny (*putting her hand in her pocket*). Would you believe it? Look! My garnets! Why didn't he take them? I—I wanted him to have them. And I thought he looked so happy when I gave them to him.

JOHN (*taking out compass and staring at it*). My compass is back in my pocket. I'd like to know how—

JAMES (*pointing to* PAUL). Say, look at Paul's pin, right back in his tie! It's a miracle. (*Reaches into his pocket and takes out watch.*) Why, say, here's my watch right in my pocket! Well, I say!

KATE (*holding out her arms to show her bracelets*). My bracelets!

MARY (*after a search, produces her vanity case*). Here's my vanity. Oh, Miss Angelica, this all couldn't have been— just a dream?

SARAH (*looking down at her feet*). It's my scarf. I felt it slip from my neck. (*Picks up scarf and holds it up for audience to see.*) Now how do you suppose—? I certainly gave it to the little boy.

AMY. That's nothing. Look! Here's my ring right back on my finger. (*Holds up her hand.*) You know I gave it to him.

HARRY. And I've got my medal back. (*Pulls out his coat lapel to show medal.*) When I gave it to him, it seemed a lot. I'm sorry he didn't keep it.

FANNY. I'm sorry he didn't want my garnets. It hurt to part with them, but after I'd put them in his hand, I felt so happy. He made me see things differently. I can't understand how all our—you know—how we got these things back.

MARY (*looking around at the others*). Why, where have all the wreaths gone?

JOHN. They've gone—every last one of them. This must have been a dream.

KATE. Or a miracle!

SARAH. A miracle! And the little boy!

MARY. Our giving him those things did make him happy. His eyes were bright and shining with joy when he went away. I wonder—

JOHN. It couldn't have been that he didn't want our gifts.

MISS ANGELICA. Oh, children, don't you see? Do you remember what we came here for?

AMY. We came to sing carols.

HARRY. And light the candle.

PAUL. And let the little Jesus know we were up to welcome Him.

JOHN. We were hoping He would come to us.

JAMES. He did come. Don't you understand? I thought it out long ago.

SARAH (*startled*). You mean?

JAMES. Little Jesus—

FANNY (*bursting in excitedly*). Oh, Miss Angelica, it was a miracle. I know that that was the little Jesus.

(MISS ANGELICA *nods assent.*)

MARY. Now, I wonder why He didn't want our gifts.

MISS ANGELICA. Oh, children, don't you understand? It's because we didn't know it was He that makes what we did worth while. He came and we received; that's what makes us happy. That's what made Him happy. It wasn't our lockets and watches and vanities and rings He wanted. He wanted our hearts. Did you give Him these?

ALL THE CHILDREN (*in concert, eagerly*). Yes, yes.

MISS ANGELICA. That's why He went away so happy. That is why He left us His blessing.

FANNY. It wasn't a dream. It was true, and I shall remember Him all my life long. He said He would be my friend.

MISS ANGELICA. No, it was no dream. He is your friend, Fanny, and mine—a friend to each one of us.

MARY. Our King!

MISS ANGELICA. Yes, and we must serve Him in love not only at this glad season, but all our lives long.

KATE. Miss Angelica, that makes me think of "Hark! What Mean Those Holy Voices?" Let's sing that now.

(NOTE.—*Any other appropriate Christmas carol may be substituted, if desired.*)

MISS ANGELICA. Our last carol, children; then we must be leaving. (*She goes to the piano and plays while the chil-*

dren, gathering around her, sing softly "Hark! What Mean Those Holy Voices?" As they are singing the last stanza, the curtain begins to descend slowly, while the chimes heard earlier in the play may be rung off stage, blending with the singing.)

CURTAIN

A CHRISTMAS CAROL

A PLAY IN THREE SCENES

Adapted from Charles Dickens'
immortal story

By

WALTER BEN HARE

PRODUCTION RIGHTS

A CHRISTMAS CAROL

For ten men, seven women, four boys, two girls, and extras

CHARACTERS

(In the order of their first appearance)

BOB CRATCHIT.........................*Scrooge's clerk*
EBENEZER SCROOGE..................*A miserly merchant*
FIRST WAIT.................*Leader of the carol singers*
FRED ....*Scrooge's nephew*
FIRST LASS }
SECOND LASS } ....*Collecting for the mission*
THE GHOST OF JACOB MARLEY..........*Scrooge's partner*
FIRST SPIRIT...............*The Ghost of Christmas Past*
FEZZIWIG..........................*A jolly old merchant*
EBENEZER......................*Scrooge as a young man*
DICK................................*His fellow clerk*
OLD FIDDLER...............*Who plays for the Fezziwigs*
MRS. FEZZIWIG...............*One vast, substantial smile*
BELLA......................*Scrooge's first and only love*
SECOND SPIRIT..........*The Ghost of Christmas Present*
MRS. CRATCHIT.............................*Bob's wife*

BELINDA
PETER
BOB
BETTY } ....*The Cratchit children*
MARTHA
TINY TIM
THIRD SPIRIT.........*The Ghost of Christmas Yet to Be*

Five men, five women, and a small boy for the Fezziwig tableau, and chorus of waits (boys to sing Christmas carols)

TIME—*Christmastide in the nineteenth century.*

PLACE—*The counting house of Scrooge and Marley.*

TIME OF PLAYING—*Forty minutes.*

SYNOPSIS OF SCENES

SCENE 1. The counting house office of Scrooge and Marley at front of stage, about five o'clock in the afternoon before Christmas. During the scene, the rear curtains are opened, revealing the Fezziwig workshop at rear of stage.

SCENE 2. Same as opening of Scene 1, shortly after the close of Scene 1. During the scene, the rear curtains are opened, revealing the Cratchit kitchen at rear of stage.

SCENE 3. Same as opening of previous scenes, the morning of Christmas Day. Early in the scene, the rear curtains are opened, revealing a churchyard with Scrooge's tombstone in the foreground, with quick return to original office setting.

COSTUMES AND CHARACTERISTICS

Cratchit is a meek and kindly man of about forty, wearing a very shabby dark suit, neatly patched, in much the same style as that of Scrooge, but much shabbier, with a long, white woolen muffler around his neck. For outdoors, he dons an old cap. For Scenes 1 and 2 he wears a sprig of mistletoe or holly on his coat.

Scrooge is a thin, gray-haired, sour-faced man in his late forties, with a lined countenance. In Scene 3, his expression changes to one of benevolence. He wears a shabby dark suit, with no sign of jewelry. If the characters are costumed in the Victorian period style, he should wear very tight dark trousers, low-cut brown vest, shabby black full-dress coat, soft white shirt, black stock tie, and high collar made by taking an ordinary turn-over collar and turning it up.

First Wait is a boy of about twelve, wearing a white smock, ragged trousers, old shoes, and felt hat twined with red and green ribbons.

Fred is a bright, cheerful young man of twenty-two, with a loud and happy laugh. He is dressed in a dark suit similar in style to Scrooge's, with ruffled shirt, stock tie, high collar, overcoat and top hat.

First and Second Lass are girls in their early twenties, wearing dark skirts, long dark capes, and dark blue poke bonnets with red ribbons across the front.

Marley's Ghost is an elderly man who speaks in a subdued monotone and wears a long black robe with a black hood and chains about his waist weighted down with several toy money banks. If desired, he may wear a skeleton false face, or his face may be made up as a skeleton's with white, black, and gray grease paint. At his entrance his face is hidden in the black hood.

First Spirit is a little girl of ten, with long light hair, dressed in white Grecian draperies trimmed with tinsel and with a crown of tinsel.

Fezziwig is a short, stout, middle-aged man, always laughing and moving about. He wears a white colonial wig, short black trousers, white shirt, white stockings, low shoes with pasteboard buckles covered with tinfoil, and fancy colonial coat and hat.

Ebenezer should be played by a young man of Scrooge's height and general build, since he represents Scrooge as a young man. He and Dick are youths of about twenty, dressed much alike in colonial costume, without wigs.

Old Fiddler is a man of sixty, with white wig and whiskers, dressed in a long white smock and a hat trimmed with ribbons. Preferably the player of this rôle should be able to play simple dance tunes on the violin, but if he cannot, a violinist off stage in the wing nearest him may play the music while he goes through the motions of playing on his instrument.

Mrs. Fezziwig is a middle-aged woman in a white colonial wig and a gay-colored colonial gown tucked up over petticoats.

Bella is a pretty girl of twenty or more, with her hair in curls, wearing a neat colonial costume of pink and white.

Second Spirit is an old man with a white beard, dressed in a red robe trimmed with sprigs of green pine, with a white cotton border to represent snow, and wearing a peaked red cap trimmed with white cotton.

Peter, aged fourteen, wears a large white collar. Mrs. Cratchit is a middle-aged matron, jolly and good-natured. The other Cratchits include Belinda, aged eighteen, Bob, aged eleven, Betty, aged nine, Martha, aged seventeen, and Tiny Tim, aged four, who is a pathetic little cripple. The whole family wear old-fashioned costumes, faded and worn, but bright with cheap lace and gay ribbons. Martha makes her entrance wearing a bonnet, with a shawl over her dress.

Third Spirit, who appears only in pantomime, having no lines to speak, may use the same costume and make-up as Marley's Ghost.

The extras who appear in the Fezziwig tableau are costumed in the same style as the principals, the three Fezziwig girls, the cook, and the housemaid wearing dresses much like Mrs. Fezziwig's and the three escorts of the girls, the baker.

and the milkman wearing suits on the same order as Fezziwig's, while the small boy's costume resembles young Bob Cratchit's except for the fact that it is not old and ragged. The band of waits, who may be any number of teen-age boys, wear costumes exactly like that of First Wait, and each carries a branch of holly.

PROPERTIES

For CRATCHIT—Small coin.
For SCROOGE—Handful of coins.
For FIRST LASS—Subscription paper.
For FEZZIWIG—Handful of coins.
For OLD FIDDLER—Violin.
For SECOND SPIRIT—Torch in which a red light burns.
For MRS. CRATCHIT—Dish of pudding decked with holly.
For TINY TIM—Crutch.
For BOB and BETTY—Roast goose in baking pan (may be made of cardboard and painted).
For each wait—Branch of holly.

STAGE DIRECTIONS

Up stage means away from footlights; *down stage,* near footlights. In the use of *right* and *left,* the actor is supposed to be facing the audience.

SCROOGE · BOB CRACHIT · MARLEY'S GHOST · SECOND SPIRIT

THIRD SPIRIT · WAIT · MISSION LASS · FRED · FIRST SPIRIT

MRS FEZZIWIG · FEZZIWIG · BELLA · COSTUME OF EBENEZER & DICK · FIDDLER

PETER BETTY, BELINDA and Mrs CRACHIT · THE CRACHIT FAMILY · MARTHA · BOB · TINY TIM

THE SCENERY

A CHRISTMAS CAROL

SCENE 1

SCENE: *The counting house of* SCROOGE *and* MARLEY. *A dark, dreary office is constructed across the front of the stage, enclosed by brown curtains at sides, with two entrances at right and left respectively and brown curtains at rear. These rear curtains should be arranged to be parted, showing the tableau stage back of the real stage. The tableau stage is elevated a few feet above the real stage. This makes a better picture but is not absolutely necessary. A high desk is at right facing the right wall. A tall stool stands at this desk, and a ledger, quill pen, ink, candle are on the desk. A small, old desk is down left, facing audience, with a desk chair back of it. Two common wooden chairs are at right center and left center respectively. A ledger, quill pen, books, and a candle stuck in an old dark bottle are on desk down left. On the wall above the desk at right hangs a clock, which strikes on cue, when someone off stage back of it taps out the hour on a gong. The stage lights are half up, reinforced by the dim light of the two candles, for which electric bulbs should be used.*

Before the curtain rises, waits are heard off left, singing the "Christmas Carol," music of which is given at the end of this book. At rise of curtain, BOB CRATCHIT *is discovered seated on stool, bent over ledger at right desk, working by the light of the candle. As the waits sing,* CRATCHIT *turns and listens.*

Enter SCROOGE *from right in a towering passion, slam-*

ming door behind him. CRATCHIT *hurriedly returns to his work.* SCROOGE *crosses to left door and flings it open angrily.*

SCROOGE (*calling off left*). Get away from my door. Begone, ye beggars! I've nothing for you.

FIRST WAIT *sticks his head in door at left.*

FIRST WAIT. Only a shillin', sir, for a merry Christmas, yer honor.

SCROOGE. Get away from there or I'll call the police.

FIRST WAIT. Only a shillin', sir.

SCROOGE. Not a penny. I have other places to put my money. Go on, now. You don't get a cent. Not a penny!

FIRST WAIT. All right, sir. Merry Christmas, just the same, sir. (*Exit, left.*)

SCROOGE (*comes down to his desk at left, muttering*). Howling idiots! Give 'em a shilling, hey? I'd like to give 'em six months in the work'us—that I would. Paupers! I'd show 'em what a merry Christmas is. (CRATCHIT *gets down from stool and starts to slink off at left.*) Hey!

CRATCHIT (*pauses, turns to* SCROOGE). Yes, sir.

SCROOGE. Where you going?

CRATCHIT. I was just going to get a few coals, sir. Just to warm us up a bit, sir.

SCROOGE. You let my coals alone. Get back to work. I'm not complaining about the cold, am I? And I'm an older man than you are. Back to work!

CRATCHIT (*sighs, pauses, then speaks meekly*). Yes, sir. (*Resumes work.*)

SCROOGE. You want to let my coals alone if you expect to keep your job. I'm not a millionaire. Understand? (*Loudly.*) Understand?

CRATCHIT. Yes, sir, I understand. (*Shivers, wraps long white woolen muffler closer about throat, and warms hands at candle.*)

SCROOGE. Here it is three o'clock, the middle of the afternoon, and two candles burning. What more do you want? Want me to end up in the poorhouse?

FRED (*calling from off left*). Uncle! Uncle! Where are you? Merry Christmas, uncle.

FRED *enters at left, laughing, and comes down center.*

SCROOGE (*looking up from his work*). Oh, it's you, is it?

FRED. Of course it is, uncle. Merry Christmas! God save you!

SCROOGE (*with disgust*). Merry Christmas! Bah! Humbug!

FRED. Christmas a humbug, uncle? You don't mean that, I'm sure.

SCROOGE. I don't, hey? Merry Christmas! What cause have you got to be merry? You're poor enough.

FRED (*laughing good-naturedly*). Come, then. What right have you got to be dismal? You're rich enough. So, merry Christmas, uncle.

SCROOGE. Out upon your merry Christmas! What's Christmas time to you but a time for paying bills without money—a time for finding yourself a year older, but not an hour richer? You keep Christmas in your own way and let me keep it in mine.

FRED. Keep it? But you don't keep it!

SCROOGE. Let me leave it alone, then. Much good may it do you! Much good has it ever done you!

FRED. Christmas is a good time, uncle—a kind, forgiving, charitable, pleasant time—the only time I know of, in the long calendar of the year, when men and women seem by one consent to open their shut-up hearts freely and to think of people below them in the social scale. And therefore, uncle, though it has never put a scrap of gold or silver in my pocket, I believe that it has done me good, and will do me good; and I say, "God bless it. God bless Christmas!"

CRATCHIT (*who has been listening eagerly, claps his hands*). Good!

SCROOGE (*to* CRATCHIT). Let me hear another sound

from *you* and you'll keep your Christmas by losing your job. Get to work!

CRATCHIT. Yes, sir. (*Resumes his work on the ledger.*)

SCROOGE (*to* FRED). You're quite a powerful speaker, sir. I wonder you don't go into Parliament.

FRED. Don't be angry, uncle. Come and dine with us to-morrow.

SCROOGE. Dine with you? Me? I'll see you hanged first. Dine with you? I'll see you in— (CRATCHIT *sneezes violently*. SCROOGE *turns to him.*) What's the matter with *you*? (SCROOGE *turns back to* FRED.) I'm a busy man. Good afternoon.

FRED. Come, uncle. Say, " Yes."

SCROOGE. No.

FRED. But why? Why?

SCROOGE (*savagely*). Why did you get married?

FRED. Because I fell in love.

SCROOGE. Bah! (*Resumes his work.*) Good afternoon.

FRED. I want nothing from you. I ask nothing from you. But why can't we be friends?

SCROOGE. Good afternoon.

FRED. Uncle, I won't part in anger. My dear mother was your only sister—your only relation. For her sake, let us be friends.

SCROOGE (*savagely*). Good afternoon.

FRED. I'll still keep the Christmas spirit, uncle. A merry Christmas to you.

SCROOGE (*busy at ledger*). Bah!

FRED. And a happy New Year.

SCROOGE. Good afternoon!

FRED (*goes to* CRATCHIT). And a merry Christmas to you, Bob Cratchit.

CRATCHIT (*getting down from stool and shaking hands with* FRED *warmly*). Merry Christmas, sir. God bless it!

FRED. Ay, God bless it! And a happy New Year.

CRATCHIT. And a happy New Year, too! God bless that, too.

FRED. Ay, Bob. God bless that, too. (*Exit, left.*)

SCROOGE. Cratchit, get to work!

CRATCHIT. Yes, sir. (*Resumes work.*)

SCROOGE (*looks at him*). Humph! Fifteen shillings a week and a wife and six children, and he talks about a merry Christmas. Humph! (*Works on ledger.*)

Enter two mission lassies at left. They come down center. FIRST LASS *carries a subscription paper.*

FIRST LASS. Scrooge and Marley's, I believe? Have I the pleasure of addressing Mr. Scrooge or Mr. Marley?

SCROOGE. Mr. Marley has been dead these seven years. He died seven years ago this very night.

FIRST LASS. We have no doubt his liberality is represented by his surviving partner. (*Hands him the subscription paper.*)

SCROOGE. Liberality? Humph! (*Returns paper to her.*)

SECOND LASS. At this festive season of the year, Mr. Scrooge, we are trying to make some slight provision for the poor and destitute, who are suffering greatly. Hundreds of thousands are in want of common comforts, sir.

SCROOGE. Are there no prisons?

SECOND LASS (*sighs*). Plenty of prisons, sir.

SCROOGE. And the workhouses—are they still in operation?

FIRST LASS. They are, sir; but they scarcely furnish Christmas cheer for mind and body. We are trying to raise a fund to buy the poor some meat and drink and means of warmth.

SECOND LASS. We chose this time because it is a time when want is keenly felt and abundance rejoices. What shall we put you down for?

SCROOGE. Nothing.

FIRST LASS. You wish to be anonymous?

SCROOGE. I wish to be left alone. I don't make merry myself at Christmas. I don't believe in it. And I can't afford to make idle people merry. They should go to the poorhouse.

SECOND LASS. Many of them would rather die, sir, than do that.

SCROOGE (*savagely*). If they would rather die, they'd better do it and decrease the population. And besides, I am a very busy man.

FIRST LASS. But, sir—

SCROOGE (*interrupts*). Good afternoon.

FIRST LASS. I'm sorry, sir—sorry.

SCROOGE. Sorry for them?

FIRST LASS. No, sir. I'm sorry for you, sir. Good afternoon. (*Exit at left, followed by* SECOND LASS.)

SCROOGE. Sorry for me, hey? (*There is a pause. He works. The clock strikes five.*) Sorry for me!

CRATCHIT (*closes his book and blows out candle*). Is there anything more, sir? (*Comes to center.*)

SCROOGE. You'll want all day off to-morrow, I suppose?

CRATCHIT. If it's quite convenient, sir.

SCROOGE. Well, it isn't; and it's not fair. If I'd dock you a half a crown for it, you'd think I was ill using you, wouldn't you?

CRATCHIT (*nervously*). I don't know, sir.

SCROOGE. And yet you expect me to pay a full day's wages for no work.

CRATCHIT. It only comes once a year, sir—only once a year.

SCROOGE. A poor excuse for picking a man's pocket every twenty-fifth of December! But I suppose you've got to have the whole day. But you be here all the earlier next morning.

CRATCHIT. Oh, yes, indeed, sir.

SCROOGE. I'll stay here a bit and finish up the work.

CRATCHIT *goes off at right, returning immediately wearing his hat. He turns up his coat collar, wraps the long white woolen muffler around chin, and pulls hat down over his face.*

CRATCHIT (*crosses to door left*). I'm going, sir.

SCROOGE. All right.

CRATCHIT (*shields face with arm as though he were afraid* SCROOGE *might throw something at him*). Merry Christmas, sir! (*Runs off at left.*)

SCROOGE. Bah! Humbug! (*He works at ledger, then finally drops his head on his arms and sleeps. The light of his candle goes out.* SCROOGE *may blow it out, unseen by audience.*)

The stage is now in darkness. A musical bell tolls off left. After a pause, another bell tolls off right. The clinking of chains is heard. When the stage is completely darkened, the GHOST OF MARLEY *slips on at right and sits in plain wooden chair at right center. He is entirely covered with black, face and all, so as to be quite invisible. Mysterious music sounds. A sudden clap of thunder is heard. A green light from the wings at right is thrown on the ghost's face. The thunder dies away. The clanking of chains is heard. The ghost groans.*

SCROOGE (*starts up, looks at ghost, and pauses*). How now? What do you want with me?

MARLEY'S GHOST. Much.

SCROOGE. Who are you?

MARLEY'S GHOST. Ask me who I was.

SCROOGE. Well, who were you, then?

MARLEY'S GHOST. In life I was your partner, Jacob Marley. It is required of every man that the spirit within him should walk abroad among his fellow-men, and if that spirit goes not forth in life, it is condemned to do so after death.

SCROOGE. You are fettered. Tell me why.

MARLEY'S GHOST. I wear the chain I forged in life. I made it link by link, yard by yard—the heavy chain of avarice. Now I must make amends for the opportunities I neglected in life.

SCROOGE. But you were always a, good man of business, Jacob.

MARLEY'S GHOST. Business? Mankind should have been

my business. Kind actions, charity, mercy, benevolence, love—all should have been my business. I am here to-night to warn you—to warn you, Ebenezer Scrooge, that you have yet a chance of escaping my fate.

SCROOGE. You were always a good friend to me.

MARLEY'S GHOST. You will be haunted by three spirits.

SCROOGE. If it's all the same to you, I think I'd rather not.

MARLEY'S GHOST. Without their visits, you cannot hope to escape my fate. Expect the first when the bell tolls one.

SCROOGE. Couldn't I take it all at once and have it over, Jacob?

MARLEY'S GHOST. Remember my warning and heed the message, and you may yet be saved. My time is over. (*Chains rattle.*) Farewell, farewell, farewell! (*Loud crash of thunder. The green light is quenched, and* MARLEY'S GHOST *exits at right, unseen by audience.*)

After a pause, the bell off stage tolls one. Enter SPIRIT OF CHRISTMAS PAST, *right, in a strong white light streaming from off right. She comes down right.*

SCROOGE (*trembling*). Are you the spirit whose coming was foretold to me?

FIRST SPIRIT. I am.

SCROOGE. Who and what are you?

FIRST SPIRIT. I am the Ghost of Christmas Past.

SCROOGE. Long past?

FIRST SPIRIT. No, your past.

SCROOGE. Why have you come here to me?

FIRST SPIRIT. For your own welfare. I must teach you the first lesson of consideration.

SCROOGE. But I *am* considerate.

FIRST SPIRIT. Are you a kind master to your clerk?

SCROOGE. Well, I'm not unkind.

FIRST SPIRIT. Do you remember your own first master, one Fezziwig by name?

SCROOGE. Indeed, I do. Bless his dear, old heart! He was the kindest master that ever lived.

FIRST SPIRIT. Then why haven't you followed his good example? Would any of your clerks say that you were the kindest master that ever lived?

SCROOGE. Well, times have changed; that's it. It's all the fault of the times.

FIRST SPIRIT. It's all the fault of a squeezing, wrenching, grasping, scraping, clutching, covetous old sinner, hard and sharp as flint, from which no steel has ever struck out a generous fire! No wind that blows is more bitter than he, no falling snow is more intent upon its purpose, no pelting rain less open to entreaty. And his name is Ebenezer Scrooge.

SCROOGE. All I ask is to edge my way along the crowded path of life. I want to be left alone. That's all—left alone.

FIRST SPIRIT. I have come to save you, Ebenezer Scrooge. I have come to kindle into life the stone that once was your heart. First, I will show you the kind heart and generosity of your old-time master. Behold the warehouse of Fezziwig and Company.

(*The rear curtains are drawn apart, revealing a workshop, with two doors at right and left respectively and with a desk down right, facing front, with two desk chairs back of it. A barrel is up left, with a number of long festoons of Christmas greens lying on it. A sign on rear wall reads, " Fezziwig and Company." Two young men, EBENEZER and DICK, are discovered happily working at desk. FEZZIWIG stands up left looking off left. Waits are heard off left at rear, singing the " Christmas Carol," the music of which is given in the back of this book.*)

WAITS (*singing, off left*).
         Christ was born on Christmas Day,
         Wreathe the holly, twine the bay;
         Light and life and joy is He,
             The babe, the son,
             The Holy One
                Of Mary.

FEZZIWIG (*flinging them a handful of coins*). That's right, my lads. Sing away. Merry Christmas to you.

WAITS (*in concert, off left*). Thank ye, sir. Merry Christmas and happy New Year! Thank ye, sir. (*They sing and the song dies away in the distance.*)

SCROOGE (*down right with* FIRST SPIRIT). Why, it's old Fezziwig. Bless his dear, old heart! It's Fezziwig alive again.

FEZZIWIG (*comes merrily down center*). Yo-ho, my boys! No more work for to-night. Christmas Eve, Dick! (*Throws his arms over the shoulders of the two boys.*) Christmas Eve, Ebenezer! God bless Christmas.

DICK. Ay, ay, sir.

EBENEZER. Ay, ay. God bless Christmas.

FIRST SPIRIT. Did you hear that, Scrooge? That is yourself; and you said, "God bless Christmas."

SCROOGE. That's true. That was thirty years ago.

FEZZIWIG (*bustling about*). The missus and the girls are downstairs, so let's clear away before you can say, "Jack Robinson." (*They push desk back, and decorate rear stage with the strings of Christmas greens on the barrel,* FEZZIWIG *talking all the time.*) Yo-ho! That's right, Dick. String the Christmas greens. Here you are, Ebenezer. We're going to have the merriest time in all the kingdom. (*Dancing a step or two.*) I'll show ye how to enjoy life. That's it. Now we're all ready. (*Sings.*) "Wreathe the holly, twine the bay!" Let's have lots of room. Clear away, Dick. Here comes the fiddler now.

Enter OLD FIDDLER *at right. He sits on barrel at rear and starts to tune up.*

OLD FIDDLER. Merry Christmas, sir.

FEZZIWIG. The same to you, granfer, and many of 'em.

Enter MRS. FEZZIWIG, *left.*

MRS. FEZZIWIG. Lawsy, lawsy! I thought we'd be late.

(*Goes to the two boys and puts her arms over their shoulders.*)   And how's my merry boys to-night?

DICK.   Finer'n a fiddle.

EBENEZER.   Merry Christmas, Mrs. Fezziwig.

MRS. FEZZIWIG.   The same to you, dear lads.

FEZZIWIG.   Where's the girls, mother?

MRS. FEZZIWIG.   Here they come—Flora, Felicity, and little Fanny May.

Enter the three Fezziwig girls with three escorts at left. Everybody bustles around shaking hands.

ALL (*in confused chorus*).   Merry Christmas!   Merry Christmas!

FEZZIWIG.   And here's the housemaid and her cousin, the baker.

Enter housemaid and 'baker at left.

FEZZIWIG.   The cook and the milkman, and the lonesome little boy from over the way!   And Ebenezer's young lady, Miss Bella.

Enter BELLA, cook, milkman, and small boy at left.

FEZZIWIG.   And now, mother, what do you say to a rollicking game of Puss in the Corner?

(*All play Puss in the Corner, with much loud laughter, clapping hands, running about, etc.   OLD FIDDLER plays.*)

MRS. FEZZIWIG.   Oh, I never was so happy in all my life. This is the real spirit of Christmas.

FEZZIWIG (*hanging a bit of mistletoe from a festoon draped across center of stage*).   And here's the mistletoe.

(*All form a ring and play a ring game, with much noise and confusion.*)

EBENEZER (*catching* MRS. FEZZIWIG *under the mistletoe*). I've got ye! (*Kisses her.*)

MRS. FEZZIWIG. God bless the boy!

EBENEZER. And God bless the merry Christmas!

FEZZIWIG. And now a dance, my hearties. Yo-ho for the old-time Christmas dance!

(*They dance a few figures of Sir Roger de Coverley or the Virginia reel, while* OLD FIDDLER *plays. All are dancing wildly, swinging, etc., with plenty of loud laughter, clapping of hands, etc., as the rear curtains are drawn. Note: Use brilliant lights from right and left upon the rear stage.*)

FIRST SPIRIT. What a small matter to make these silly folks so full of gratitude and happiness!

SCROOGE (*astonished*). Small? It was the happiest time in my life.

FIRST SPIRIT. And yet your master only spent a few pounds of your mortal money—three or four, perhaps. And yet he kindled the true spirit of Christmas in all your hearts.

SCROOGE. He could have made us miserable, but he made every day we worked for him seem like Christmas.

FIRST SPIRIT (*gazes steadily at* SCROOGE, *who becomes uneasy under the look*). What's the matter now?

SCROOGE (*trying to appear unconcerned, but failing*). Oh, nothing!

FIRST SPIRIT (*gazing at him*). Something, I think.

SCROOGE. No, nothing; only this: I wish I could say a word or two to my clerk just now. That's all. Poor fellow! I'm afraid I've been a little hard on him. Poor Bob Cratchit!

FIRST SPIRIT. My work is thriving, but my time grows short. Quick! I have another picture for you.

(*Soft music sounds. The curtains part, showing the scene as before, but only* EBENEZER *and* BELLA *are discovered. Soft music is played all through this scene.*)

BELLA. It matters little to you—very little. Another idol

has displaced me; that's all. If it can comfort you and cheer you in time to come, as I would have tried to do, I have no just cause to grieve.

EBENEZER (*irritated*). What idol has displaced you in my heart?

BELLA. An idol of gold.

EBENEZER. Well, I must make money. You know that. Poverty is the hardest thing in the world.

BELLA. I have seen your nobler instincts fall off, one by one. Now nothing remains in your heart but the love of gold. Therefore I am releasing you from your engagement. (*Takes ring from her finger and hands it to him.*)

EBENEZER. Have I ever sought release?

BELLA. In words, no; but in everything else, yes. I am penniless. If you married me, you would probably regret it. So I release you with a heart full of love for the noble man you once were.

EBENEZER. But, Bella—

BELLA (*interrupts*). You will soon forget me. Your time and your mind will be full of business, seeking after gold. The idol of gold has driven love from your heart, but may you be happy and contented in the life you have chosen.

(*The rear curtains are drawn.*)

FIRST SPIRIT. And are you happy and content in the life you have chosen, Ebenezer Scrooge?

SCROOGE. No, a thousand times, no. I threw away her love, the one pure thing in my life, for gold. And now I'm alone—alone. (*Sinks in chair at desk and sobs.*)

FIRST SPIRIT. I have shown shadows of times that are passed. Have you learned a lesson from the Spirit of Christmas Past?

SCROOGE. I have, I have; a bitter, bitter lesson.

FIRST SPIRIT. And will you see more?

SCROOGE. No, no. Show me no more. Torture me no longer.

FIRST SPIRIT. Remember the lesson you have learned.

Remember the kindness of your old master. Remember the love of your old sweetheart. Your life is barren and bitter, but there is yet time for repentance. (*Bell tolls twice.*) The signal! My hour is past. On the stroke of six, my brother, the Spirit of the Christmas Present will visit you. Remember! Repent! Believe! Farewell, farewell, farewell!

THE FRONT CURTAIN SLOWLY FALLS.

SCENE 2

SCENE: *Same as in Scene 1. Lights are half up, but candles are not burning. The rear curtains are closed.* SCROOGE *is discovered asleep at his desk. The* SPIRIT OF CHRISTMAS PRESENT *sits at right center, a red light shining on him. He carries a torch, in which a red light burns. The bells off stage toll six times.* SCROOGE *suddenly awakens and gazes at* SECOND SPIRIT.

SECOND SPIRIT. Arise, arise, Ebenezer Scrooge, and learn to know me better.

SCROOGE (*frightened*). I don't believe I ever met you before.

SECOND SPIRIT. Probably not. I am the Spirit of Christmas—the Ghost of Christmas Present.

SCROOGE. The Ghost of Christmas Present?

SECOND SPIRIT. I am a brother of the little Spirit of Christmas Past who visited you before.

SCROOGE. And are you going to show me all my past misdeeds?

SECOND SPIRIT. Not I. I am going to show you your present misdeeds. It is my mission to show you the love and comradeship of Christmas of to-day. I travel among the common people. My torch is their benediction. If there is a slight quarrel or if there are any misunderstandings on Christmas Day, I simply throw on them the light of my torch. And then they say it is a shame to quarrel on

Christmas Day—the day of peace and love. And so it is God bless it! God bless Christmas Day!

SCROOGE. And what do you intend to show me?

SECOND SPIRIT. I intend to show you the House of Happiness.

SCROOGE. Is it a wonderful palace of gold?

SECOND SPIRIT. It is a humble little kitchen. In fact, the kitchen of your poor clerk, Bob Cratchit. Bob, with his fifteen shillings a week, with his wife and six children, with his shabby clothes and his humble, shabby manners—Bob, with his little four-room house and his struggle to keep the wolf from the door. The Ghost of Christmas Present blesses his abode. Behold!

Bright, cheerful music is heard, off stage. SCROOGE *and* SECOND SPIRIT *cross to down right. The rear curtains open, showing the interior of the Cratchit kitchen, with two doors at right and left respectively. Everything is neat, but shows extreme poverty. A fireplace is in back flat up center, with a kettle boiling on a crane on the hearth. A table is at left center, with red cloth and lighted lamp. A cupboard filled with dishes and silverware is up right. Old chairs are scattered around stage. A shabby armchair is down right. Several pots of bright flowers are in evidence on mantelshelf and cupboard. A row of hooks for wraps is in the wall near right door. A bird in a cage is singing over the mantelshelf.* PETER *is discovered watching the potatoes boiling in the kettle at the fireplace. Enter* MRS. CRATCHIT *and* BELINDA *at left.*

MRS. CRATCHIT. Hurry, Belinda. We must set the table right away. How's the 'taters, Peter?

PETER (*peeps into the kettle*). Boiling, mumsy, boiling.

MRS. CRATCHIT. Here, carry the lamp over there.

BELINDA. Yes, ma'am. (*Puts lamp on cupboard.*)

MRS. CRATCHIT. And now where's the white tablecloth?

BELINDA (*getting it from cupboard drawer*). Here it is, mumsy.

(MRS. CRATCHIT *and* BELINDA *get castor, dishes, silverware, etc., from cupboard and place them on table during the following scene.*)

MRS. CRATCHIT. Whatever has got your precious father, I wonder? He and Tiny Tim have been at the church these three hours.

Enter BOB *and* BETTY *from right. They run down and kiss* MRS. CRATCHIT.

BOB. Oh, mumsy, we saw the goose—we did. We peeped in through the bakery window and we saw the goose—we did.

BETTY. And we smelled him, too. And we went inside— we did. And the baker asked us what was wantin'. And Bob said he wanted to know which goose was the Cratchit goose.

BOB. And he pointed to the very biggest one, mumsy. Didn't he, Betty?

BETTY. And it was all nice and brown on top. And he said it 'ud be ready in 'bout twenty minutes. Didn't he, Bob?

BOB. And it was the best-looking goose I ever saw—it was. It just made me hungry to see him and to smell him baking.

BETTY. And it had sage and onion stuffing, mumsy. Didn't it, Bob?

MRS. CRATCHIT. I'm sure there never was such a goose before, and I'm sure there never will be such a goose again. How's the 'taters, Peter?

PETER (*looks in kettle*). Boilin', mumsy, boilin'.

BOB. Oh, Peter's got on pa's shirt collar—he has. Peter's got on pa's shirt collar.

PETER. If I didn't have to mind these 'taters, I'd show you!

MRS. CRATCHIT. I can't think what's keeping your father and your brother, Tiny Tim. And Martha wasn't as late last Christmas Day by half an hour.

Enter MARTHA *at right.*

MARTHA. Here's Martha, mumsy.

BOB (*dragging her down to* MRS. CRATCHIT). Here's Martha, mumsy.

BETTY. Oh, Martha, there's such a goose! Isn't there, Bob?

MRS. CRATCHIT (*hugging and kissing* MARTHA). Why, bless your heart alive, my dear, how late you are! (*Takes off* MARTHA'S *bonnet and shawl and hangs them on wall hooks.*)

MARTHA. We'd a deal of work to finish up last night. I was on my feet all day. Oh, why won't people learn to do their Christmas shopping early? If they'd only stop to give a moment's thought to the poor clerks!

MRS. CRATCHIT. There, there, my dear, sit ye down. Here's the big chair, Martha. (BOB *has been sitting in the armchair at right, but* MRS. CRATCHIT *simply turns it forward, letting* BOB *slip to the floor, and seats* MARTHA *therein.*) Well, never mind, as long as you're home at last, Martha. Draw your chair up to the fire and warm yourself. God bless you. How's the 'taters, Pete?

PETER (*looking in kettle*). Boilin', mumsy, boilin'.

MARTHA (*sitting in front of the fire*). Oh, mumsy, ain't this heavenly? Be it ever so humble, there's no place like home.

BETTY (*looking off at right door*). Father's coming! Father's coming.

BOB. Hide yourself, Martha. Here, here! (*Pulls her to left.*)

BETTY (*helping her*). Hurry up. Hide, hide!

Exit MARTHA *at left, just as bright music begins. Enter* CRATCHIT *at right, carrying* TINY TIM *on his shoulder.* TINY TIM *carries a little crutch.*

CRATCHIT (*coming down center*). Why, where's our Martha?

MRS. CRATCHIT (*down left*). Not coming.

CRATCHIT. Not coming? Not coming—on Christmas Day? (*Sets* TINY TIM *on floor*.)

MARTHA *rushes on at left*.

MARTHA. No, father, it's only a joke. Here I am, father; here I am. (*Rushes into his arms*.)

BETTY (*taking* TINY TIM'S *hand*). Come on, Tiny Tim, out to the wash-house. We've got something to show you— we have. Ain't we, Bob?

BOB. You bet we have, Tiny Tim. Come and hear the Christmas pudding singing in the wash boiler. Come on! (*Exit* BOB *at left, followed by* BETTY *and* TINY TIM.)

MRS. CRATCHIT (*taking* CRATCHIT'S *hat and muffler and hanging them up on wall hooks*). And how did Tiny Tim behave in the church, father?

CRATCHIT. As good as gold and better. Somehow he gets thoughtful, sitting by himself so much, and thinks the strangest things you ever heard. (*Sits at left, surrounded by all the others*.) He told me, coming home, that he hoped the people saw him in the church, because he was a cripple, and it might be pleasant to them to remember, upon Christmas Day, who it was who made lame beggars walk and blind men see. (*In a trembling voice*.) Little Tim is growing stronger and more hearty every day.

Enter TINY TIM *at left*.

TINY TIM. I heard the pudding singing a song in the wash boiler—I did.

MRS. CRATCHIT. Everything is ready. Bob, you and Betty run across the street to the baker's and fetch the goose.

BOB. Come on, Betty. (*Runs off at right with* BETTY.)

MRS. CRATCHIT. I've got the gravy to heat, right away. Peter, mash the potatoes. Belinda, sweeten the apple sauce. Martha, the hot plates!

(*All bustle around, placing dishes on table.* CRATCHIT, *with* TINY TIM *on his knee, sits before the fire.*)

BELINDA. We haven't got enough chairs, mumsy.
CRATCHIT. This young shaver can sit on my knee.
MRS. CRATCHIT. Peter, set up the chairs.

PETER *places seven chairs around the table. Enter* BOB *and* BETTY *at right, carrying a roast goose in a baking pan, while* PETER *places the chairs around the table.*

BOB. Here it is, mumsy.
BETTY. Here's the goose.

(MRS. CRATCHIT *takes goose from pan and puts it on platter on table.*)

BELINDA. What a wonderful goose!
MARTHA. And how big it is!

(*All take seats around table.*)

BOB. And doesn't it smell good?
BETTY. Hurray for the Christmas goose!
TINY TIM. Hurray!

(CRATCHIT *gives a signal, and all bend heads for a silent grace.*)

CRATCHIT (*after a pronounced pause*). And God bless Christmas Day.
TINY TIM. God bless us all, every one.

(CRATCHIT *and* MRS. CRATCHIT *serve the meal. All eat.*)

CRATCHIT. I've got a situation in my eye for Master Peter.
PETER. A situation for me?

CRATCHIT. Yes, sir, for you. Full five-and-sixpence weekly.

ALL THE OTHERS (*except* PETER). Oh, Peter!

BOB. Peter will be a man of business. Won't you, Peter?

PETER. What'll I do with all that money?

CRATCHIT. Invest it, invest it, my lad. It's a bewildering income.

MARTHA. Who do you think was in the shop yesterday? You'll never guess. A countess and a real lord.

ALL THE OTHERS (*except* MARTHA, *in concert*). Martha!

MARTHA. A real, live lord, as fine as silk and just about as tall as Peter here.

PETER (*pulls his collar up high and tosses his head*). As big as me?

(*Waits off right sing two stanzas of " Christmas Carol," as before.*)

CRATCHIT (*goes to right door*). Here's a sixpence for you, and God bless you all. (*Takes coin from his pocket and tosses it off right.*)

WAITS (*calling in unison from off right*). Thankee, sir. Merry Christmas, sir.

BELINDA. And now the pudding.

BETTY. Oh, suppose it should break in turning it out.

MARTHA. Or suppose it isn't done enough.

BOB. Suppose somebody should have got over the wall of the backyard and stolen it while we were in here eating the goose.

MRS. CRATCHIT. Nonsense! I'll get the Christmas pudding. (*Exit at left.*)

BOB (*very much excited*). Oh, I can smell it—I can. I smell the pudding.

Enter MRS. CRATCHIT *at left, bearing dish of pudding, decked with holly.*

CRATCHIT. Oh, it's a wonder, mother; it's a wonder.

BETTY. It looks like a little speckled cannon-ball.

BOB. But just wait till you taste it; that's all.

(MRS. CRATCHIT *serves pudding to all.*)

CRATCHIT (*rises*). I have a toast. Mr. Scrooge! I'll give you Mr. Scrooge, the founder of the feast.

MRS. CRATCHIT (*indignantly*). The founder of the feast indeed! I wish I had him here. I'd give him a piece of my mind to feast upon, and I hope he'd have a good appetite for it.

CRATCHIT (*remonstrating gently*). My dear, the children! Christmas Day!

MRS. CRATCHIT. He's an odious, stingy, hard, unfeeling man. You know he is, Robert. Nobody knows it better than you do.

CRATCHIT (*mildly*). My dear, Christmas Day!

MRS. CRATCHIT. Then I'll drink his health, for your sake and the day's, not for his. Long life to him! A merry Christmas and a happy New Year! He'll be very merry and happy, I've no doubt.

CRATCHIT. And now a merry Christmas to us all, my dears. God bless us.

ALL THE OTHERS (*rising and speaking in concert*). A very merry Christmas.

TINY TIM. And God bless us, every one!

(*The tableau curtains are slowly drawn, hiding the dinner scene.*)

SCROOGE. Spirit, tell me if Tiny Tim will live.

SECOND SPIRIT. I see a vacant seat in the poor chimney corner, and a little crutch without an owner. If these shadows remain unaltered by the future, the child will die.

SCROOGE. No, no, kind spirit! Say he will be spared.

SECOND SPIRIT. If he be like to die, he had better do it and decrease the surplus population. Your very words, Scrooge. Decrease the surplus population. (SCROOGE *hangs his head in shame.*) Man, if man you be in heart, forbear that wicked cant. Will you decide what men shall live and what men shall die? It may be that in the sight of Heaven you are more worthless and less fit to live than millions like this poor man's child.

SCROOGE. Forgive me. Forgive me!

SECOND SPIRIT. You have seen the spirit of Christmas bless this poor dwelling. They were not a handsome family; they were not well dressed; their clothes were scanty and their shoes far from being waterproof, but they were happy, grateful, pleased with one another, and contented with the Christmas time. They are my children. Have you learned your lesson? (*Chimes ring off stage.*) My hour is spent.

SCROOGE. I have learned the lesson, Spirit of Christmas. I have seen happiness, in spite of poverty—a happiness that all my gold cannot buy. I have seen the Christmas spirit. Forgive me that I ever dared to utter a word against Christmas. Forgive me! Forgive me! ' (*The chimes continue ringing. SECOND SPIRIT glides off at right. SCROOGE kneels in prayer, still muttering.*) Forgive me! Forgive me!

CURTAIN

SCENE 3

SCENE: *Same as in Scene 1, with the rear curtains drawn together. SCROOGE is discovered seated at his desk, his head buried in his hands. The THIRD SPIRIT stands at center, with ghastly green light on him from off right. This is the only light on the stage. The bells off stage toll six.*

SCROOGE (*awakens and looks at the ghost*). I am in the presence of the Ghost of Christmas Yet to Come? (THIRD SPIRIT *inclines his head.*) You are going to show me the shadows of things that are to happen in the future? (THIRD SPIRIT *inclines head.*) I fear you more than any I have yet seen. But I know you are working for my welfare, so I will see your visions with a thankful heart. Will you not speak to me? (THIRD SPIRIT *points downward with right hand.*) No word for me. Well, have you anything to show me?

(THIRD SPIRIT *points up center. The curtains part, showing rear stage draped in white sheets, with bare trees at right and left. A grave with carved headstone is up center. Blue lights from off stage illumine the scene. Artificial snow is falling, being scattered from the flies. Bells are heard tolling in the distance.*)

SCROOGE. A churchyard! (THIRD SPIRIT *goes to rear and points to tombstone.*) Before I draw nearer to that stone to which you point, answer me one question: Are these the shadows of the things that will be, or are they the shadows of things that may be only? (THIRD SPIRIT *points to stone.* SCROOGE *creeps tremblingly toward it, moving very slowly, bends over, reads name, and screams.*) Ebenezer Scrooge! My tombstone, my grave! No, spirit, no, no! (*Rushes to desk and sinks into chair.*) I am not the man I was. I am not past all hope. I will honor Christmas in my heart and try to keep it all the year. Save me, save me! (*The rear curtains are slowly closed, hiding* THIRD SPIRIT. SCROOGE *rises.*) I will keep Christmas in the past, the present, and the future. The spirits of all three shall strive within me. Heaven be praised for this Christmas warning! (*Laughing.*) I don't know what to do. I'm as light as a feather. I'm as happy as an angel. I'm as merry as a schoolboy. A merry Christmas to everybody. A happy New Year to all the world. Hip, hurrah!

(*Christmas chimes are heard off right. Waits are heard singing " Christmas Carol" in the distance.*)

WAITS (*singing more loudly*).
            Christ was born on Christmas Day;
            Wreathe the holly, twine the bay;

> Light and life and joy is He,
> The Babe, the Son,
> The Holy One
> Of Mary.

SCROOGE (*rushes to left door*). Merry Christmas! Merry Christmas! God bless ye! (*Flings them a handful of coins.*)

FIRST WAIT *appears in left doorway.*

FIRST WAIT. Thankee, sir.

SCROOGE (*grabs him and brings him down center*). What day is this, my merry lad?

FIRST WAIT. Hey?

SCROOGE. What day is this, my lad?

FIRST WAIT (*loudly*). To-day! Why, Christmas Day!

SCROOGE. Do you know the grocer's in the next street?

FIRST WAIT. I should hope I did.

SCROOGE. Do you know whether they've sold the prize turkey that was hanging up there? Not the little prize turkey, but the big prize turkey.

FIRST WAIT. What! The one as big as me?

SCROOGE. Yes, my buck.

FIRST WAIT. It's hanging there now.

SCROOGE. Is it? Go and buy it.

FIRST WAIT. Aw, go on!

SCROOGE. No, no; I'm in earnest. Go and buy it and tell 'em to bring it here, that I may tell 'em where to take it. Come back with the man, and I'll give you a shilling. Come back with him in less than five minutes, and I'll give you half a crown.

FIRST WAIT. Watch me. (*Rushes off at left.*)

SCROOGE. What a fine little fellow! See him run. I'll send the turkey to Bob Cratchit's. He shan't know who sends it. It's twice the size of Tiny Tim. Bob should be here by now.

Enter CRATCHIT *at left.*

CRATCHIT. 'Morning, sir. (*Takes off cap and muffler, goes to desk, and starts to work.*)

SCROOGE (*at desk*). What do you mean by coming here at this time of day?

CRATCHIT. I'm very sorry, sir. Very, very sorry.

SCROOGE. Sorry? (*Sarcastically.*) Yes, you are! Come here! Come here at once! Understand?

CRATCHIT (*comes to* SCROOGE'S *desk*). If you please, sir—

SCROOGE (*interrupts*). I'm not going to stand this sort of thing any longer. And therefore (*rises, dances toward* CRATCHIT, *and digs him in ribs*)—and therefore I am about to raise your salary.

CRATCHIT. Heavens! The master has gone plumb crazy.

SCROOGE. I'm going to help you and your family. I'm going to be a godfather to all of 'em—the two girls and Master Peter, Bob, Betty, and to dear Tiny Tim. Home to your family, now. Home to them, Bob Cratchit; and merry Christmas to you and yours. God bless you.

Enter FRED *at left.*

FRED. Here I am again, uncle. Merry Christmas.

SCROOGE (*rushes to him and shakes his hands heartily*). And the same to you, my lad, and many of 'em. I'm going to eat Christmas dinner with you this day. I'm going to honor Christmas in my heart and keep it every day in the year. I will live in the past, the present, and the future. The spirits of all three shall strive within me. (*Stands at center,* FRED *on his right and* CRATCHIT *on his left. He takes their hands.*) Merry Christmas, boys, and God bless us!

FRED *and* CRATCHIT (*in unison*). The same to you, sir. God bless us.

(Rear curtains are drawn back, showing the Cratchit family seated around the table. TINY TIM *stands on table.)*

TINY TIM. God bless us every one!

(All unite in singing " Christmas Carol.")

SLOW CURTAIN

CHRISTMAS CAROL.

J. M. NEALE.
THOMAS HELMORE.

1. Christ was born on Christ-mas day, Wreathe the hol - ly,
2. He is born to set us free; He is born our
3. Let the bright red ber - ries glow Ev - 'ry-where in

twine the bay, Light and life and joy is He, The
Lord to be; Car - ol, Chris-tians, joy - ful - ly; The
good - ly show, Light and life and joy is He, The

Babe, the Son, the Ho - ly One of Ma - ry.
God, the Lord, by all a - dored for - ev - er.
Babe, the Son, the Ho - ly One of Ma - ry.

Christian men, re-joice and sing; 'Tis the birth-day of our King.

CHRISTMAS CAROL—Continued.

CHRISTMAS CAROL—Concluded.

Mid-night scarce-ly passed and o - ver, Draw-ing to the

ho - ly morn; Ver - y ear - ly, Ver - y ear - ly, Christ was born.

Sing out with bliss, His name is this: Em - man - u - el!

As 'twas fore-told, In days of old, By Ga - bri - el.

THE HOLY SEARCH

A CHRISTMAS PLAY IN ONE ACT
AND FOUR SCENES

By

ROBERT ST. CLAIR

PRODUCTION RIGHTS

Copies of this play are available in single pamphlet form. The right to produce this play by one group of amateur players is authorized only by the purchase of eight copies (one copy for each speaking part) at the current price of 50c each.

It is dishonest and illegal to copy parts.

THE HOLY SEARCH

THE CHARACTERS

For eleven players

THE NARRATOR (*either male or female*)
HEROD, *the wicked king*
A PRIEST
A BEGGAR
A ROMAN SOLDIER
MELCHIOR,
BALTHAZAR, } *the three wise men*
CASPER,
MARY
JOSEPH
THE ANGEL GABRIEL

NOTE: Where a larger cast is desired, more attendants may be used in Herod's palace scenes such as a fan bearer and a Nubian slave.

THE SCENES

SCENE ONE
    A room in Herod's palace.

SCENE TWO
    The stable of an inn at Bethlehem.

SCENE THREE
    Herod's palace again.

SCENE FOUR
    The stable.

PRODUCTION NOTE: The entire play may be performed without any actual scenery whatsoever. All that is needed is a set of masking draperies and the properties such as the crib, Herod's throne chair, etc. When the play is presented in a church, these necessary things will be used on the chancel and colored spotlights will be hidden and trained on the playing space to give the proper light effects. In this case, the lights are turned out at the end of each scene and will, of course, be turned on again after the Narrator has finished speaking. For musical effects, a small group of singers may be offstage—when the entertainment is *given* on a stage. In a church, however, the actual choir may be used, and it will not destroy the effect of the play if the singers remain seated in the choir stalls throughout the performance.

THE HOLY SEARCH

AT THE BEGINNING: *The choir, or singers offstage, sing an appropriate Christmas hymn that should not last over three minutes. Then the* NARRATOR *(who may be either male or female) appears at the left side of the stage or platform, dressed in Biblical garments and bathed in a rose-colored light. The offscene music, but not the singing, continues softly while the* NARRATOR *speaks. The narration may be read from a scroll or committed to memory.*

NARRATOR. When Jesus first came into the world, and while He was still lying in a manger at Bethlehem, three Wise Men came out of the East on a search to find and worship Him. The names of these Wise Men, or Magi as they were called in those days, were Melchior, Balthazar and Casper. Where they first met, no one knows. But each followed the great new star that they had been miraculously told would guide them on their journey and take them safely to the newborn King. Their arrival in Jerusalem was, quite naturally, reported to the wicked King Herod, who had already heard that the long awaited birth of the Deliverer of the Jews had arrived. However, no one seemed to know just where the birth had taken place and Herod, who feared that his throne was in danger, was frantically trying to discover where the infant Jesus' was. There had been much talk of a Jewish rebellion in the land, and now that they had a King to lead them, Herod was desperately afraid they would try to overthrow him and the Roman rule. Since Melchior, Balthazar and Casper informed every one they encountered just *why* they were taking their long journey, Herod sent for them to come to his palace, hoping that

at last he could find out more about this mysterious child
and perhaps have Him assassinated. Let us hear what
transpired in Herod's audience chamber that day. . . .
(*The rose-colored light goes out, the music rises, the*
NARRATOR *disappears in the darkness and the lights come
on for* . . .)

SCENE ONE

*A room in Herod's palace. No actual stage setting is
required, merely a cyclorama or draperies. These may
be parted at the back to show a painted cut-out representing the roof-tops of Jerusalem, and a couple of
Oriental hangings may be pinned onto the draperies at
either side of the Center opening to give color and
atmosphere to the setting. There is a small, rug-cov-
ered dais, or platform, at Right Center. On this is a
Roman type chair. Beside the chair is a taboret, or
low pedestal, with a bowl of fruit. A low, ornate bench
stands down Left Center. No other furniture is required. Where the play is being performed in a church,
the dais and bench may be dispensed with and instead
of the main curtain parting, or rising, the lights will
come up and go out between each scene.*

DISCOVERED: HEROD *sits on the dais, talking earnestly to
a* PRIEST *who stands at Center.* HEROD *absently
munches on a peach as he frowns and talks. He is a
gross, animalistic-looking man garbed in a white toga
trimmed in gold, and he has gold sandals on his feet.
His dark and oily, tightly curled hair is held in place
by a golden circlet. The music fades away as he speaks.*

HEROD (*As if continuing a conversation.*) And you say
these men know where the parents and child are hiding?
PRIEST. That is what our spies report they have said,
Your Majesty.
HEROD. Where did the men come from?
PRIEST. The East, people say.

HEROD (*Impatiently.*)   *Where* in the East?

PRIEST (*Shrugging his shoulders.*)   No one seems to know.

HEROD (*Grimly.   Leaning back in his chair.*)   Well, we shall soon find out.   They'll be here before long.   And *then—*   (*His voice trails away.*)

PRIEST.   They have a number of camels, sire—one for each of them to ride and several heavily laden with gifts, they say.

HEROD (*Looking up.   Quickly.*)   Gifts?

PRIEST (*Nodding a slow affirmative.*)   Presents for this child they're on their way to worship.   The—er— newborn King, *they* call Him.

HEROD (*Lowly.   Thoughtfully.*)   King of the Jews! (*In sudden, angry disgust.*)   Pah!   What nonsense!   I'm getting tired of the Jews and their preposterous superstitions.   How do *they* know that this mysterious infant is any different from the hundreds of *other* Jewish babies which are born every day in the year?

PRIEST.   Because of the prophecies, Your Majesty. The ancient Scriptures foretell the coming of a Savior, a Messiah, and many of the people believe that at last he has arrived.

HEROD (*Leaning forward.*)   In the shape of a baby? What utter stupidity!   (*Rises, steps down off the dais and moves Left, toward the bench, as he continues talking.*)   They must all have the intelligence of children to believe such folk tales.   It's small wonder that they have been held in captivity and persecuted for so many ages. (*Turning, in front of the bench, to face the* PRIEST.) Look you here!   If there *is* such a God as they believe in—which *we* know there *isn't*—do you not think He would have the power to appear on earth as a fully grown *man* instead of going through all the trouble of being born of woman and waiting to grow to manhood before He could wrest my throne away from me?

PRIEST (*Nodding a quick, obsequious affirmative.*) That seems reasonable, Your Majesty.   (*Moves a step closer to* HEROD.)

HEROD.   To be sure it's reasonable.   We Romans are

a *practical* people. That is why *we* have so *many* gods. Ours are gods of *convenience*—we have one for every occasion. However, we would be fools to take them seriously. To the thinking man, they are nothing but interesting legends. If we are displeased with one, we can turn to another. That is why we are so powerful and why we rule the world. *We* believe only in what we can see, hear, feel and smell. However— (*Once again, his voice trails away and he frowns in thought as he moves over to the Right.*)

PRIEST. Your Majesty is the wisest of men. (*A SOL-DIER enters briskly down Left and comes to attention with a quick, Roman salute.*)

SOLDIER. Your Majesty—

HEROD. Yes?

SOLDIER. The Magi are here.

HEROD. Good. I will see them at once. (*Quickly resumes his seat on the dais.*)

SOLDIER. Yes, Your Majesty. (*Salutes, turns on his heel and exits the way he has come.*)

PRIEST. Shall I go, sire? (*Backs toward the Left.*)

HEROD. No. I want you to remain throughout the interview. You are well acquainted with all their beliefs and ridiculous prophecies. They will be cautious, evasive, self-conscious and ill-at-ease. However, I'll draw them out if I have to threaten them with punishment. They shall not be permitted to leave the palace until they have told me all I wish to know. (*Settles himself in his chair, absently helping himself to another bit of fruit. He is nibbling on this as MELCHIOR, BALTHAZAR and CASPER enter down Left, where they pause for the initial greetings. The PRIEST moves up Center, where he turns to watch the proceedings. The SOLDIER follows the Wise Men and remains at attention down Left.*)

MELCHIOR (*The first to enter. Raises one hand in greeting.*) Hail, Herod—

BALTHAZAR (*Raising his hand.*) Mighty ruler of Jerusalem—

CASPER (*Imitating the others.*) Peace be unto you. Your Majesty, and unto your rule.

HEROD (*Nodding. Assuming a friendly smile.*) And peace be unto *you,* my friends. You have journeyed far, I hear. (*Exchanges meaning glances with the* PRIEST *and waits for the answer.*)

BALTHAZAR (*Going closer to the dais.*) Far indeed, Your Majesty—

MELCHIOR (*Also going closer to* HEROD.) From Egypt and beyond—

HEROD (*Leaning forward, his manner now tense.*) For what purpose, may I ask?

CASPER. We are on a holy search—

BALTHAZAR (*Calmly.*) We are seeking to find the King.

HEROD (*Drawing himself up. Arrogantly.*) I am the king.

MELCHIOR (*Quietly.*) We mean the King of the Jews.

HEROD (*With assumed casualness. As if just remembering.*) Oh, yes. I understand. I've heard the stupid rumor about the so-called miraculous birth of an infant that is supposed to be the Jews' long-awaited Deliverer. (*Laughs, shortly.*) How amusing! (*With a quick transition of manner, he leans forward and barks—*) What is the name of this child? What is He called?

BALTHAZAR. He is called—the Christ.

PRIEST (*Going quickly closer to* HEROD. *As if reminding him.*) The Messiah, Your Majesty.

MELCHIOR (*To* HEROD.) And his name·is Jesus.

HEROD. Who are his parents?

CASPER. That, we do not know.

HEROD (*Surprised.*) You have not been told the names of such important people?

PRIEST (*Smiling at the Wise Men. Dry-washing his hands together. In an oily tone of voice.*) Surely you must know where they live?

BALTHAZAR. No.

HEROD. Then how do you know where to search?

MELCHIOR. We each had a strange dream, and in the dream we talked with an angel—an angel who told us to rise up and follow a star.

HEROD (*Astonished.*) A star? What star?

CASPER. A new star, Your Majesty—one that has never been seen before. That is why we travel at night, for the star is not in the heavens during the daylight hours. Every night it appears and is always before us, showing us the way.

HEROD. Amazing! (*His voice silky, his mouth smiling craftily.*) And it was this star that led you to Jerusalem? (*The three men nod solemnly.*) Then the child you seek is *here?* (*He and the* PRIEST *wait with bated breath for the answer.*)

BALTHAZAR. No, Your Majesty. The child is in Bethlehem.

HEROD (*Amazed.*) Bethlehem?

PRIEST (*Sarcastically.*) That miserable pig-sty of a town? (*To* HEROD.) A wonderful birthplace for the savior of a race, eh, Your Majesty? (*They laugh, rudely. The Wise Men exchange significant glances.*)

HEROD (*Turning serious again.*) What makes you think that your search will come to an end in Bethlehem?

MELCHIOR. Because it was over Bethlehem that the star was hovering the last time we saw it yesterday before darkness covered the land.

HEROD (*Leaning back, with his elbow on the arm of the chair and his chin resting on his fist. Thoughtfully.*) Bethlehem, eh?

PRIEST (*Moving closer to the Wise Men.*) Rome has been taking a nation-wide census and thousands of people have been moving in and out of Bethlehem for days, even as they are going in and out of Jerusalem. Many children have undoubtedly been born there recently, the same as *here.* How will you be able to discover *which* child you see is the great Deliverer you wish to acknowledge? (*Smiles at* HEROD, *who nods a slow, smiling approval of the question. The Wise Men again exchange looks,* MELCHIOR *and* BALTHAZAR *nod to* CASPER *to speak.*)

CASPER. The star will let us know. The star will shine down on the place of His birth. It has always moved before us heretofore. But when we have reached the end of the search, it will remain stationary, and—we shall know. (*There is a short, awkward pause during*

117

which HEROD *frowns and taps his fingers on the arm of the chair. Then he comes to a decision, straightens and smiles again.*)

HEROD. So be it. I am not in sympathy with your quest, but it is a wonderful mission and I sincerely hope that you are well-rewarded for your pains. (*Rises, steps down off the platform and goes closer to the Wise Men.*) I am grateful to you for accepting my invitation to come to the palace so that I may have this talk with you. And I'll admit that I have been greatly impressed by what I have learned. Before you leave, however, I should like to ask a small favor of you. (*Lowers his voice a trifle, choosing his words with care.*) Undoubtedly you will pass through Jerusalem again on your return journey to your native lands. If you find the child, I would like you to come to me and tell me where *I* may locate Him so that *I* may go to worship Him *also.* (*Beams at* BALTHAZAR *and lays a friendly hand on his shoulder.*) And now you may depart. Peace be unto you, my friends.

BALTHAZAR. And unto *you*, Your Majesty. (*The Wise Men bow slightly and exit down Left. As soon as their backs are turned,* HEROD *gives the grinning* PRIEST *a broad wink and—the lights go out. Instantly, the off-scene music fades in and continues while the* NARRATOR *enters in the darkness.*)

END OF SCENE ONE

NARRATOR (*Speaking as soon as the rose-colored light comes on to illuminate his, or her, figure.*) And so it came to pass that the three Wise Men again took up the search the following night, and soon they had arrived in Bethlehem. It was not difficult to find the Child once they had made known the object of their search, for many in Bethlehem had already seen and worshipped Him. However, because they all knew that Herod had many spies about, those who had seen Jesus kept the place of His birth a secret from any but the Jews. But once they had heard the story of the star, they knew that *these* men

were friends and *believers*. *They* knew about the star.
They had heard the story of the Shepherds, and some
had even seen the star itself, shining down on the stable
of the wretched inn. And so the Wise Men came to the
end of their holy search, and presented the child with
gifts of gold, frankincense and myrrh. . . . (*The* NAR-
RATOR *stops speaking, the light goes off and he, or she,
exits in the darkness. The music changes to "Silent
Night," and the lights come on to reveal* MARY, JOSEPH
and the manger. MARY *is sitting behind the crib, gazing
into it tenderly.* JOSEPH *stands behind the crib, smiling
at the Wise Men as they kneel with their offerings held
in outstretched hands. No word is spoken. The characters merely hold the tableau until the singing has ceased,
and then . . . the lights go out again and the* NARRATOR
*re-appears. The music is soft as a background to the
rest of his, or her, speech. THE TABLEAU IS
SCENE TWO. As the* NARRATOR *begins speaking, the
rose-colored light comes on again.*) The Wise Men did
not return to Jerusalem after finding and worshipping the
newborn King. They were much *too* wise to play into
Herod's hands like that. *They* knew what the wicked
monarch had in mind. So they left Bethlehem in the
dead of night, successfully eluding the soldiers that Herod
had sent after them to spy on their movements. When
Herod heard about this, he went almost insane with frus-
tration, and into his evil mind came one of the most horrible plans ever conceived by man. (*The light goes out,
the music fades, the* NARRATOR *disappears, and the lights
come on for . . .*)

SCENE THREE

SCENE: *Herod's palace again, the same as before. Herod
sits on the dais, eating another piece of fruit. The*
SOLDIER *enters down Left and salutes.*

SOLDIER. Hail, mighty Herod.
HEROD. What is it? Speak.

SOLDIER. There is a man who insists upon seeing you. He is a filthy beast, dressed in beggar's rags—not fit to come into your august presence. And yet, even though we beat him with sticks, he will not be turned aside.

HEROD. A beggar with that impudence? What is his mission?

SOLDIER (*Advancing closer to* HEROD.) He will not tell us, Your Majesty. All he says is that he has come from Bethlehem—

HEROD (*Sitting quickly upright.*) Bethlehem!

SOLDIER (*Continuing. Holding out a small coin.*) And he asked me to give you this coin.

HEROD. Let me see it. (*Snatches the coin and examines it.*) If there is a locust scratched on one side— (*Excitedly.*) There *is!* (*Talking rapidly.*) The man is not a beggar. He is one of my spies—a soldier whom I trust. Bid him enter—quickly—then leave us alone. (*Rises.*)

SOLDIER (*Saluting.*) Yes, Your Majesty. (*Turns in military fashion and exits down Left.* HEROD *steps down off the dais, grinning like the cat who swallowed the goldfish. The* SOLDIER *returns with a bronzed, bearded and dirty man, dressed in beggar's rags.*)

MAN. Hail, mighty Herod. Hail. (*The* SOLDIER *exits.*)

HEROD (*Eagerly meeting the man at Center.*) Quickly now. Your report. What have you learned? Where can we find the child?

MAN. I do not know, Your Majesty.

HEROD (*Explosively.*) You do not—*know?*

MAN (*Perceptibly cringing.*) The three Magi we were to watch left Bethlehem last night—secretly—while my men were asleep. No one knows in what direction they went. It was as if they had vanished into thin air.

HEROD. Fools! *Fools!* I told you never to let them out of your sight.

MAN. They had already found the Child by the time *we* arrived in Bethlehem, Your Majesty. When we last saw *them* they were inside an *inn*, getting rooms for the night. I posted a guard outside the inn door, but *they*

must have left the *back* way. Those men are magicians,
Your Majesty, and I've heard it said that magicians from
the East have the power to make themselves *invisible*—

HEROD (*Grasping the man by the throat. Raging.*)
You feeble-minded lout! I'll have your eyes burned out
of their sockets with hot *irons* for letting those men slip
away from you!

MAN (*Gaspingly. Clutching at the strong hands about
his throat.*) Majesty! Majesty—

HEROD (*Livid with anger. Shaking the man as he
would a puppy. The man slowly sinks to his knees.*)
Your superstitious tongue shall be torn out by the roots!
I'll have wooden splinters forced under your fingernails!
You let them get *away!* (*Almost shrieks the last word,
flinging the man away from him to the floor and walking
up Center.*)

MAN (*Weakly. Fearfully.*) They vanished. They
vanished—

HEROD (*Pacing furiously up and down Center.*) The
Jews are afraid of me. That's why they refuse to talk.
That's why they're keeping this child hidden. Their plan
is to raise Him in secret until He is old enough to assume
leadership. Then they'll rise up in *revolt* to overthrow
all Roman rule so they can place this—this *Messiah* in
power! (*Pauses at Center, raising his clenched hands.
He is practically shouting in his insane rage.*) But *I'll*
put a stop to their mad scheme. I'll thwart them in their
purpose if it's the last thing I ever do on *earth!* (*To the*
MAN.) Arise! Don't lie there like a whipped dog! I
still have use for you. Get to your feet! (*The* MAN
does so, quickly.) In spite of everything the Jews can
do I'll find their holy infant and *kill* him! (*Claps his
hands smartly together. At once, the* SOLDIER *enters
down Left and snaps to attention. The spy backs hurriedly upstage as* HEROD *strides toward the* SOLDIER.)
Look, you, and mark well my words! Somewhere in the
village of Bethlehem there is a newborn male Jewish
child—a child I wish to-find and do *away* with. You,
¬s Captain of the Guard, will organize a detachment of

soldiers to go with you *immediately* to carry out this order.

SOLDIER. How shall we find this Child, Your Majesty?

HEROD (*Lowly, rapidly and breathlessly.*) Surround the village, search through every house and building. Whenever you come across a Jewish *man*-child—*slay* him —slay him without *mercy!*

SOLDIER (*Horrified.*) Your Majesty! You want us to—?

HEROD (*Interrupting.*) Every male Jewish child in the entire *village* must die! Hah! Your face blanches with fear! Perhaps you do not care to undertake this unpleasant task?

SOLDIER (*Quickly. Well knowing the penalty for disobeying* HEROD's *orders.*) It isn't that, Your Majesty. It's just that—Bethlehem is crowded with the census taking. There must be *many* newborn babies. Surely— surely there must be some *other* way of locating the one you seek than to—?

HEROD (*Cutting in.*) You will kill them all! *All!* Do you hear me? *Then* we are *sure* to get the one I seek. You will spare only the *girl* children. (*Lowly, breathing heavily as he points down Left.*) And now—go. The work must be carried out before another nightfall. (*The* SOLDIER *hesitates.* HEROD *screams.*) Well, what are you waiting for? You have heard my orders. See to it that they are obeyed. If you fail, your *own* life shall be forfeited. (*The* SOLDIER *salutes, wheels about and exits.* HEROD *immediately starts walking up and down, Left Center, muttering his dark thoughts aloud, while the* MAN *up Center cringes back with an expression of stark terror on his face.*) I'll show them how miraculous their little King is! I'll show them what happens when they try to cross *me! This* will stop their talk of rebellion. *This* will make them tremble at the very mention of my *name* for the next thousand *years!* (*Strikes a pose of incarnate evil as* . . . *the lights go out.*)

END OF SCENE THREE

NARRATOR (*Entering in the darkness again. Soft music once more fades in as a background to the* NARRATOR'S *speech as the rose-colored light comes on.*) All was serene and quiet in the stable at Bethlehem where Jesus had been born. Neither the gentle Mary nor her husband, Joseph, had the faintest inkling of the dreadful plot that had just been hatched in Herod's palace. And yet Joseph was worried for the safety of the Babe, and was anxious to get the census business finished with as soon as possible so that he and Mary and their precious charge could return to Nazareth, where he felt they would all be secure. But a strange thing was to happen to them that night, and it would be a long, long time before they would set foot in Nazareth again. (*The light goes out, the* NARRATOR *exits, and the offstage music segues into* "O, *Little Town of Bethlehem*." *This continues until otherwise indicated.*)

SCENE FOUR

SCENE: *The stable again, the same as before.* MARY *sits quietly behind the crib, smiling down at the imaginary infant as* JOSEPH *enters quickly down Right.*

JOSEPH (*Speaking as he enters.*) Still awake, Mary?

MARY. Yes, Joseph. I've been waiting for you to return.

JOSEPH (*Going closer to her.*) When *I* left you were sleeping on your bed of straw.

MARY (*Smiling up at him.*) I know. But something awakened me and I got up to look at the Child.

JOSEPH (*Looking down into the crib.*) He sleeps—his face is tranquil and serene.

MARY (*Lowly.*) And see the gentle smile, my husband?

JOSEPH (*Introspectively.*) One has only to gaze upon His lovely features to know that here is indeed a living miracle. (*Bringing his thoughts back to the present.*) Well, Mary, we have registered for the census—our work in Bethlehem is finished. Tomorrow we must start out on the return journey to Nazareth and my carpenter shop. I am eager to get back to the business of earning shekels again. I hope everything has been all right with the shop during our absence. (*Sighs and moves to Right Center.*)

MARY (*Quietly. Rising.*) Something is worrying you, Joseph—

JOSEPH (*Interrupting. Forcing himself to smile.*) It is nothing—

MARY (*Continuing. Moving closer to him.*) —and it is not the fear that perhaps thieves might have stolen from us during our absence. What is it, beloved?

JOSEPH (*Tenderly. Placing his hands on her upper arms.*) I can keep nothing from you. You read my very thoughts.

MARY (*Softly.*) Tell me—

JOSEPH (*Sighs again and moves to Left Center.*) Herod has been trying to find the Child.

MARY (*Widening her eyes in sudden fear.*) Herod?

JOSEPH (*Nods a slow, frowning affirmative.*) You remember what the three Wise Men from the East told us about their interview with him?

MARY. Yes—

JOSEPH. Well, friends have just told me that spies were sent to follow them.

MARY (*Quickly. Fearfully. Taking a step closer to him.*) Then they *know*—?

JOSEPH (*Shaking his head.*) No. The Magi managed to leave the village without the spies seeing them. And they arrived too late to be able to follow our friends when they came *here*. However, Herod's men—in very poor disguises—have been going about the village, asking for information about us. Up to now, no one has told them where we *are*.

MARY. What do you think it means?

JOSEPH. I only wish I knew. (*Goes behind the crib, looking into it.*)

MARY (*Thoughtfully. In her innocence, thinking only of the best.*) It is only natural that Herod has heard of the ancient prophecies, and that he should have been told of the *signs*. Perhaps he is merely curious to *see* the Son of—

JOSEPH (*Turning. Quickly.*) No, Mary. Herod is evil, and the coming of your Son means the deliverance of our people from their bondage. (*Going closer to her.*) The temple priests are constantly inciting him against us. Who knows what terrible things they may be plotting? (*Smiles and places a comforting hand on her shoulder as he sees her look of fear.*) But there, do not be afraid, Mary. God will protect us and His Son. You are weary, and so am I. Let us cast all worries aside and go to our rest.

MARY (*Smiling.*) As you say, my husband. (*They move behind the crib, only to come to a sudden stop as the music swells and changes to a more dramatic Christmas hymn. At the same time, the curtains at the back open to reveal the imposing figure of* GABRIEL, *who stands with uplifted hand while a brilliant white light illuminates him. N. B. When the play is performed in a church, the angel merely steps suddenly into view from the right side of the chancel.*)

GABRIEL (*In loud, commanding tones. The music softens as he speaks.*) Arise, Joseph. Arise, and take the Child and His mother and fly into Egypt; and be there until I shall tell you. For this will come to pass—that Herod *will seek the child to destroy Him!* (MARY *and* JOSEPH *stiffen. He places his arms about her, protectingly.* GABRIEL'S *voice softens.*) But do not fear. The Lord God will protect you. Many shall die, but in Egypt you and the Child will be safe. The ancient prophecies will be fulfilled and Christ Jesus will live to become the Savior of the world! (*The characters hold their positions for a picture effect as the music rises, segues into a hymn of praise, which may be sung by the offscene voices. Then, the lights go out, or the curtains fall, or close in.*)

CURTAIN

JOY TO THE WORLD

A CHRISTMAS PLAY IN
THREE SCENES

By

ROBERT ST. CLAIR

PRODUCTION RIGHTS

JOY TO THE WORLD

CAST OF CHARACTERS

For two men, two women, and extras

JOSEPH, *a carpenter of Nazareth*
MARY, *his young wife*
ELIZABETH, *Mary's elderly cousin*
AN INNKEEPER *in Bethlehem*
RACHEL, *his daughter*
AN ELDERLY SHEPHERD
A MIDDLE-AGED SHEPHERD
A BOY SHEPHERD
AN ANGEL
THE NARRATOR (*either male or female*)

SYNOPSIS OF SCENES

SCENE ONE
    Joseph's carpenter shop in Nazareth.

SCENE TWO
    Outside an Inn in Bethlehem.

SCENE THREE
    A stable under the Inn.

DESCRIPTION OF THE STAGE SETTING

The author has arranged the play so that it may be produced on any stage or platform, or even in a church. Where it is performed on a stage, draperies or a cyclorama may be used as a background. The various locations are indicated by a few "set" pieces and the furniture. The main curtain is lowered and raised in the darkness, as indicated in the text, and the Narrator reads his lines from *in front* of the curtain, at one side of the stage, in a small spotlight. However, when the play is performed in a church, or in a hall without any stage, the few small changes of furniture, etc., will have to be done in the darkness. In the latter case, the flashback in Scene Three will be done in front of the altar, and there will have to be a screen located near by for the angel to hide behind until it is time for his (or her) appearance.

COSTUMING

Simple, Biblical costumes may be inexpensively made from cheap cotton materials where they cannot be rented from a regular costumer. Colored pictures of Mary, Joseph and the shepherds may be examined for the colors and patterns to be used. Any typical Jewish Biblical styles will do for the Innkeeper and his daughter, Rachel, while the angel's garment may be made of white cheesecloth. Elizabeth's costume is somewhat like Mary's, only of different, drabber colors.

JOY TO THE WORLD

AT THE BEGINNING, *soft organ music is played as the auditorium lights go out and the* NARRATOR *enters in the darkness, taking his—or her—place at one side of the stage. The* NARRATOR *is dressed in simple, graceful Biblical garments, and he—or she—may either commit the lines to memory or read them from a scroll. A soft, rose-colored light comes on to illuminate the individual and the music softens.*

NARRATOR. Many years ago, in the little town of Nazareth, there lived a strong but gentle carpenter by the name of Joseph. Joseph had recently wed Mary, the lovely young daughter of an elderly couple living at the edge of town. Shortly before their wedding, Mary had had a soul-shattering experience. An angel had appeared to her in her father's house one evening and had told her that she was about to have a child. This was not to be Joseph's child, the angel said, but was to be given to her by the Lord, who had looked deep into Mary's soul and had found her full of grace. Now Mary was frightened upon hearing this strange news, so she fled in the dead of night to her elderly cousin, Elizabeth, who lived not far from Nazareth. Mary felt that Elizabeth would understand her mysterious experience because a similar miracle had happened to Elizabeth and her husband, Zacharias, who had also been visited by the angel. Zacharias had been told that Elizabeth would have a son, and *his* name was to be called *John*. John was destined to be a great prophet, but Mary's Son, who was to be called Jesus, would be hailed as the Messiah, the Son of the Living God! Now Elizabeth induced Mary to go back to Nazareth and tell Joseph and her family of the miraculous thing that had come upon her. And this Mary did. Joseph believed, and soon after their marriage the words of the angel came true, for Mary had conceived and it would not be long until Jesus should be born. Then one day, while Joseph was working in his shop, Elizabeth came to call . . . (*The music rises, the rose-colored light goes out, and the curtain goes up, or the lights come on, for*

SCENE ONE

The music fades away as the lights come up and we see the brawny, golden-bearded JOSEPH *sitting on a three-legged stool over Right, in front of his work bench, hammering at the spokes of a wagon wheel. He is tall, muscular and deeply tanned. His brown tunic is drawn in at the waist with a brown cord, or length of hemp. His golden, brown hair falls almost to his shoulders. His tunic has no sleeves, but his outer garment has, and this is lying across the upstage end of the work bench. He looks up in pleased surprise as* ELIZABETH *enters from the Left. She is a seventy-year-old woman, with white hair and a wrinkled skin. But she is still vital and active, and her eyes are young.*

ELIZABETH. Peace be unto you, Joseph.

JOSEPH. And to you, Elizabeth. It is good to see you so far away from home. Mary will be pleased— (*Places his hammer on the work table behind him.*)

ELIZABETH (*Moving to Center stage.*) Is she here?

JOSEPH. No— (*Rises.*)

ELIZABETH. Then do not let me interfere with your work, Joseph.

JOSEPH (*Bracing the wheel up against the work bench.*) But she is not far away. And she would be unhappy if she didn't see you, Elizabeth. I'll call her. (*Moves toward the entrance down Right.*)

ELIZABETH (*Sitting on the three-legged stool that is down Left.*) To whom does the wheel belong?

JOSEPH (*Pausing down Right.*) A merchant from Jerusalem. He is in a hurry to have it mended so he can overtake his caravan before nightfall. (*Calling offstage.*)

Oh, Mary, your cousin, Elizabeth, is here. (*To* ELIZA-
BETH. *Moving closer to her.*) You will stay and eat
with us?

ELIZABETH. Oh, no. I must return to Ain Karim
immediately. If I am not home before dark, Zacharias
will wonder what has happened to me.

JOSEPH. He is well?

ELIZABETH (*Nodding a smiling affirmative.*) Unusually well. Happier than I ever remember seeing him
before, praise God. His voice has returned in full measure and he is conducting services in the synagogue again.

JOSEPH. Praise God indeed! And the baby—little
John?

ELIZABETH (*Seriously.*) He is a miraculous child,
Joseph—in more ways than one. He is the strongest boy
baby I have ever seen. Yesterday he took his first steps—

JOSEPH (*Greatly surprised.*) At such a tender age?

ELIZABETH. It is true, Joseph. His little hands have
tremendous power. He will be a very strong man some
day.

JOSEPH. He will need great strength if he is to undergo
the hardships of a prophet, Elizabeth. (*Goes to the
upstage end of the work bench to pick up his robe and
put it on.*)

ELIZABETH. Is Mary well?

JOSEPH (*Smiling.*) Oh, yes. Wonderfully well.

ELIZABETH (*Thoughtfully.*) I'll never forget that
night—almost nine months ago now—when she came
rushing into our house with the strange tale about the
angel who had visited her, and what he had told her. It
was at that moment—when she mentioned the coming of
this child—that *I* first felt *life* within me.

JOSEPH (*Lowly. Moving slowly down to Right Center.*) We are all of us faced with great responsibilities,
Elizabeth—

ELIZABETH (*Nodding a slow, thoughtful affirmative.*)
Yes, Joseph. Especially you and Mary. How very curious. Here, when all Israel is bent under the yoke of the
pagan Roman conquerors and is crying out for a deliverer,
our Mary—a simple country girl—is even now about to

bring one into the world. Do you ever doubt, Joseph? Do you ever wonder—?

JOSEPH (*With earnest, quiet conviction.*) I have read the scripture, and the prophet, Isaiah, said, (*Looks into space as he softly quotes.*) "Therefore a virgin shall conceive and bear a son." (*Goes closer to* ELIZABETH *and lays his hand on her shoulder.*) This is what is happening to Mary, Elizabeth. It could be no other way. Look at what has happened to you and Zacharias. At your ages you have had a son. We believed when he told us what the angel had said to *him* in the tabernacle, and *that* miracle has come to pass. Why should we not believe the holiness of Mary's child?

ELIZABETH. Ah, but will the *people* believe?

JOSEPH (*Looking troubled.*) I don't—know. The Lord will reveal the truth to them in His own good time. (*Moves up Center. Slowly, thoughtfully.*)

ELIZABETH. Perhaps, if you were to tell the priests—

JOSEPH (*Turning quickly.*) No. That would not be wise. They would only say we were mad—or worse. (*Moving downstage on a line with her again.*) Mary and I must go on living like any ordinary, normal couple for a while, Elizabeth. God will give us a sign of some kind when things are to be changed. Meanwhile, we must be content to go on doing our everyday tasks—and wait.

ELIZABETH (*Sighs and rises.*) You are right, Joseph. It would be sinful to question the ways of the Lord.

MARY (*Entering down Right. Quietly smiling.*) Elizabeth!

ELIZABETH (*Holding out her arms.*) Mary!

MARY (*Moving closer to receive the elderly woman's embrace.*) Peace be unto you, cousin.

ELIZABETH. And to you, Mary. Such blessed peace.

JOSEPH. What were you doing, Mary?

MARY (*Smiling.*) Milking the goat and feeding the chickens.

JOSEPH (*Reproachfully.*) I asked you to let *me* do those things—

MARY (*Turning to lay a gentle hand on his arm.*) It

did me no harm, my husband. And I knew you were working hard to get the wagon wheel finished in time. (*To* ELIZABETH. JOSEPH *frowns, worriedly, and moves down Right.*) Poor Joseph. He fears my coming ordeal.

ELIZABETH (*Smiling.*) All young husbands have the same fears, Mary. Your father had them before *you* were born, and mine, I've heard, was the same way. (*Turning serious.*) But your time draws near, and you should rest a lot.

JOSEPH (*With an expressive gesture.*) That's what *I've* been trying to tell her. But she is up at daybreak and does not go back to bed again until *I* do. There are others who could do our scrubbing and mending—

MARY (*Interrupting.*) Not when I feel so wonderfully strong and composed, Joseph. (*Moves up Center.*)

ELIZABETH (*Going closer to* JOSEPH.) Isn't it about time to consult a good midwife?

JOSEPH. I have already arranged for one, Elizabeth. (*Smiling toward* MARY.) Mary shall receive the very best of care.

ELIZABETH (*To* JOSEPH.) What if she should be taken to her bed while you are in Bethlehem?

MARY (*Surprised. Moving down Center.*) Bethlehem? Joseph! You are going to Bethlehem?

JOSEPH (*Looking worried again.*) I must, Mary.

MARY. When?

JOSEPH. The day after tomorrow. (*To* ELIZABETH.) I am greatly worried over *that*.

MARY. What does it mean? *Why* are you going to Bethlehem?

ELIZABETH (*Going closer to her.*) Have you not heard, Mary? Rome has ordered a nation-wide census to be taken of our people.

JOSEPH. I told you, Mary. Caesar Augustus, the Emperor *himself,* has ordered it.

MARY. Yes. I remember your speaking about it.

ELIZABETH. It is so they can increase the taxes again. As if we were not *already* taxed more than we can sometimes *pay.* (*Shakes her head and goes up Center.*) It will be a heart-breaking burden on our poor people.

MARY (*Moving closer to* JOSEPH.) But what does that have to do with your going to Jerusalem, Joseph?

JOSEPH. Under the ruling every person must be registered in the city of the *tribe* to which he belongs. And I belong to the House of David.

MARY. I, too, Joseph. What about *me* then? Am *I* not supposed to go and register?

JOSEPH (*Lowly.*) I have wondered how I was going to tell you this, Mary. You *are*. (MARY *looks thoughtful.*)

ELIZABETH (*Moving quickly down Center.*) But that will be impossible when you are about to have a child—

JOSEPH. Impossible? It's *unthinkable.* (*Going closer to* ELIZABETH, *via the front of* MARY.) This will be no ordinary child.

ELIZABETH. And surely she would not be missed. What is one person among so many? Why, there will be thousands—everything will be confusion. It would be unjust.

JOSEPH. I went to the synagogue today—

MARY. What for, Joseph?

JOSEPH. To see if perhaps they wouldn't make an exception in your case—

ELIZABETH (*Eagerly.*) What did they say, Joseph? (*He lowers his eyes, unhappily. There is a short pause.*)

MARY (*Quietly.*) What did they say?

JOSEPH (*Taking a quick step closer to her.*) Do I have to tell you, Mary?

MARY (*Very softly.*) What did they say?

JOSEPH (*Lowly.*) They said they could not help us. They told me that if you remain behind and fail to register the soldiers will come and—(*His voice sinks to a whisper.*)—punish us.

MARY (*Calmly.*) Then, of course, I must go with you, my husband.

JOSEPH (*A quick, frantic note creeping into his voice.*) But, Mary! How can you? The journey is long and hazardous. The dust and heat will be stifling. I should never forgive myself if something happened to you on the way.

MARY. I will not have to walk?

JOSEPH. Oh, no. We have the donkey—

MARY (*Smiling serenely. Taking his hand.*) Remember, beloved—we are under the divine protection of God. One of the first words the angel said to me that wonderful, mysterious night he came to me in my father's house was, "Fear not, Mary." So I am not afraid. The Lord will take care of me, Joseph. The Lord and you. And who knows but what it is His *wish* to have the child born in the city to which our tribe belongs.

ELIZABETH (*Quickly. Her tone is one of awe as she remembers.*) Joseph! There is a prophecy! I remember Zacharias reading it to us from the Scriptures many moons ago. It concerned the coming of the Messiah— (*Breaks off, looking at* MARY *with a new, almost reverent intentness.*)

JOSEPH (*Going closer to her.*) Yes, Elizabeth?

ELIZABETH (*Laying a trembling hand on his arm.*) The prophecy declared that the Savior *is* to be born in Bethlehem!

JOSEPH (*Overawed.*) In—Bethlehem!

ELIZABETH (*Excitedly.*) That is why Mary is required to go there with you—so that the prophecy may be *fulfilled!*

MARY (*Quietly. Moving closer to the dazed-looking* JOSEPH.) You see, beloved? It is all coming to pass as the angel said. Should we be afraid?

JOSEPH (*There is a short, dramatic pause while he looks deep into her eyes. Then he relaxes, smiles and enfolds her gently in his arms. The music of "Oh, Little Town of Bethlehem" fades in as a background to the balance of the scene.*) No, Mary. All fear has left me now. The ways of the Lord are mysterious and my heart is at peace. We shall go to Bethlehem—*together.* (*The lights go out and the curtain falls.*)

CURTAIN

NOTE: When the play is produced in a church, or a hall where there is no main curtain, the lights will merely go out and the Narrator will enter in the darkness. As soon as he—or she—is in position, the small, rose-colored light comes on to illuminate the Narrator again, the music seques into another hymn, and the Narrator begins to read.

NARRATOR. Bethlehem was a distance of about seventy-five miles from Nazareth. That made a three-day journey in those days. People by the thousands cluttered the highways, riding in caravans, on donkeys or walking over the hot, dusty roads. At night they slept in the fields under the brilliant stars. Joseph did everything possible to make Mary as comfortable as he could, and although she must have suffered greatly, she remained serene and calm. It was night when at last they entered the narrow, noisy streets of the little city, and the crowds were so great that they found it difficult to get through them. Time and time again they tried to get lodgings, only to find that all the inns were crowded to overflowing. Joseph was getting frantic, for, in spite of his faith, he could see that Mary's time was getting dangerously close, and they had no place to stay. Then, in a little side street, near the edge of town, they stopped in front of another hostelry. If they could not find lodgings *here,* they would have to leave the city again and spend the night in the hills. (*The music rises, the rose-colored light goes out, the* NARRATOR *exits and the stage lights come on for Scene Two.*)

SCENE TWO

IN FRONT OF THE INN. *Other than a backless bench down Left, there is no furniture on the stage. The Inn may be a "set piece" on the Right, painted to represent rough-dressed stone, with an archlike door. Or the entire setting may be left to the audience's imagination. The stage lights are quite dim, and should be blue to give a night effect. When the Inn door is opened a brilliant ray of amber-colored light will come on off Right, and this will be sufficient to illuminate the characters.*

JOSEPH (*Entering with* MARY *down Left, speaking to her comfortingly. He has his right arm about her shoulders. In his left hand he carries a bundle. The music offstage dies out as he speaks.*) Have courage, beloved. There must be some place for us to stay. God has carried us through safely so far, and I am sure that He will provide lodgings for us in the place He has prepared. (*They pause at Left Center, looking toward the Inn, or the Right entrance, as a sudden burst of raucous laughter comes from offstage.*) Listen to the drunken revelers in there!

MARY. We must close our ears to their merrymaking, beloved. I am faint. My time draws near.

JOSEPH (*Leading her to the bench.*) Sit here and rest yourself, Mary, while I talk with the Innkeeper. I shall offer him twice the regular price. (*As he moves toward the Inn door, or the Right entrance.*) Oh, Jehovah! We pray that this is the end of our search. (*Calling off Right.*) Innkeeper! Ho! I would a *word* with you. (*The loud masculine laughter is heard again.* JOSEPH *looks off Right, hopefully.*)

MARY. Mayhap he is in another *room*—

JOSEPH. No. He is there, serving wine to a group of men around a table near the door. (*Stepping closer to the door, or entrance. Calling loudly as the laughter dies down.*) Innkeeper! Have you any rooms?

INNKEEPER (*Coming to the door, or entrance. He is a big, coarse-looking man in a sleeveless tunic and a bright red scarf. His skin is swarthy and hairy, and his beard is black. He speaks with leering sarcasm.*) Have I any rooms? Have I any rooms! (*Disgustedly.*) Hah! The town is overflowing with people wanting rooms.

JOSEPH. I know. We have tried everywhere—

INNKEEPER (*Gruffly.*) There is no room *here.* (*Turns as if to exit.* JOSEPH *restrains him by quickly grasping his arm.*)

JOSEPH. Wait! My wife is ill. We must find lodgings soon.

INNKEEPER. Must? Hah! So must hundreds of others But many of them will have to sleep in the streets

138

.'his night, or out in the fields on the hills. I tell you we are full. (*Again turns to exit.*)

JOSEPH (*Keeping a firm grip on the man's arm. Desperately.*) You must have some place. Even a dark corner with a pallet of straw and a curtain hung before it for privacy. My wife's baby is about to be born.

INNKEEPER (*Sharply. Looking past him toward* MARY.) Her baby, you say? (*There is a tense pause while* MARY *rises and moves closer to* JOSEPH.)

MARY (*To the* INNKEEPER. *Softly.*) Help us—we beg of you.

INNKEEPER (*Shortly.*) It is a trick; a scheme to get a room. Away with you! (*Brushes* JOSEPH's *hand off his arm and turns to exit, but stops short as his daughter,* RACHEL, *appears in the door, or from the entrance, behind him.* RACHEL *is about eighteen; pretty in an unkempt, soiled sort of way.*)

RACHEL. What is it, Father?

INNKEEPER. More people looking for a room.

JOSEPH (*Desperately. Now holding* MARY *close to him with his left arm around her shoulders.*) I will give you twice your regular price—

INNKEEPER. Every spare inch in the building is taken. People are even sleeping on the roof. (*To* RACHEL.) He says his wife is about to have a baby.

RACHEL (*Lowly.*) A—baby? (*Goes closer to the pathetic-looking couple, brushing in front of the* INNKEEPER.)

INNKEEPER (*Sharply.*) Rachel!

RACHEL (*To* MARY.) Tonight?

MARY (*Softly.*) Soon.

RACHEL (*Turning to the* INNKEEPER.) Father—

INNKEEPER (*Interrupting.*) Go back inside! Give that rich merchant from Jerusalem more wine.

RACHEL (*Going closer to him.*) Father. They can have *my* room.

INNKEEPER. Your room is already taken. I have given it to four men. You will have to go over to your cousin's for the night. Now come on, you stupid wench— (*Once more turns to exit, but pauses as the girl speaks again.*)

JOSEPH. Please—for the love of God.

RACHEL. Wait, Father! There is one place you have overlooked.

INNKEEPER. Where is that? (JOSEPH *begins to look hopeful.*)

RACHEL (*Eagerly.*) The stable, Father! It is warm and dry. They should be quite comfortable there.

JOSEPH. This child cannot be born in a stable!

MARY (*Quietly.*) Why not, Joseph? *I* would be content.

JOSEPH. But, Mary—

MARY (*Continuing.*) A bed of straw will serve me well, beloved. It will be soft, sweet-smelling, and we shall be alone except for the gentle animals that may be there. God has led us to this place and has provided us with shelter—in time. The inn is filled with rowdy men who will be staying up late to sing their drunken songs and laugh at their coarse, ribald jokes. I would much sooner have my child in a stable than in the same building with company such as that. At least we shall be alone where it is quiet, peaceful and warm. (*Going closer to* RACHEL, *via the front of* JOSEPH.) Thank you, Rachel, and God bless you for your kindness to us this night. (*Turns back to* JOSEPH.)

RACHEL (*To the* INNKEEPER. *In a loud, half-whisper.*) Who *is* this woman who speaks with such wondrous peace and calm? (*He shrugs his shoulders. Softly, the music of "It Came Upon the Midnight Clear" fades in and continues playing as a background to the rest of the scene.*)

JOSEPH (*To* MARY.) So be it, Mary. There is much wisdom in your gentle words. (*To the* INNKEEPER.) Where is the stable?

INNKEEPER. It is a roomy cave that extends under the whole building of the inn. (*Nods down Right.*) If you wish to go ahead, I shall get a lantern and leave it with you for light. (JOSEPH *again puts his arm around* MARY'S *shoulders and they exit down Right, quietly, during the following lines.*)

RACHEL (*To the* INNKEEPER.) And I shall remain with her to be of help in her hour of toil—

INNKEEPER. No! You must attend to the wants of the other guests.

RACHEL (*Laying a coaxing hand on his arm.*) Please, Father. I want to see that she is made comfortable. That is what Mother would do if she were alive. (*Talks at a more rapid tempo as he frowns.*) I'll fetch her linen and a comforter, and a pillow for her head. I— (*Breaks off to jerk her head up and looks around the stage in puzzled wonder.*) Do you hear music, Father?

INNKEEPER. Music? No.

RACHEL (*Moving slowly toward Center.*) I hear it quite plainly—

INNKEEPER. Some of the guests, no doubt, singing with their wine— (*Turns as if to exit, but pauses as she speaks again.*)

RACHEL (*Standing at Center. Speaking like one in a trance.*) No. It is not that kind of music. It is more like the music one *feels* instead of *hears*. It seems to be coming out of the *air!* (*Looks upward.*)

INNKEEPER (*Going closer to her.*) What manner of talk is this? The next thing I know you'll be saying you hear mysterious *voices*—

RACHEL (*Breathlessly.*) I *do*, Father! *Singing* voices; so sweet and joyous-sounding. (*Suddenly pointing upward.*) Look! They seem to be coming from up *there!*

INNKEEPER (*Looking upward.*) From the heavens?

RACHEL (*Barely breathing the word.*) Yes!

INNKEEPER (*Still looking upward. The sound of the music rises.*) What is that bright star up there? I've never noticed *that* one before.

RACHEL. It seems to be hovering over the city!

INNKEEPER. So close. So close. One feels they could almost reach out and touch it! (*Sudden, loud laughter offstage breaks the momentary spell. The music dies down. He mentally shakes himself and moves toward the inn door, or entrance.*) What nonsense! You are a fool, Rachel. Better not say these things to other people or they will think you mad. (*Pausing near the entrance.*) I shall get the lantern for those folks in the stable now. You can make the woman a bed of fresh straw close to the inner wall where it is dry. (*Shaking his head as he exits slowly.* RACHEL *stares upward, supposedly toward the star.*) There is something strange about that pair. What is it, I wonder? Coming, Rachel?

RACHEL (*Lowly, moving slowly toward the door, or exit, but keeping her gaze turned upward.*) Yes, Father, I'm coming. (*The lights go out, the music seques into another old hymn and rises, the* NARRATOR *enters, and the curtain falls.*)

CURTAIN

NARRATOR (*Speaking as soon as the rose-colored light comes on to illuminate the* NARRATOR. *The music dies down, but continues to play as a background to the following speech.*) And it was in the stable, amidst the braying of donkeys and the bleating of gentle sheep, that the infant Jesus was born that night. There was nothing unusual in the actual birth, and no angels appeared in the stable to announce the child's arrival with joyous praise. But when Joseph looked upon the child who was not his Son, he knew that there was something miraculously different about the smiling babe. Then, while Mary rested, Joseph, the carpenter, built a crude little manger and filled it with fresh hay. And it was in this that he placed the newborn infant before he, too, lay down to sleep. A short while later, he was suddenly awakened by the sound of excited voices and the shuffling of feet outside. Then the daughter of the Innkeeper came breathlessly into the cave. . . . (*The music rises, seques into "Silent Night" and continues playing this as the rose-colored light goes out, the* NARRATOR *exits and the curtain goes up for Scene Three.*)

SCENE THREE

THE STABLE. *The stage lights are quite dim—either amber or straw-colored this time. An antique lantern stands on a small stool at Right Center. This should*

*be a small electric globe inside the lantern, with a cord
running offstage along the floor so that it may be
turned out and on again offstage for the flashback
scene. The manger is over at Left Center. This is
filled with straw, and there is a small white electric
light globe lying on a piece of tin within the manger
which will come on to suggest the divinity of the infant
Jesus later on. The child itself is not seen. There is
a small, three-legged stool behind the manger, and a
pile of straw near by, on which* MARY *is lying—on a
soft white sheet, with a pillow for her head and a quilt
to cover her, as* RACHEL *has said. The sound of excited
men's voices is heard off Right, and* RACHEL *is supposedly knocking on the entrance to the cave.* JOSEPH
*is standing near the manger, putting on his outer gar-
ment and looking toward the entrance down Right.*
MARY *half rises.*

MARY. What is it, Joseph?

JOSEPH. Sounds like a group of men—soldiers perhaps.

MARY (*Rising to a sitting position.*) Have we done
something wrong? Have we broken a law? Oh, Joseph!
If they should want to take the child! (*In spite of her
weakened condition, she manages to rise and move closer
to the manger, protectingly.*)

JOSEPH. Peace, Mary. No one knows about the birth
except the Innkeeper and his daughter. (*As the knocking
sound comes again. Calling offstage as he moves down
Right.*) One moment. I'm coming. Peace! Peace!
What do you want?

RACHEL (*Entering quickly down Right.*) Forgive me,
I did not want to awaken you—I know your wife needs
rest. But these shepherds came into the inn— (*Indicates the* FIRST SHEPHERD, *an elderly man, who enters
behind her at that moment.*)

JOSEPH (*Wonderingly.*) Shepherds?

FIRST SHEPHERD. The Lord be unto you. We come
in peace. We have no wish to make trouble. We know
the hour is late, but we have some questions to ask—

RACHEL (*Going closer to* JOSEPH, *who is just to the*

Right of Center. During this, MARY *sits weakly on the stool behind the manger.*) About your child.

JOSEPH (*Surprised.*) The—*Child?*

MARY (*Fearfully.*) Joseph!

FIRST SHEPHERD (*Indicating* RACHEL.) This girl tells us that one has recently been born in this place.

JOSEPH. That is true— (*Looks toward* MARY, *reassurance in his eyes.*)

RACHEL (*To* JOSEPH.) I asked him why they should be interested in the birth of a strange child, but he would not tell me. He said he wished to *see* the child for *himself.* (*Moves toward* MARY *and the manger, going behind* JOSEPH.)

JOSEPH (*To the* SHEPHERD. *Indicating the manger.*) The child is there. (*Watches the man narrowly, ready for any emergency.*)

SHEPHERD (*Eagerly.*) Is it a man-child?

JOSEPH (*With an almost imperceptible nod of his head.*) It is.

SHEPHERD (*Raising his voice in thanksgiving.*) Praise God! It is true! (*Calling off Right.*) Come in! Come in! It is true! The child is here! (*Backs closer to* JOSEPH *as two more* SHEPHERDS *come in, one a middle-aged man, the other a boy of twelve or thirteen.*)

SECOND SHEPHERD. A man-child—?

THIRD SHEPHERD (*Eagerly.*) Born only a little while ago?

FIRST SHEPHERD (*Nodding a quick affirmative.*) In a *manger!*

JOSEPH (*Quickly.*) There was no cradle to be bought. The town is crowded. There was no other place I could take my wife—

FIRST SHEPHERD (*To* JOSEPH.) Wait! Be not alarmed. We have recently seen a marvelous sight—an unbelievable sight, and it has to do with you and your child.

MARY (*Softly.*) Our—child?

JOSEPH (*To the* SHEPHERDS. *Backing toward the manger.*) Come no closer! (*Goes behind* MARY *to place a protecting hand on her shoulder.*)

SECOND SHEPHERD. *Believe* this thing we tell you—

144

THIRD SHEPHERD. We were all out on the hills tending our flocks. It was our turn to watch them tonight.

FIRST SHEPHERD. It was quite clear, the air was cool and the stars bright—everything was just as usual.

SECOND SHEPHERD (*The music of "It Came Upon the Midnight Clear" fades in as a background to the rest of the scene.*) We were talking about the census and how the town was so crowded with people. We had watched them moving along the roads all day—

FIRST SHEPHERD (*To* JOSEPH. *Taking up the tale.*) When, suddenly, my son here interrupted our talk and pointed excitedly toward the sky.

SECOND SHEPHERD. I had seen a great white light—

THIRD SHEPHERD. When we all looked up it almost dazzled us—

FIRST SHEPHERD. And in the light there was a *form*—

SECOND SHEPHERD. It was the form of an angel!

JOSEPH (*To* MARY. *Awed.*) An *angel*, Mary!

THIRD SHEPHERD. Then we heard a voice—

SECOND SHEPHERD. It came down from the white light—

RACHEL. A sign! A heavenly sign!

JOSEPH (*To the* SHEPHERDS.) What did the voice say?

FIRST SHEPHERD. It told us not to be afraid.

JOSEPH (*To* MARY.) The same words that the angel, Gabriel, spoke to *you*, Mary, when he first told you about the coming of the Child! (MARY *smiles.*)

FIRST SHEPHERD (*During this line, the stage lights dim out, the lantern goes off and the music rises to a joyous crescendo.*) We were dazed. None of us could move. Then the angel seemed to come closer to earth until he was hovering so near we could almost reach out and touch him. He said that he had glad tidings—that *the Savior of the World was being born!* (*By this time, the stage is completely dark. The music is playing loudly. The draperies at the back up Center are drawn quickly aside and the shepherds hurry upstage so that they are standing together in a close group at the right side of the opening, where a blue light dims up to show the* ANGEL, *standing on an elevation, looking down at the* SHEPHERDS,* *with one hand upraised.* MARY, JOSEPH *and* RACHEL *remain in fixed positions. The music softens as the* ANGEL *speaks.*)

ANGEL. Fear not, for behold, I bring you good tidings of great joy, which shall be unto all people. For unto you is born this day in the city of David a Saviour, which is Christ the Lord. And this shall be a sign unto you; Ye shall find the babe wrapped in swaddling clothes, lying in a manger. (*At once, a brilliant white spotlight comes on to illuminate the* ANGEL, *and—where possible— the voice of an offstage choir sing jubilantly, "Hark, the Herald Angels Sing." As soon as this is over, the lights all go out again, the music changes to "O Come, All Ye Faithful," the* SHEPHERDS *assume their former positions, the draperies drop back in place, and the stage lights come on as before and the* FIRST SHEPHERD *goes on speaking.*)

FIRST SHEPHERD. Then the whole heaven seemed to open up, the curtain of night was split like a tent, and through the opening we saw—

SECOND SHEPHERD. Let me tell them, Father. (*To* JOSEPH.) It could not have been imagination for we all saw and heard the same things. Through the opening we saw a host of angels that seemed to fill the whole sky, and they were all singing—

RACHEL (*Interrupting.*) I heard singing, too!

FIRST SHEPHERD. Then the light grew dim, the angels vanished and all was as it had been before.

THIRD SHEPHERD. We left our sheep and ran into the city—

SECOND SHEPHERD. Asking everywhere, "Tell us. Where can we find the newborn King?"

FIRST SHEPHERD. We went from inn to inn—

THIRD SHEPHERD. Every one looked at us as if they thought us mad—

SECOND SHEPHERD. At last we came here, and the Innkeeper's daughter told us about you—

FIRST SHEPHERD (*To* JOSEPH.) Do you believe?

JOSEPH (*Going quickly closer to them.*) Yes! It was the sign we have been waiting for. (*Indicating the manger. As he speaks the white light within it comes on and shines up in* MARY'S *face.*) *There* is the child you have come to worship. His name is Jesus, and he is indeed the Son of God. Look upon His sleeping face and you will know that He is no ordinary child. You have come, full of humble faith, and now you shall rejoice as the heavens have rejoiced at the birth of Mary's Son. Come, ye faithful—come and adore Him. (*The* SHEPHERDS *move silently and reverently toward the manger and kneel with bowed heads in attitudes of worship.* RACHEL *does the same. And while the music rises to a joyous note the curtain falls.*)

CURTAIN

THE MEANING OF CHRISTMAS DAY

A CHRISTMAS PLAY IN ONE ACT

By

Merlo Heicher

PRODUCTION RIGHTS

Copies of this play are available in single pamphlet form. The right to produce this play by one group of amateur players is authorized only by the purchase of nine copies (one copy for each speaking part) at the current price of 50c each.

It is dishonest and illegal to copy parts.

CAST OF CHARACTERS

Margaret*

Jane*

Harry*

Sam*

Mary*

Joseph

The Babe

A Shepherd, Amos*

Other Shepherds, young and old, 4 or 5 in number

A Wise Man, Melchoir

Two other Wise Men

Simeon

Anna

Angel*

Heavenly Host *(Singing.)* (Not essential, but effective if a choir can be used offstage.' However, a recording will serve the purpose.)

Production Note: *The play is performed within a church. There are no special effects or properties outside of a crib, supposedly containing the Infant Jesus, and a stool for* Mary *to sit on. A half-trimmed Christmas tree is used, with extra ornaments in cardboard boxes on two chairs. Careful attention should be paid to the lighting arrangements, however, for these are an important— almost vital—part of the production. Outside of the four modern characters, the costumes are all Biblical.*

THE MEANING OF CHRISTMAS DAY

PROLOGUE

SCENE: *In a church.*

TIME: *The present. Christmas time.*

AT THE RISE OF THE CURTAIN: *The lights go out and soft organ music is heard, playing a Christmas song. In the darkness, four people take their places around the Christmas tree that stands in front of, and at one side of, the chancel. These people are* MARGARET, *a middle-aged woman;* JANE, *a young woman;* HARRY, *a middle-aged man, and* SAM, *a young man. They are supposedly church members who have volunteered to trim the tree. As they get into their positions around the tree, a spot-light comes on to illuminate the space around the tree, which is more than half-trimmed. The people take ornaments, etc., out of the boxes on two chairs near by to go on trimming the tree as they talk. The music fades away.*

MARGARET. Do you folks realize that this is the fifth year in a row that we have decorated this chancel for Christmas?

JANE. It doesn't seem that long, but I guess you're right.

MARGARET *(With a sigh.)* Well, this is my last year. I'm fed up on Christmas. Christmas is a headache. It's rush, rush, rush . . . too many presents . . . too many cards. Now, when *I* was a little girl . . . *(The two men look around at her, as much as to say "Do we have to listen to that again?" She sees their reactions and shrugs.)* Oh, what's the use in going into that? I'm not a little girl now. *(She puts an ornament on the tree.)*

HARRY. Christmas's getting too commercialized. Now there are Christmas sales even before Thanksgiving. At the rate we're going they'll soon begin in August! *(He goes on trimming the tree lazily, without thinking much about what he is doing.)*

SAM *(Cynically.)* I still go through the motions. I suppose I'll be here helping to decorate the chancel next year. But the thrills are gone. It's just a habit. There's no meaning in Christmas for me any more.

JANE. You're all getting old . . . *(They all look at her, a trifle resentfully.)* . . . that's what's wrong with you. There's nothing wrong with Christmas. It's wrong with *you*. Why, there's lots of meaning left in Christmas.

SAM: Just what?

MARGARET. Yes—tell us, Jane.

JANE *(Thoughtfully. Walking away from the tree toward the middle of the chancel a few steps.)* Well, I like to make Christmas a happy day for the children . . . and the family means something. *(Turns, facing the others again.)* And doesn't it give you a thrill to see the decorations in the store windows—and the Santa Clauses on the streets?

SAM. That's surface, sentimental stuff. Like this pageant business we always have in the church. *(He points up onto the chancel.)* Mary, Joseph, the Babe, the Shepherds, the Wise Men . . . kind of threadbare, don't you think? People playing parts, dressed in fancy costumes. What does all this mean to *you?*

HARRY, *(He has been standing on a chair to reach the top of the tree. He now gets down.)* What is the true *meaning* of the Christmas day? I'd like to *know*.

MARGARET. So would we all.

JANE *(Moving closer to the others.)* I see what you mean. I guess I'm pretty shallow. The real significance of Christmas—yes—what *is* it? *(All look thoughtful as they slowly go on trimming the tree.)*

SAM. It's too bad to lose the meaning out of Christmas. Of course, we know . . . in a general way . . . what it means. But the real significance . . . that's different.

(Suddenly snaps his fingers as he has an idea.) Look! I
have a suggestion. *(They all gather around him ad libbing,
"You have, Sam?" "What is it?" etc.)* Let's each of us
go on a kind of quest during the year. Why, we might
even travel to the Holy Land! *(The others ad lib, scoff-
ingly, "The Holy Land?" "Are you crazy?" etc. He
laughs, shortly.)* I'm fooling. That's impossible, of course.
But we *could* go on some sort of a quest so that each could
discover, in his or her own way, the meaning of Christmas
and report to each other what we've found when we meet
here again to decorate the chancel *next* year.

MARGARET *(Enthusiastically.)* That's a fine idea, Sam!

HARRY. Agreed!

MARGARET. We'll do it!

HARRY. Yes! We'll start right away! *(HARRY, MAR-
GARET and SAM get into a little huddle as they continue to
talk, in animated, low-voiced ad lib, about the quest. Soft
organ music fades in while they are doing this, and JANE
moves away from the group a few steps.)*

JANE *(Lowly, thoughtfully.)* If only I could ask Mary
what it means! *(The lights go out and the four people exit.
JANE runs around to the front of the church. During this,
the proverbial crib is placed in the middle of the chancel
and the characters take their places.)*

SCENE ONE

SCENE: *The traditional Christmas tableau which shows
MARY posed on a stool beside the crib, with JOSEPH
standing behind it. The lights come up to reveal the
tableau . . . while the music is still playing something
appropriate, such as "O, Little Town of Bethlehem."
Then the lights go out again, briefly, and JOSEPH exits.
The music continues playing as a spotlight comes on at
the back of the church to illuminate JANE, who moves
slowly down the aisle.*

SCENE TWO

(JANE on the quest to find the meaning of Christmas. As she moves slowly down the aisle toward the chancel, MARY remains unmoved.)

JANE. I take the road to Bethlehem,
I pass the place where Rachel shed her tears
When Ben-oni was born, her son of woe,
At Rachel's death, named by his father, Benjamin,
The son of my right hand. *(She pauses, looking around the church.)*
'Tis saddening memory at Rachel's tomb,
Recalling all those mothers of the world,
Who, giving life to babes, lost theirs,
Who ne'er beheld the issue of their pain
Nor saw the satisfaction of their souls. *(She moves onward toward the chancel.)*

On down the road toward Bethlehem, the House of Bread
On either side, the fertile fields
Whose harvest gave the town its name,
With joy supplanting sorrow in my heart,
For *I* am an expectant *quest,*
In search of answer when succeeding years
And men of *future* days might ask
"What is the meaning of the *Christmas* Day?"
    (She pauses again, as if at some interesting location.)

I pass the spring by Bethlehem's gate,
From which three warriors, breaking through
A hostile troop of jeopardy of life,
With crystal water filled a cup
And tinged it red with their life's blood,
And brought it back to David, Jesse's son;
With happy thought of David and his days
I *pass* the gate, the spring, the inn,
To enter David's town, where David's son was born.

(She goes to the steps leading up onto the chancel and throws out her arms as if she had found the stable.)

Ah! Here beyond the square I find the stable cave!
The low of cows and scent of hay;
I wish that I could ask from Mary first
The burdening question of my heart—
"What is the meaning of the Christmas Day?"

(The light on MARY *comes up. She remains unmoving, looking down at the* BABE. JANE *calls softly to* MARY.*)*
Holy Mother! *(*MARY *doesn't answer.* JANE *speaks a bit louder.)* Goddess! *(Still the form remains unmovable.* JANE *stretches out her arms and kneels with one knee on the steps.)* Peasant girl from Galilee! *(*MARY *turns, smiles, rises and moves softly closer to* JANE.*)* Mary! Mary! Give answer to my plea. What is the meaning of the Christmas Day?

MARY *(Slowly, deliberately, thoughtfully.)* 'Tis *pain,* the meaning of the day!

JANE *(Surprised, she rises, half-turning to face the audience.)*
Such answer I did not anticipate:
The piercing thrust of sword, deep *pain!*
The pain of travail, Rachel's pain, *(Turning to* MARY, *as if suddenly understanding.)*
I understand . . . a woman's *memory!*

MARY *(Sighs slightly, and smiles, sadly.)* Ah, *deeper* pain!
The anguish Bethl'em mothers knew
When wicked Herod killed their baby sons; *(Hand over heart, a look of anguish on her face.)*
The pain that stabbed my soul when *He*
Came running with outstretched arms,
(Gesturing.) Made shadow on the roadside, shadow of the *Cross;*
(Softly, clearly.) Each Christmas holds a *Calvary.*

JANE *(Bows her head a bit.)* Vivacious *pain,* the meaning of the day,

That purchases the now and *higher* good.
All blood and sweat and tears, and toil,

MARY. Not good for which *ignoble* men will die,
Not good of gold, or oil, nor selfish *gain*.

JANE *(Eagerly.)* But good of faith, and peace, and . . .
liberty?

MARY. All pain that mothers and their sons endure
for these, the meaning of the day. *(The music rises and
the lights go out.* JANE *exits and* MARY *sits behind the
crib again.* JOSEPH *enters to take up his former position
behind the crib and the* SHEPHERDS *enter to assume their
attitudes of adoration.*

SCENE THREE

THE TABLEAU OF THE SHEPHERDS ADORING THE BABE.
*(This is held, like living statuary, until the end of the
hymn has been reached. Then the lights go out.* MARY,
JOSEPH *and all the* SHEPHERDS—*except one,* AMOS—*exit.
He remains standing in a fixed position, leaning on his
crook. When all is in readiness, the spotlight at the back
comes on to illuminate* HARRY.*)

SCENE FOUR

HARRY ON HIS QUEST TO FIND THE MEANING OF THE
CHRISTMAS DAY. *(The music fades away as* HARRY *starts
walking slowly down the aisle toward the chancel.)*

HARRY. How came I *here,* I scarcely know;
Am I in dream or vividly awake?
As I stand here in these Judean fields,
These fields where once gleaned the golden grain. *(He
pauses, looking around.)*
On down and down below the level of the sea;
Here looking north an ancient city gleams,
Jerusalem, all pinnacles and domes.
I seek an outcome of my quest—

To sum the meaning of the Christmas Day. *(He moves a few steps closer to the chancel.)*
Some shepherd I would seek, a son
Through generations of some ancient one
Who heard the heavenly host when Christ was born;
(Seeing AMOS, *as the light on the chancel comes up.)*
Ah! *there* he stands before me! *(He moves closer to the chancel, indicating* AMOS, *who remains unmoving.)*
He might be the very one
Who first bent knee before the Child,
His crook in hand, with sandles on his feet,
And mantle made of white sheep's wool.
Greetings, shepherd!

AMOS *(Turning.)* Greetings! I see that you are a stranger in this land. *(Points off scene.)*
Yon mountain to the north, Jerusalem! *(Points up the aisle.)*
And here, the land dips down to Sea of Salt.
Are you, my friend, on pilgrimage or quest?

HARRY. On quest. Perhaps 'tis ended now. *What is the meaning of the Christmas Day?*

AMOS *(Spontaneously. In a loud, happy voice.)* 'Tis joy! High *joy's* the meaning of the day! *(He exits and* HARRY *watches after him.)*

HARRY. Unto this hour I do not understand
How one so separate from human kind
Could know so much of human *history.*
(To the audience, now standing on the steps.)
His name was Amos, counterpart
    of *prophet* Amos long ago,
Who tended goats upon these very hills,
For life he knew, and men, and history.
(Looking after AMOS *again.)*
His theme of joy became a fugue
Rehearsing all the story of that night
When his forebears were stricken down with fear,
As angels brought them messages of joy,

157

(To the audience again.)
Good tidings of a Savior, born
That very night, that very *hour,*
So snugly wrapped in swaddling clothes
And lying in a manger.
(He moves up onto the chancel, taking the "stage.")
He told of *later* days and deeds
When Bethl'em's Babe to manhood grew
And cared for *men* as shepherds care for sheep,
When one is lost they *leave* the nine and ninety
To seek the *hundredth* one,
To find and bring it in their arms
Securely to the fold,
That all might then rejoice
Because a wanderer is found.
(Pointing after AMOS *again.)*
This Amos then recalled the names of men
From that day even unto this,
Whose lives redeemed, were changed,
Ennobled by the Savior Christ;
And how the *joy then* touched the pens of men,
And how it moved the brushes in the hands
Of those who drew the mother and her babe,
How joy had lifted temples from the earth
And made them *shout* with Hallelujah chorus;
(Directly to the audience.)
How this man knew I do not understand,
But by his discourse I shall ne'er forget
That *Christmas* Day means *Joy! High . . . joy!*
*(Raises his hand in a dramatic gesture as the music fades
in and the lights go out. Instantly* HARRY *exits, and in
the darkness* MARY *and* JOSEPH *take up their positions at
the crib again. Also, the* WISE MEN *come onto the
chancel. When all is in readiness, the music changes to
"We Three Kings," or a similar appropriate theme, and
the light on the chancel comes up.)*

SCENE FIVE

The Tableau of the Wise Men Adoring the Babe..

(As the music finishes, the lights go out again. Mary *and* Joseph *exit. The three kings remain.)*

SCENE SIX

Sam's Quest.

(The spotlight comes on to illuminate Sam *as he walks slowly toward the chancel.)*

Sam. I know not why I take this desert road.
'Tis not by choice, some urge of soul
Restrains me from the town of Bethlehem.
With purple Moab capturing my eyes
My feet descend e'en to the bitter sea,
And wading Jordan's tumbling stream,
My mind is all a-ponder with my quest—
What is the meaning of the Christmas Day?
(He pauses, halfway down the aisle, as he sees the kings.)
I soon caught up—three men of dignity
Gave greeting . . . *(The* Wise Men *hold up their hands
in salute.)* . . . dismounted from their steeds;
Seemed glad to share their rich supply
Of food for body and for soul,
For these were men of wisdom and of grace,
'Twas their similitude to those who saw a star
And traveled westward 'cross these very sands
Impelled the mention of some ancient names,
Including those of Herod and the Christ.
Yes, they had heard the names and more,
With fine exactitude they traced
The ancient track of Magi 'cross the sand.
They told of Jordan's ford, the road from Jericho
To Herod's house, where inquiry was made
About the birthplace of the King.
This prompted me to ask,

Aware that wisdom's answer would be given, —
(To MELCHOIR.*)*
Pray, tell me, *what is the meaning of the Christmas Day?*

MELCHOIR *(Moving to the center of the chancel, directly
above* SAM.*) Direction* is the meaning of the day.

SAM. Perplexed am I—I do not understand.

MELCHOIR *(Soft music fades in as a background to this
truly beautiful speech, which must be carefully learned
and delivered.)*
In ancient legend I will make you understand,
It was like this, so long ago
Three men much like ourselves, yet far more wise,
Were following hard the star, betokening a birth,
When tall Melchoir, whose name *I* bear,
Was also youngest of the three,
A-lingering behind the caravan
Espied a *plant* beside the track
Abundantly a-bloom with flowers . . . white and blue,
(Descriptively.) The blue like that of eastern morning sky,
The white like that of foam of western sea,
Incomparable in loveliness.
(Gesturing.)
Melchoir dismounted from his beast,
And stooping, plucked the tender flowers
To stom them gently in his saddle-bags,
Then *marked* the spot that on *return*
He might *uproot* the plant
To grace the garden of his distant home.
(Gesturing.)
He traveled westward with the star,
Each eventide he reveled in the white and blue
As merchants gloat o'er precious *stones,*
For neither did the flowers *wilt nor fade,*
And thus he brought them to Jerusalem.
(He walks slowly away from SAM *and back again.)*
Temptation came to lay them down
Before the mighty Herod as a *gift,*
In pledge of their *return* to him

When they should find the birthplace of the King.
But some strange hand restrained his own;
It was by *lack* of this restraint
And *more* than lack, an *urge* upon his *soul,*
He laid the flowers on his gift of *frankencense*
And gave them to the Infant Savior, King.

SAM *(Breathlessly interested. Lowly.)* Instead of
mighty Herod, he gave the flowers to the Babe!

MELCHOIR *(Continuing.)* 'Twas *then* that having knelt
before the Child,
Intending to *return* to Herod's house
That they might tell the glorious news
Concerning the Christ, His time and place of birth,
The spirit that had *urged* the *gift*
Now gave command, *forbade* return,
Forbidding too, the same road to the *East.*
This prompting came like the knell of *death,*
'Twas the seal of doom
Upon the soul of young Melchoir.
'Til then he had not plumbed
The depth of his desire to find again
The *plant* that bloomed beside the desert track,
The blue like that of eastern morning sky,
The white like that of foam of western sea.

With joy because of having found the King,
With *pain* on having lost a *prize,*
The young man traveled homeward with his friends
A *different* road, a weary road,
Yet led it to his own door step,
(Gesturing—his voice rising to a climax.)
And there, *beside* it, rooted deep,
He found a *plant* abundantly in bloom,
The blue like that of eastern morning sky,
The white like that of foam of western sea! *(The music
has risen to a climax along with* MELCHOIR'S *voice. It
now dies away.)*

SAM *(Nodding, reflectively.)* Magi of old were wont
to travel ancient roads,

The road named Wisdom taught by Greece,
Or that of Empire built by Rome.
The road that Jews had trod was Holy Law,
But *this* road for you and *me*, Melchoir—
Direction given by the Christ—the road is *Love!*

MELCHOIR *(Nodding, slowly.)* Yes, love is the meaning of the Christmas Day. *(The lights go out, music fades in and* SAM *and* MELCHOIR *exit. While the music is still playing, the characters assume their positions on the chancel.)*

SCENE SEVEN

The lights come on to reveal the tableau of the presentation of Jesus according to Luke 2:21-39. We see MARY *carrying the infant Jesus, and* JOSEPH *with a wicker cage of pigeons. They are standing on either side of* SIMEON, *who is dressed as a priest.* ANNA, *an old woman, stands beside* MARY. *The characters hold their positions until the music has finished playing, then the lights go out and all except* SIMEON *exit. He remains immovable with the spotlight coming on at the back of the church to illuminate* MARGARET.

SCENE EIGHT

MARGARET *(Walking down the aisle toward the chancel.)*
I made my way to David Street
In old Jerusalem, and up the steps
To temple side, where now the Mosque of Omar stands,
That, resting by a parapet,
A passing pilgrim greeted me. *(The light on the chancel comes up as* SIMEON *turns to see* MARGARET *approaching, and smiles.)*

SIMEON. Greetings, my daughter. Hast traveled far?

MARGARET *(Pausing at the bottom of the chancel steps.)*
Yes, I have traveled far, on search
To find the meaning of the Christmas Day.

SIMEON. Now lettest Thou thy servant go to rest
According to thy word in peace,
Mind eyes have seen salvation
Planned before the face of all the race.

MARGARET *(Startled.)* These are Simeon's words!—
Who blessed the Lord Christ Jesus here
So long ago, ere this the temple site
Had been profaned by Moslem Mosque.

SIMEON *(Nodding, slowly.)* The words of Simeon,
yea, for that's my name
The meaning of the Christmas Day is *Light!*
The *word* is Light! *Revealing* light!
To Gentiles such as thou, a stranger, art,
For thou doest lack the profile of a Jew. *(He bows in a
dignified manner and slowly moves away.)*

MARGARET *(To the audience.)* The night was falling
as with deep salaam
This bearded pilgrim spoke his final word.

SIMEON *(Pausing near the exit.)* He is the light no
darkness can put out. *(He exits.)*

MARGARET *(Moving up onto the chancel.)* He said his
name was Simeon, he seemed too real
To be the ghost of ancient patriarch
Who blessed the Mother and the Babe,
And yet I thought I saw resemblance.
'Tis only this I know, he said that *Light*
Is the meaning of the Christmas Day! *(She slowly exits
as the light go out and the music fades in again. During
this,* JANE, SAM, HARRY *and* MARGARET *surround the
Christmas Tree again and the light that illuminates the
tree comes on.)*

THE EPILOGUE

(As soon as the light comes on and the music finishes, the characters start talking in an animated and excited manner.)

HARRY. Well, here we are—back where we started from!

SAM. Once more decorating the chancel for Christmas.

JANE. Did you all go on the quest?

OTHERS *(Ad libbing.)* Oh, yes! . . . Of course! . . . Certainly . . . *(Etc.)*

MARGARET. Well, what is the meaning of the Day?

HARRY. Joy! High joy's the meaning of the day!

SAM. Oh, no! It's *Love!* Love's the meaning of the Christmas Day.

JANE. You're wrong! Wrong! It's *pain.*

MARGARET. No! It's *Light!* Revealing light's the true meaning of the day! *(They all start to argue, excitedly, "Oh, no!"— "It's love"—"Pain"—"Joy"—etc. As their voices rise shrilly they are suddenly silenced by a loud fanfare played on the organ, and turn to stand transfixed as a white spotlight comes on to illuminate the majestic figure of an angel, who suddenly appears at one side of the chancel with upraised arm. All hold their positions until the fanfare stops, then the angel advances to the center of the chancel and speaks.)*

ANGEL *(In ringing tones, while inspiring music plays.)*
'Tis not in Bethlehem fields nor an *ancient* place
That final answer to your quest is given
About the meaning of the Christmas Day.
Above the busy marts of men
Enwrapped in ruin wrought by shot and shell;
Above the country-sides where women meet
At cross-roads, moaning loss of son or mate;
You must hear the Heavenly Host advancing
Singing, shouting: *"Peace on Earth!*
And round the earth *Good Will!"* *(Here a choir should*

start singing a triumphant hymn off scene.)
'Tis *God* who knows the meaning of the Day
'Tis only He could shout above this awful din of war
The cry of *Peace!* and set aflame men's hearts with *Hope.*
For *Hope* is the meaning of the Christmas Day!
Enduring Hope, which *ever* shall *God's* angels sing *(Looks pointedly around at the audience.)*
'Til men like you . . . and *you* . . . God's peace shall bring
By *Pain's* travail, and *Joy's* surmise,
By life of *Love, see?* . . . coming in the skies . . .*(Points upward to the back of the church, where a brilliant white light comes on.)* Through darkest cloud, the gleam of *Light* . . . never to be extinguished by another night! *(All look toward the white light . . . as if it were the star of Hope . . . and hold their positions until the music reaches a triumphant climax and the lights go out. All the characters disappear in the darkness, and the lights come on again.)*

THE END

THE SILVER STAR OF CHRISTMAS

A NATIVITY PLAY IN ONE ACT
AND TWO SCENES

By

ESTHER BALDWIN YORK

PRODUCTION RIGHTS

THE SILVER STAR OF CHRISTMAS

For three men and five women

CHARACTERS

(In the order of their first appearance)

SHELAH..............*Daughter of a Bethlehem shepherd*
DEBORAH.........*Her friend, handmaiden to Herod's wife*
RUTH ⎫
TIRZAH ⎬ ....*Other royal handmaidens*
MIRIAM ⎭
SETH..*A page*
NATHAN.............................*A young scribe*
JACOB..........................*The father of Shelah*

TIME—*The period of Christ's birth.*

PLACE—*Ancient Judea.*

TIME OF PLAYING—*Twenty-five minutes.*

168

SYNOPSIS OF SCENES

SCENE 1. A room in King Herod's palace in Jerusalem. It is morning a few days before the first Christmas. During the scene, the curtain is dropped for a minute to indicate the lapse of two weeks, and the time changes to evening.

SCENE 2. A room in the cottage of the shepherd Jacob in Bethlehem. It is evening of the following day.

COSTUMES AND CHARACTERISTICS

The costumes are the long, loose, gracefully flowing robes worn by the ancient Hebrews, consisting chiefly of the tunic, or inner garment, and the mantle, or outer garment. The tunics had wide, open sleeves and were caught in at the waist with woven belts or bright-colored cords. Men's tunics hung a little below the knees, while women's reached the floor. The mantle was a piece of cloth nearly square, which was wrapped around the body or tied over the shoulders. For this play, costumes may be made of cheesecloth and designed in various bright colors to make an attractive stage picture. As white was widely worn among persons of wealth and high station, the five royal handmaidens should wear white tunics, each with a mantle in a becoming color, as expressive as possible of the personality of the wearer. On their heads they may wear veils fastened to bead-trimmed head bands, or a scarf headdress. Both men and women wear sandals, preferably in brown or some other dark color. The men wear colored or striped tunics and their mantles should be in deeper and more brilliant hues than those of the women.

The five handmaidens are pretty girls between the ages of eighteen and twenty-one, Shelah being the sweetest and brightest-looking. Tirzah has a spoiled and arrogant expression, in keeping with her character. Shelah, the only character for whom a change of costume is absolutely necessary, should wear a rich-looking costume for the palace scene, changing to a much simpler one and in more subdued colors for the last scene, in the shepherd's cottage. Seth, a lively boy in his early teens, wears a knee-length tunic and sandals with thongs laced up his legs. Nathan, who is in his early twenties, is good-looking and has an air of distinction. He wears a pouch hanging from his belt and a turban to match the rich coloring of his mantle. Jacob, a man of about fifty with gray hair and beard, wears a shepherd's costume in brown, maroon, or some other neutral color, the tunic reaching to his calf. He also wears a turban to match his mantle.

———

PROPERTIES

GENERAL

Divan, with pillows
Low, ornate table
Four low stools or cushions
Window draperies
Rugs
Jewel box, with necklaces and bracelets
Table scarf
Candelabra and vases
Bowl of fruit
Small bells to imitate camel bells, ringing off stage
Plain, rude table
Several small benches
White tablecloth
Unlighted candle

PERSONAL

For SHELAH—Lighted candle.
For DEBORAH—Sewing materials; embroidery.
For RUTH—Pair of bracelets; half-finished woven belt of colored cords.
For TIRZAH—Bouquet of flowers.

For NATHAN—Scroll, made of heavy paper fastened to two parallel sticks and rolled; pouch containing coin.
For JACOB—Knotted rope.

STAGE DIRECTIONS

Up stage means away from footlights; *down stage,* near footlights. In the use of *right* and *left,* the actor is supposed to be facing the audience.

THE SILVER STAR OF CHRISTMAS

SCENE 1

SCENE: *A room in the palace of King Herod at Jerusalem in ancient Judea, a few days before the birth of Christ. It has two doors: an outer door in the right wall leading to the street, and an inner door in the left wall leading to the royal apartments. A window with rich draperies is in the center of the back flat, supposedly overlooking a courtyard. The furnishings are ornate. Up right is a divan piled with pillows. Down left is a low, ornate table, on which are placed a table scarf, an unlighted candelabra, a vase or two, a bowl of fruit, and a large jewel box filled with necklaces and bracelets. On the floor near the table, a little back of it, is a low stool or a cushion, and three more stools or cushions are at left center, up left, and down extreme right respectively. Rugs may be used freely to make the room look more luxurious. Large ones cover the floor and smaller ones hang on the walls, suggesting tapestries. As it is a bright morning, the footlights, borders, and bunch lights off stage at doors and window are full up, yellow and amber bulbs being used.*

At rise of curtain, DEBORAH is alone on the stage, being seated on the divan at work on a piece of sewing. Immediately SHELAH enters at left and walks slowly around the room, examining the furnishings with awe. Once or twice, DEBORAH glances up at SHELAH with an amused smile. SHELAH finally stops at the divan and sits beside DEBORAH.

SHELAH.   Pinch me, Deborah, so I may be sure I am

awake. Is it true that I am really in the palace of a king?!
(*Looks around wonderingly.*) Nay, I must be dreaming.

DEBORAH (*leans over and tweaks her hair laughingly*). Of
course you are really here, Shelah. Why should you doubt
it?

SHELAH. But such glory is not for the eyes of the daughter of a humble Bethlehem shepherd. Oh, Deborah, if you
but knew how often I have fancied this, and now it has come
true! How can I ever thank you?

DEBORAH. Do not thank me. When Rachel, one of the
other handmaidens, received word that her mother was ill,
she was accorded permission to go to her for a brief stay.
The Queen is very particular. We had to find someone
immediately to take Rachel's place. It was natural that I
should turn to my childhood friend.

SHELAH. But I am not a gentlewoman.

DEBORAH (*shrugs*). What makes a gentlewoman? Birth
usually, but not always. I am not of high birth. It was only
that I had a kinswoman known to Herod's wife—a woman
of influence, who had me selected as one of the royal handmaidens. Had fate been otherwise, it might just as well
have happened to you.

RUTH, MIRIAM, *and* TIRZAH *enter at left, talking among
themselves in pantomime.* DEBORAH *turns to them.*

DEBORAH. Ruth, Miriam, · Tirzah, this is Shelah, my
friend, here to take Rachel's place while she is gone.

(RUTH *and* MIRIAM *greet* SHELAH *informally with a
smile or a handclasp, but* TIRZAH *regards her with silent
distaste.*)

RUTH. Welcome, Shelah.

SHELAH. Thank you. I'm sure I shall be happy here.

TIRZAH (*dubiously*). Perhaps.

(TIRZAH, RUTH, *and* MIRIAM *seat themselves on cushions
or stools up left, at left center, and down left respectively.*)

SHELAH. And what will be my duties here?

DEBORAH. To wait upon the Queen; to go on whatever errands she may request of you.

RUTH (*wearily*). To minister to her slightest whims.

MIRIAM. To do her thinking for her, but not to let her be aware that you do it.

TIRZAH. Remembering not to bring plans quite to completion until she has changed her mind at least five times.

SHELAH (*laughing*). Oh, really! Is it as bad as all that? You make her sound like an ogress. I'm afraid I shall be all of a tremble when I am first ushered into her presence.

SETH *enters at left.*

DEBORAH (*looks up from her sewing*). It looks as though that time has come.

SETH. The Queen wishes to see the new handmaiden. (*Goes off at left.*)

(DEBORAH *and* SHELAH *rise and cross to down left.*)

DEBORAH. I thought so. (*She surveys* SHELAH *from head to toe, turning her around.*) You need a necklace. (*Puts one on her from the box on the table.*)

RUTH. Here, take one of my bracelets. (*Takes one of her bracelets off and gives it to her.*)

MIRIAM (*fusses with* SHELAH'S *hair*). There. You look very sweet.

(TIRZAH *sits, watching, not offering to help.*)

SHELAH. It is good of you all. Do I look too frightened? I'm afraid the Queen will hear my heart pounding, it is making so great a tumult.

(SHELAH *and* DEBORAH *go off at left, talking in pantomime.*)

TIRZAH (*after a pause*). And where did *she* come from?

RUTH. From Bethlehem. She is a friend of Deborah's. Her father is a shepherd.

TIRZAH. What! That village?

MIRIAM. I think she is very gracious. She may be of humble station, but she does not pretend nobility, as do some people I know.

RUTH. She has all the manners of a gentlewoman.

TIRZAH. H'mph!

RUTH. Let us be especially thoughtful and kind. Everything here is new and strange to her.

TIRZAH. She has much to learn. But she will get no sympathy from me. Since when has the royal household included a shepherd's girl?

MIRIAM. You will do well to hold your tongue, Tirzah. You know how the Queen dislikes ill temper.

TIRZAH (*flippantly, as she saunters over to the window*). On the other hand, she must be very fond of it, since she harbors it so often in her own bosom. (*Looks out of the window idly at first, then with sudden interest.*)

MIRIAM. What do you see?

(*They all run over to the window for a look.*)

RUTH. That handsome youth in the courtyard—who is he?

TIRZAH. The scribe Nathan, I believe. How tall he is! He comes on business with the King. Perhaps I—er—we shall meet him. (*She smiles, straightens her robe, and turns toward the right exit.*) Well, I must go to the garden to gather flowers for the Queen's chamber. (*Goes off at right.*)

RUTH (*mischievously*). To gather flowers for the Queen's chamber and perchance to gain a closer view of the handsome stranger?

(*Both laugh.*)

MIRIAM (*musingly*). A scribe, she says. The King seems to be having business with many scribes of late. I wonder why.

RUTH. It has something to do with the prophecies of the ancient Scriptures, I think. Something about a king.

Their conversation is interrupted by the entrance of DEBORAH *and* SHELAH *at left, talking as they enter.*

DEBORAH. Well, here we are, and none the worse for having braved the lioness in her den. (*Seats herself on stool up left center.*)

SHELAH (*sitting on stool up left near* DEBORAH). I think you must have been jesting. She really wasn't so frightful.

(RUTH *and* MIRIAM *return to their places on divan.*)

RUTH. You come back quickly. Tell us about it.

DEBORAH. Her esteemed Majesty was in an extraordinary humor this morning.

MIRIAM. She must have enjoyed the excellently prepared food which I served her for breakfast.

RUTH (*giving her a sidelong glance*). What do you usually serve her?

DEBORAH (*ignoring the interruption*). We performed the ceremonial bow at her door. There was perfect silence.

SHELAH. She appeared not even to see us.

DEBORAH. She was fondling a pet bird perched on her finger. Presently she said, still looking at the bird, " Come here, child. What is your name? "

SHELAH. So I went over to her and told her.

DEBORAH. She had Shelah walk across the room to fetch her a comb, and watched her every step of the way.

SHELAH. When I returned to her side, she took the comb, said, " You will take Rachel's place while she is gone," and dismissed me with a wave of her hand. I know not whether I pleased her or not.

MIRIAM. She approved, or you would have known otherwise.

RUTH. She is rarely in so mild a humor.

SHELAH. What a pity! She is a great lady, and her home

is a palace. She has everything to make her happy. (*Sighs.*) And a king for a husband!

DEBORAH. Even kings have their faults, Shelah. And this king has more than his share.

MIRIAM. Not the least of which is a terrible temper. Haven't you heard what a reputation Herod has for that? He is sometimes very cruel.

SHELAH. Some day there will be another king over Israel. I have heard of him ever since I was a child. When he, the Messiah, comes, he will not be despotic or cruel. He will be great and noble and kind. Oh, if he would only come in our time!

DEBORAH. King? Messiah? What do you know of this?

RUTH. Yes, tell us. I have heard there was to be one.

SHELAH. I know only what I have heard my father say. It is a favorite topic among the shepherds. Often as a little girl, I have crept out and sat in the circle of their campfire and listened as they talked. There under the stars God seemed so near that I just knew those Scriptures must be true.

MIRIAM. What do the Scriptures say? Do you know them?

SHELAH. No. I wish that I did. Being a girl, I could not go to school. Sometime I hope to find out the exact words. I do know that there is to come a Saviour who will redeem our people from their sins. His kingdom will be one of truth and righteousness. The day of his birth will be a happy one for Israel.

RUTH. Perhaps that is what King Herod is worried about lately. He has been calling in scribes to confer with him. Scribes, you know, are versed in the Scriptures.

TIRZAH *enters at right carrying a bouquet of flowers.*

TIRZAH (*to the flowers*). It is too bad that you must leave the sunlit luxury of your garden home to grace the Queen's chamber. Most likely she will not even notice you, fair flowers.

SHELAH. (*admiringly*). What lovely blossoms! They go

177

well with your beauty, Tirzah. Such a picture should lift the spirits of even an angry queen.

TIRZAH (*pleased in spite of herself*). A pretty compliment, Shelah. Would that certain others were of like opinion. (*Glances significantly toward the window, then starts toward left door.*) I go to arrange these flowers. If we are summoned for any reason, let me know.

MIRIAM. We will, Tirzah. (TIRZAH *goes off at left.* MIRIAM *rises and stretches.*) I think I should like a bit of fresh air myself. Let's go out for a few minutes while we have the opportunity.

(RUTH *and* DEBORAH *rise.*)

DEBORAH. Yes, let's go out to the garden. The boy will let us know if we are needed. (DEBORAH, RUTH, *and* MIRIAM *start off at right. There is a sound of a man's voice off left.* SHELAH *looks in that direction, lags behind the others, but still walks toward the right door. The other girls go off at right.* DEBORAH *calls from off right.*) Coming, Shelah?

SHELAH (*calls back*). I will meet you in the garden presently, Deborah. Don't wait for me.

NATHAN *enters at left. He is reading silently to himself from a scroll.* SHELAH *steps back to escape his notice, watches him cross the stage, and then steps forward suddenly to address him.*

SHELAH. Forgive me, sir. But I— (*Hesitates.*)

NATHAN (*startled*). So I am not alone!

SHELAH (*alarmed at her own boldness*). Oh, sir, I'm sorry to intrude. I—

NATHAN (*interrupts, smiling*). Is that what you were doing? I hardly recognized the offence in such charming company. You see, I wasn't expecting anyone like you in Herod's palace. Do you mind telling me your name?

SHELAH. It is Shelah, sir. I am handmaiden to the Queen.

NATHAN. And mine is Nathan. Rather more pleasing than " sir," don't you think?

SHELAH (*shyly*). Yes, sir.

(*Both laugh.*)

NATHAN. You were about to ask me something as I came in. Now that the introductions are over, shall I go back and come in again? This time I promise to answer you properly.

SHELAH (*laughs*). I only wanted to ask if you are a scribe.

NATHAN. I am, and one very much out of favor with King Herod. I just came from reading him this Scripture. (*He indicates the scroll.*)

SHELAH. Is it about the Messiah?

NATHAN (*suddenly serious*). Yes. And do you know about the Messiah?

(*They seat themselves on the divan.*)

SHELAH. All my life I have heard of him. He is to be a great and good king, they say. Maybe some day he will live in this very palace. Would it be too much to ask, Nathan, for you to read those words to me?

NATHAN. I shall be glad to. (*Reads.*) " For unto us a child is born, unto us a son is given; and the government shall be upon his shoulders; and his name shall be called Wonderful, Counsellor, the mighty God, the everlasting Father, the Prince of Peace. Of the increase of his government and peace there shall be no end, upon the throne of David, and upon his kingdom, to order it, and to establish it with judgment and with justice from henceforth, even forever. The zeal of the Lord of hosts will perform this." Those are the words of the prophet Isaiah.

SHELAH (*repeats*). " And his name shall be called Wonderful." How the people would reverence a king like that! How they would look up to him and love him!

NATHAN. Which is something they can't do for our present monarch. (*Looks around cautiously before continu-*

ing.) I think Herod fears that this king of prophecy will displace him. That is why he rages so furiously at all who tell him what the Scriptures say. Herod is not a man who loves God. Rather, he fears God. He tries to cover this up by blustering.

SHELAH. And so he sent you away in anger?

NATHAN. Yes. Many scribes are cunning enough to twist the words of God into a permanent contract for a court position. But, to me, the Scriptures are too sacred for that.

SHELAH. I am so glad you feel that way about them.

NATHAN. I have a strange assurance that the fulfillment of this prophecy is not far off. Perhaps your eyes and mine, Shelah, will see the promised Messiah.

SHELAH. Does it say where he will be born, Nathan? Most likely he will come to this royal city of Jerusalem.

NATHAN. Not if these words are true. Listen. (*Reads.*) " And thou Bethlehem, in the land of Juda, art not the least among the princes of Juda; for out of thee shall come a Governor, that shall rule my people Israel."

SHELAH. Bethlehem! (*Repeats the word soundlessly with her lips.*)

TIRZAH *starts to enter at left, sees them, pauses in door-way, and watches jealously.*

NATHAN (*smiles*). A mere five miles from here. (*Rises.*) And now I must go. (SHELAH *rises.* NATHAN *looks at her earnestly.*) May I come again to see you? There are yet other words of prophecy which you might like to hear.

SHELAH. Oh, yes, Nathan. I should like very much to hear them and (*shyly*)—to see you.

NATHAN. To-morrow, then, at this same time. Until then, good-bye. (*He takes her hand, bows, and goes off right.*)

(TIRZAH *disappears off left.*)

SHELAH (*aloud, to herself, exultantly*). In Bethlehem— my little town—a king!

THE SILVER STAR OF CHRISTMAS

(*The curtain is lowered for a minute or two, to indicate a lapse of about two weeks. When it rises again, the time is evening, and the stage lights are more subdued than in the previous scene, the candles are lighted, yellow bunch lights are burning at the door off left, and blue offstage above the right door and outside of window up center, to indicate moonlight. Otherwise, the scene is unchanged. At rise of curtain,* SHELAH *stands by the window, looking off up center,* DEBORAH *sits on the divan working on some embroidery,* RUTH *sits beside her weaving a belt of various colored cords,* MIRIAM *is down left at the table sorting necklaces and bracelets and putting them into the jewel box, and* TIRZAH *lounges on the cushion down left, watching the other girls.*)

SHELAH. That bright star to the south has been shining for a number of nights now. It is so brilliant that it dazzles one's eyes to look at it. Yet it holds my attention strangely.

MIRIAM (*rises and crosses to window to look*). I never remember having seen it before just recently. Isn't it beautiful?

RUTH. They say that some men make a study of the heavens over their whole lifetime. They are very wise. For them the stars have mysterious meanings. If only we had such a sage scholar in court, we might ask him the significance of this new star. But such men live far in the East.

(MIRIAM *and* SHELAH *sit on divan.*)

TIRZAH (*pointedly*). Perhaps Shelah's scribe could give her the information.

DEBORAH. Hush, Tirzah. Would you have us believe you are jealous?

RUTH (*teasingly*). Nathan *has* been to the palace often of late. I'm sure it was not to see King Herod.

MIRIAM. Nor to visit Ruth, Deborah, Tirzah, or me, although he has been very charming to all of us.

SHELAH (*embarrassed*). I'm afraid that you mock me. Nathan came to read me the prophecies in which I am so interested. He has been very kind.

DEBORAH. Never mind us, Shelah. It is only that you blush so beautifully.

(*Camel bells are heard off right.*)

RUTH. What is that? (*She hurries to the window.*) Camels! Three of them! And upon them ride three men in costly garments. Who are they?

(*All the others rise and go to the window to look off up center.*)

MIRIAM (*excitedly*). Even the trappings of the camels are of gold and precious stones. See how they sparkle in the starlight!

TIRZAH. Where are they from? They look almost like kings.

SHELAH (*playfully*). Maybe they are some of Ruth's wise men, here to make her wish come true and tell us about the star.

(*All the others laugh in protest.*)

RUTH. Seriously, though, they do look as I've always imagined them.

DEBORAH. That's strange. I'm certain the King was not expecting any royal visitors. Surely preparation would have been made. The Queen would have told us. (*They turn away from the window.*) Perhaps we had better go at once and see if there is anything we can do.

All go off at left, talking excitedly in pantomime. After a moment, NATHAN *enters at right.*

NATHAN (*calls*). Shelah! (*Waits for a moment.*) Shelah! (*Pauses, then calls.*) Boy!

SETH *enters at left.*

SETH. Yes, sir?

NATHAN. Where is Shelah?

SETH. There are guests at the palace, sir. She is busy attending the Queen.

NATHAN (*taking coin from purse at his belt and giving it to* SETH). Then here is a coin. Be sure that you give her this message: "The King is born." Is that clear?

SETH. Yes, sir. "The King is born."

NATHAN. Also bid her send me return word at her earliest opportunity.

SETH. I will, sir.

NATHAN. That is sufficient. (*Goes off at right.*)

SETH *walks idly about the room. He eats a grape or two from the fruit bowl, then eases himself down on the divan. He lifts one foot tenderly and feels of it, yawns and stretches, lifts both feet upon the divan, lies down, and sleeps.* SHELAH *enters at left as if to get the jewel box. Discovering the sleeping boy, she bends over him tenderly. Her hand smooths a stray lock from his forehead. Then she straightens up, glances uncertainly toward the door and back at the boy, and finally leans over and shakes him gently.*

SHELAH. Seth! (*Shakes him.*) Seth!

SETH (*awakens and sits up quickly*). Oh, Shelah! I—I'm sorry!

SHELAH. Sh! It is all right, Seth. I wanted to let you sleep, but I didn't want you to be caught and punished. (*Sits on divan beside him.*)

SETH. Thank you, Shelah. Why are you so kind to me?

SHELAH. Because I once had a little brother like you.

SETH. Where is he now?

SHELAH. He died. I think he is up there with God somewhere beyond the stars. Sometimes I fancy I see his smile in their friendly twinkle.

SETH. I wish he were here where I could meet him. (*Gasps.*) Oh, good gracious, Shelah! I nearly forgot!

SHELAH. Forgot what?

SETH. That I have a message for you from Nathan. I

knew I couldn't give it to you while you were busy with the Queen.

SHELAH. Quickly! What did Nathan say?

SETH. Only this: "The King is born." And you are to send Nathan back some word.

SHELAH (*rises*). The King is born! (*Turns and places her hands on* SETH's *shoulders.*) Oh, Seth, do you know what that means? The Messiah has come! He will save our people from their sins. He will be a good king, full of kindness and love.

TIRZAH *enters at left and regards them coldly.*

TIRZAH. It seems to me that there is little time for loitering, with so much to be done for the royal visitors. And there is no need for you to get excited over this fabled Messiah. These very men within our gates have traveled miles seeking him. They have not found him yet. They even asked Herod if the child were here.

SHELAH (*wonderingly*). They must have seen the star!

TIRZAH (*scornfully*). They leave to-night, and if they do find such a babe, they are to tell King Herod where he is, so that he can "go to worship the Messiah, too." But do you want to know why he really is anxious to find out? It is so that he can have the child slain. (*Crosses to go off right, and flings the words back over her shoulder.*) And then where do you think your Saviour—your Messiah of the Scriptures—will be? (*Goes off at left.*)

SHELAH (*frightened*). Seth, quickly! I must send two messages. Will you go on two errands for me?

SETH. Yes, yes! What shall I do?

SHELAH. One is to find Nathan and tell him to come here at once. The other is more difficult.

SETH. I will do it. What is it?

SHELAH. We must save the newborn King, Seth. Already we are called upon to serve him. Now listen. (*Looks around carefully.*) Watch until the three kings of the East leave to-night. When they are outside the palace gates, approach them. Tell them that a humble worshipper of the

Messiah sends them this word: "King Herod is false of heart. He seeks to know the babe's whereabouts to slay him. Return not to tell Herod of his birthplace." Can you remember that?

SETH. Yes, Shelah.

SHELAH. Then go; and God bless you!

SETH. I go.

SHELAH *goes off at left, and he starts to exit at right, but meets* TIRZAH *as she is entering at right, and is pushed back into the room by her.*

TIRZAH (*angrily*). No, you don't go! Not now. I thought it would be like this; so I went around to the outer door and listened. You should be ashamed to raise your head, boy. Plotting with this impostor, this—sheep herder's daughter against your king! (*She shakes him and boxes his ears.*) You will not deliver the messages—not either of them. Do you hear?

SETH. But I must! Let me go! I have promised!

TIRZAH. Such promises are better broken. This puts you in line for a good flogging, and it will not be gentle for a matter as serious as this. Perhaps I had better turn you over to the palace guard.

SETH. No, no! They will beat me!

TIRZAH. Then come with me. I will see that you are safely locked up until she is gone and all this is over. (*She leads him off at right by the arm.*)

After a minute, SHELAH *enters at left. She straightens things on the table, rearranges the pillows on the divan, etc. Then she walks anxiously back and forth. Camel bells sound off right. She hurries to the window and looks off up center, anxiety and eagerness in her bearing. Meanwhile,* TIRZAH *enters at left.*

TIRZAH (*half to herself, half to* SHELAH). At last they are leaving! It's a wonder we wouldn't be informed of these things ahead. (*Grumbles.*) No less than three foreign monarchs dropping in on the palace at once! (SHELAH *continues to look off up center.* TIRZAH *briskly changes things around on the table.*) What are you standing there mooning about?

SHELAH. I was watching them go. They are magnificent, Tirzah, and yet so humble in their quest.

TIRZAH. What nonsense! They are gone now. Come away from the window.

SHELAH. I am watching for— (*Hesitates.*)

TIRZAH. Nathan, I suppose. Well, Nathan is not coming.

SHELAH. Nathan—not coming? But why?

TIRZAH. He has found out that you are not really a royal handmaiden. He knows now that you are only a shepherd's daughter, a pretender in the palace. A scribe, you know, has to be careful whom he selects for friends.

SHELAH (*trying to hide her chagrin*). Oh—I see.

TIRZAH. It is unfortunate, of course, that all this has happened. A king also has to be careful whom he harbors in his palace. Any seeds of disloyalty have to be rooted out.

SHELAH. You are asking me to leave?

TIRZAH. Yes.

SHELAH. But the Queen expects me to fill Rachel's place until she returns. The Queen has not dismissed me.

TIRZAH. We had word to-day that Rachel returns to-morrow. There is really no longer any need of your remaining. You will find a donkey saddled in the courtyard and two servants ready to accompany you home.

SHELAH. I understand. (*Slowly she removes her bracelets and necklace, laying them on the table while* TIRZAH *stands watching.* SHELAH *starts toward the right exit, then turns back.*) I—I should like to say good-bye to Deborah and the others.

TIRZAH (*crisply*). They are busy. I will tell them.

SHELAH. Very well. (*She looks around the room once more, her glance lingering.*) Good-bye, Tirzah. (*Exit at right.*)

CURTAIN

SCENE 2

SCENE: *A room in the home of the shepherd Jacob in Bethlehem, on the evening of the following day. It has two doors: one at right leading outdoors, and another at left leading to the rear of the house. A window is in the back flat up center. The furnishings are very simple and meager. At center is a plain table covered with a white cloth, with a small bench on the upstage side of it and two similar benches at right and left of it respectively. On the table is an unlighted candle. All stage lights are dim, to give the illusion of twilight, brightening a little after the lighting of the candle.*

At rise of curtain, JACOB *is seated at left of table, holding a knotted rope and trying to untie the knots.* SHELAH *enters at left, carrying a lighted taper.*

SHELAH. Father! It is dark. You should not try to use your eyes in this gloom. Here, wait till I light this candle. (*She lights the candle on the table from her taper. The stage lighting should become brighter at this point.*)

JACOB. My old eyes are used to the dark of the fields at night. (*Laughs softly.*) I declare, Shelah, you treat me like a child. (*Looks down at the rope.*) I was just getting the knots out of this rope so I can use it on the door of my sheepfold.

SHELAH. Well, I have put away the supper bowls, and now I shall have time to help you. (*She crosses and stands beside* JACOB.)

JACOB. No, my fingers are stronger for this. That was a good meal to-night—a good meal. You don't know how I've missed you, daughter.

SHELAH (*teasingly*). Oh, so that's the only reason you're glad I'm home: on account of my cooking.

JACOB (*pats her hand*). Shelah! Shelah! You know it's more than that. (*She smiles and puts her arm around his shoulder.*) You're all I have, but your happiness is mine, my child. I tried to think of you as having a wonderful time in the King's palace.

SHELAH (*sits down beside him*). I did at first, father. It was thrilling to think of myself as the Queen's handmaiden. And my surroundings reached my highest dreams of splendor and luxury. But there was something missing.

JACOB. In what way?

SHELAH. In the atmosphere, I think. The Queen was spoiled and discontented. The King was selfish and cruel. Tirzah, the handmaiden who sent me away, was displeased at my presence there. There just wasn't the harmony one would expect to accompany such beauty. Why, father, there is more loveliness here or in the dwellings of any of our humble neighbors than at the royal court!

JACOB. I'm glad you see that, Shelah. It is a lesson few learn.

SHELAH (*sadly*). Once I would have said Nathan would understand it, but—

JACOB (*interrupts*). Ah, Nathan again, it is, daughter? (*He lifts her chin with his hand.*) You have spoken much of him since you came home. You love him; don't you?

SHELAH. To do so is to step out of my place. But I shall always remember him as one who taught me more about God than I have ever known before.

JACOB (*rises*). And God works all things out for the best. You can depend on that, Shelah. Well, I must go out and take care of my sheep for the night. (*Exit at right.*)

(SHELAH *remains seated thoughtfully for several moments. Suddenly* NATHAN'S *voice is heard as if from a distance.*)

NATHAN (*calling from off right*). Shelah! Shelah!

SHELAH *starts, rises, and turns toward the right, a glad surprise lighting her face.* NATHAN *enters at right.*

NATHAN (*holds out his arms*). Shelah!

SHELAH. Nathan! (*Goes to him.*)

NATHAN. Oh, Shelah, I looked everywhere! Why did you leave the palace so suddenly?

SHELAH (*remembers and draws away from him*). Rachel was to return to-day. I was no longer needed.

NATHAN. But to go away like that without letting me know—

SHELAH (*interrupts*). Tirzah told me that you would not come again and that shepherds' daughters and scribes do not mix.

NATHAN. Foolish one! I suppose you believed her.

SHELAH (*smiles*). I'm afraid so, Nathan.

NATHAN. Perhaps in the course of time I can help you to change your mind. (*He takes her hand and leads her to the bench at right of table, where they sit.*)

SHELAH. How did you find me, Nathan? Did Seth give you my message to come to the palace?

NATHAN. No, the poor little fellow was discovered and locked up overnight by Tirzah.

SHELAH. How cruel of her! And then what?

NATHAN. Deborah found him this morning and released him. She told me you had gone home. Tirzah was severely reprimanded. She will be more careful after this.

SHELAH. I am glad she was not discharged. I am too happy to wish anyone ill luck. My place is not in Herod's palace, Nathan. I shall be happier here in Bethlehem serving another king.

NATHAN. And so shall I.

SHELAH. You have seen the child? Where is he?

NATHAN. In a little stable in back of the inn. You see, because of all the people coming to be taxed, there was no room left anywhere else.

SHELAH. A little king in a cattle manger!

NATHAN. But his presence makes it glorified. A majesty is there, Shelah, and you feel that nothing is so wonderful as the King himself.

SHELAH. It is almost as though you brought some of his glory here with you. You are somehow different, Nathan.

NATHAN. I am not the same person I was before I went to the manger. He who once looks into the face of the Christ must ever be changed. The words of the Scriptures then become a reality.

SHELAH. We are on the threshold of a new life. God has come to earth! Father told me that the angels sang the night when the babe was born. He and the other shepherds left their sheep to go to the manger. Since then, many have come to worship the King, among them the wise men. (*She suddenly looks alarmed.*) Nathan!

NATHAN. What is it? What is the matter?

SHELAH (*frightened*). The wise men did not get my message!

NATHAN. About Herod? Yes, they did, but not through Seth. Those at the stable told me that the three kings were warned by God in a dream and have gone home by another road.

SHELAH. God works in wonderful ways! But will not Herod make further attempts on the babe's life?

NATHAN. By that time, his parents, Mary and Joseph, will have taken the little Messiah to a place of safety. God will take care of them.

(*There is a rap at right door.*)

SHELAH. Who can that be? (*Goes to right door and throws it open.*)

SETH *enters at right, out of breath.*

SETH. Shelah! Nathan!

NATHAN. Seth!

SHELAH. Seth! How did you get here?

SETH. I ran away, Shelah. Don't send me back. Please!

SHELAH (*puts her arm around him*). Of course not, Seth. But why did you do it?

SETH. I do not like it at the palace. I want to serve the real King. But I have no other home. And you have no little brother. Could I be your little brother, Shelah?

SHELAH (*embraces him*). Yes, Seth. And you and Nathan and I will work together for the little Messiah's new kingdom.

(*" O Little Town of Bethlehem "* is played softly on the organ, or voices hum the melody softly, off stage. The music continues pianissimo to end of the play.)

NATHAN (*quoting*). "And his name shall be called Wonderful, Counsellor, the mighty God, the everlasting Father, the Prince of Peace."

SHELAH. He will be no ordinary king. Nations will look to him and call him blessed. He will speak truth, and the ages will listen. The world will never forget his birthday.

SETH. Even the children will love him.

SHELAH. Take us to worship him, Nathan.

NATHAN. The air is like crystal to-night. The hills lie silent as in adoration. High in the heavens over your Bethlehem, God's silver star is shining. And the way to the manger is not far. Shall we go?

(*Slowly and reverently the three exeunt at right. The music swells in a finale as—*)

THE CURTAIN FALLS.

THE SHEPHERDS AND THE WISE MEN

A NATIVITY PLAY IN ONE ACT

By

ADDISON LEROY PHILLIPS

PRODUCTION RIGHTS

THE SHEPHERDS AND THE WISE MEN

For nine men, one little boy, two women, and
a choir of women's voices

CHARACTERS

THE FATHER.....................................*An old
man who has had an assurance of the coming Messiah*
CALEB.......*The eldest son, next in authority to his father*
REUBEN ....*Second
son, shares his father's hope concerning the Messiah*
EPHRAIM ....*The
business manager, interested in selling some sheep*
HEBER ....*The
doubter, mainly concerned with the care of the flock*
GAD ....*An excitable
fellow who rages about the cruel oppression of Herod*
THE ANGEL......................................*The
one who announces to the shepherds the birth of Christ*
JOSEPH ....*An elderly
man, only half aware of the greatness of the event*
MARY ....*Who appears
with the babe in the closing scene but has no lines*
THE THREE WISE MEN..............................
..............*Who bring gifts with song and lines*
THE CHOIR OF WOMEN'S VOICES.....................
.......*In the midst of the Choir the Angel appears*

TIME—*The First Christmas Eve.*

PLACE—*Bethlehem.*

TIME OF PLAYING—*Forty minutes.*

THE STAGE SETTING

The back stage, which is the stable, is shut off by a curtain which opens in the middle. (Screens may take place of the curtain.) During the first part of the performance this curtain is kept closed. The front stage, which should be roomy, is the field where the shepherds are grouped around an open space.

If the front curtain is dispensed with, the shepherds take their places in a half circle, sitting, or reclining, or asleep. The Old Shepherd lies upstage on a mat or blanket, fast asleep, and The Little Shepherd near him. Gad and Heber are about halfway down stage, and Caleb and Ephraim are down front, their talk directed toward the audience so as not to disturb their father.

The back stage, the stable, needs only a bench or stool for Mary. If a manger is added, the boards should not look too startlingly new. Mary holds the Babe, a large life-like doll wrapped in a blanket. Joseph stands beside her except for a moment, when he goes forward to greet the Wise Men.

If the stage lacks a dressing room, some tall screens will be needed where the shepherds may withdraw.

For a touch of realism, a covered basket and jug of water may be placed in the space around which the shepherds are grouped.

SUGGESTIONS FOR COSTUMES AND MAKE-UP

Costumes

The shepherds wear knee-length smocks, the shins wrapped with cloth puttees of tan or brown color. Turbans of bright colors are effective. The Old Shepherd and the Little Shepherd should wear long robes (jubbahs). All wear girdles and sneakers or soft slippers.

The Wise Men have rich robes and splendid turbans. Dressing gowns of good materials will answer, but they should not be too suggestive of the bath.

Joseph's costume is a plain robe of dark stuff, suitable for a carpenter's dress on the Sabbath.

Mary wears a long white robe with wide sleeves, has a blue silk scarf draped over her head.

The Angel should be golden-haired, wear a white robe, and may have a wreath of tinsel on her head.

MAKE-UP

Dark powder is preferable to grease paint to give a swarthy complexion. The father should have a full gray beard. Reuben and Caleb should have dark beards; Ephraim, Heber, and Gad should have but little beard. If preferred, one of the wise men may be given a very dark complexion. Mary should have but little color. Joseph's beard should be graying.

PROPERTIES

Heber should have a sheep-stick. Reuben also should carry one when the group go to Bethlehem; this he should give to his father when the old man goes to the door of the stable. If crooks are wanted, green rods may have the small end bent and held with a fine wire. A little cutting along one side will make them bend easily.

A few rugs, blankets, car robes for the shepherds to lie on, and a bundle for the father to take with him.

THE GIFTS

A gilt jewel box will be suitable for the first Wise Man; a wide-mouthed vase with ears or handles will be suitable for the frankincense (a gum); an ornate flask or carafe carried on a platter, to hold the myrrh.

STAGE DIRECTIONS

Up stage means away from the footlights; *down stage,* near the footlights. In the use of *right* and *left,* the actor is supposed to be facing the audience.

THE SHEPHERDS AND THE WISE MEN

SILENT NIGHT! HOLY NIGHT!
(This hymn, first played softly by the organist and then sung by the choir, is a fitting prelude to the play.)

Silent night! Holy night!
All is dark save the light
Where the mother a vigil keeps
O'er the Babe who in silence sleeps;
Sleep in heavenly peace!
Sleep in heavenly peace!

Silent night! Holy night!
Darkness flies, all is light;
Shepherds hear the angels sing
"Hal-le-lu-jah! Hail the King
Christ the Savior is born,
Christ the Savior is born!"

Silent night! Holy night!
Son of God, love's pure light
Radiant beams from thy holy face,
With the dawn of redeeming grace,
Jesus, Lord, at thy birth,
Jesus, Lord, at thy birth.

(When the hymn is ended and while the organ continues playing the air softly, the shepherds take their positions on the stage, some sitting, some lying down. Caleb and Ephraim, one on either side of the stage, stand looking off into the night [the darkened house].)

For the Prelude the organist plays "Silent Night," softly

*for atmosphere, and a choir of girls offstage sing the hymn.
The singing finished, the music should continue, growing
softer until it dies away. With the last strain* CALEB *stirs
and after a moment sits in a listening attitude.*

CALEB (*now on his feet*). Hark! (*Pause.*) I think I
heard a wolf. (*He speaks to* EPHRAIM, *who is across from
him, downstage.*) Ephraim, I think I heard a wolf. The
moon has gone down and it has grown so dark a wolf
might easily steal upon the flock.

EPHRAIM (*rising*). I heard it too; but it's a long way
off. Up toward Rachel's tomb, wasn't it? (*He goes and
shakes* HEBER.) Hey, Heber, get up. There's a wolf about.

CALEB (*looking Left*). Somewhere near the tomb, but
a little more toward the town, I think. Sounded like one,
but there may be more. You never can tell.

HEBER (*coming forward*). What's that you say? A
wolf?

EPHRAIM. Yes, it's a wolf we heard howling off yonder.
(*Makes a gesture.*) Up among the hills. We'd better walk
out in that direction.

HEBER (*taking up a staff*). Never you mind, I'll make
the circuit. No use of both going. You are pretty tired,
aren't you? (*He goes briskly to Left, whistling for the
dog, and disappears behind the screens.*)

EPHRAIM. Our sheep are likely to bring us good money
now. The crowds that are coming into Bethlehem will
make brisk market for all we have to sell.

CALEB (*still standing*). Yes, and we need money badly.
Our taxes were never so heavy. We can't afford to lose a
single head.

EPHRAIM. We ought to be able to sell a good many.
You know, the travelers haven't all arrived yet. The roads
are choked with them, Reuben said. I wonder where they
are all going to sleep? The old inn won't hold them all.

CALEB. Oh, Reuben said the inn was full already, and
people were being turned away. Many will have to camp
out, and little comfort they'll find I'm thinking. The nights
are growing chilly, and they won't be prepared to camp.

They ought to have a few of our sheepskins. I wonder, Ephraim, if we ought to take a few pelts with us?

EPHRAIM. Might be a good idea. About how many do you think we ought to sell?

CALEB. We have about five and twenty wethers that we ought to dispose of now and, if the prices are good, we might sell a few lambs.

THE LITTLE SHEPHERD (*moving quickly and grabbing* CALEB'S *arm*). You won't sell my lamb, will you, Father? You won't let them have my pet lamb?

CALEB. You needn't fret, young one; we won't sell your lamb. We don't have to sell everything. (*He takes the child back.*) Now cover up and go to sleep, or we won't let you watch with us again.

(GAD *sits up and listens.*)

EPHRAIM. Yes, we had better take a few lambs with us. I doubt not the market will be good. Herod has made no provision to feed the crowds.

GAD (*on his feet and talking excitedly*). Herod make provision! Man alive! These people come here to be bled, not to be fed. It's a fine big tax he will be rolling up for the benefit of his Roman friends.

EPHRAIM. Right you are, Gad. The king is after their gold. But there is no use getting so excited about it. You will wake up Father with your noise.

GAD (*more excited and noisy*). We are slaves! Slaves of a cruel and bloody king. He's a monster. Uncle Amos said he had hired a villain to strangle his own sons. He's afraid they might push him off the throne.

CALEB. Hush, brother, not so loud, or he'll be having you strangled. The very stones have ears. Herod's spies are everywhere. We must bear our yoke as best we can. Grumbling won't help us.

GAD (*gesturing with his fist*). Bear it! How long? I ask you, how long? (*He lowers his voice a little.*) How many years—O God, how long ago it was that we were promised a deliverer, a king of our own, one who would be wise and just. The prophets said he was to be born right here in our Bethlehem. Why doesn't he come?

(REUBEN, *awakened by* GAD'S *noise, comes down Center, near* GAD.)

HEBER (*returning*). Everything is quiet, boys. Shep didn't get any scent of the wolf, so I guess it must have gone off in another direction.

(*He goes back and lies down.*)

EPHRAIM (*doubtfully*). Yes, Gad, we know what the prophets have said—born in Bethlehem and of the House of David. All nonsense! What family in Bethlehem would pretend that a drop of the great king's blood is flowing in their veins? We know everybody in the village. They are just common folks like us.

REUBEN (*silent while he looks from one to the other*). What you know, or what any one of us knows, amounts to very little. We are ignorant shepherds. The ways of the Lord are past finding out. Our part is to be faithful and trust in his promises. Rest assured, our king *is* coming, and a powerful king he will be. He won't be like this bloody Herod; he will be gentle and merciful. What was it the prophet Isaiah said?—"One who would bear our sorrows and carry our griefs."

(THE OLD SHEPHERD *rises quietly and comes forward.*)

THE OLD SHEPHERD (*his hand on* REUBEN'S *shoulder*). Well said, Reuben. The wisest word you have heard here tonight, lads. Listen to me. (HEBER *comes forward and all take listening attitudes on either side of the father.*) This is something I have long wanted to tell you. It is a kind of revelation—a vivid dream that I had many years ago. It came to me while I was watching sheep in these fields and you were little boys at home with your mother. I was alone on just such a night as this. I had been praying for the coming of the King, the Prince of Peace, who would save Israel from the wrongs of the oppressor. We had waited so long; and we needed him sorely. All at once it came upon me—a great calm. I felt a deep assurance that he would come, and that I would live to see him with these eyes. It has remained with me all these years—a steadfast assurance. So, my sons, put away your doubts. Our King will come. I have a strange feeling—that—that he will come this very night. I feel that his time is at hand. (*He looks up and clasps his hands.*) O God, that my heart be not misled! Oh, my sons, prepare your hearts for the coming of the Prince of Peace. Harbor no unkind thoughts, no envying, nothing dishonest, nothing unclean— else when he comes you will not be able to look upon his face.

REUBEN (*speaking slowly and thoughtfully*). Why shouldn't he come now, my brothers? Why not tonight? (*He looks up toward the heavens.*) Did you ever see a more beautiful sky? And the world is beautiful—or would be if it were not filled with cruelty, hatred, and strife. The humble and weak are scorned—are trodden under foot. There is no one to befriend the poor, no one to see that they have justice. The poor man is robbed of what little he has; and Israel groans under a foreign yoke—never so much in need of a Judge and a Redeemer as at this very hour.

(*The old man raises his hands in prayer; all except* HEBER *bow their heads.*)

THE OLD SHEPHERD. Oh God, God of our fathers, hear us we most humbly beseech thee. Send a deliverer to thy wretched people. We have waited long—oh, so long!

(HEBER *looks disgusted, goes and gets his staff and stands at Left, remaining silent for a little while.*)

HEBER (*thumping the ground with his staff*). Father, don't you think you had all better settle down and go to sleep? You are all tired, and we will have to be stirring early if we take a flock of sheep into town. You all go to sleep. I'll keep guard. (*They all lie down on their blankets, and* HEBER *goes out Left. Behind the screen he talks to the dog.*) Come, Shep, you lazy old cur. That wolf may be sneaking around. Use your nose. (*The star at the rear of the auditorium is flashed on, and a moment later* HEBER *rushes in shouting excitedly.*) Hey, fellows, look! (*Pointing at the star.*) See that strange light. Did you ever see anything like that?

(*All are on their feet looking, the old man shading his eyes with his hand.*)

THE OLD SHEPHERD (*his voice shaking*). I told you, my sons. I told you! That star is the sign of his coming. It looks as if it had come right down out of the heavens.

REUBEN (*with conviction*). It is a star, though—a most brilliant star. Unlike any we have ever seen. And, see! It is right over Bethlehem.

HEBER (*quite calm now*). Yes, it is a star; and quite wonderful, to be sure. But don't become so excited about it, or you will have no sleep tonight. And you all need rest.

(*He goes out, whistling for the dog to follow.*)

EPHRAIM (*studying the star*). Yes, it's over Bethlehem. And that is where it should be. That's where the King was to be born.

CALEB. No, not quite over the town, is it? It's at one side—must be back of the old inn. Hark!

(*All stand still, looking up and listening. The organist begins playing very softly "O Come All Ye Faithful." The shepherds kneel quietly. When the organist has played through the air, the choir, remaining seated, sing two stanzas: "O come," etc. And "Sing, Choir of Angels."*)

ANGEL (*rising from the midst of the choir*). Be not afraid; for I bring you good tidings of great joy, which shall be to all people. For there is born to you this day in the City of David, a Saviour, who is Christ the Lord. And this is the sign by which you shall know him: You will find the babe wrapped in swaddling clothes and lying in a manger.

(*As the music of the organ gradually dies away, the shepherds rise, one after another.*)

CALEB (*quite overcome*). The prophecy is fulfilled!

REUBEN (*equally awed*). It is just as Father said it would be! Our King and Redeemer *has* come at last. High honor it is that an angel of the Lord should come down to make it known to us poor shepherds. Was that a part of your dream, Father?

THE OLD SHEPHERD (*ignoring the question*). He will heal the sick; he will give sight to the blind; he will bind up the broken heart; he will preach good tidings to the poor.

EPHRAIM (*slowly and reverently*). Just to think—God sent his angel—to bring the news to humble men like us! Let us go straight and find the King.

(HEBER *enters quite unconcerned.*)

CALEB. Oh, Heber, you should have been here. An angel appeared with a heavenly host and told us that the Christ is born in Bethlehem. That *is* his star, sure enough. And we are going to the town to find him.

HEBER (*looking around at them, much amused*). Are you fellows awake? It seems to me that you have all had a wonderful dream while I was gone.

REUBEN. Dream, brother! No dream. It actually happened. We are going to Bethlehem right now to find the babe.

HEBER (*not impressed*). Well, I'll stay here and maybe get a little rest. And I'll need it; for you will wear yourselves all out tramping around. Possibly I'll have a little dream all my own.

CALEB. Is it well that one should stay alone? You had better keep him company, Ephraim.

(EPHRAIM *shakes his head and looks disappointed.*)

HEBER. Go 'long, Eph. I don't need you. Caleb thinks I'm afraid to stay here alone.

THE LITTLE SHEPHERD (*tugging at* CALEB'S *arm*). I want to go too, Father. I don't want to stay here. I want to take the baby my lamb. You don't care if I take him my lamb, do you?

THE OLD SHEPHERD. The child is right. We should take a gift. I wish we had something fitting to take. Of course, if I understand the meaning of his coming, it is our loyalty, the love of honest hearts, that will please him best. Still, I wish we had some precious thing which would show our love.

THE LITTLE SHEPHERD (*joyfully*). Then I may take him my lamb? Oh, I want to take it. Say yes, Father.

CALEB. Very well, you may. We will get it as we pass the sheep pens. Are we ready to go?

THE OLD SHEPHERD. Wait a minute. You know, his family must be among the strangers who have come to Bethlehem to be enrolled. They will be far from home and perhaps are not well provided for this cold weather. I'll take a few blankets. (*He gets the bundle.*) And a sheepskin will make a warm bed for the baby to lie on.

(*As they go out,* EPHRAIM *stands looking at the star. After a moment* HEBER *gives him a push.*)

HEBER. I say, go 'long, Eph. No use your staying here.

EPHRAIM (*smiling*). I do want to go. (*He hurries out.*)

HEBER (*pondering*). Of all the wonders! Still, it might be possible. Father feels so certain about it. (*He pauses to study the star.*) Well, I'd better be stirring. (*As he disappears he calls, "Come, Shep!"*)

(*To mark passage of time while the shepherds foot it to Bethlehem, the Choir sings: "While Shepherds Watched Their Flocks."*)

> While shepherds watched their flocks by night,
>   All seated on the ground,
> The angel of the Lord came dowr
>   And glory shone around,
>   And glory shone around.

"Fear not," said he, for mighty dread
  Had seized their troubled mind;
"Glad tidings of great joy I bring
  To you and all mankind,
  To you and all mankind.

"To you in David's town, this day,
  Is born of David's line
A Saviour, which is Christ the Lord,
  And this shall be the sign,
  And this shall be the sign.

"The heavenly Babe there you shall find
  To human view displayed,
All meanly wrapped in swathing bands
  And in a manger laid,
  And in a manger laid."

Thus spoke the seraph, and forthwith
  Appeared a shining throng
Of angels, praising God on high,
  Who thus addressed their song,
  And this shall be the sign:

"All glory be to God on high,
  And to the earth be peace;
Goodwill henceforth from heaven to men
  Begin and never cease,
  Begin and never cease."
      (*Air by Handel, found in all hymnals.*)

(*While the choir are singing the first stanza, the stage
should be cleared. When the song is finished, the shepherds come from behind the screens and hesitantly approach
the stable. If a front curtain has been closed, the stable, if
made of screens, may be moved forward a little. This is
only necessary if the stage is very deep.*)

CALEB (*with his father, leading*). This is the old stable.
(*They halt.*) I doubt we shall find the little Prince here.
It is not a suitable place.

(REUBEN *and his father cross to the farther side of the door, so that the two groups stand facing each other. They must not turn backs to the audience.*)

GAD. Let's not stop here. Let's go into the village and inquire of Rabbi Samuel. He will know where these people are staying—probably at his house. If not, he will know where they are.

THE OLD SHEPHERD. No, no! You have forgotten what the angel said—the sign he spoke of—the manger. We are to find the baby lying in a manger.

CALEB. That's true. So this must be the place. Who will go and knock at the door? I don't know how one should speak to a prince or to his noble parents.

REUBEN. Father, you go. The spirit that informed you of the coming of the Prince of Peace and has kept your faith alive all these years—trust that spirit to lead you now and give you the words you ought to say. (*He gives his father his staff.*)

THE OLD SHEPHERD (*shaking his head*). If it should be a king—the Prince's father—I shouldn't know what to say. I don't know how to begin.

(*They all fall back a little, leaving the old man alone before the door. He turns and looks to those on his right; then slowly turns to* REUBEN, *as if he expected help. He then bows his head as in prayer.—Time for this.—Then he taps the floor gently with his staff.* [*Pause.*] *He taps louder. Presently the curtain opens and* JOSEPH *peers out cautiously. The old man moves back beside* REUBEN, *so as not to have his back to the audience and to give* JOSEPH *the stage.*)

JOSEPH (*slowly looking them over, fearing an emissary from Herod*). Friends, what is it you want?

THE OLD SHEPHERD. Sir, as we were watching our flocks in the field tonight—scarcely an hour ago—an Angel appeared to us and said that a babe was born here—the one promised of old—a Prince who should bring peace on earth to all mankind. We have come here to find him,

JOSEPH (*speaking slowly*). It is true—a child *was* born here tonight.

THE OLD SHEPHERD. Are you—may I ask, if you are descended from King David?

JOSEPH. I am of David's line. That is why we had to come to Bethlehem for the enrolling.

(*The shepherds see that they need not stand in awe of* JOSEPH *and come nearer and speak more freely.*)

CALEB. Pray tell us, sir, what signs and wonders you have seen tonight.

JOSEPH (*shaking his head, puzzled*). Signs? I don't know what you mean.

CALEB. Have you had no signs from heaven? As my father has just said, an Angel spoke to us—yes, and a host of angels sang to us. And we saw a star, a strange, brilliant star, which has led us to this place.

JOSEPH. Yes, we have had visions, my wife and I. But I—I don't know what to say. We do not feel sure that we know what the visions mean. (*Pause.*) You say you came to see the child?

REUBEN. Oh, sir, if we may be so bold. (*He touches his father's arm.*) This is our father. He has waited many years to see the redemption of Israel. It was revealed to him many years ago that he should not die till he had seen with his own eyes the Prince of Peace, the one who was coming to save us from our sins. Kind sir, may we—may we be permitted to behold him?

JOSEPH (*nodding, with an understanding look*). Wait, friends, and I will go in and speak with the child's mother.

(*He disappears, closing the curtain.*)

CALEB. Shall we tell him about Herod? He may not know of the danger. If the old king should hear of the birth of this child and have the least hint of the prophecy—

GAD (*impetuously*). Oh, you must tell him! You must! That old murderer would destroy the little Prince.

REUBEN. If he comes from far away, he probably has

not heard of the crimes the old tyrant has committed. We know how he guards his throne against every suspected rival. Of course, we must ask if he knows.

THE OLD SHEPHERD. Yes, yes. We must warn him. Herod has his spies in almost every village—very likely a spy right here in Bethlehem.

JOSEPH (*looking out as he holds the curtain aside*). Yes, my friends, you may come in.

(*The curtain is closed and the choir sings the hymn, "There's a Song in the Air." When the song ends, the curtain is opened wide showing the Holy Family, MARY seated holding the babe, and JOSEPH standing beside her. At their left are all the shepherds, part of them kneeling, part standing. The audience will forget about the lamb, and we may do so too. From the rear of the auditorium the WISE MEN enter and begin singing as they advance up the left aisle. They carry their gifts about shoulder high. An accompaniment is unnecessary.*)

THE WISE MEN (*singing and keeping step with the melody*).
> We three Kings of Orient are;
> Bearing gifts we traverse afar,
> Field and fountain, moor and mountain,
> Following yonder Star.
>
> Oh, star of wonder, star of might,
> Star with royal beauty bright,
> Westward leading, still proceeding
> Guide us to the perfect light.

(*They pause at the Right of the stage and JOSEPH comes forward looking alarmed.*)

FIRST WISE MAN (*arm raised high, hand open, palm down, placed against the forehead as if shading the eyes*). Peace be unto you, and to all who are here assembled; and perfect peace to the infant Prince. Ours the joy that we have found him.

(JOSEPH *stands with his hands clasped in wonderment, looking inquiringly from one Wise Man to another. At last he bows a little in acknowledgment of their august presence and motions for them to take their places at the right side of the stage, balancing the Shepherds at the left. The* FIRST WISE MAN *stands nearest to* JOSEPH, *who now has taken his place beside* MARY.)

FIRST WISE MAN (*continuing*). We are three kings from the far East. In a mysterious way it has been revealed to us that a Prince, one who is to be King over all the world, was to be born at this time and in this land. We have come to find him, that we may pay him homage.

SECOND WISE MAN (*bowing slightly and slowly*). Peace and blessing of the Most High God be upon you all. For many days we have journeyed, following a star—a wonderful star—which seemed to be leading us on. (*In a tone of ecstasy.*) And this is the blessed Babe who is to be the light of the world!

THIRD WISE MAN (*with a half step forward*). Blessed art thou, Son of David! Hear, we pray thee, a word of warning. We have been at Jerusalem, thinking to find the Babe there. We had audience with Herod the King, who was eager to learn about our mission. When he heard what we had to say, he flew into a terrible rage. Then, all suddenly he put on an air of great piety and said: "Pursue your quest, noble sirs, and when you have found the child you must bring me word, that I may go and worship him also." But, oh sir, go not to Jerusalem; though the king's voice was soft, his eyes were fierce and bloody.

FIRST WISE MAN. And, sir, we beseech you not to tarry in this place. For when Herod learns that we have gone away into our own land without giving him a report, he will be still more suspicious, and he will search, and he might find you here. He is not to be trusted; he fears a rival to his throne. Best that you flee from this place and leave no word about where you have gone.

JOSEPH. Thanks, gentle friends. We shall take good heed of your warning. We had not learned of the danger till these good shepherds told us; for we come from **far-off**

Nazareth, in Galilee. And we arrived here only yesternight.
We heard nothing in Galilee except that we had to be taxed
and that we must come here for the enrolling. When that
is done, we shall depart quickly. (*He turns to* MARY,
who has been looking at him anxiously.) We shall go
away into a strange land.

FIRST WISE MAN. Then all will be well. (*He moves a
half-step forward.*) Long, long we three have prayed for
a better world. At last, it seems that our prayers will be
answered. Something within me says that this is the
Redeemer we have been praying for—this child is the hope
of all mankind. For him we have brought our gifts, little
gifts to show our love. And we have prepared a song of
praise. When we have rendered this we shall depart. (*He
moves forward just perceptibly and sings:*)

> Born a king on Bethlehem's plain,
> Gold I bring to crown him again;
> King forever, ceasing never
> Over us all to reign,—

(*Kneeling, he places his gift at* MARY'S *feet and, taking
his place with the other two, they sing the chorus: Oh, Star
of wonder, Star of might, etc.*)

SECOND WISE MAN (*moving a half-step forward and
singing.*)

> Frankincense to offer have I;
> Incense owns a Deity nigh;
> Prayer and praising all men raising,
> Glory to God on high.

(*Having placed his gift, he remains a moment, gazing
with rapture at the babe. Then, tatking his place, he with
the other two repeat the chorus: "Oh, Star of wonder," etc.*)

THIRD WISE MAN (*singing, his tones full of grief*).

> Myrrh is mine, its bitter perfume
> Breathes a life of gathering gloom;
> Sorrowing, sighing, bleeding, dying,
> Sealed in the stone-cold tomb.

(*With an air of profound sadness he places his gift and, having glanced at* MARY *and the babe, he returns to his place, hands clasped against his breast and head bowed. He remains silent while the other two sing the chorus:* "Oh, Star of Wonder," *etc. The Wise Men now descend from the stage, pause, and facing the Holy Family, make a salaam; then facing the audience, they sing the last stanza:*)

Glorious we shall see him arise,
King and Priest, and Sacrifice,
Heavenly hosts sing "Hal-le-lu-jah!"
Joyfully earth replies.

(*Followed by the shepherds, the* WISE MEN *pass down the aisle singing the chorus:* "Oh, star of wonder," *etc. If used in a church performance, the play may be fittingly followed by the congregation singing* "Joy to the World.")

CURTAIN

THE TREE

A CHRISTMAS COMEDY IN ONE ACT

By

ELLEN LAURA McMARTIN

PRODUCTION RIGHTS

Copies of this play are available in single pamphlet form. The right to produce this play by one group of amateur players is authorized only by the purchase of eight copies (one copy for each speaking part) at the current price of 50c each.

It is dishonest and illegal to copy parts.

CAST OF CHARACTERS

For four men and four women

JAMES DAVIES................a middle-aged, businessman, father of the five young people in the play

MAUDE DAVIES..his wife

KAY DAVIES............................their daughter, a freshman at State College, a typical co-ed

DICK DAVIES............................Kay's collegiate brother, the usual type of freshman

VIRGINIA DAVIES......a younger sister, a pert high school girl

NED DAVIES............................the high school brother, rather brusque in a boyish way

BUDDY DAVIES..........the "kid brother," in the seventh grade

MOLLY PENDLETON....Kay's chum, home from the University

*   *   *

SCENE: The living room of the Davies home.

TIME: The afternoon of December twenty-fourth.

PLAYING TIME: Thirty-five minutes.

214

LIST OF COSTUMES AND PROPERTIES

JAMES DAVIES—Wears a conservative, gray business suit, overcoat, hat and gloves. Newspaper. Billfold. Christmas tree on a standard.

MAUDE DAVIES—Wears a dark silk dress. Apron to wear over dress. Wristwatch. Sewing material. Letter. Rolling pin. Plate of cookies.

KAY DAVIES—Wears a fur coat; a smart, bright-colored silk or wool dress. Hat, gloves and purse. Sorority pin. Traveling cases. Christmas tree.

DICK DAVIES—Wears a coon coat or an overcoat, and a snappy suit. Hat and gloves. Fraternity pin. Traveling bag.

VIRGINIA DAVIES—Wears a skirt and sweater in a bright color, preferably red, with a leather jacket and beret. Changes to a bright, pretty dress and coat. If preferred, to eliminate changes, she may wear a jacket over the dress when she first enters, making only a change from the jacket to a coat necessary. Gloves and scarf. Skates. Christmas tree.

NED DAVIES—Wears a pull-over sweater, leather jacket, trousers and a cap at the first entrance. Changes to a good-looking suit. It is possible to make this change in the manner suggested for Virginia. Skates. Piece of cake. Christmas tree.

BUDDY DAVIES — Wears cap, sweater, and knickers. Skates. School books. Hockey sticks, football, skates, tennis racket, overshoes, mittens, etc., to throw from the closet. Christmas tree.

LIST OF COSTUMES AND PROPERTIES—(Contd).

MOLLY PENDLETON—Wears a fur coat and a smart dress, similar to Kay's. Hat, gloves, purse. Sorority pin. Magazine to pick up from the table.

MISCELLANEOUS PROPERTIES — Framed pictures of Kay and Dick on the table; books on the table; wreaths at the windows; greens banked on mantel; candles and candlesticks on the mantel; lamps, pillows, pictures, etc., to brighten up the room.

THE TREE

THE SCENE: *Is the living room of the home of* MR. *and*
MRS. JAMES DAVIES *in a midwestern city. It is the after-*
noon of December twenty-fourth. There are Christmas
wreaths at the two windows on either side of the door at
the rear. A fire is burning in the grate at Right. Ever-
green boughs bank the mantel, and red candles are in the
candlesticks on the mantel. A davenport, drawn up near
the fireplace, faces the front. At Center and a little to
the Left is a table, on which there are framed photo-
graphs of KAY *and* DICK, *books and a lamp. At the Left*
of the table is an easy chair. A stairway at the back
leads off to the Left. A chair and lamp placed at the Left
below the stairway will help to make the room seem more
homelike. The door at Center leads to the street; the
stairs are upstage Left. At the lower Left, a door leads
to the kitchen; and at lower Right there is the impor-
tant door to the clothes closet. The wreaths, the green-
trimmed mantel, everything gives the effect of being all
prepared for the Christmas festivities. The room is a
homey room, arranged in excellent taste. Pictures, rugs,
books, lamps, cheery draperies at the windows, etc., show
that a family lives here and enjoys it.

AT THE RISE OF THE CURTAIN: MAUDE DAVIES, *a rather*
plump woman of forty-five, is standing at the window,
upper Left, arranging a wreath. MRS. DAVIES *is rather*
inclined to sentiment, but is far from being devoid of a

*sense of humor and thoroughly enjoys her family.
Throughout the play she wears a simple, dark dress,
which is now covered with an apron. As she pats the
wreath, she hums one of the old Christmas hymns.*

MRS. DAVIES *(Giving the wreath a last pat.)* There now.
*(Stands back to survey her work, then ' goes over to
straighten a candle that has fallen into the mass of greenery
on the mantel.)* It looks really Christmas-like now. Everything except no tree. But Buddy will want to help Father
get it. Christmas! *(Goes over to the table, straightens the
two photographs on it.)* Kay's and Dick's first Christmas
homecoming! I do hope Father will get back in time to
meet the train. I'd hate to send Ned and Jimmy down with
the car, with the streets so slippery. They'll come on the . . .
*(She takes a letter from her apron pocket. One can see that
she remembers its contents perfectly, but wants an excuse to
read the letter again.)* Let's see . . . the five o'clock train.
I hope Dad won't be late. *(Sound of stamping snow off
outside Center door.)* There he is now. *(JAMES DAVIES
enters from outside, Center. He is a man of fifty, his hair
well-sprinkled with gray. He is a tall man, but is a little
bent and care-worn with hard work to give his family the
best in life. His peaceful, happy expression shows, however, that he feels his sacrifice has more than paid. He is
wearing an overcoat and hat and a conservative, gray business suit.)*

MR. DAVIES. Hello, Mother! *(Goes over to kiss her affec-
tionately. Straightens up, sniffs the air.)* Are you trying to
burn the house up?

MRS. DAVIES. Oh, my Christmas cakes! I forgot *all*
about them! *(Dashes off to the kitchen. MR. DAVIES removes his hat and overcoat, puts them in the clothes closet
at Right, removes a paper from his pocket as he does so.
He looks around the room, enjoying it, then sits down at
the davenport in front of the fire. Lays the paper on the*

davenport, rises, putters with the decorations until MRS.
DAVIES *re-enters.)*

MRS. DAVIES. Well, I saved them, I think. I'm afraid I'll
have to trim the edges, though. I'm sorry there isn't time
to make another batch.

MR. DAVIES. They'll never know the difference. *(Indicates the room.)* It looks grand, Maude—the real Christmas spirit.

MRS. DAVIES. Everything but the tree. I thought you
and Buddy would like to pick that out when you go to
meet the train. *(MRS. DAVIES is continually straightening
something as she talks. She wants the house spic and span
when her children get home.)*

MR. DAVIES. When do the young scalawags come in?
(MRS. DAVIES has an excuse to read the letter again.)

MRS. DAVIES. On the five o'clock, James.

MR. DAVIES *(Musing.)* It's strange to think of them coming home from college for Christmas.

MRS. DAVIES. Yes, isn't it? Why, it was just yesterday,
it seems, that they had their first tree. Remember how
darling they looked — baby Kay and little Dick in their
creeper suits coming downstairs to see what Santy left
them?

MR. DAVIES. It couldn't have been more than a year or
so ago that Bud crept downstairs at two in the morning
and found his mouth organ and woke up the whole house
tooting it! *(Both are laughing.)*

MRS. DAVIES. Yes, and he slept the rest of the night on
the davenport with his train tucked under his chin. *(Laughs
again.)*

MR. DAVIES. Then there was the time when Jinny and
Ned set the tree on fire with their prancing. *(Stops, thinking.)* By the way, where are they now?

MRS. DAVIES. Off skating with some of their high school
chums.

MR. DAVIES *(Just a bit sternly.)* Maude, didn't you make Virginia help you?

MRS. DAVIES *(Indulgently.)* Oh, it's vacation now, James. *(Laughs.)* Remember the time when Jinny *did* try to help?

MR. DAVIES. I'll say so. I'll never forget those cookies!

MRS. DAVIES. James, our happiest times have always been at Christmas with the children, haven't they? *(Gets up, looks out of the window at Left.)* Why, there comes Buddy now!

MR. DAVIES. Well, I'll be getting the car out. *(Exit MR. DAVIES at Center, and a moment later MRS. DAVIES at lower Left.)*

MR. DAVIES *(Off Center.)* Hello there, son!

BUDDY *(Also off Center.)* Hi, Dad! *(BUDDY, a typical boy about twelve years old, slides into the room a moment after MR. DAVIES goes out. Skates across the room, tosses his hat on the lamp and the books on the table, and executes a handspring all in one bound. BUDDY is wearing knickers and a pull-over sweater.)* No more of that trash for two weeks! *(As he tosses the books.)* No more "gerund-is-a-verb-in-ing" or "the capital of Peru is Chili" or "the square root of twenty-five is five." Whoopee! *(The handspring on this exclamation.)* Just skating and hockey 'n' ... *(Sees MRS. DAVIES entering with a plate of cookies and makes a dive for them.)* Gee! Cookies!

MRS. DAVIES. Yes, Buddy, you may have one. *(But he already has two or more and, talking between bites, is gobbling them down.)* You're late, Buddy.

BUDDY. Yes, school party. Had to be Santa Claus. *(Contemptuously.)* Santa Claus! Where's my skates?

MRS. DAVIES. I picked them up off the hearth and put them into the clothes closet yesterday. *(MRS. DAVIES picks up the plate and goes back to kitchen. BUDDY goes into the closet at lower Right.)*

THE TREE

BUDDY *(From the closet.)* Ma! *Ma! (No answer.)* Mother!

MRS. DAVIES *(From the kitchen.)* What is it, Buddy?

BUDDY. Where'd you say those skates were?

MRS. DAVIES. In the closet.

BUDDY. Well, I can't find 'em. *(Overshoes, tennis rackets, mittens, footballs, hockey sticks—everything comes flying out.)* They aren't here, Ma—Mother!

MRS. DAVIES *(Resignedly, from the kitchen.)* I'll have to find them, I suppose. *(Enters, lower Left.)* Why, James Davies, Junior, what do you think you're doing?

BUDDY *(Muffled, from the closet.)* Trying to find those skates.

MRS. DAVIES. Here, let me get them. *(BUDDY backs out into the room. MRS. DAVIES exits to the closet.)*

BUDDY. They just aren't in there anywhere, Mother. I looked all over and I couldn't find 'em. *(MRS. DAVIES comes out almost immediately.)*

MRS. DAVIES *(As BUDDY looks at her in a puzzled manner.)* Right on the shelf where I told you they were. Now put everything right back where it came from.

BUDDY. Aw, gee, Mother! Aw, criminy, I have to go skating.

MRS. DAVIES *(Firmly.)* Back in the closet, Buddy. *(BUDDY throws the things back the same way he threw them out. MRS. DAVIES, watching him, stands toward the kitchen. MR. DAVIES enters Center.)*

MR. DAVIES. Coming with me to get that Christmas tree now, Buddy?

BUDDY. Aw, who wants an old Christmas tree? I want to go skating. *(There is a whistle from offstage.)* There's the gang whistling for me now.

MRS. DAVIES *(Mildly surprised.)* But aren't you going to meet Dick and Kay?

BUDDY. Aw, we'll see enough of them the next two weeks. Dick'll play football with my ping pong set 'n' Kay'll try to curl my hair'n' . . .

BOY'S VOICE *(From outside.)* Did they need sharpening?

SECOND BOY'S VOICE. Are you coming, or aren't yuh? *(Also outside.* NOTE: *If desired, these two boys of* BUDDY'S *age, wearing stocking caps, sweaters, and knickers, and carrying skates, may poke their heads in the door at Center as they speak.)*

BUDDY. Yeh, I'm coming. Wait a minute! *(Dashes off.* MR. *and* MRS. DAVIES *are too astonished to say anything for a moment. Then* MRS. DAVIES *goes over to the door to shut it after him.)*

MRS. DAVIES *(Slowly, as she comes down from the Center door.)* Maybe Buddy doesn't want a tree.

MR. DAVIES. Oh, he was just in a hurry, Mother. *(Looks at his watch.)* Well, I'll have to go to meet the train now. *(Brightly.)* Why don't you have Jinny and Ned get it while I'm gone?

MRS. DAVIES. They'd like to, I'm sure. I'll tell them when they come. Do hurry back, Father.

MR. DAVIES *(Going to the door.)* Good-bye, Maude!

MRS. DAVIES *(Following him to the door. This speech and her previous one, "Do hurry back, Father," should follow each other immediately.)* Now, Father, don't drive too fast. *(Starts back to the kitchen.)*

MR. DAVIES *(Off Center.)* How was the skating?

NED *(Also off Center.)* Just great!

MR. DAVIES *(Still off Center.)* I think your mother wants to see you.

VIRGINIA *(Off Center.)* We're just looking for her, Dad! *(*VIRGINIA *and* NED, *the typical high school boy and girl, rush in and drop their skates on the davenport.* VIRGINIA *is a dark, vivid girl, of the always-alert type.* NED *is rather brusque, with that mask of harshness and bravado which is* *often noticed in the high school youth. Both are peppy and always moving.* VIRGINIA *is wearing a leather jacket over a bright sweater and skirt, preferably red, with a matching beret. If desired, she may wear her jacket over a dress, which will eliminate the necessity of changing when she goes out later for the evening.* NED *wears ordinary trousers, a sweater, and a leather jacket—or he may wear a high school athletic sweater with a monogram.)* Oh, Mother ...

MRS. DAVIES *(Comes back from the kitchen door.)* Oh, here you are now. Wouldn't you like . . . ?

NED. Some supper? Yes. We're starved. Is it ready yet?

MRS. DAVIES. Why, no, we're waiting for Kay and Dick to come home. Remember, it's Christmas eve.

NED. Gee, we can't wait. Must get going. Got any grub around loose? Any kind of handout will do. *(Starts to make a dash for the kitchen,* VIRGINIA *following.)*

MRS. DAVIES. But there's no hurry. It's Christmas eve ...

VIRGINIA. Surely. We know it. That's why we're in such a rush. We've just time to grab a bite and change our duds and get over to Lil's to meet the gang. *(She is flinging the beret and gloves and jacket and scarf as she speaks.)*

MRS. DAVIES. Lil's? The gang?

NED. Yes. Large evening, Mums. We're all meeting at Lil's and then going to the show and then wind up with a party over at Thelma Gray's.

MRS. DAVIES. But you'll wait until Kay and Dick get home? I thought we'd all have supper here and then all go to the Sunday school exercises together. The program's going to be very good.

VIRGINIA *(Astonished.)* The Sunday school program!

NED. The Sunday school program! Ah, Mother, you're kidding us!

MRS. DAVIES. No, I . . . *(NED and VIRGINIA have grabbed up part of their clothes and are starting up the stairs.)*

VIRGINIA *(Over the banister.)* Just leave us something on the kitchen table, Mother.

MRS. DAVIES *(Hesitantly. She has begun to wonder what has come over her family.)* Will you do something for me?

NED *(Coming back.)* Yes, of course, Mums. Why didn't you say so before? What is it?

MRS. DAVIES *(Trying to be bright and looks as if she expects them to do what she is asking.)* Won't you go out and get the tree, so the rest of us can trim it this evening?

NED *(Scornfully.)* Tree! Gee, Mother, what d'ye think we are, kindergarteners? Next thing you'll want us to hang up our socks and read "The Night Before Christmas" to us!

MRS. DAVIES *(Shocked that her son should speak this way to her.)* Why, Ned . . .

VIRGINIA *(Trying to smooth things over a bit, yet blundering as she does it.)* Don't you see, Mother? It's different now. Nobody does those old things any more. They're out—just out. *(Starts upstairs, then turns back.)* Is my good dress back from the cleaners yet?

MRS. DAVIES. It's hanging in your wardrobe, Virginia. *(VIRGINIA has already gone on upstairs. MRS. DAVIES sighs and picks up the skates and clothes, puts them into the clothes closet. Commotion, laughing and chatter outside. MRS. DAVIES breathlessly removes her apron and takes it to the kitchen, returns just as KAY and DICK burst in, followed by MR. DAVIES, who is carrying their bags. DICK has one of the bags which he slides across the floor. Both are typically collegiate, gay, pseudo-sophisticated, and yet underneath each is to be found true character and worth. KAY wears a fur coat, a bright, smart turban, a chic, collegiate dress of wool or silk, and carries a smart purse and gloves. DICK wears either a coon coat or an overcoat, a hat, and a snappy suit.)*

DICK. Hi, Mums!

MRS. DAVIES. My dears! Dick! Katherine! *(Rushes to them and tries to embrace both at once.)*

KAY. Greetings, Mother! Gee, it's gr-rand to be home again!

MRS. DAVIES *(Holding her off, looking at her, then turning to* DICK. *There are tears of happiness in her eyes.)* I'm so glad to have you back home again! You haven't changed a bit, have you? *(This is a real question, and she stresses the "you" without being aware of it.)*

DICK. Why, do we *look* any different? Boy, the old place surely looks the same. And darn good, too.

KAY *(Flopping on the davenport.)* And am I a wreck? The dance last night after all those exams, and then the train . . .

MRS. DAVIES. You may rest all you want while you're home, Kay.

KAY. Don't worry, I will. *(Stretches out luxuriously, then sits up suddenly.)* Hope there'll be something doing during vacation—dances and parties. I'm ready for a keen time! Wonder who else of the gang is home yet? I'm just *dying* to sport my sorority pin and my fur coat. See, Mother, Dad! *(Goes over to show them the pin.)*

DICK. You don't eclipse me, kid. Take a peek at this, will you? It's good!

MRS. DAVIES. Yes, children, they're very lovely.

MR. DAVIES. But isn't it costing you a good deal of money?

DICK. Oh, yes, but you see . . . *(During the last two speeches,* MOLLY PENDLETON, KAY'S *chum, who is also home from college for the first time, has entered and slipped her hands over* KAY'S *eyes.* MOLLY'S *clothes and outward personality are very similar to* KAY'S *although she lacks the inherent sweetness that* KAY *has, and she also has a tendency to be a little patronizing, to show that she knows she has more money and a better social position than* KAY.*)*

KAY *(Squealing as she pulls the hands off.)* Why, Molly! *(During the following scene,* MOLLY *and* KAY *are at Right, back of the davenport, while* DICK *and* MR. *and* MRS. DAVIES *are at Center, a little to left of the outside door.)*

MOLLY. Oh, honey, it's good to see you! Hello, Mrs. Davies! It's good to be here again!

MRS. DAVIES. And it's good to have you here, Molly.

MOLLY. How do you do, Mrs. Davies?

MR. DAVIES. How do you do, Molly?

MOLLY. And Dick, what damage have you done besides breaking all State's football records, and smashing the co-eds' hearts, and everything?

DICK. Well, well, if it isn't the same old Molly! Do they call that snappy repartee down at the U? You'd better come to State and get an education. *(She makes a face at him.)*

KAY *(To* MOLLY.*)* Don't mind him, sweet. That's just his childish way of demonstrating his affection. You're a perfect duck to come over so soon.

DICK *(Explaining to his mother and father.)* Well, the reason I finally pledged was that all my crowd went Zeta. Anyway, all the *big guns* belong.

KAY. Honestly, Molly, aren't you just cr-razy about college?

MOLLY. Oh, the University's just too thrilling for words!

DICK. Too bad you missed the Carter game, Dad.

MR. DAVIES. They said it was good . . .

DICK. Good! Sa-ay, was it good!

KAY. You pledged a sorority?

MOLLY. Of course, Phi Lambda—it rates at the U.

KAY. I didn't care for their girls at State. I went Kappa Tau.

DICK. Did I tell you, Dad, the fellows want me to go out for the swimming team . . . ?

MRS. DAVIES. Now, Richard, try to remember that you're at college primarily for an education.

MOLLY. Oh, Kay, I had the keenest date for our last dance.

DICK. Well, Mother, at that I think I'm going to rate a B in my chemistry course. But, boy, did I have to polish the apple for the old fossil who teaches it . . . !

KAY. Oh, but, Molly, isn't vacation just the grandest thing ever?

MOLLY. And the best part of all is outside. *(Draws KAY to window at Right.)* Take a look!

KAY *(Ecstatically.)* Oh, Molly! Dick, look outside! Hasn't Molly the *duckiest* car?

MOLLY *(Swelling, yet trying to be modest, as all crowd to the windows.)* Yes, I rather like it. It's a present from Dad.

KAY. Are you giving *me* one, Daddy?

MR. DAVIES. Sorry, Kay. You'll be lucky if you get a month's supply of streetcar tokens. *(MOLLY and KAY put their heads together, talking in undertones. VIRGINIA and NED appear on the stairs.)*

NED. Did I hear *car?*

VIRGINIA *(All curiosity.)* Where? Who? What are you all shouting about?

NED *(To VIRGINIA.)* Aw, pipe down. *(To KAY and DICK.)* Hi, there, collegiates!

KAY. Hello, kids! *(As she looks up at them.)*

DICK *(Making a dive for her.)* Hi, Sis!

VIRGINIA. Hello there, Kay! Dick, don't be such a bear!

DICK. How are all the high school boy friends, Jinny? Boy . . . *(As he whirls her about.)* . . . but you've gotten to be the young lady! I could almost take you to our winter dance.

VIRGINIA. Oh, Dick, *would* you?

DICK *(At Left again.)* Oh, in a dozen years or so, when you grow up!

VIRGINIA. Conceited! *(*MR. *and* MRS. DAVIES *finish their talk as they stand at Left; then* MR. DAVIES *picks up the bags and goes upstairs.* MRS. DAVIES *is picking up wraps.)*

KAY. Listen, Dick! We're going for a spin in Molly's car. Then there's a keen dance on. We're all going. You and Molly, and . . .

DICK. Since when do you make *my* dates, Kay?

MOLLY *(With an assumed injured air.)* Well, Kay, it seems I'm jilted!

KAY *(To* DICK.*)* Oh, all right, if you don't want to go! It won't be hard to find a substitute! *(*VIRGINIA *and* NED *listen disgustedly, then move off toward the kitchen.* MRS. DAVIES *at lower Left.)*

NED. How about the grub, Mums? No use listening to that bunch jabber. *(*MRS. DAVIES *follows them as they exit to the kitchen.)*

DICK. And anyway, just who said I *didn't* want to go?

KAY. You change your mind often.

DICK. My privilege. Let's get started.

KAY. Just a minute. We must get unpacked and cleaned up a bit. Oh, our bags are gone.

MR. DAVIES *(Coming downstairs.)* I took them up, Kay.

KAY. Thanks, Dad. *(As he sits down in the chair left of the table with his paper, she sits on the arm, puts her arm around him, and pats his shoulder.)* You're a peach!

MRS. DAVIES *(Coming in from the kitchen.)* I'll unpack for you, Kay. Don't you and Dick and Molly want to get the tree before you go—if Molly'd like to? *(During the following scene* MOLLY, *realizing that she is listening in on a family quarrel, is a little embarrassed. She picks up a magazine, looks at it, puts it down, fumbles with her coat, etc.)*

KAY. The tree?

DICK. Tree?

MRS. DAVIES. Yes, our Christmas tree, you know.

DICK. Oh, Mother, we don't need a tree this year. There aren't any kids in the family now.

KAY. And, Mumsy, the needles all fall off so soon and litter up everything. It's hardly worth the effort.

DICK. Let's not bother with it this year.

MRS. DAVIES. But I want to bother with it.

DICK. Well, if you want it, Mother, but we just haven't time to get one tonight. Won't tomorrow do just as well?

MOLLY *(Rises and moves toward the door at Center. Speaks in an embarrassed manner.)* Well, I must be running along.

KAY. Well. don't be gone too long.

MOLLY. I won't. I'll come back as soon as I pick up Larry. *(KAY walks to the door with her.)* Good-bye!

KAY. 'Bye, hon! See you in a jiff.

DICK. Now see what you did. What'll Molly think?

MRS. DAVIES. But don't you want a tree? It's somewhat of a family tradition, you know.

NED *(Coming in the kitchen door with a piece of cake he is munching. VIRGINIA follows.)* Are you people sounding off on the Christmas tree gag again?

MR. DAVIES *(Who has been silently reading his paper all this time. Looks up and speaks severely.)* Ned!

NED. Oh, all right! *(Jamming on his hat.)* Only I think you're making a big fuss over a good deal of—of . . .

KAY. Sentiment.

NED. That's it exactly. Well, look for us when we get in. I'll bring the car around to the front, Virginia, so meet me out there. I can have it, can't I, Dad? *(This is an afterthought, said over his shoulder as he goes out the kitchen door.)*

MR. DAVIES *(Sighs.)* I suppose so. *(*VIRGINIA *exits Center.)*

DICK *(Snaps his fingers.)* Just like that! Well, come on, Kay. Molly'll be back in a second and all that time wasted! Scram! *(They dash upstairs.* MRS. DAVIES *watches them go up, then turns and stands in front of the stairs.)*

MRS. DAVIES *(Crying softly.)* What's the matter with them? They always wanted a tree before.

MR. DAVIES *(Rises and pats her shoulder comfortingly.)* There, Mother, they're just growing up, I suppose.

MRS. DAVIES. Well, maybe sentiment is out of style.

MR. DAVIES. Sentiment is just for the very young and the very old, I imagine, Mother. I'd like to get a tree for just us, though. Shall I?

MRS. DAVIES. Yes, do, Father. Well, perhaps I'd better help them unpack. *(Exit* MRS. DAVIES *upstairs.* MR. DAVIES *is putting his hat and coat on.)*

MR. DAVIES *(To himself, unaware of* DICK, *who is on the stairs.)* I don't believe the youngsters are half so worldly as they think they are. They'd be disappointed if I didn't get a tree.

DICK *(Coming downstairs.)* No, Dad, we really don't want a tree. It's so much fuss and lasts such a short time, and we're here so little. The gang always wants to get together for vacation anyway, you know. It isn't that we don't appreciate your thoughtfulness and everything. We surely do—heaps, but you know . . . *(This is palaver.* DICK *realizes that what he is saying doesn't mean anything, but it is his way of paving the way for what he is going to say in a moment.)*

MR. DAVIES. That's all right, Son.

DICK. Gee, Dad, you know you're a great guy! And

that's the point—we'd rather see you 'n' Mother a little, rather than have you fuss around so much for us. At least, I would. We do appreciate everything and all that, you understand, but we just couldn't work on the tree tonight. The gang always has this big Christmas dance, and we couldn't possibly miss that. You know how it is, Dad.

MR. DAVIES. Yes, Dick.

DICK. Thanks, Dad, I knew you'd understand. *(Starts off, as if to go outside, then comes back immediately.)* Say, Dad, you couldn't possibly spare me a five, could you? That dance is going to put me back some!

MR. DAVIES *(Severely, yet indulgently. These children get almost everything they want.)* This is going over your allowance, Richard. *(Reaches into his pocket.)*

DICK *(Accepting the bill.)* Thanks, Dad, you're a brick. *(Goes over to the stairs.)* Coming, Kay?

MR. DAVIES *(Puts the billfold back into his pocket and exits at Center.)* Anyway, one old custom still seems to be popular! *(Exits.)*

KAY *(Calling from above.)* Okay! In a minute. *(Comes downstairs. Turns to call back upstairs.)* Thanks for unpacking for me, Mother.

MRS. DAVIES *(From the stairs.)* Don't be out too late, dear.

KAY. We won't.

DICK *(As they exit Center.)* Don't bother to wait up for us, though. *(*MRS. DAVIES *comes downstairs, picks up the things the children have left lying about, and passes on to the kitchen.)*

MRS. DAVIES *(At the kitchen door.)* I'm afraid Father and I will have to eat Christmas eve supper alone. *(Exits. As she is going out,* BUDDY *pops his head in, backs out, pops in again, watches her leave, then enters stealthily, dragging a Christmas tree.)*

BUDDY *(At the door.)* There! Maybe she's gone now!

(Dragging the tree in, looks for a safe place to put it.)
Gee, whillikins, tree, it wouldn't be Christmas without yuh,
would it? Gee, but the fellers would laugh if they saw me
now, but I fooled 'em—telling 'em I had to take a tree to
a sick orphan or my dad wouldn't give the rifle he promised me. Now, where'll I put yuh? Right here, I suppose.
*(He is now on the side of the fireplace nearest the clothes
closet.)*

MRS. DAVIES *(From the kitchen.)* Is that you, Father?
Did you get a good-looking tree?

BUDDY. Gee, whillikins, now what? She surely would
laugh at me after what I said! *(Looks around wildly, then
dashes towards the closet door.)* I know! *(Dodges into
the closet with the tree just as* MRS. DAVIES, *all floury and
carrying a rolling pin, enters from the kitchen.)*

MRS. DAVIES. Why, that's strange! I would have sworn
I heard someone talking. *(*BUDDY *comes out of the closet.)*

MRS. DAVIES. Oh, it's you, Buddy! What are you doing
in there?

BUDDY *(Very much embarrassed.)* Just a—a—putting
my skates away.

MRS. DAVIES. Such a good boy! "But jest 'fore Christmas, I'm as good as can be," eh, son? *(Tweaks his ear.)*

BUDDY *(Ducking.)* Gee, don't, Mother, you're getting me
covered with flour!

MRS. DAVIES *(Going over to lower Left.)* Come on, get
ready for supper. There's Dad now. *(*MR. DAVIES *enters
at Center.)*

BUDDY. Where's the rest of the howling mob?

MRS. DAVIES. They've all gone out for the evening.

MR. DAVIES *(As they go to the kitchen.)* I just bought
a tree, Bud. It's outside the kitchen door. Want to help
Mother and me trim it tonight?

BUDDY. Huh? You did? Trim an old Christmas tree?
Me? *Naw!* I'm going to be *busy!* *(N. B.—Curtain is*

drawn briefly at this point, for the purpose of indicating a lapse of several hours. As the curtain is raised again, MR. and MRS. DAVIES are seated on the davenport in front of the fireplace. He is seen reading and she sewing, but both are doing more nodding than anything else.)

MR. DAVIES *(Looking up from his paper and yawning.)* It says here that the community Santa Claus fund is presenting five hundred Christmas baskets tomorrow.

MRS. DAVIES. When do you suppose the youngsters will be in? We don't want to trim the tree before they do come in. Trimming Christmas trees doesn't seem to be a very popular pastime in the Davies' home this evening.

MR. DAVIES. Not before two o'clock, judging from the way they were talking.

MRS. DAVIES *(Yawning.)* I don't see how I'll ever be able to keep awake that long. I'm sleepy now. *(Yawns again.)*

MR. DAVIES. I wonder what Buddy was going to be so busy at. I don't think he left the house.

MRS. DAVIES. I haven't the slightest idea. Maybe he was just tired and went to bed.

MR. DAVIES. That was probably it. *(Yawns. Looks at the paper again. MRS. DAVIES half-heartedly takes a few stitches.)*

MRS. DAVIES. Is the tree behind the back porch?

MR. DAVIES *(Nodding.)* What? Oh, yes. *(A pause. He reads and nods. She sews and nods.)* Mother . . . *(No answer.)* Oh, Mum-m-m! *(He, too, drops off to sleep. BUDDY appears at the top of the stairs.)*

BUDDY. Gee, they're sitting up late. Gee, what'd they have to go and do that for? *(Slips back upstairs.)*

MRS. DAVIES *(Starting up.)* What was that?

MR. DAVIES *(Also sitting up suddenly.)* Wh-what? It's getting late, isn't it? *(But MRS. DAVIES does not answer. Both drop off to sleep again. Presently VIRGINIA appears at*

Center, backs out again. As she slips out, NED *appears at the kitchen door, backs out again. In a moment, both reappear, each dragging a Christmas tree. Both start guiltily, try to back out; then, realizing each has seen the other, they walk in slowly, laughing softly.)*

VIRGINIA *(At Center, towards the front,* NED *at Left. She points to her mother and father, sleeping on the davenport.)* S-sh! *What are you doing,* Mr. Ned Davies?

NED. Why don't you speak for yourself, Jin?

VIRGINIA *(Giggles.)* Funny, isn't it?

NED. There seems to be rather a wave of Christmas trees. Dad has one parked out on the back step.

VIRGINIA. Why'd you do it, Ned?

NED. Why'd *you* do it, Jinny? I thought you were at the party.

VIRGINIA. I thought you were. But I began to think of getting up in the morning with no tree, and having our presents handed out to us like charity orphans, and it just didn't seem like Christmas at all. So I just told Billy I had a headache and to take me home. And you?

NED. Well, I rather wanted the tree all the time, too, only I thought nobody else did and I didn't want you to think I was silly.

VIRGINIA. But what are we going to do with both of them?

NED. We'll have to hide one and . . .

VIRGINIA. S-sh! What was that?

NED. I don't know. Here, take yours and put it into the closet there quickly. If Mother and Dad wake up I can tell them I saw Dad's tree out there on the back porch and felt so sorry for it, that I brought it in to keep the poor, starved, homeless little thing from freezing to death. *(*VIRGINIA *has shoved the tree into the closet. Take care that neither* VIRGINIA *nor those who go to the closet later look into it.)*

VIRGINIA. I heard something! I'm going to look! *(Goes to the door at Center.)*

NED. Christmas tree thieves, maybe!

VIRGINIA. Listen, Ned, it's Kay! Get that tree into the closet quickly, and scamper upstairs. You can't let the college wise-guys see you with a *Christmas tree* in your hands. Hurry! *(*NED *is already halfway across the floor and* VIRGINIA *is disappearing around the corner upstairs. He makes a dash for the stairs and gets out of sight just as* KAY *enters. She. stops and looks at the room, touches a wreath at the window at Right, then goes and bends over the davenport where her mother and father are sleeping.)*

KAY *(Tremulously.)* You darlings! *(She watches them a moment, then drops her hat and gloves on the table and goes over to the Left window, looks out pensively.* DICK *enters and finds her there.)*

DICK *(Crossing to her, back of the davenport.)* Kay, you home? Where's Larry?

KAY. I suspect he went back to the dance. I made him take me home. It got tiresome.

DICK. I thought so, too.

KAY. It's nice being back home, isn't it, Dick? Is'nt it pretty? *(Draws him to the window.)* Look . . . the lawn out there with the funny, little, round evergreen covered with snow. Mother's made wreaths, too.

DICK. Just like always.

KAY. Isn't it good to be back here? *(She sits on the steps.)* With no first hour classes to get to and no house matron to crab when you get in too late and no roommates who are homesicker than you are to comfort . . . ?

DICK *(Entering into her mood.)* And no military drill, and no bossy sophomores!

KAY. I like it here. Really, I do. Everything's always the same. Just the same as when we were kids . . . everything except . . . why, Dick?

DICK *(Alarmed.)* What? *(Then he realizes what she means.)* Kay! The Christmas tree! There isn't one!

KAY *(Softly.)* There could have been.

DICK. We were little idiots. I wanted to . . .

KAY. I know. You wanted to impress Molly with how sophisticated you'd become after your semester away from home. She did the same thing.

DICK *(Half under his breath.)* I'll say she did!

KAY. And I did, too. I seemed to have the idea Christmas trees weren't in style any more.

DICK. The joke was on us. Did you see the one in Central park?

KAY. And the one in the hotel lobby at the dance. I really wanted one all the time. Didn't you?

DICK. We'll have to do something about that. Come on! *Some* place ought to be open, even if it *is* late at night.

KAY. All right. We'll get a tree and come home and then after Mother and Dad go to bed, we'll come down and trim it. Shall we?

DICK. It's rather fun to be kiddish. Only I'd feel foolish as heck if anyone caught me. *(They go out, Center, laughing softly.)*

VIRGINIA *(Peeking around the corner of the stairs, NED behind her.)* She's gone now. Somebody was here talking to her.

NED. It couldn't have been Mother or Dad. They're sound asleep.

MR. DAVIES *(Staring.)* What did you say, Mother? *(Seeing that MRS. DAVIES is asleep.)* Oh, I thought you were saying something, Mother. *(NED and VIRGINIA slip back upstairs very quietly.)*

MRS. DAVIES. *(Stirs, mumbling in her sleep.)* Now put the star on that one.

MR. DAVIES. What? Why, Mother, you're talking in your sleep!

MRS. DAVIES *(Sleepily.)* Oh, maybe I was dreaming. I thought we had a lot of Christmas trees, about a hundred, all in a line, and the children were all in their little creeper suits, putting bright stars on the trees. It was so pretty.

MR. DAVIES *(Just a bit irritably.)* Well, I wish they'd come in, so we could trim the tree.

MRS. DAVIES. It'll be a long time yet. I'm—so—sleepy. *(They doze off again.* BUDDY *comes down, looks in.)*

BUDDY *(Disgustedly.)* Gosh all fish hooks! Are they going to stay there all night? Swell chance I have to play Santa Claus with them sitting there. Well, I suppose I'll have to pretend to sleep some more. *(Goes back upstairs.* KAY *and* DICK *enter with a tree.)*

DICK. Boy, that was quick work!

KAY. We were lucky! Now what are we going to do?

DICK. I don't know! The folks evidently are sitting up for us.

KAY. It certainly looks that way.

DICK. Tell you what. We can put the tree into the clothes closet so they won't see it when they wake up. Then when they find we're in, they'll go to bed. Wonder why we didn't wake them up with all our noise?

KAY. They're probably just dead tired. I'll bet Mother's been baking for a week.

DICK *(As he puts the tree into the closet.)* It'll be safe in there, I think.

KAY. You listen when they come up, and let me know, so we can go down and trim it.

DICK. Okay, Sis. *(They go upstairs.)*

MR. DAVIES. Yes, I think so. *(Then realizes no one was talking to him.)* Didn't you say something?

MRS. DAVIES *(Waking suddenly.)* What's that, Father? Goodness, I must have fallen asleep again! *(Looks at her watch.)* Why, it's twelve o'clock!

MR. DAVIES. They won't be in for an hour yet, Mother.

MRS. DAVIES. Shall I make a cup of coffee to keep us awake?

MR. DAVIES. That would be a good idea, Mother.

MRS. DAVIES *(Starts across the room, but gets only as far as the table.)* Why, they must have come in while we were asleep! Here's Kay's hat and gloves and Dick's hat, too.

MR. DAVIES. That's odd. I didn't hear them.

MRS. DAVIES. I'll go up and see if all the kiddies are in while you go and get the tree, Father. *(Exit MR. DAVIES, lower Left. MRS. DAVIES picks up the things from the table and goes upstairs. MR. DAVIES enters with the tree. This tree is on a standard.)*

MR. DAVIES *(Starts over toward the fireplace.)* Imagine this would be about the best place to put it. No, over there would be better. *(Finally sets it down at upper Left in front of the stairs. MRS. DAVIES comes downstairs.)*

MR. DAVIES. Where are the decorations, Mother?

MRS. DAVIES. On the shelf in the clothes closet. *(He goes over to the closet.)* It's a very pretty tree, Father. *(MR. DAVIES opens the closet door and the four Christmas trees fall out on him with a great clatter.)*

MR. DAVIES *(Simply astounded.)* Jum-pin' Jehosaphat!

MRS. DAVIES *(Screams.)* Heavens! What is it? *(All the noise should bring the five DAVIES children running down the stairs. They are all clamoring at once.)*

KAY. What has happened?

DICK. What's all the racket about?

VIRGINIA. What is it?

BUDDY. Is there a burglar?

NED. Why the big rumpus?

MR. DAVIES *(Picking up the trees.)* Well, I'll be hornswoggled! *(There is a twinkle in his eye. He has caught*

on immediately, and is enjoying the situation immensely.)
This is almost the hundred trees you dreamed about,
Mother. How do you suppose there happened to be so
many? *(The children are downstairs, crowding around.)*
Do any of *you* know anything about this?

MRS. DAVIES *(Not understanding yet.)* Did the noise
awaken you?

DICK. I'll tell the hand-embroidered football it did!

VIRGINIA. I should think so!

NED *(Trying to look surprised.)* What happened, anyway?

MR. DAVIES. Don't *you* know anything about it, Ned?
Buddy?

BUDDY *(Sheepishly.)* Uh-huh. I—uh—just decided we
had to have a tree, and nobody was getting one, and so I
went down and brought one home. *(Picks up a tree.)* It's
a rather good tree.

VIRGINIA *(Picking up a tree.)* I think this one's mine.

NED *(Grinning, but sheepishly, as he picks his tree out.
All are embarrassed.)* Well, I brought this in.

KAY *(As NED acknowledges the last of the trees.)* And
Dick and I are responsible for this.

DICK. I feel like a five-year-old in a kindergarten program.

MRS. DAVIES. Well, now what are we going to do with
all these trees?

NED. Throw 'em outside and donate them to the starv-
ing Chinese in the morning.

KAY. Now that's not a half-bad idea. We can find some
poor people who haven't any trees and take these to them.

VIRGINIA. That would really be heaps of fun!

BUDDY. I know some people who live down by the river
that would be . . .

KAY. Here, Dick and Ned, take them outside, won't you?

VIRGINIA. Mother, where are those trimmings? Let's all decorate it together!

MRS. DAVIES *(Happy again. She goes to the closet and comes back with a box of decorations.)* Here they are! I'm coming with them!

DICK *(Going out Center with two trees. NED has the other two.)* Don't use everything up before we get back! *(Everyone makes a dive for the big box—MR. and MRS. DAVIES included.)*

VIRGINIA *(Hanging a large red ball on the tree.)* This always was my favorite one! *(DICK and NED dash back in.)*

DICK. Here, Buddy and Dad, don't get so frisky with those icicles!

NED. Hey, let me at it!

KAY. Don't be a pig!

MRS. DAVIES *(Mildly reproving. She and MR. DAVIES are thoroughly happy.)* Children!

NED. Gosh, Dad, but you look snappy with that tinsel dangling over one ear!

MR. DAVIES *(Jovially.)* Now let me you it isn't every old man that can wear tinsel over his ears with the dash that your dad can! *(All laugh.)*

VIRGINIA. Here, Dick, you put this star on the top. You're tall.

DICK *(Reaching up with the star.)* I feel like a regular kid!

KAY. Oh, yes, and isn't it fun? *(All are talking and laughing hilariously as the curtain drops.)*

CURTAIN

THE WHITE CHRISTMAS

A NATIVITY PLAY IN ONE ACT

By

WALTER BEN HARE

PRODUCTION RIGHTS

Copies of this play are available in single pamphlet form. The right to produce this play by one group of amateur players is authorized only by the purchase of ten copies (one copy for each speaking part) at the current price of 50c each.

It is dishonest and illegal to copy parts.

A CHRISTMAS MORALITY PLAY IN ONE ACT.

Originally produced by the Quadrangle Club of the University of Missouri.

CHARACTERS.

MARY ....*The Maiden Mother*
JOSEPH..................*Cf the House of David*
SIMEON ....*An Old Shepherd*
TIMOTHY.......*A Shepherd, the Husband of Anna*
ISAAC......................*A Young Shepherd*
ANNA........*The Wife of Timothy, the Shepherd*
THOMAS.......................*Her Little Son*
RUTH.....................*Her Little Daughter*
DEBORAH.........*Hostess of an Inn at Bethlehem*
RACHEL................*A Maiden of Bethlehem*
PRISCILLA ....*Her Cousin*
MELCHOIR. ⎫
GASPAR.... ⎬.......*The Wise Men from the East.*
BALTASAR.. ⎭

A Concealed Choir.   The Prologue.

For description of costumes, arrangement of the scene, etc., see "Remarks on the Production" at the end of the play.

TIME OF PLAYING—*About* **Thirty Minutes.**

———

SCENE I: *Before the play begins the* PROLOGUE *steps in front of the curtains and addresses the congregation.*

PROLOGUE.

The earth has grown old with its burden of care,
But at Christmas it always is young,
The heart of the jewel burns lustrous and fair,

And its soul, full of music, bursts forth on the
    air,
    When the song of the angels is sung.

It is coming, Old Earth, it is coming tonight!
    On the snowflakes which cover thy sod
The feet of the Christ Child fall gentle and
    white,
And the voice of the Christ Child tells out with
    delight,
    That mankind are the children of God.

On the sad and the lonely, the wretched and
    poor,
    The voice of the Christ Child shall fall;
And to every blind wanderer open the door
Of hope that he dared not to dream of before,
    With a sunshine of welcome for all.

—Phillips Brooks.

And it came to pass in those days, that there went
out a decree from Cæsar Augustus, that all the world
should be taxed. And this taxing was first made
when Cyrenius was governor of Syria. And all went
to be taxed, every one into his own city.

And Joseph also went up from Galilee, out of
the city of Nazareth, into Judea, unto the city of
David, which is called Bethlehem, because he was of
the house and lineage of David. To be taxed with
Mary his espoused wife. . . . .

And so it was, that, while they were there, the days
were accomplished that she should be delivered. And
she brought forth her first born son, and wrapped
him in swaddling clothes, and laid him in a manger;
because there was no room for them in the inn.
(*Exit* PROLOGUE.)

(*Soft chimes. As these chimes die away in the distance a concealed choir is heard singing.*)

O COME, COME, AWAY.

O come, come away
From labor now reposing,
Let busy care a while forbear;
O come, come away.

(*The front curtains are drawn, showing a winter street in Bethlehem. No one appears on the stage, but the choir continues singing outside at right front.*)

Come, come, our social joys renew,
And thus where trust and friendship grew,
Let true hearts welcome you,
O come, come away.

RACHEL *and* PRISCILLA *enter from the inn at right front, arm in arm. They go to the center, then to the rear of the stage, turn and face the inn, pause a moment or two, listening to the choir, and then go out, at rear left. The choir continues:*

From toils and the cares
On which the day is closing,
The hour of eve brings sweet reprieve,
O come, come away.
O come where love will smile on thee,
And round its hearth will gladness be,
And time fly merrily,
O come, come away.

While the choir is singing the last three lines of the song, SIMEON *and* ISAAC *enter from rear left, leaning on their shepherd's crooks. They pause at*

*rear center and listen to the singing.   When the song
is finished the organ continues the same music softly.*

SIMEON.

> Make haste, my son, the hour is waxing late,
> The night is cold, methinks our sheep await.

ISAAC.

> Nay gran'ther, I would liefer tarry here.
> The town is gay, the inns are full of cheer.

SIMEON (*points to rear right*).

> But there our duty lies, the wind grows cold!
> Come, let's away and put the sheep in fold.

ISAAC.   (*Starts off right.*)

> Nay, Simeon, wait! What means this crowd of
>   men
> And women here in peaceful Bethlehem?

SIMEON (*comes to him*).

> Herod the King hath issued a decree
> That each and all his subjects taxèd be;
> And every one who in this town saw light
> Must here return and register tonight.
> From all Judea, aye, from th' distant land,
> Each Bethlehemite must come at his command.

ISAAC (*comes to the doorway of the inn and peers in*).

> The town is full of people, great and small,
> Each inn is crowded to its very wall.

SIMEON (*comes down center and takes his arm*).

> But come, we're wasting time, 'tis very late.
> Make haste, my son, I know the flocks await!

ISAAC.

> Thou speakest true, though I would rather stay,
> Our duty calls, so to the hills, away!

> > (*They go out at rear right.*)

The concealed choir repeats the first stanza of the song softly. After a slight pause DEBORAH *enters from the inn.*

DEBORAH (*coming down to right front*).
    My inn is crowded to the doors. The heat
    Is stifling, but out here the air is sweet.
                                (*Looks upward.*)
    The bright stars twinkle with mysterious light,
    Methinks there's something strange about the
        night.

She sits on the bench in front of the inn. TIMOTHY *enters from rear left.* DEBORAH *continues her soliloquy.*

    The air is still, the night is very cold,
    The shepherds seek the hills to watch the fold.
                                (*Sees him.*)
(TIMOTHY *goes out at rear* R.)

DEBORAH.
    Some strange, unearthly voice seems calling me.
    Methinks this night portends great things to be.

Enter RACHEL *and* PRISCILLA *from rear right, then come down center and address the hostess.*

RACHEL.
    Hail, hostess of the inn, my cousin here
    Hath lodgings at your inn. We'd seek its cheer.

DEBORAH (*rises*).
    Enter within. My guests tonight are gay
    And fain would turn this winter's night to day.

RACHEL *and* PRISCILLA *enter the inn, followed by* DEBORAH. *The organ music continues softly. After a slight pause enter* ANNA *from rear left. She leads* RUTH *and* THOMAS *by the hand.*

THOMAS (*at rear center*).

Oh, mother, hark! There's music in the inn!

ANNA.

'Tis not for us—their noise and merry din.

RUTH.

Our little town is crowded, joyous, gay.

THOMAS.

So many travelers came this way today.

RUTH.

The night is chill and cold, I much do fear
The little sheep will shiver by the mere.

ANNA.

Too cold it is for thee, I fear, in truth,
Return and get thy cloak, my little Ruth.
We'll wait for thee upon the little hill.

(*Points off R.*)

But speed thy steps, the cold will work thee ill.

RUTH.

I'll fly, dear mother, like an arrow home.

(*Runs out at L.*)

ANNA.

We must not tarry. Come, my Thomas, come!

(*She leads him out at rear R. There is a pause.
The music changes to a mysterious plaintive air.
The old German song, Holy Night, may be effec-
tively introduced as an organ solo.*)

Enter from rear right, JOSEPH, *walking with a
staff and supporting* MARY.

MARY.

Here is a place, now I must rest awhile!
For many a league, for many a weary mile,
We've trudged along since break of day began.

JOSEPH.

> 'Tis true, and I'm an old and ancient man,
> My joints are stiff, my bones are waxing old—
> And the long night is bitter, bitter cold.
> Here take my cloak and keep thee warm within.
> And wait thee here while I search out an inn.

(*He wraps his cloak around her and seats her on the bench or stool in front of the manger. He goes out at rear left. The music changes to the Magnificat, to be found in all Episcopal hymnals.*)

MARY (*sings*).

> My soul doth magnify the Lord: and my spirit hath rejoiced in God my Saviour.
>
> For he hath regarded: the lowliness of his handmaiden.
>
> For behold, from henceforth: all generations shall call me blessed.
>
> For he that is mighty has magnified me: and holy is his Name.
>
> And his mercy is on them that fear him: throughout all generations.
>
> He hath showed strength with his arm: he hath scattered the proud in the imagination of their hearts.
>
> He hath put down the mighty from their seat: and hath exalted the humble and meek.
>
> He hath filled the hungry with good things: and the rich he hath sent empty away.
>
> He remembering his mercy hath holpen his servant Israel: as he promised to our forefathers, Abraham and his seed, forever.

Enter JOSEPH *from rear L.*

248

JOSEPH.

>For hours I've trudged the street in fruitless quest,
>Here is an inn, mayhap at last we'll rest.

Enter DEBORAH *from the inn.*

MARY.

>Husband, I'm faint; I can no farther go.
>Methinks I'll rest me here upon this loe.
>>(*Sits in front of the manger.*)

JOSEPH (*assisting her*).

>Have courage, Mary, here's the hostess here.
>>(*Comes to* DEBORAH *at right.*)
>We'd lodge with thee tonight.

DEBORAH.

>Alas, I fear
>My inn is crowded to the very wall,
>Soldiers and scribes, the rich, the great, the small!

JOSEPH.

>Is there room for us? My wife is ill.

DEBORAH.

>My heart is sad and it is not my will
>To send you hence, but naught is left to do.
>Perhaps some other inn will shelter you.

JOSEPH.

>Alas, the other inns are all the same!

DEBORAH.

>Never was seen the like in Bethlehem.
>>(*Laughter and noise at* R.)
>My guests are merry, hear their jovial din!
>>(*Goes to* R.)
>I pity you, there's no room at the inn.
>>(*Exits into the inn.*)

MARY.

> Our last hope gone! Now, what shall we do?
> My strength is leaving!   (*Bows head.*)

JOSEPH.

> Would I could succor you.
> I'll wrap thee warm. Now rest thee here a while.
> We've traveled far, full many a weary mile.

Enter RUTH *from rear L., hurrying along.*

JOSEPH.

> Maiden, I fain would stop thee in thy flight—
> Can'st tell where we could lodge this winter
>   night?

RUTH.

> That inn is crowded. There's one upon the hill.

JOSEPH.

> I've tried them all, my wife is very ill.

RUTH.

> That little stable there upon the loe,
>
> > > (*Points to L front.*)
>
> 'Tis snug and warm. 'Twill shield thee from
>   the snow.

MARY (*rises*).

> God's blessing on thy little head, sweet child!
> Come, Joseph, for the wind now waxes wild.
>
> > > (*Exits L. front.*)

(JOSEPH *leads her to exit L., then turns and looks
off R.*)

JOSEPH.

> > O little town of Bethlehem,
> >   How still we see thee lie!
> > Above thy deep and dreamless sleep

The silent stars go by.
Yet in thy dark streets shineth
        (*Turns toward manger.*)
The everlasting Light;
The hopes and fears of all the years
Are met in thee tonight.
(RUTH *stands at rear C., watching him.*)
    The curtains slowly fall.

SCENE II: *Hymn by the congregation.*

WHILE SHEPHERDS WATCHED THEIR FLOCKS.

While shepherds watched their flocks by
    night,
    All seated on the ground.
The angel of the Lord came down,
    And glory shone around,
    And glory shone around.

"Fear not," said he,—for mighty dread
    Had seized their troubled mind,
"Glad tidings of great joy I bring,
    To you and all mankind,
    To you and all mankind."

"To you in David's town this day,
    Is born of David's line,
The Saviour, who is Christ, the Lord,
    And this shall be the sign,
    And this shall be the sign."

"The heav'nly babe you there shall find
    To human view displayed,
All meanly wrapped in swathing bands,

And in a manger laid,
And in a manger laid."

Thus spake the seraph—and forthwith
Appeared a shining throng
Of angels, praising God, who thus
Addressèd their joyful song,
Addressed their joyful song:—

"All glory be to God on high,
And to the earth be peace;
Good will henceforth, from heav'n to men,
Begin and never cease,
Begin and never cease."

The Prologue *appears before the curtains and speaks.*

PROLOGUE.

There's scarlet holly on the streets, and silver
mistletoe;
The surging, jeweled, ragged crowds forever
come and go.
And here a silken woman laughs, and there a
beggar asks—
And, oh, the faces, tense of lip, like mad and
mocking masks.
Who thinks of Bethlehem today, and one lone
winter night?
Who knows that in a manger-bed there
breathed a Child of Light?

There's fragrant scent of evergreen upon the
chilling air;
There's tinsel tawdriness revealed beneath the
sunlight's glare;

There's Want and Plenty, Greed and Pride—
a hundred thousand souls,
And, oh, the weary eyes of them, like dull and
sullen coals.
Who knows the town of Bethlehem, once
gleamed beneath the star,
Whose wondrous light the shepherds saw
watching their flocks afar?

And yet above the city streets, above the noise
and whir,
There seems to come a fragrant breath of frank-
incense and myrrh.
I saw a woman, bent and wan, and on her face
a light
The look that Mary might have worn that other
Christmas night.
And as the little children passed, and one lad
turned and smiled,
I saw within his wistful eyes the spirit of the
Child.
            —*Caroline Reynolds.*

And there were in the same country shepherds
abiding in the field, keeping watch over their flock
by night. And, lo, the angel of the Lord came upon
them, and the glory of the Lord shone round about
them; and they were sore afraid.

And the angel said unto them, Fear not: for, behold, I bring you good tidings of great joy, which
shall be to all people. For unto you is born this day
in the city of David a Saviour, which is Christ the
Lord.

And this shall be a sign unto you: Ye shall find
the babe wrapped in swaddling clothes, lying in a
manger.

And suddenly there was with the angel a multitude of the heavenly host praising God, and saying, Glory to God in the highest, and on earth peace, good will toward men.

And it came to pass, as the angels were gone away from them into heaven, the shepherds said one to another, Let us now go even unto Bethlehem, and see this thing which is come to pass, which the Lord hath made known to us.

And they came with haste, and found Mary and Joseph, and the babe lying in a manger. (*Exit* PROLOGUE *at L.*)

(*Soft chimes are heard. The* SHEPHERDS, *accompanied by the concealed choir, are heard singing*:)

LEAD, KINDLY LIGHT

Lead, kindly Light, amid th' encircling gloom,
    Lead Thou me on!
The night is dark and I am far from home;
    Lead Thou me on!
Keep Thou my feet, I do not ask to see
The distant scene; one step enough for me.

As the SHEPHERDS *begin on the second stanza of the hymn, the curtains rise disclosing the same scene as before.* SIMEON, TIMOTHY *and* ISAAC *discovered seated in a group at rear center, singing.* THOMAS *stands by his father.*

So long Thy pow'r hath blest me, sure it still
    Will lead me on
O'er moor and fen, o'er crag and torrent, till
    The night is gone,
And with the morn those angel faces smile
Which I have loved long since, and lost a-while.

SIMEON.

Methought I heard a whir of wings on high.

TIMOTHY.

I see naught save the snow and starry sky.

ISAAC.

We've come a long and mighty step today,
From o'er the frosty hills and far away.

THOMAS (*pointing over the manger*).

Look, father, dost thou see that shining star
That seems to stand above the town so far?
'Tis like a wondrous blossom on a stem,
And see, it ever shines o'er Bethlehem!

TIMOTHY.

A brighter star, I'm sure I never saw—
And perfect form, without a speck or flaw.

SIMEON.

A stranger star! It never shone before,
It standeth still above that stable door.

Enter ANNA *and* RUTH *from rear left.* ANNA
carries a little lamb.

ANNA (*joining the group*).

Look ye, I've found a little lamb new-born.

TIMOTHY.

Poor little beastie! Wrap him well and warm.

SIMEON.

An ill night to be born in, frost and snow,
Naught but cold skies above, cold earth below.
I marvel any little creature should be born
On such a night.

ANNA.

I found it all forlorn,
Crying beside its mother in the storm.

SIMEON (*comes down a little to right front*).
> Hark, I thought I heard a sound of mighty
>   wings!
> Listen! Is it the winter sky that sings?

ISAAC (*with the group at rear center*).
> Nay, gran'ther, I heard naught. You're old
>   and gray
> And weary with the miles you've walked today.

SIMEON.
> At noon I met a man who tarried in the shade,
> He led a mule, and riding it a maid—
> A maiden with a face I'll ne'er forget,
> A wondrous face, I seem to see it yet
> Lit with an inward shining, as if God
> Had set a lighted lamp within her soul.
> Many have passed all day, but none like these,
> And no face have I ever seen like hers.

TIMOTHY.
> Belike the man and maid were strangers here,
> And come to Bethlehem at the king's command.

RUTH (*comes down to* SIMEON *and takes his hand*).
> Methinks I met that very man and maid—
> A maiden with such wondrous dove-like eyes,
> I saw them near this place, all tired and worn,
> Trudging about the town, seeking an inn.

SIMEON.
> And did they find one?

RUTH.
> Nay, not so!
> For every inn was crowded to its doors.
> Hard by Deborah's inn there is a little barn,
> All full of cattle, oxen, cooing doves—
> I showed it to them, and they went therein.

THOMAS (*standing at rear L. with* ANNA).

Mother, that star! That wondrous, wondrous
    light,   (*Points up.*)
It turns the night to day, it shines so bright
I am afraid! It cannot be that any star,
Only a star, can give so great a light.
It frightens me.

ANNA.

All things are strange tonight.
The very sheep are restless in their fold,
They watch the star and do not mind the cold.

SIMEON (*puts hand to right ear, bends toward right
    and listens*).

Again I heard a singing in the sky!

TIMOTHY.

You heard the tinkling bell of some stray sheep,
The night grows late, come let us all to sleep.

SIMEON.

Yea, all ye lie down and take your rest,
I'll keep the watch alone, this night is blest.

(*The others recline at the rear.*)

ANNA (*comes to* SIMEON).

Here, take the little sheep and keep it warm

SIMEON.   (*Lies down.*)

Poor little new-born beast, I'll guard from harm
Again I marvel that you should be born
On such a night, poor little lamb forlorn.

(SIMEON *walks toward the manger with the sheep
in his arms. The others sleep.*)

The Lord is my shepherd: I shall not want.

He maketh me to lie down in green pastures: he
leadeth me beside the still waters.

He restoreth my soul: he leadeth me in the paths
of righteousness for his name's sake.

Yea, though I walk through the valley of the shadow of death, I will fear no evil: for thou art with me; thy rod and thy staff they comfort me.

Thou preparest a table before me in the presence of mine enemies: thou anointest my head with oil; my cup runneth over.

Surely goodness and mercy shall follow me all the days of my life: and I will dwell in the house of the Lord for ever.

(*Soft Music.*)

Hark! There's music in the wind! And that
strange light
There in the east, it brightens all the night!
I seem to hear again the whir of wings,
Awake, awake! It is an angel sings!

(*He arouses the others. They listen wonderingly, standing or reclining.*)

VOICE (*an unseen soprano chants softly*).

Glory to God in the highest!
Fear not!
For behold I bring you glad tidings
Of great joy.
For unto you is born this day
In the city of David, a Saviour
Which is Christ, the Lord.
And this shall be the sign unto you:
Ye shall find the heavenly Babe
Wrapped in swaddling clothes,
Lying in a manger.
Glory to God in the highest,
And on earth peace,
Good will toward men!

TIMOTHY.

'Twas a fine voice, even as ever I heard.

ANNA.

The hills, as with lightning, shone at his word.

SIMEON.

He spoke of a Babe here in Bethlehem.
That betokens yon star!
Full glad would I be,
Might I kneel on my knee,
Some word to say to that Child.

TIMOTHY.

See! In the east there breaks the day.

ANNA.

Let us tarry no longer; away, then, away!

(ANNA *goes out at rear, behind the stable, with*
TIMOTHY, RUTH *and* THOMAS.)

ISAAC.

Come, gran'ther, let us go and see this thing!

SIMEON.

But first get gifts to take the new-born King!
Glory to God in the highest,
And on earth peace,
Good will toward men.

(*They follow the others out at rear.*)
The curtains fall.

SCENE III: *Hymn by the congregation:*

HARK! THE HERALD ANGELS SING.

Hark! The herald angels sing,
"Glory to the new-born King!
Peace on earth, and mercy mild,
God and sinners reconciled."
Joyful, all ye nations, rise,
Join the triumph of the skies;

With th' angelic host proclaim,
"Christ is born in Bethlehem."

Christ, by highest Heaven adored;
Christ, the everlasting Lord;
Late in time behold Him come,
Offspring of the favored one.
Veiled in flesh, the Godhead see;
Hail th' incarnate Deity:
Pleased, as man with men to dwell,
Jesus, our Immanuel.

Hail! The Heav'n-born Prince of Peace!
Hail! The Son of Righteousness!
Light and life to all He brings,
Risen with healing in His wings.
Mild He lays His glory by,
Born that man no more may die:
Born to raise the sons of earth,
Born to give them second birth.

Enter PROLOGUE *before the closed curtains.*

PROLOGUE.

Now when Jesus was born in Bethlehem of Judea
in the days of Herod the king, behold, there came
wise men from the east to Jerusalem, saying, Where
is he that is born King of the Jews? For we have
seen his star in the east, and are come to worship him.

When Herod the king had heard these things, he
was roubled, and all Jerusalem with him. And
when he had gathered all the chief priests and
scribes of the people together, he demanded of them
where Christ should be born.

And they said unto him, In Bethlehem of Judea:
for thus it is written by the prophet, And thou Beth-

lehem, in the land of Juda, art not the least among the princes of Juda: for out of thee shall come a Governor, that shall rule my people Israel.

Then Herod, when he had privily called the wise men, inquired of them diligently what time the star appeared.

And he sent them to Bethlehem, and said, Go and search diligently for the young child; and when ye have found him, bring me word again, that I may come and worship him also.

When they had heard the king, they departed; and, lo, the star, which they saw in the east, went before them, till it came and stood over where the young child was.

When they saw the star, they rejoiced with exceeding great joy.

And when they were come into the house, they saw the young child with Mary his mother, and fell down, and worshipped him: and when they had opened their treasures, they presented unto him gifts; gold, and frankincense, and myrrh.

The White Christmas.

As the three wise men rode on that first Christmas night to find the manger-cradled Babe of Bethlehem, they bore gifts on their saddle-bows. Gifts of gold, frankincense and myrrh. And so the spirit of Christmas giving crept into the world's heart. We bring our gifts to the children. Rich children, poor children! The children of the high and the children of the humble! Poor little sick children—and the ragged children of the slums of our cities. Let us remember them all.

So go ye, all of ye, into the highways and byways, and seek out the poor and the distressed, the humble and the afflicted, seek out the ragged children and the outcasts and the aged ones, and in the name of Him who was born on Christmas day, carry some sunshine into their hearts! Give unto the poor and the afflicted, and your hearts shall glow with that inward peace that passeth all understanding.

Then—and then only—will you be able to sing with all the company of Heaven, Glory to God in the highest, peace on earth, good will toward men! And this will be your pure white Christmas. (*Exit* Prologue *at L.*)

Soft chimes are heard. The curtains are drawn, disclosing the same scene as before. Deborah *sits before her inn, deep in thought.*
Deborah (*reading a scroll*).

This is the ancient prophecy. Therefore the Lord himself shall give you a sign; behold, a virgin shall conceive, and bear a son, and shall call his name Immanuel.

Butter and honey shall he eat, that he may know to refuse the evil and choose the good.

For before the child shall know to refuse the evil, and choose the good, the land that thou abhorrest shall be forsaken of both her kings.

Enter Gaspar *from behind the inn. He comes down center.*

Gaspar.
    I pray thee, tell me, Lady Bethlehemite,
    If any wonders you have seen this night?
Deborah (*rises*).
    I've seen a wondrous silver shaft of light
    Come from a star, and blinded is my sight.

GASPAR.

> Tell me, for thou art native of this place,
> What dost thou know about the **King of
>   Grace**—
> King of the Jews?

DEBORAH.

> Aye, in Jerusalem
> He dwells, and not in Bethlehem.
> He sits upon his mighty judgment throne,
> Cruel and stern, his heart a living stone.

GASPAR.

> I mean a new-born King, of love and peace;
> His is the star—His reign shall never cease.

DEBORAH.

> All things tonight seem passing strange to me,
> I have just read an ancient prophecy
> That this, our Bethlehem, King David's town,
> Shall be the birthplace, e'er of great renown,
> Of one called Councillor of King David's line
> Whose coming is foretold in words divine.
> And now you come with words of mystery!
>
> > > (*Muses.*)
>
> Why should thy questions, which are dark to me,
> Cause me to think of Him?

GASPAR.

> The star! The star!
> No more it moves about the heavens afar,
> It standeth still. O, hostess, kneel and pray,
> For Jesus Christ, the Lord, is born today!
>
> > > (*Hurries out right.*)

DEBORAH.

> His words are fraught with mystery; I'll within
> And seek protection in my humble inn.
>
> > > (*Exits right front.*)

After a short pause, MELCHOIR, GASPAR *and* BALTASAR *enter from rear right.*

MELCHOIR.

> Three kings came riding from far away,
>> Melchoir, Gaspar and Baltasar;
>
> Three wise men out of the east were they,
> And they traveled by night and they slept by
>> day,
>> For their guide was a beautiful, wonderful
>> star.

BALTASAR.

> The star was so beautiful, large and clear,
>> That all other stars of the sky
>
> Became a white mist in the atmosphere;
> And by this they knew that the coming was
>> near
>> Of the Prince foretold in prophecy.

GASPAR.

> Of the child that is born, O Baltasar,
>> I begged a woman to tell us the news;
>
> I said in the east we had seen His star,
> And had ridden fast and had ridden far
>> To find and worship the King of the Jews.
>> *—Adapted from Longfellow.*

MELCHOIR.

> Brothers, our quest is ended; see the star
> Is standing still over this lowly hut.

BALTASAR.

> Methinks it is a stable. Knock and see!

GASPAR (*knocks on the door of the manger*).

> What ho, within!

> JOSEPH *enters from the L. rear.*

JOSEPH.

> Sirs, whom seek ye?

MELCHOIR.

> We have journeyed from afar
> Led by the shining of yon splendid star.
> We are Gaspar, Melchoir and Baltasar.

BALTASAR.

> We seek a new-born King,
> Gold, frankincense to him we bring.
> And many a kingly offering.

JOSEPH *draws back the curtain and reveals the interior of the manger.* MARY *is seen bending over the crib. The* SHEPHERDS *are kneeling in the background. Very soft music heard in the distance, with faintly chiming bells at intervals.*

GASPAR.

> Behold, the child is clothed in light!

MELCHOIR.

> Our journey ends, passed is the night.

BALTASAR.

> Now let us make no more delay,
> But worship Him right worthily.

> (*They enter the manger and kneel.*)

SIMEON.

> Hail, hail, dear child
> Of a maiden meek and mild.
> See, he merries!
> See, he smiles, my sweeting,
> I give thee greeting!
> Have a bob of cherries.

> (*Places a spray of cherries on the crib.*)

TIMOTHY.

> Hail, little One we've sought,
> See, a bird I've brought,
> See its feathers gay.

Hail, little One adored,
Hail, blessed King and Lord,
    Star of the day!
(*Places a bird on the crib.*)

ISAAC.

Hail, little One, so dear,
My heart is full of cheer,
    A little ball I bring,
Reach forth thy fingers gay,
And take the ball and play,
    My blessed King.
(*Places a ball on the crib.*)

*Enter all others from the Inn. They kneel out
side the manger.*

ALL (*sing, with concealed choir*).

CHRISTMAS CAROL.

Christ was born on Christmas day,
Wreathe the holly, twine the bay,
Light and life and joy is He—
    The Babe, the Son,
    The Holy One
        Of Mary.

He is born to set us free;
He is born our Lord to be;
Carol, Christians, joyfully;
    The God, the Lord,
    By all adored
        Forever.

Let the bright red berries glow,
Everywhere in goodly show,
Life and light and joy is He,

The Babe, the Son,
The Holy One
Of Mary.

Christian men, rejoice and sing;
'Tis the birthday of our King,
Carol, Christians, joyfully;
The God, the Lord,
By all adored
Forever.

THE THREE KINGS.
Hail, King of Kings!

GASPAR.
I bring Thee a crown, O King of Kings,
And here a scepter full of gems,
For Thou shalt rule the hearts of men.
(*Places crown and scepter on crib.*)

MELCHOIR.
For Thee I bring sweet frankincense!
(*He swings a smoking censor.*)

BALTASAR.
And I bring myrrh to offer Thee!
(*Places casket on the crib.*)

GASPAR.
The greatest gift is yet ungiven,
The gift that cometh straight from Heaven.
O, Heavenly King,
Heart's love we bring.

MELCHOIR.
Not gold nor gems from land or sea
Is worth the love we offer Thee.

BALTASAR.
And lowly folk who have no gold,
Nor gift to offer that is meet,

May bring the dearest thing of all—
A loving heart and service sweet.

(*All join in singing "Joy to the World."*)

Curtain falls.

THE WHITE CHRISTMAS.

WHAT IT MEANS.

How to make a pleasant, *helpful* Christmas for the Sunday School is an annual problem. A tree with gifts, Santa Claus coming down the chimney, a treat of candy and nuts—these and many other schemes have been tried with a greater or less degree of success. But the criticism is often made that the true significance of the celebration of the birth of Christ is lost in the mere idea of bartering Christmas presents. "She didn't give me anything last year, so I'm not going to give her anything this year."

One wise superintendent determined to teach his Sunday School pupils the precious lesson of the beauty of giving. He called his teachers together a few weeks before Christmas and proposed to eliminate entirely the idea of "getting something," and in its stead to try to teach something of the true spirit of Christmas, the blessedness of giving.

The children were told that while at home they would receive all the usual presents, of course they would not get anything whatever from the Sunday School. The story of Jesus and how He gave His life, and how He liked best the gifts that cost us something, love, thought, foresight, charity, money —was told to the children and they were asked to save their pennies, instead of spending them for candy and nuts, to brighten the Christmas Day for God's poor and unfortunate.

It was put to a vote and every little hand was raised, although it may be confessed that a few went up a little reluctantly.

Teachers and young ladies met a few evenings later and made little stockings out of cheap cambric, with a cord put into the top of each in such a manner that it could be drawn together so the pennies would not be lost out. The stockings were about five inches long, and of various bright colors, and there were enough for every child. These were given out two weeks before Christmas.

On Christmas Eve, near the close of the regular program, a large tree was disclosed, but without a single present on it. The Minister made a short talk on the joys of giving to the poor and the children marched up, singing a Christmas carol, and attached their little stocking-bags to the tree.

Six little boys and girls passed among the congregation with larger stockings, collecting donations for the tree. These stockings had their tops neatly sewed around little circles of wire to keep them open.

The program consisted of Christmas hymns and carols, interspersed with recitations—all breathing the spirit of the White Christmas.

REMARKS ON THE PRODUCTION.

SCENERY.

Hang the rear and the sides of the stage with dark blue curtains, spangled with small silver bits of tinfoil, to represent very tiny stars. If the blue curtains are not available, use white sheets.

Cover the floor with white sheets. Have two or

three small evergreen trees at rear, covered with white calcimine and diamond powder. Soak long rags, shaped like icicles, in a strong solution of alum, and then let them crystallize, then attach them to the trees.

Down right, near the audience, is a doorway, supposed to be the entrance to the inn. This may be simply an opening between two wooden columns, with a step or two leading in. A lantern hangs over the door. A small bench stands by the inn.

Down left, near the audience, is the manger, a building extending out from left about seven feet. It has a back and one side of scenery or dark draperies and a thatched roof, covered with twigs or evergreen branches. There may be a door leading into the manger from the stage, but this is not necessary, as the characters can go out behind the manger. A front curtain, of dark goods, conceals the interior of the manger from the audience until it is withdrawn by Joseph.

The interior of the manger is covered with hay. Rude boxes and farm implements all around. A large upturned chair with wooden legs may simulate the crib, if it is concealed by enough straw. An electric light bulb is concealed in this straw and shines on the face of Mary, bending over the crib.

If desired, the manger scene may be presented in the choir loft, the manger hidden by curtains until revealed by Joseph. In this case have the evergreen trees at the left of the stage and arrange the manger scene at the rear and elevated above the other scene. This will prove most feasible in churches where the choir loft is immediately behind and above the platform.

LIGHTS.

Dim all the lights in the audience. Have a powerful searchlight, engine headlight or two powerful auto lights shining on the stage from a concealed elevation at the left. Shade these lights with a blue isinglass shield, thus casting a blue light over the entire stage. Use a strong yellow light on the manger scene, the rest of the stage being in darkness.

PROPERTIES.

If it is possible have bits of white confetti or finely cut paper fall from above during the shepherds' scene in Act II.

The bases of the trees should be covered with cotton.

Three rough crooks for the shepherds.

Chimes to ring off the stage. A dinner gong or set of chimes will answer.

For the lamb use a white muff, being careful to shield
it from the direct gaze of the audience.

A spray of cherries.

A small bird of blue feathers.

A ball.

A crown and scepter made of gilded wood.

A censor made of metallic butter dish suspended by
chains.

A fancy jewel case, supposed to contain myrrh.

Bench in front of inn.

Rude box in front of manger.

COSTUMES.

MARY—A sweet-faced blonde. Long tunic of light
blue, falling straight from neck to the ankles.
White stockings. Sandals. Hair in two long braids
either side of face. White veil draped around head
and shoulders, bound about the brow with circlet.
Dark red mantle, fastened to left shoulder and
draped around body. This mantle may trail on the
ground. The tunic may be made of cotton crepon,
the mantle of dyed muslin.

JOSEPH—A virile, bearded man of about fifty.
Sandals. Long black cassock, easily obtained from
an Episcopal choir. Striped couch cover may serve
as mantle. This should be draped about head and
body. Long staff.

SIMEON—An old man with white hair and beard.
Tunic of potato sacking falling in straight folds
from neck to ankles. Large gray shawl serves as
mantle, draped on head and body. Long crook.
Sandals.

TIMOTHY—Man of forty. Costume similar to
Isaac's. Striped mantle.

ISAAC—Man of twenty. Shorter tunic similar to Simeon's. Fur rug draped over left shoulder. Dark red drapery on head. Sandals. Brown stripes criss-crossed on legs. Crook.

ANNA—Long tunic of brown. Take a square white sheet and stripe it with bands of dark blue. This serves as a mantle, draped over head and body. Hair hanging. A woman of thirty-five. Sandals. If desired, a blue veil may be draped around the head and neck and the mantle draped over the body.

THOMAS—A boy of seven. Sandals. Brown strips criss-crossed on legs from sandals to hips. Short white tunic cut like a boy's nightgown, but coming only to knees. Dark blue mantle. Small crook.

RUTH—A girl of eleven. Blue tunic hanging in straight folds from neck to three or four inches above ankles. Border of figured goods, to simulate oriental embroidery, around bottom of robe and down the front. This should be about two inches wide. Sandals. White stockings. Hair hanging. White veil draped around head and shoulders. Later she enters with striped mantle.

DEBORAH—A dignified matron of about forty-five. Sandals. Long kimono of solid color. Sash of yellow. Hair in two long braids on either side of face. Yellow drapery over head and shoulders. Rich striped mantle draped over the costume.

RACHEL—Sandals. White tunic trimmed with red figured cloth to simulate oriental embroidery. Red sash. Wreath of red roses on head. Mantle made of a square white sheet with stripes of red sewed on it. Bracelets, armlets and anklets of silver paper.

PRISCILLA—Sandals. Light green tunic. Dark green mantle. Gold paper armlets, etc.

MELCHOIR—Tall, dark man with dark mustache. Long black cassock may be borrowed from an Episcopal Church. Over this is a red or yellow kimono. Sandals. Turban on head. This turban may be made from a calico covered crown of an old derby, with red and white striped rim. He wears many rich ornaments. Curtain chains around neck and on arms. This costume may sometimes be borrowed from a lodge of Shriners, Knights Templar, Royal Arch Masons or Odd Fellows.

GASPAR—Similar to Melchoir. He is a young king aged about twenty-two. Wear white drapery on head and over it a golden (paper) crown. May wear sword. Sandals.

BALTASAR—Old king with white hair. Long rich robe or kimono over a cassock. Red sash. · Red head drapery. Golden crown. Sandals.

ANGELS—Invisible to the audience.

PROLOGUE—Stately lady in trailing Grecian robe of white. Hair powdered. This character should be played by a lady with distinct dramatic ability.

NOTE.—If it is desired to simplify these costumes, kimonos, cassocks and cottas from Episcopal choirs, draperies of sheets and couch covers, and sandals made of a sole bound to foot with brown cloth cords, will answer admirably in the dim blue light.

Nightgowns, dressing gowns, fur rugs, fur muffs opened, fur stoles, opera capes, spangled tunics, window cords and chains, etc., will make valuable substitutes for the oriental garments.

CHRISTMAS CAROL.

J. M. NEALE.
THOMAS HELMORE.

Maestoso.

1. Christ was born on Christ-mas day, Wreathe the hol - ly,
2. He is born to set us free; He is born our
3. Let the bright red ber - ries glow Ev - 'ry-where in

twine the bay, Light and life and joy is He, The
Lord to be; Car - ol, Chris -tians, joy - ful - ly; The
good - ly show, Light and life and joy is He, The

Babe, the Son, the Ho - ly One of Ma - ry.
God, the Lord, by all a - dored for - ev - er.
Babe, the Son, the Ho - ly One of Ma - ry.

Christian men, re-joice and sing; 'Tis the birth-day of our King.

CHRISTMAS CAROL—Continued.

Car - ol, Christians, joy - ful - ly; The God, the Lord, By

all a-dored For-ev - er. Night of sadness, Morn of glad-ness

Ev - er-more: Ev - er, Ev - er, Aft - er man - y

troub-les sore, Morn of glad-ness ev - er-more, and ev - er-more.

CHRISTMAS CAROL—Concluded.

Mid-night scarce-ly passed and o - ver,. Draw-ing to the

FINE.

ho - ly morn; Ver - y ear - ly, Ver - y ear - ly, Christ was born.

Piu lento.

Sing out with bliss, His name is this: Em - man - u - el!

a tempo. D. S.

As 'twas fore-told, In days of old, By Ga - bri - el.

JOSEPH   MARY   SIMEON

TIMOTHY   ISAAC   ANNA   THOMAS

RUTH   RACHEL   DEBORAH   PRISCILLA

MELCHOIR   GASPAR   BALTASAR   PROLOGUE

WHEN THE LITTLE ANGEL SANG

A ONE-ACT CHRISTMAS PLAY

By

LILLIAN DUNLAP GEORGE

Author of

"Aunt Martha Pays"

PRODUCTION RIGHTS

WHEN THE LITTLE ANGEL SANG

For two men and three women

CHARACTERS

(In the order of their first appearance)

LITTLE SHEPHERD....................*Faithful to his flock*
LOST OLD MAN.................*An unfortunate traveler*
LITTLE ANGEL.....................*Of the heavenly host*
THIEF......................*A fugitive from conscience*
MARY ....*Mother of Jesus*

Chorus of the heavenly host, to sing off stage

NOTE.—*The rôles of Little Shepherd and Little Angel are to be played by women. Mary has no lines to speak, but only a Christmas lullaby to sing in the tableau at close of play.*

TIME—*Morning after the birth of Christ, just before dawn.*

PLACE—*A hillside near Bethlehem in Judea.*

TIME OF PLAYING—*Twenty-five minutes.*

COSTUMES AND CHARACTERISTICS

Little Shepherd, played by a girl or woman, appears to be a youth in his middle teens, with short black hair and a brown make-up for face, legs, and arms. Wears a sleeveless tunic of burlap, falling to the knees and held in by a rope girdle, with a sheepskin over his shoulders and a brownish turban-like headpiece reaching to the shoulders in the back. Both legs and arms are bare.

The Lost Old Man appears aged, with a bent figure, a long gray beard, and a light brown facial make-up. He wears a long, flowing robe of deep, rich blue, with a gold-stencilled design on sleeves and hem and around the neck and a wide, striped girdle, also a close-fitting headpiece of white falling below the shoulders in the back, and sandals. He makes his first appearance without his cloak and turban, which he recovers late in the play from the Thief. The cloak is of deeper blue than the robe, sleeveless, open at the front, and gold-stencilled in an all-over design, and the turban is of blue silk, ornamented with sparkling beads and imitation precious stones.

The Little Angel, played by a girl or woman, is a spiritual-looking youth with shoulder-length yellow hair and a delicate blond make-up, wearing a long, shimmering white robe of rayon or metalline, with wide sleeves and no girdle. Between the shoulder blades are fastened a pair of wings of heavy wire covered with white muslin, buckram, or several thick-nesses of building paper, with strips of white crêpe paper feathers pasted upon this foundation. A golden halo made of heavy cardboard or buckram covered with gilt paper and fastened about the forehead with a flesh-tinted elastic is also worn. The feet may be bare or white sandals may be worn.

The Thief is a rather fierce-looking man in his early thir-ties, with a brown or black beard and with a brown make-up for face, hands, and feet. He wears a dull brown robe reaching six or eight inches below the knee, with a striped girdle; a brown cloak striped with black, sleeveless and open at the front; a brown head cloth and brown sandals. He makes his entrance wearing the Lost Old Man's rich cloak over his poor garments and the latter's jeweled turban on his head.

Mary is a sweet-faced young woman, with dark hair and a brunette make-up. She wears a soft full white robe over a rose-colored foundation, a long, flowing white veil over her dark hair, and a dull blue mantle with a gold-stencilled border, covering her head and most of the veil and falling to the hem of her robe, which reaches the floor. She should have a good singing voice.

NOTE.—The Tissot pictures of Old and New Testament characters are accurate representations of biblical costumes and may be consulted in the designing of the costumes. The publishers of this play do not handle the crêpe paper suggested for one of the costumes, but it may be obtained at the stores of practically all towns of ordinary size throughout the country.

PROPERTIES

For Little Shepherd, lamb, shepherd's rod, goatskin water bag, lantern (all on stage from beginning). For Thief, leather money bag full of coins. For Mary, large-sized doll swathed in white to represent baby.

How to Make Properties.—The lamb may be made of creamy canton flannel, stuffed with cotton, and wrapped in pieces of burlap or similar coarse cloth. The shepherd's rod is a wooden rod about two feet long with one end thickly padded like a knob, with nails protruding through the dark brown covering of the padding. The goatskin water bag is a slender pouch made of canvas. The lantern is a medium-sized can with a design cut in its sides with tinsmiths' shears or punched out with a large nail. A socket for holding a piece of candle is soldered to the bottom of the can and a wire handle is fastened to the top. The leather money bag may be made of soft leather or heavy canvas, fastened with a drawstring around the top. The coins may be gilded lead button molds and weights, gilded buttons of various sizes, and enough real money to make the proper jingle.

LIGHTING PLOT

Except for the red glow from the open fire, the play opens in darkness, which quickly changes to the semi-darkness of approaching dawn, indicated by blue and amber foot-lights and bunch lights above the stage off right and left, with the blue lights predominating. As the dawn pro-gresses, a few amber and rose bulbs may be added. Care should be taken that the scene is not made so dim as to obscure the movements of the characters. When the Little Angel enters, a white spotlight should be thrown on him and kept in play most of the time he is on the stage. The fire, which is made by crossing several sticks of wood above a double socket containing two electric bulbs, one red and the other orange, or white bulbs with gauzy red and orange cloth stretched above them, should be carefully arranged so that its glow will fall upon the Thief and the Little Angel in the scene in which they examine the coins, and again upon the Little Shepherd as he sits beside the fire with his lamb at the close of the play. When the vision of Mary is to appear, concealed lights on both sides of the manger are turned on, blotting out the gauze back drop and revealing Mary seated beside the manger. One of these lights may be covered with amber gelatine and the other with pink gelatine, to obtain a delicate radiance. If director has any difficulty in obtaining theatrical gauze, a plain, dark drop curtain may be substi-tuted, to be raised or drawn aside for the final tableau.

MUSIC

The song of the heavenly host, the lyric of which is pro-vided at the beginning of the play, should be sung off stage either by a good mixed quartet or a chorus choir, with all four parts represented, if possible. It is also sung as a solo by the Little Angel. Piano accompaniment should be used in all the singing unless the voices are unusually good or well trained. The music recommended for this song is that of the carol, "What Child Is This?" All music sung off stage during the dialogue should be kept very soft. For Mary's song at the close of the play, any appropriate Christmas lullaby may be selected. If the singer has no choice of her own, either Reinecke's "The First Christmas" or the well-known Luther's Cradle Hymn, "Away in a Manger," is suggested for this number. All these three songs may be found in *"Denison's Christmas Songs and Carols,"* which collection of old Christmas favorites may be obtained from the publishers for the price of 50 cents, postpaid.

STAGE DIRECTIONS

Up stage means away from footlights; *down stage,* near footlights. In the use of *right* and *left,* the actor is supposed to be facing the audience.

WHEN THE LITTLE ANGEL SANG

SCENE: *A hillside at some distance from Bethlehem in Judea, just before dawn of the morning after the birth of Christ. The stage is set with wings or sides of the setting painted to represent hilly pasture land showing an occasional tree. The back drop is made of several thicknesses of dark blue theatrical gauze, representing a night sky, in which are a few stars, one very bright and hanging low on the horizon. The effect of stars is obtained by placing white bunch lights back of a plain blue canvas drop curtain behind the back drop and letting them shine through small holes pierced in the curtain. Immediately back of the gauze drop curtain is placed the manger, a rough wooden box filled with straw, which is invisible to the audience until the lights with which it is wired are turned on. There are two exits, up right and left respectively, where the sides of the set or the wings approach the back drop. Near the right exit stands a clump of trees, which may be cut cedars or firs mounted on standards, which are concealed by dark green cloth or grass mats. Near the left exit stands a lone tree similar to the others. At left center is a large rock, made by covering wooden boxes first with an irregular padding of papers and cloth to the desired shape and size and then with gray canvas, painted dark green or black near the base. Down center is an open fire made of crossed sticks and electric bulbs, its glow dimmed and some of its sticks collapsing to indicate that it is dying. Near it lies a stick with which to stir it. The* LITTLE SHEPHERD'S *lantern stands near the fire, and his rod is leaning against the rock at left center. The water bag is lying against a tree up right. The stage floor may be covered with green baize and grass mats, with a few smaller rocks here and there, if desired. As it is the hour just before dawn, the play opens with the stage dark, except for the light of the fire down center.*

At rise of curtain, the lamb is lying at right of the fire, swathed in cloths, while in front of fire the LITTLE SHEPHERD *stands motionless, facing a little up right, listening raptly to the song of the heavenly host, which is heard off up right, softly as if far away. The choristers off stage sing the entire song once, using the melody of "What Child Is This?" with the following words:*

SONG OF THE HEAVENLY HOST

1.

Oh, fear ye not, oh, fear ye not,
  Who serve in places lowly,
For unto you is born this day
  The Savior, Christ most holy.

CHORUS

He lies in a cattle stall,
  Bright angels bending o'er him.
Go, haste ye to Bethlehem
  To worship and adore him.

2.

Rejoice ye now, rejoice ye now,
  Whose hearts know sin and sadness,
For unto you is born this day
  The Prince of Peace and Gladness.

(*As the last tones of the melody die away, the* LITTLE SHEPHERD *turns and looks around him, then speaks to the lamb.*)

LITTLE SHEPHERD. 'Tis the most beautiful song I ever heard. I wish it might go on forever, little lamb. Then the night wouldn't seem so lonely and cold, and I could forget that I'd been left behind. (*He pokes the embers of the fire with the stick, then kneels beside the lamb, lying at the right of the fire. Blue and amber footlights and off-stage lights are gradually turned on.*) Did you hear the voices, little lamb? They sang of a Savior in a cattle stall in Bethlehem. And there was a light all about—a glorious, silvery light like— Oh, I can't tell you what it was like; 'twas so soft and radiant. I could even see the highway which leads to Bethlehem. (*Sighs.*) The highway that Benjamin and the rest have taken. (*Catches his breath sobbingly.*) Oh, why couldn't I have gone with them? There will be angels at the cattle stall, little lamb. I want to go! Oh, I want to go! (*He buries his face in the lamb's soft wool for a moment, then lifts his head and hugs his pet more tightly.*) And yet —and yet you do need me to care for you. You were such a careless lamb to venture to the cliff. I could never have saved you if you had not caught in the thicket. (*A faint noise of crackling branches is heard off left. The* LITTLE SHEPHERD *looks around, startled.*) What is that? (*The noise is now more distinct. The boy lays down the lamb, then hastens to pick up his rod lying against the rock at left center. He listens.*) 'Tis not the tread of a wolf. (*He picks up his lantern, peers forth into the darkness, and calls.*) Is it you, Benjamin?

The LOST OLD MAN, *dazed and unsteady of step, enters at left. His headdress and cloak are missing and his rich gown is soiled and torn. He comes to left center, halting on left side of rock.*

LOST OLD MAN (*swaying*). The gold! The gold!

LITTLE SHEPHERD (*dropping lantern and running to him*). The gold, sir? What gold?

LOST OLD MAN (*sinking down against the rock*). I was bearing it—in a bag. 'Tis gone! 'Tis gone! (*Rousing himself suddenly.*) Did you take it?

LITTLE SHEPHERD (*standing over him*). I? No, oh, no, sir!

LOST OLD MAN. You do not know where it is?

LITTLE SHEPHERD. I have not seen it, sir.

LOST OLD MAN. You—are not—lying?

LITTLE SHEPHERD. Before Jehovah, I speak the truth, sir. Where did you lose it?

LOST OLD MAN (*weakly*). I—have—forgotten—forgotten. (*He leans against the rock, motionless, his eyes closed.*)

LITTLE SHEPHERD (*shaking him gently*). Wake! Please wake! (*There is no response. He speaks coaxingly.*) Can you not remember about the gold? Perhaps I could find it for you. (*He strokes the* LOST OLD MAN'S *head gently.*) Oh, I wish Benjamin were here! (*He takes the sheepskin from his shoulders, places it around the shoulders of the* LOST OLD MAN, *stirs the fire, then returns to the side of the stranger.*)

LOST OLD MAN (*faintly, without moving*). Water!

(*The* LITTLE SHEPHERD *runs up right for the water bag lying against the tree.*) ·

LITTLE SHEPHERD. Here is sweet, cool water. (*He holds the bag that the* LOST OLD MAN *may drink.*) Oh, the bag is empty. (*Drops it beside the rock.*)

LOST OLD MAN (*unheeding*). Water!

LITTLE SHEPHERD (*kneeling beside the* LOST OLD MAN). I am so sorry. When the dawn comes, I will find a well of clear water. (*The song is heard again softly, now sung by one high, sweet voice—that of the* LITTLE ANGEL. *The* LOST OLD MAN *stirs.*) 'Tis the song again! (*Rises.*)

The song is now clearer and sweeter. The LOST OLD MAN *stirs again. The* LITTLE ANGEL *appears at right, in a light that makes him appear all shining radiance.*

LITTLE SHEPHERD. O-o-o-h! (*The* LITTLE ANGEL *sees the* LITTLE SHEPHERD *and stops singing.*) Oh! Oh!

LITTLE ANGEL. Why do you say, "oh" in that tone of voice?

LITTLE SHEPHERD. You are so white—and so shining! And you have wings!

LITTLE ANGEL. Most certainly. Haven't you?

LITTLE SHEPHERD (*turning about to show him*). Of course not.

LITTLE ANGEL (*looks at* LITTLE SHEPHERD'S *back and shoulders*). That's very strange!

LITTLE SHEPHERD. Not at all. Angels are the only people who have wings.

LITTLE ANGEL. I am an angel. But I thought perhaps mortals had them, too. You are a mortal, are you not?

LITTLE SHEPHERD (*hesitating, not exactly sure as to what a mortal is*). I'm a shepherd.

LITTLE ANGEL (*nodding his head*). I have heard of them, though I'm sure I never met one before. Just what does a shepherd do?

LITTLE SHEPHERD. He cares for his sheep. He finds fresh pastures and clear streams for them each day. At night, he keeps them safe from the wild beasts.

LITTLE ANGEL. How very interesting! One can learn something new every day. Can't one? Where are your sheep?

LITTLE SHEPHERD. All but one are on the hillside just below, near the olive grove.

LITTLE ANGEL. And the other one? (*Looks toward the lame lamb.*)

LITTLE SHEPHERD (*kneeling beside the fire*). He is here. He fell from a cliff and cannot walk. I must care for him until he is well again.

LITTLE ANGEL (*coming closer and examining the lamb*). He's a beautiful, soft creature.

LITTLE SHEPHERD. He's my own little lamb. See! He knows me.

LITTLE ANGEL. Oh, I like him. I must find a lamb when I go home. (*Bends down to pat lamb.*)

LITTLE SHEPHERD. Home? You mean heaven?

LITTLE ANGEL. Of course.

LITTLE SHEPHERD. I thought angels always stayed in heaven. Why are you here?

LITTLE ANGEL (*standing erect again*). The Christ child is born in Bethlehem to-night. We wanted all the earth to know, so we came to sing the heavenly song. Of course you heard me.

LITTLE SHEPHERD. I can hear the song in my heart now.

LITTLE ANGEL. It is a song you remember.

LITTLE SHEPHERD. But there were many voices. Where are the others?

LITTLE ANGEL. They are still singing, I presume.

LITTLE SHEPHERD. You should be with them.

LITTLE ANGEL. I wondered what sort of place the Christ child had come to live in, so I stayed behind to see.

LITTLE SHEPHERD. You will be lost!

LITTLE ANGEL. I am quite safe. There's a long, shining path all the way back. (*The* LOST OLD MAN *groans and stirs.*) Who is there? (*Looks toward* LOST OLD MAN.)

LITTLE SHEPHERD. An old man. He has lost some gold, and he is hurt. (*Running to* LOST OLD MAN.) Can I help you, sir?

LOST OLD MAN (*gasping*). Water. I thirst.

LITTLE SHEPHERD (*shaking his head*). There is none. (*He inverts the bag to show that it is empty.*) Morning will come soon. Then I will find fresh water for you.

LITTLE ANGEL (*taking the bag from the hands of the* LITTLE SHEPHERD). There is always water! Drink!

(*He pretends to turn the bag upward, and water apparently trickles forth. The* LOST OLD MAN *drinks greedily. Then he slumps down into his former position against the rock.*)

LITTLE SHEPHERD (*amazed*). How can that be? I am sure the bag was empty! (*Takes bag from* LITTLE ANGEL *and examines it.*)

LITTLE ANGEL. That is easily done. When one wishes something good, it happens—if one is an angel.

LITTLE SHEPHERD. Being an angel must be nicer than being a shepherd, then.

LITTLE ANGEL. It's more convenient, certainly.

LITTLE SHEPHERD (*wistfully*). When we want something, we wish first and then we work, oh, so hard! After all, what we want doesn't happen sometimes.

LITTLE ANGEL. Oh, that's very disappointing.

LITTLE SHEPHERD. I wished and wished that I might follow the star to-night. I watched over the sheep so carefully, that I might go with the other shepherds—and then —and then— (*He sighs.*)

LITTLE ANGEL. And then?

LITTLE SHEPHERD (*shaking his head sadly*). Benjamin said I was needed here.

(*The* LOST OLD MAN *sits up and looks about him in bewilderment.*)

LOST OLD MAN. Timon! Timon! Here, boy!

LITTLE SHEPHERD (*turning to him*). What do you wish?

LOST OLD MAN. I called Timon. Where is he?

LITTLE SHEPHERD. I do not know, sir. I have not seen him.

LOST OLD MAN. Who are you?

LITTLE SHEPHERD. I am the younger brother of Benjamin. And this (*pointing to the* LITTLE ANGEL) is a shining angel.

LITTLE ANGEL. My name is Asmiel.

LOST OLD MAN (*to* LITTLE SHEPHERD). How came you here in my garden?

LITTLE SHEPHERD. This is not your garden, sir. You are on the hillside which rises from the plain near Tekoa. Yonder lies Bethlehem.

LOST OLD MAN (*bewildered*). Bethlehem! I have heard the word; yet I cannot recall— 'Tis as if I had dreamed— (*Breaks off, shaking his head.*)

LITTLE ANGEL. You must have heard us singing about Bethlehem. (*Sings chorus of song of the heavenly host.*)

LOST OLD MAN (*his face alight*). Somewhere from out the night that song came to me. A light flamed in the sky. Then I heard a soft fluttering, like angels' wings.

LITTLE ANGEL (*eagerly*). I am sure you could have seen me if you had looked carefully.

LOST OLD MAN. I heard the song as I journeyed past great vineyards, through a wide plain—then—then—I forget. Tell me: How came I to this place?

LITTLE SHEPHERD. You came stumbling through the darkness. You must have followed the light of the fire. You were looking for some gold.

LOST OLD MAN. I bore a leathern bag, filled with golden coins. (*Distractedly.*) I do not know where it has gone.

LITTLE SHEPHERD. Your cloak is missing. And your turban, too.

LOST OLD MAN (*putting his hand to his head*). Aye, 'twas jeweled. (*To* LITTLE ANGEL.) Sing the words again. Perchance I shall remember the rest. (*The* LITTLE ANGEL *sings first stanza of the heavenly song.*) It all comes back to me. I was journeying toward Bethlehem.

LITTLE SHEPHERD. Why, Benjamin has gone to see the Christ child in a cattle stall there. A star led him. Did you see it?

LOST OLD MAN. I was following its gleam when the robber came upon me.

LITTLE SHEPHERD (*looking around him apprehensively*). Robbers about?

LOST OLD MAN. He stripped my outer garments from me and took my camel and my bag of coins.

LITTLE ANGEL (*amazed*). I never heard of such a thing!

LOST OLD MAN (*wailing*). My gold! My treasure! Gone! Gone!

LITTLE SHEPHERD. Surely he did not take all you possessed.

LOST OLD MAN. The hoarded wealth of years! My gift of adoration to the new Messiah.

LITTLE SHEPHERD (*comfortingly*). You can worship the child without the treasure. He will understand.

LOST OLD MAN. All my life I have waited for the moment when I might kneel before the Holy One of Israel and offer my choicest gift. And now—to go empty-handed! No! No! I cannot! (*He rises painfully.*) I must find the thief and recover my golden coins.

LITTLE SHEPHERD. When Benjamin returns, he will help you.

LOST OLD MAN. I cannot tarry. I might be too late. Where lies Carmel?

LITTLE SHEPHERD (*pointing off right*). Far beyond that line of hills.

LOST OLD MAN. And Bethlehem?

LITTLE SHEPHERD. Yonder beneath that gleaming star. The road is winding. You could not follow it in the darkness.

LOST OLD MAN. I must return toward Carmel to find that cursed thief. (*He raises his arm in malediction.*) May the undying wrath of Jehovah pursue him! (*He trembles with the violence of his wrath.*)

LITTLE SHEPHERD. You are not strong. Wait for the shepherds. They will return before the day is far gone.

LOST OLD MAN. Do not urge me. I might miss the child.

LITTLE SHEPHERD. Then I must guide you to the plain. The path is so narrow.

LITTLE ANGEL. The Christ child will welcome you without your gift. But I hope you may find the coins.

LOST OLD MAN. Jehovah grant your wish!

LITTLE SHEPHERD. Will you care for my little lamb while I am gone, dear angel? (*Picks up lamb and holds it out to* LITTLE ANGEL.)

LITTLE ANGEL (*taking the lamb in his arms*). He will be perfectly safe with me. (*Exeunt* LOST OLD MAN *and* LITTLE SHEPHERD *at right.* LITTLE ANGEL *pats the lamb and addresses it thoughtfully*). Lamb, this is a most distressing situation. I thought everyone was happy here. Then I found you with your wounds, and a little shepherd who can't see the Christ child, and an old man who **has lost** his treasure. It is very disillusioning. (*He sighs.*) I wonder if the child will enjoy this earth. (*Lays down lamb near fire, sits on rock at left, and is silent for a moment. Then he sings softly the second stanza of the heavenly song.*)

He has just finished when the THIEF *breaks through the trees at right. Over his poor garments he wears the jeweled headdress and rich cloak of the* LOST OLD MAN. *In his hand he carries the old man's leather money bag full of coins.*

THIEF (*aloud, with a groan*). That cursed, piercing song again! Wherever I go, it beats upon my ears.

LITTLE ANGEL (*rising and coming towards the* THIEF). Good evening! Or perhaps I should say, "Good morning."

THIEF (*pauses, startled*). Who are you?

LITTLE ANGEL. My name is Asmiel.

THIEF. No shepherd certainly.

LITTLE ANGEL. Not exactly, though I am caring for some sheep at present.

THIEF. Are you alone here?

LITTLE ANGEL (*nodding*). Except for this lamb and the sheep below the hill.

THIEF (*menacingly*). If anyone asks you who passed this way to-night, you have seen no one.

LITTLE ANGEL. How could I forget you in that beautiful headdress and shining robe?

THIEF. You know my meaning.

LITTLE ANGEL. If I wore such beautiful garments, I'd want to be seen. And your leathern bag—is it filled with golden coins? (*Looks pointedly at bag.*)

THIEF (*roughly*). Hold your tongue! The contents of the bag are nothing to you.

LITTLE ANGEL. I have never seen a golden coin.

THIEF (*incredulously*). You've never seen one? You cannot mean that!

LITTLE ANGEL. I do, indeed.

THIEF. They speak to you with their gleam. They lure you until you could not resist them if you would.

LITTLE ANGEL. They must be very beautiful.

THIEF. Aye. They dazzle one.

LITTLE ANGEL. You make me very curious.

THIEF (*hesitating*). I should not tarry longer—but— (*Opens the bag.*) You shall see these. (*He opens bag and takes out the coins in handfuls, fingers them covetously, and lets some of them slip back into the bag with a jingling sound.*)

LITTLE ANGEL. How they glitter in the firelight! You must have been saving them for years. There are so many!

THIEF (*uneasily*). Yes. Oh, yes.

LITTLE ANGEL (*touching them gently*). They are so shining. And they make such a pleasant sound.

THIEF. Aye. Their jingle is music in one's ears. (*He puts the last coin into the bag, then hesitates.*) Here, I will give you one of these for your own. (*He takes out a coin and hands it to the* LITTLE ANGEL.)

LITTLE ANGEL (*taking the coin*). How kind you are! But I have nothing to give you in return, except—a song. I should be delighted to sing for you.

THIEF (*hastily*). No, no! I must journey on.

LITTLE ANGEL (*coaxingly*). Everyone thinks I sing rather well. And I do enjoy singing.

THIEF. Very well, then. A coin for a song. About shepherds?

LITTLE ANGEL. About a child. (*Sings second stanza of heavenly song part way through, but is stopped in middle of third line.*)

THIEF (*interrupting in agitation*). Stop! Stop! I cannot bear it.

LITTLE ANGEL (*surprised*). I thought you would like it.

THIEF. Those words have pursued me all night long.

LITTLE ANGEL. That song helped an old man remember how he became lost.

THIEF. I have tried for hours to escape that melody, and now you—you— (*He starts towards left.*)

LITTLE ANGEL (*going to* THIEF *and holding out the coin*). I have changed my mind. I cannot keep it. If you meet an old man who has lost his gold, give the coin to him. Some one stole his gift to the Christ child. He has gone to look for it.

THIEF (*with a furtive side glance*). When—when did he lose his gold? (*Takes coin and puts it back in bag.*)

LITTLE ANGEL. To-night. As he was following the star, he met a robber. The old man had saved the money for many years that he might some day give it to the new Messiah.

THIEF. I cannot understand how you have learned all this.

LITTLE ANGEL. The old man has been here, wounded, beside this fire. Now he has gone to recover his gift, if he can. A robber would never have taken the gold if he had known 'twas meant for the Christ child. Would he?

THIEF (*distracted*). I do not know! I do not know!

(*The song is sung again softly by many voices off right. The* THIEF *sinks to the ground and buries his face in his hands. After a moment the song dies away.*)

LITTLE ANGEL. You should not grieve. The song is meant to bring happiness.

THIEF. Happiness! There is none. Only wasted days—remorse—bitterness!

LITTLE SHEPHERD (*calling from off right*). See! The fire is just ahead. Now you may rest.

The LOST OLD MAN *and* LITTLE SHEPHERD *enter at right.*

LOST OLD MAN. You were right, lad. I must wait until morning. I need a guide for the whole journey. (*The* THIEF *has started up at the sound of voices. Instinctively he conceals the bag beneath his cloak. The* LOST OLD MAN *stretches out his hands to the fire.*) Ah, the fire is cheering. I should not mind the cold had I my— (*He sees the* THIEF.) My cloak! My jeweled turban! (*Advances towards the* THIEF, *with both arms raised.*) Then you—you are the man who—?

THIEF (*falling on his knees before the* LOST OLD MAN). The man who robbed you? Yes.

LOST OLD MAN. Most cursed thief!

THIEF. Forgive me! Oh, forgive!

LOST OLD MAN. No! Vile, wicked, wretched! You ruin my life's hope, then ask forgiveness. Never!

THIEF (*pleadingly*). See! I return your bag of coins. Not one is missing. Count them. (*Holds out bag.*)

LOST OLD MAN (*seizing it*). My treasure! (*Opens bag and feverishly counts coins.*)

(*Many voices are softly singing the song of the heavenly host off right. Keep music pianissimo. At this point,* MARY, *with the doll, may take her place beside the manger behind the back drop, ready for her song.*)

THIEF. The price of the camel is there, also.

LOST OLD MAN. The Messiah's gift. Tell me why you have returned it.

THIEF. I heard a song of peace and good will. I remembered days long ago when peace and good will had been even in my heart.

LOST OLD MAN. And you found me here.

THIEF. I did not know where you had gone. I ran blindly. The song would not leave me. I could not forget that I had wronged you. Speak! Say that I am forgiven. (*The first light of dawn appears, as stage lights gradually go up. The heavenly host are still singing very softly.*) Listen! The voices! Nay, I will not ask forgiveness. Punish me as thou wilt.

(*The* LOST OLD MAN *listens, hesitates, then helps the* THIEF *to rise.*)

LOST OLD MAN. Come! Your sin shall be remembered no more between us. Truly a song has brought healing to the earth this night.

LITTLE ANGEL. I knew the world would be happier because we sang.

THIEF (*removing the robe and headdress and placing them upon the* LOST OLD MAN). I am not worthy even to touch your garments.

LOST OLD MAN. Speak no more of this. See! I give the money into your hands. Guide me to Bethlehem. We will worship the new Messiah together.

(*The song dies away. The* THIEF *takes the bag and bows low before the* LOST OLD MAN *in humility.*)

LITTLE SHEPHERD. Will you not wait to break bread with us?

LOST OLD MAN (*shaking his head*). Dawn comes swiftly, and the hours are precious. We must be on our way.

LITTLE SHEPHERD (*eagerly, clasping his hands*). Oh, I want to see the child and his mother and the angels!

LOST OLD MAN. Then come, lad.

LITTLE SHEPHERD (*shaking his head*). The flock will need care. And my own little lamb—he would be so lonely.

LOST OLD MAN. Perchance your brother will give you leave to go when he returns.

LITTLE SHEPHERD. He will say the distance is too great. Tell the little child that, when my lamb is grown, its fleece shall make a soft coverlet for his bed.

LOST OLD MAN. I will not forget.

LITTLE SHEPHERD. Jehovah guide your steps, sir.

LOST OLD MAN. You have richly blessed an old man to-night. (*Extends outstretched hand over* LITTLE SHEPHERD'S *head.*) May the favor of the Most High be yours forever!

LITTLE ANGEL (*to* LOST OLD MAN). Some day I will sing again for you. (*Exeunt* LOST OLD MAN *and* THIEF *at left. The* LITTLE SHEPHERD *looks after them wistfully for a moment, then turns to the fire as he tries to stifle a sob. The* LITTLE ANGEL *goes to him and tries to comfort him.*) Do not cry. You shall see the Christ child yet.

LITTLE SHEPHERD. Bethlehem lies too far away.

(*The song is heard again very softly, off right.*)

LITTLE ANGEL. They are singing again. I ought to go. Perhaps they miss me. (*He starts off right.*) You know, I like this world, after all. The mortals I have met are very charming. Some day, I think I shall come back. (*Exit at right, waving his hand in farewell.*)

(*The* LITTLE SHEPHERD *watches the* LITTLE ANGEL *depart, stands motionless for a moment, then, going slowly to the lamb, picks it up and seats himself beside the fire.*)

LITTLE SHEPHERD (*tenderly, to the lamb*). Your wound is healing. Oh, do hurry and get well! When you are older, your fleece shall make a coverlet for the Christ child. Then we—you and I—shall journey to Bethlehem bearing a gift.

(*The heavenly song has died away. As the light of dawn grows brighter, the lights above the manger just back of the drop are turned on, revealing the manger, with the baby lying on the straw in plain view and* MARY, *the young mother, leaning lovingly over it. The radiance from the lights envelopes her, and she is singing a Christmas lullaby. The* LITTLE SHEPHERD *rises to his knees and waits motionless, rapt, until she has finished the song. Then she turns to him, smiles, and holds out her hand. Carrying his lamb, the* LITTLE SHEPHERD *starts towards her as—*)

THE CURTAIN FALLS.

BEGGARS CAN'T BE CHOOSERS

By

LINDSEY BARBEE

PRODUCTION RIGHTS

Copies of this play are available in single pamphlet form. The right to produce this play by one group of amateur players is authorized only by the purchase of nine copies (one copy for each speaking part) at the current price of 50c each.

It is dishonest and illegal to copy parts.

BEGGARS CAN'T BE CHOOSERS

For eight women and one man

CHARACTERS

(In order of their first appearance)

MISS PRATT.........*Secretary of the Ladies' Aid Society*
MRS. BROWN.............................*The hostess*
MRS. DIGBY.................*Chairman of the committee*
MRS. LEWIS..........*Another member of the committee*
DORA BROWN...................*Daughter of Mrs. Brown*
ROSE DIGBY...................*Daughter of Mrs. Digby*
KATE LEWIS...................*Daughter of Mrs. Lewis*
MRS. ALLEN......................*The minister's wife*
MR. KELLY ....*An expressman*

SCENE—*Mrs. Brown's living room.*

TIME—*The week before Christmas.*

TIME OF PLAYING—*About twenty-five minutes.*

STORY OF THE PLAY

A Christmas box for a mountain minister is being packed by the Ladies' Aid Society. Donations for the box prove to be a collection of most unsuitable and unattractive garments, all of which are included in the packing. In the midst of the proceedings, the young daughters of three of the committee members appear; and while the guests repair to the other room for tea, the trio takes a hand in thrusting Hope into Pandora's box of evils. Just how they do this is characteristic of impulsive schoolgirls. Each girl contributes one of her most cherished possessions; and as a result, the box is transformed into a real Christmas offering, with two unexpected gifts hidden therein.

COSTUMES

Modern and appropriate to the age of the characters.

PROPERTIES

Table with books, lamp, box of cigars, hammer.

Desk with desk chair, telephone, tissue paper, Christmas ribbons and cards.

Davenport, two large chairs, a smaller rocking chair.

Work table heaped with articles, among them, a fancy negligée, boudoir cap, dancing slippers, fan, opera hat.

Pedestal table with fern.

Collection of garments for box (among them a coat, fur piece, khaki colored sweater, gown).

Square wooden packing box; also lid with nails.

Letter for Miss Pratt.

Tam, books, fur coat, white sweater for Dora.

Beads for Rose.

Sport stockings for Kate.

SCENE PLOT

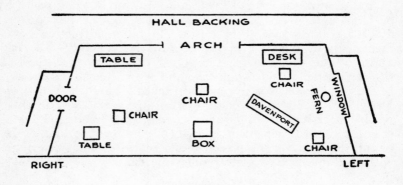

STAGE DIRECTIONS

Up stage means away from footlights; *down stage,* **near** footlights. In the use of *right* and *left,* the actor is supposed to be facing the audience.

BEGGARS CAN'T BE CHOOSERS

SCENE: *Living room of* MRS. BROWN'S *home, where an important business meeting is in session. The members of the committee are engaged in packing a Christmas box for the family of a worthy but needy minister whom fate has assigned to an obscure mountain district. This committee, a division of the Ladies' Aid Society, after soliciting various articles of apparel for the family, has assembled the booty and to the pleasant accompaniment of frank comment upon the contributions and of a judicious flavor of gossip, are assigning the articles to the depths of the heavy wooden box.*

MRS. BROWN'S *pretty living room, with its cheerful rugs and draperies, is a pleasant place for the task. A curtained arch in the rear reveals a hall beyond; on one side of the archway is a long table bearing its lamp, its books, its magazines; on the other side is a desk with telephone, which is heaped with tissue paper and Christmas ribbons. The large wooden box in the foreground, square and uncompromising, has to its right a low rocking-chair and a worktable loaded with contents for the box; to its left, a davenport also bearing its burden of miscellaneous garments and articles. Back of center is a large armchair; left of the davenport is a similar chair. A door at right leads into an adjoining room; a curtained window at left forms the background for a pedestal table with its spreading fern.*

As the curtain rises, MRS. BROWN *and* MRS. DIGBY *are seated upon the davenport, busily sorting the accumulation thereon;* MRS. LEWIS *by the worktable, is similarly engaged;* MISS PRATT, *in the chair by the davenport, is consulting a letter of information.*

MISS PRATT. The minister himself is six feet, two inches, and needs a warm overcoat. (*Turns to* MRS. BROWN.) We have that, haven't we, Mrs. Brown?

MRS. BROWN (*patting a melancholy heap of garments*). We have all the garments for the minister, Miss Pratt. (*Pauses.*) Mr. Brown's old overcoat isn't beautiful, but it's warm. Why, he wore it into the country the other night and said it kept him absolutely comfortable. (*Again she pauses; perhaps it's a prick of conscience.*) Of course, he has a better one which he has discarded; but I think this will do. Don't you, Mrs. Digby?

MRS. DIGBY. Perfectly. When we pack these boxes for poor ministers and their families we can't expect to have new things. (*Pauses.*) My husband is only five feet, eight inches, but his suit is being sent. Six feet, two inches is uncommonly tall, and no man of that height can hope to have his clothes made to order. Beggars can't be choosers.

MISS PRATT (*consulting the letter*). Warm underwear.

MRS. LEWIS. Plenty of that.

MRS. BROWN. Who gave it, Mrs. Lewis?

MRS. LEWIS. It belonged to old Mr. Scroggins and has been shrinking every time it's been washed. So Mrs. Scroggins donated it.

MISS PRATT. Shoes.

MRS. BROWN. A size too small, but perfectly good. It seemed a shame not to use them.

MISS PRATT. Hat.

MRS. LEWIS (*as she holds up an opera hat*). Only this was sent in. (*It collapses.*) Some way, it doesn't seem quite appropriate. Sort of a shut-up effect.

MISS PRATT. Shut-up effect is most appropriate for the victim if he happens to be long-winded. (*Referring to her letter.*) The wife is only five feet, five. (*Fretfully.*) Why can't we have matched-up people!

MRS. BROWN. It really doesn't make any difference when it comes to clothes, does it? We must use what we can get.

MISS PRATT (*referring to letter*). Coat.

MRS. BROWN. One of mine. (*She displays it.*) Such a pretty coat when it was new.

(*A silence.* MRS. LEWIS *looks critically at the unfortunate garment.* MISS PRATT *frankly elevates her nose.*)

MRS. DIGBY. How can you remember so far back?

MISS PRATT (*returning to the inventory*). Dress.

MRS. LEWIS. Mrs. Strong gave us one of hers.

MISS PRATT. *Mrs. Strong?* The two-hundred pound Mrs. Strong?

MRS. LEWIS (*with dignity*). There is only one Mrs. Strong in the congregation.

MISS PRATT. But this minister's wife is registered as five feet, five. Surely she is not correspondingly broad.

MRS. LEWIS. I don't know, I'm sure. Anyway, if the dress doesn't fit, all she has to do is to take it up here— and there—

MISS PRATT. And everywhere. (*As she meditates.*) Great heavens!

MRS. BROWN. We have a fur piece to go with the dress. (*She throws it for effect around her own shoulders.*)

MRS. DIGBY. Ugh! (*Holds her handkerchief to her nose.*) Something is flying.

MRS. BROWN. Dust, probably.

MISS PRATT. Dust? (*Emphatically.*) Moths. (*Flourishes her letter.*) What's been reserved for the seventeen-year-old daughter?

MRS. BROWN. A warm sweater; such a good one, too. Not a worn place in it. (*She exhibits a heavy, unattractive sweater of khaki hue.*)

MISS PRATT (*sarcastically*). Such a pretty color! Looks just like a young girl!

MRS. DIGBY. The petticoat—

MISS PRATT (*interrupting*). Petticoat? Where did you find one?

MRS. DIGBY. Old Mrs. Hutchins.

MISS PRATT. Relic of another generation. I thought so.

MRS. LEWIS (*thoughtfully*). Of course a petticoat these days *is* rather obsolete.

MISS PRATT. But worth reviving on this auspicious occasion. (*Pauses.*) I see. (*Consults the letter.*) What about the dress?

MRS. BROWN. Look! (*She holds up a most attractive*

and modern little gown.) I am surprised at this.

MISS PRATT. It looks ill at ease in the midst of its companions.

MRS. DIGBY (*in surprise*). Why, it's perfectly new and good! Who was so silly as to part with that?

MRS. BROWN. Mrs. Allen. She brought it this morning.

(*There is a silence, which evidently reeks with astonishment.*)

MRS. LEWIS. Mrs. Allen? Our minister's wife?

MRS. BROWN. Yes. I thought that she must have made a mistake, and I told her so.

MRS. LEWIS. How did she answer?

MRS. BROWN. In a very strange way. I couldn't quite understand.

MISS PRATT. Perhaps we can.

MRS. BROWN. She said it was a real sacrifice to part with it.

MRS. DIGBY. That's a queer thing to say.

MRS. BROWN. Isn't it? So I asked her why she gave it.

MRS. LEWIS. How did she answer that?

MRS. BROWN. She smiled and said, "Because it *is* a sacrifice." (*Pauses.*) Sometimes I don't understand Mrs. Allen.

MRS. DIGBY. Neither do I. She did a queer thing at the Ladies' Aid dinner.

MISS PRATT. What did she do?

MRS. DIGBY. Served the strawberries and the ice cream—

MISS PRATT. What's queer about that?

MRS. DIGBY. Nothing queer about the serving, but she gave such large quantities. I was forced to warn her.

MRS. LEWIS. And she paid no attention to the warning. I watched her.

MRS. DIGBY. We are never extravagant at the dinners.

MRS. LEWIS. And she knew it. (*Pauses.*) The same thing happened at the bazaar.

MRS. DIGBY. What!

MRS. LEWIS. She was on my booth, and insisted on marking the articles just what they were really worth.

MISS PRATT. I wonder if she will object to her Christmas present.

MRS. BROWN. She can't.

MRS. DIGBY. And sometimes I wish that we hadn't bothered about collecting so much money. Twenty-five dollars is a liberal Christmas gift.

MRS. LEWIS. Especially when an equal amount goes to her husband.

MISS PRATT. Has it all been collected?

MRS. BROWN. All. I wanted it in gold but Mr. Brown misunderstood and brought it home in bills.

MRS. DIGBY. Did you send it back?

MRS. BROWN. I'll do so later. There's plenty of time before Christmas. By the way, I wonder if I placed the bills in that book on the table. Do you mind looking for them, Mrs. Lewis?

MRS. LEWIS (*moving to the table*). Which book?

MRS. BROWN. The one called *My Unknown Friend*.

MRS. LEWIS (*investigating*). Yes, the money's here. (*Pauses.*) Did you write the card with it?

MRS. BROWN. Oh, I forgot that the card was there. Read it aloud.

MRS. LEWIS (*reads*). "With our Christmas greeting and the hope that this gift will be used for some little extra." (*Pauses.*) What do you mean by extra?

MRS. BROWN. Anything she wants, of course.

MRS. DIGBY (*firmly*). A minister's wife shouldn't have extras.

MRS. BROWN (*offended*). Oh, if anyone can write a better card, she's quite welcome to try.

MISS PRATT. The card's exactly right, and nobody need worry about extras. Twenty-five dollars won't go far these days.

MRS. LEWIS (*laying down the book and returning to her chair*). Having the gold pieces will make it much showier.

MRS. BROWN. I'll have it changed to-morrow.

MISS PRATT. Let's finish up this list. There's a ten-year-old boy, and also a four-year-old girl to dispose of.

MRS. DIGBY (*briskly*). They're already disposed of. (*With a flourish toward the box.*) And already packed. Children's clothes are so much easier to get.

MISS PRATT. And why?

MRS. DIGBY. They outgrow instead of outwear. (*Pauses.*) I had quantities of Jimmy's things to donate.

MRS. BROWN (*sweetly*). Oh, did you? I thought that you made over everything, Mrs. Digby. You're so handy with your needle.

MRS. LEWIS. What shall I do with this stuff? (*She hastily exhibits a fancy boudoir cap, a negligée, a delicate fan, and a pair of high-heeled dancing slippers.*) That flighty Fanny Ferris presented them.

MRS. BROWN (*firmly*). Lay them aside. They're too frivolous for this sort of a box.

MRS. LEWIS (*weakly*). But they *are* pretty and bright; and it might be all right to tuck them in the corners.

MRS. DIGBY. Not at all. We want this box to be practical.

MISS PRATT. Then you have succeeded beyond your fondest expectations.

Through the archway dashes DORA, *seventeen and soubrettish, a gay tam on her curly head, a pile of books under her arm, and a wide-open fur coat displaying a charming school frock.*

DORA. Oh, how quiet you all are! Hello, Miss Pratt. Rose is out in the hall, Mrs. Digby; and so is Kate, Mrs. Lewis. You see, we daughters are hot on your trail.

MRS. BROWN (*as the fuzzy tam is flung on the desk*). Leave your things in the hall, Dora.

DORA. But, mother— (*Crash on the table go the books.*)

MRS. BROWN. In the hall, I say.

DORA. Oh, all right. (*Exit by way of arch, carrying tam and books with her.*)

MRS. DIGBY. Hadn't we better pack these other garments before the girls rush in? They're so demoralizing.

MRS. LEWIS. And so critical.

MISS PRATT. Just the same I should like to hear what they say about this fashion display.

MRS. BROWN (*bringing the articles for the minister to the box*). We'll put these in the box first. (*She duly packs them.*)

MRS. DIGBY. And here are the wife's clothes. (*Together she and* MRS. BROWN *arrange the garments in the box.*)

At this moment, enter DORA, ROSE, *and* KATE, *by way of the arch.* ROSE *and* KATE *are the same type as* DORA. *They are gayly chattering as they enter.*

ROSE. Oh, aren't you having a good time! It looks just like a second-hand shop.

KATE (*to* MRS. LEWIS). Oh, mother! What lovely gay things! (*In a moment she has flung the negligée around her shoulders, placed the boudoir cap on her head, and seized the fan.*)

MRS. LEWIS. Stop, Kate! (KATE *dances up and down.*)

ROSE. And what darling slippers! (*Quickly she removes her own slippers and thrusts her feet into the high-heeled pair before her.*) Oh, they fit exactly. And I feel just like Cinderella.

MRS. DIGBY. You'll ruin your feet in those high-heeled things, Rose.

ROSE. Oh, no, I won't. (*She joins* DORA, *who is examining the pile of clothes laid aside for the minister's daughter.*) What's all this junk?

DORA. A pretty little dress; and everything else—perfectly, unspeakably ugly!

MISS PRATT. Those are for the minister's daughter. She's just your age.

DORA. Why, she doesn't want these things.

MRS. BROWN. Don't be foolish, Dora. It isn't a question of what she wants but what she can get.

MISS PRATT. Her name's Rose, too, so the letter of instructions says—

ROSE. My name! (*Pauses.*) I'd hate that sweater and those ugly cotton stockings, if they were mine.

MRS. DIGBY. Well, they're not yours, and it isn't necessary for you to choose for her. (*Without further ado, she bears the clothes to the box and pushes them in.*)

KATE (*joining the other girls*). Why can't we send her the negligée and the cap and the fan?

ROSE. And the slippers? She'd love the slippers.

MRS. BROWN. You silly girls! Don't you know that a minister's daughter in a little out-of-the-way mountain town can have no possible use for such things?

DORA. She can look at them—

KATE. And dress up in them—

ROSE. And what if she is in a little out-of-the-way town? She's a girl, just the same.

MRS. ALLEN *enters by the archway, bright and smiling, and radiating Christmas cheer.*

MRS. ALLEN. I came right in. I hope you don't mind.

MRS. BROWN. Why, Mrs. Allen, of course not.

MRS. ALLEN. And don't tell me that I'm too late to help in the packing.

MRS. DIGBY. The last things are just deposited.

MRS. ALLEN. Pretty things, I hope.

MRS. BROWN. Practical things, certainly. And practical things really count.

MRS. ALLEN. Do they? I wonder.

DORA. So do I.

MRS. ALLEN. We all, at some time or other, hesitate between the necessary loaf of bread for the body and the white hyacinths for the soul.

KATE. I don't know anything about that; but I *do* know that a practical Christmas gift isn't quite the same as a lovely, frilly, frivolous something that you don't need.

ROSE. And Mrs. Allen! Don't you think that the minister's daughter would love these slippers?

MRS. ALLEN. I do, indeed.

KATE. And Mrs. Allen! Don't you think it would be perfectly all right to send this negligée, and this cap and even the fan?

MRS. ALLEN. Oh, I certainly do.

MRS. DIGBY. But Mrs. Allen—

MRS. ALLEN. Now don't spoil the girls' pleasure, Mrs. Digby. A sprinkling on top of all these pretty things is like a garnish of holly and mistletoe. (*She glances at the desk.*) Oh, have you been wrapping the packages in this pretty way?

MRS. BROWN (*stiffly*). That is for my personal gifts. (*Pauses.*) Shall we go into the other room for a cup of tea? (*She leads the way to right door.*) The girls may have their chance later on. (*She stands aside as the others pass through door into the adjoining room.*) Dora! I almost forgot to tell you about the expressman. He is coming at five, and the box is to go out on the evening train.

DORA. I'll attend to him.

MRS. BROWN. And all he has to do is to nail on the top. The address is already there. The hammer is on the table.

DORA. I understand. (*Exit* MRS. BROWN *by right door.*)

(KATE *is seated on the side of the box, poking here and there among its contents and silently investigating.* ROSE, *still wearing the dancing slippers, is on the davenport, exceedingly thoughtful.* DORA *plunges into reverie.*)

KATE. Goodness—gracious—me!

ROSE. What's the matter?

KATE. This box.

DORA. Quite so. Isn't it a fright?

ROSE. And won't those poor people be frights when they put on all this toggery? (*Pauses.*) I shall never marry a minister.

DORA (*who has been reading the letter left on her chair by* MISS PRATT). He isn't a queer minister, either. This letter says that his health gave way and that he needed the mountain air. Naturally all the money goes to the health fund.

KATE. And they probably like pretty things just as well as we do.

DORA. Of course they do.

313

ROSE. It isn't so much that the things aren't pretty as it's so plainly a charity stunt. Old clothes that nobody wants—

KATE. Or would wear. (*Emphatically.*) I think it's dreadful.

DORA. And this is supposed to be a Christmas box!

ROSE. The kind that radiates peace and good will. (*Pauses.*) It's more likely to start a riot.

KATE. Unless the happy recipients have a sense of humor.

DORA. It makes me think of Pandora and her box. Do you remember the story?

ROSE. Rather. The lady was inquisitive; wasn't she?

DORA. To the extent that she opened the box when she shouldn't have done so.

ROSE. And let out all the little evils that have been pestering the world ever since.

DORA. Well, when the lid is lifted from this box, all of Pandora's little pests will seem like nothing.

KATE. But, Dora! You've forgotten the most important part of the story. At least you've left it out.

DORA. What's that?

KATE. The fact that Hope was in the bottom of the box; and when Hope flew out alongside of all the little evils they didn't have a chance.

DORA. Of course. (*Pauses:*) That *does* make a difference—a big difference. (*Suddenly.*) Girls!

ROSE. What's the matter?

DORA. Let's play Pandora up-to-date!

KATE. How?

DORA. Mix a little Hope into this pestiferous package.

ROSE. You mean—

DORA. Play Pandora up-to-date. She let Hope escape from her box. Let's turn the tables and add Hope to this collection.

KATE. Oh, I see. (*Enthusiastically.*) It would be wonderful.

ROSE. Oh, Dora! Do you mean that we can put something pretty into the box?

Dora. I certainly do. Something that will make it Christmasy and attractive and—

Kate. Do we dare?

Dora (*with a toss of her head*). Dare? I'm Dora in real life, so I might as well have Pandora for my stage name.

Rose. It would be heavenly!

Kate (*jumping up*). Then let's begin right away. The expressman may come at any time.

Rose. And we want to be sure that Hope is securely nailed in.

Dora. Now let's see. (*Quickly.*) First of all, Kate, suppose you wrap up the fan and the negligée and the cap. They're pretty, so why not send them?

Kate. Mrs. Allen said it would be all right. (*She is at the desk.*) Shall I use this paper and ribbon to wrap them?

Dora. Of course. Mother's saving them for her own packages. There are some cards there, too. Write on them.

Kate (*busily wrapping*). I'll wrap the negligée and the cap and the fan all together.

Rose. Put the fan in a separate package. One isn't warm enough in a negligée to need a fan. (*Reluctantly she removes the slippers and slips her feet into her own property.*)

Dora (*taking the slippers*). I'll tuck these slippers into a corner. They won't need to be wrapped.

Kate. What shall I write on the card?

Rose. "To Rose." Isn't that enough? (*Pauses.*) You see, we're not sending it and—

Kate. What are we going to send?

Dora. I know what I intend to donate. One look at that sweater settled me. (*She dashes through the arch into the hall.*)

Kate (*bringing her packages to the box*). These are ready now. Aren't they pretty?

Rose. Lovely. (*They place the packages in the box.*) It does make a difference. Now doesn't it?

Dora *rushes in through the arch. Over her arm is a heavy, modish white sweater.*

Kate. Why, Dora! Your new sweater!

DORA. Of course. I wouldn't send her any other kind.

ROSE. But what will you do?

DORA. Wear my old one. (*Emphatically.*) I'm glad to wear it. (*She lays it in the box, after taking out the khaki-colored atrocity and throwing it over a nearby chair.*) It's too big to wrap; and I'll stick a card on it. (*She goes to the desk.*)

ROSE (*as she takes a string of lovely beads from around her neck*). I love these beads more than anything I have. So I want *her* to have them. (*Goes to the desk.*) I'll write on the card, "From one Rose to another Rose."

DORA (*as she returns to the box*). Here's the card for my sweater. This is what I wrote. (*Reads.*) "May this gift from somebody your own age bring you real Christmas happiness." (*Places the card on the sweater.*)

ROSE. That's sweet.

KATE. Wait a minute. (*Out into the hall she hurries.*)

DORA (*inspecting the box approvingly*). It really begins to look iike something.

ROSE (*joining her*). Doesn't it, though? (*She puts in her package.*) There goes my string of beads. (*Unconsciously a little sigh escapes her.*)

DORA. Just think how crazy that girl will be when she opens that package.

ROSE. Not half so crazy as I am to send it!

Enter KATE *through arch, carrying a package, which she unwraps as she walks.*

KATE. I spent all my allowance on these; but ever since I've seen the awful stockings for that girl my conscience has pricked me. (*She displays two pair of beautiful sport stockings.*)

DORA. They're lovely. Oh, Kate, what a peach you are!

KATE (*going to the desk*). It's lots of fun just to give them.

DORA (*pondering*). Now let me see. Is there anything else here? Any little extra? Oh, I know. (*In a moment she has taken a box of cigars from the table.*) Dad has a brand new box of cigars; and he won't mind.

Rose (*a bit dubious*). But does the minister smoke?

Dora. Maybe he'd like to; and anyway he could do it at home where the parishioners couldn't see. (*Packs cigars in the wooden box.*)

Kate (*coming from desk with her package and putting it into the box*). There! (*Pauses.*) Is that all we have?

Dora (*again pondering*). Let me see. (*She wanders to the table and looks it over.*) Perhaps— (*Suddenly.*) Oh, the very thing! (*She seizes a book.*) Here's *My Unknown Friend.* We've all read it, and it will be nice to tuck it into that empty corner. (*As she suits the action to the word, the bell rings.*) That's the expressman. I'll let him in. (*Exit through arch.*)

Rose. Let's put on the cover, so that it will be ready for him to nail. (*They place the cover on the box.*) Oh, the nails are already in it; so all he needs is the hammer.

Dora *and the expressman enter from the hall.*

Dora. Here you are, Mr. Kelly.

Kate. Lid all ready for you.

Rose. Nails all there.

Dora (*bringing the hammer*). And here's the hammer.

Mr. Kelly. Sure, an' it's mighty few boxes already fixed that I'm a gettin' these days. Folks be careless-like at Christmas time. (*His words are punctuated by blows of the hammer.*) There!

Dora. Strong enough to hold, Mr. Kelly?

Mr. Kelly. Strong enough to be goin' to New York.

Kate. Oh, that's fine.

Rose. And you'll get it to the evening train?

Mr. Kelly. Sure, miss. (*He pushes the box into the hall.*) There's a-plenty of time.

Dora. I'll go to the door with you. (*The two disappear through the archway.*)

Kate (*flinging herself on the davenport*). A little while ago, I was hoping that the box wouldn't reach the minister by Christmas—it was so hopeless. But now everything's different.

Rose (*standing at the archway and looking after* Dora). Isn't it, though? (*Pauses.*) I've had such fun.

Mrs. Brown *enters from right.*

Mrs. Brown. Was that the expressman, girls?

Kate (*rising*). Yes, Mrs. Brown. Dora's just showing him out. (*A door slams off stage, center.*) There! He's gone.

Enter Miss Pratt, Mrs. Allen, Mrs. Digby, *and* Mrs. Lewis, *two by two, right.*

Mrs. Brown (*addressing them*). The box is gone, ladies, so we may feel relieved that one task is off our minds.

Enter Dora *by archway.*

(Mrs. Allen *and* Mrs. Digby *seat themselves on the davenport.* Mrs. Lewis *returns to her chair by the work table; and* Miss Pratt, *picking up the letter of instruction, is once more seated, left of the davenport. The girls withdraw to the back of the room.*)

Mrs. Lewis (*in surprise as she lifts the discarded sweater from the chair*). Girls! You've forgotten something.

Dora. Oh, no, we haven't. We left that out on purpose.

Mrs. Digby. On purpose? That good sweater?

Dora. We substituted another one.

Mrs. Brown. Another one! (*Sharply.*) Where did you get another one to substitute?

(*She may be excused for her sharp tone; she has just discovered the havoc on her desk and the surprising disappearance of tissue paper and ribbons.*)

Dora (*sitting on arm of large chair*). I gave mine instead.

Mrs. Brown. Yours? You mean the old one, I suppose.

Dora. Oh, no, I don't. I mean my new one—the white one—

Mrs. Brown. Dora!

DORA. I was just determined that the girl should not wear that ugly—despisable—sweater!

MRS. BROWN. It was not your affair.

DORA. But I made it my affair.

MRS. BROWN. Dora!

DORA. I don't mean to be saucy, mother; but I *did* want her to have my white sweater.

MRS. BROWN. Then you'll do without.

DORA. Of course. The most pleasure of all comes from doing without and giving it to her.

MRS. ALLEN (*softly*). Bravo, my dear, bravo!

ROSE (*as she sits on the other arm of the large chair*). And that's not all. (*Pauses.*) I gave my beads, mother.

MRS. DIGBY. Your birthday beads? (*Pauses.*) I don't understand why you ever did such an unnecessary, ridiculous thing.

ROSE. But I understand; and that's all that counts.

KATE (*standing back of* MRS. LEWIS). My sport stockings, mother. They've gone, too.

MRS. LEWIS. They had never been worn! (*In her tone there is the note of tragedy.*)

KATE. Of course they hadn't been worn. That's why I sent them.

DORA. And I tucked in a box of dad's cigars—

(MRS. BROWN *hurries to the table.*)

MRS. BROWN. That new box on the table?

DORA. Of course. Dad won't care. (MRS. BROWN *is evidently in a disturbed frame of mind. She hovers over the table, touching this and that and displaying a suppressed emotion and agitation.*) What's the matter, mother?

MRS. BROWN. Has any one of you seen that book— (*turns to the others*) the book we were speaking of a little while ago? Oh, you remember why I mentioned it and how I used it—and—

DORA. Do you mean *My Unknown Friend*?

MRS. BROWN. Yes, yes. (*A sudden terror seizes her.*) Dora, you didn't—you couldn't—

DORA. I sent it, too, if that's what you mean.

MRS. BROWN. Sent it? Oh, Dora, how terrible! How—— Oh, what shall I do?

DORA. Why, mother, what do you mean by "terrible"? We've all read the book.

MRS. BROWN (*wildly*). We must send for it right **away**! We must get it before the box is opened!

DORA (*rising*). How can we get it before the **box is** opened? Why, mother! You told me yesterday that **we'd** pass on the book to somebody else.

MRS. BROWN (*sinking into the chair*). But I had **hidden** something inside of that book.

MRS. DIGBY What shall we do? Oh, what shall **we do?**

MRS. LEWIS. It was a poor place to put it, Mrs. **Brown.**

MISS PRATT. And it's all quite like the irony of **fate.**

MRS. ALLEN. What dreadful thing has happened? **Do** you mind telling me?

MRS. BROWN. I suppose we shall have to tell you **now.**

MRS. DIGBY. Of course.

MRS. LEWIS. It's just too unfortunate that it's all happened.

MISS PRATT. But Mrs. Allen will see the other side.

MRS. ALLEN. I'm sure I shall.

MRS. BROWN (*after a moment*). Well, you see, Mrs. Allen, we'd planned a little Christmas gift for you—a small money gift so that you could buy just what you wanted.

MRS. ALLEN. Oh, how lovely of you!

MRS. BROWN. Wait until I finish. The money, in bills, was there in that book——

MRS. LEWIS. I still say that it was a strange place **to** put it.

MRS. ALLEN. Not at all. I can understand how **Mrs.** Brown would thrust it into the first available place——

MRS. BROWN. Until I could have it changed into **gold.** I had intended to give it to Mr. Brown to-night.

MRS. ALLEN. And Dora has packed the book. I see.

MRS. BROWN (*rising*). Of course the money will be re-placed. And——

MRS. ALLEN (*rising and going to* MRS. BROWN). Oh, no, it won't. (*Slips her arm through* MRS. BROWN'S.) Why should it be?

MRS. DIGBY. Why shouldn't it be?

MRS. LEWIS. For we had wanted you to buy some little extra for yourself.

MRS. ALLEN. Oh, my dear, kind friends! Can't you see that the most wonderful extra in the world would be—somebody else's happiness.

MRS. BROWN. You mean—?

MRS. ALLEN. That the money will bring that other minister's wife so much real happiness and satisfaction that— Oh, you couldn't have given me a lovelier thing!

MISS PRATT. An unusual point of view, Mrs. Allen.

MRS. ALLEN. Why so? Think what you've done for me.

MRS. BROWN. Through a young girl's foolishness.

MRS. ALLEN. Through a young girl's intuition. (*She reaches out a hand to* DORA.) For an opportunity is the choicest gift that can come to one. You have given me this opportunity, and I can't begin to tell you how grateful I am.

MRS. DIGBY (*a bit ungraciously*). Well, of course, if you feel that way about it, we can do nothing but let the money go in the box.

MRS. ALLEN. Of course you can't. And it is what I most want. Doesn't that mean anything?

MISS PRATT. It ought to mean a great deal as regards Christmas gifts; but it doesn't.

MRS. ALLEN. And we must confess that these three girls have been inspired in their giving by sacrifice. That's what makes this Christmas box a real one.

DORA. We called it Pandora's box, Mrs. Allen.

MRS. ALLEN. And why?

ROSE. Because all the evils were shut up in it.

DORA. And because we placed Hope with all the other things.

KATE. Pandora up-to-date, you see.

(*At this point, the telephone bell rings sharply.*)

DORA. Shall I answer it?

MRS. BROWN. No. (*She hurries to the desk and takes down the receiver.*)

MRS. ALLEN (*as* DORA *and* ROSE *pull her into the large chair and sit on either arm*). Pandora up-to-date! Then Pandora met a responsibility wisely—

MISS PRATT. And grasped an opportunity.

MRS. BROWN (*at telephone*). Yes, John, yes. (*Pauses.*) What? (*Pauses.*) In the old overcoat? The one you wore to the country the other night? (*Pauses.*) You left it there? How much? (*Pauses.*) Twenty-five dollars! Well, it's gone. (*Pauses.*) Yes, gone. In the box we've just packed. (*Pauses.*) No, the box is gone. How did I know? (*Pauses.*) And I gave the very oldest one you had. No, there's nothing to be done. I'll explain later. (*Hangs up receiver and turns to the others.*) John left twenty-five dollars in the pocket of that old overcoat.

DORA. How perfectly heavenly!

MRS. BROWN. Heavenly! Your father doesn't think so.

DORA. Wait till I explain to him. (*Pauses.*) And, mother—

MRS. BROWN. Yes?

DORA. I'm glad I heard you say, "There's nothing to be done." (*Crosses to her.*) It sounded final.

MRS. BROWN. It had to be final. The money's gone.

DORA. And won't it mean a lot to that other minister?

MRS. ALLEN. It will, indeed. Oh, it's a wonderful box! (*Rises and goes to center.*)

ROSE (*following her*). Isn't it?

KATE. With Hope all tucked away in it.

MRS. ALLEN (*half to herself*). Hope—peace—good will. (*Pauses.*) And a merry Christmas!

CURTAIN

THE CHRISTMAS DOLLS' REVUE

A ONE-ACT CHRISTMAS PLAY

By

Effa E. Preston

PRODUCTION RIGHTS

THE CHRISTMAS DOLLS' REVUE

For twenty girls and extras

CHARACTERS

(In the order in which they first speak)

NONA...............................*The nurse doll*
JULIA.........................*The fashion model doll*
PEPITA..........................*The Mexican doll*
BETTY...........................*The mamma doll*
MOLLY }
POLLY } ....*The twin dolls*
AGOONA..........................*The Eskimo doll*
MARY JANE......................*The farmerette doll*
HULDAH ....*The Dutch doll*
EDEWINA...............*The spoiled prima donna doll*
MARIE...........................*The French doll*
DORABELLA.......................*The dancer doll*
MRS. SANTA CLAUS..............*In charge of the dolls*
MISS LACY
MISS BAKS
MISS HILENE } ....*Department store buyers*
MISS WIELDS
MISS CALTMAN
TESSIE }
BESSIE } ....*Mrs. Santa's maids*

Any number of extra model dolls

TIME—*Early evening, about a week before Christmas.*

PLACE—*One of Santa Claus's stockrooms.*

TIME OF PLAYING—*Thirty minutes.*

COSTUMES AND CHARACTERISTICS

Nona, the nurse, wears a Red Cross uniform. Julia, the model, is a beautiful little girl, elaborately dressed in the height of the current style. Pepita, a dark-haired, black-eyed girl, wears a colorful Mexican costume. Betty, the mamma doll, is a plump girl, who wears a long, plain dark dress and a white apron. Molly and Polly, the twins, look and dress alike and wear their hair in curls. Their costume is a gayly colored play suit, white socks, and white slippers. They often speak in unison. Agoona, a stout, short, dark girl, wears an Eskimo suit, parka, and boots. Mary Jane, the farmerette, wears blue slacks, a white blouse, and sandals. Huldah, a blond girl, wears a Dutch peasant's costume. Edwina, a very pretty but spoiled little girl, is elaborately and expensively dressed, with a long and conspicuous string of beads around her neck. Marie, the French doll, wears an attractive French peasant's costume. Dorabella, a charming little girl with a modest, pleasing manner, wears a white, ruffled dress and a pair of black bedroom slippers, which are later replaced by bright red dancing slippers.

Mrs. Santa, the department store buyers, and the two maids are parts that should be played by tall girls, a little older than those who play the dolls. Mrs. Santa is stout and matronly, with a slightly bewildered manner, and wears a pretty flowered dress. Miss Lacy, Miss Baks, Miss Hilene, Miss Wields, and Miss Caltman wear smart street suits and hats. Tessie and Bessie wear blue uniforms, with red caps and aprons. The extra model dolls, used in Julia's fashion show, wear ultra-fashionable outfits, not quite as elaborate as Julia's.

PROPERTIES

GENERAL: A slightly raised platform, two tall, trimmed Christmas trees, eighteen or twenty straight-backed chairs.

PERSONAL: For Molly, a key; for Mrs. Santa, a large sewing bag containing Dorabella's red slippers and a pair of scissors; for Tessie and Bessie, several keys apiece, a large rubber mat of the type used in athletic stunts.

MUSIC

The music used in the play may be supplied by a piano or a phonograph located off stage in the wings. The following selections are needed:

The Dancing Doll (Poldini)—Victor Record 1981

Parade of the Wooden Soldiers (Jessel)—Columbia Record 35719

March from "The Nutcracker Suite" (Tschaikovsky)—Victor Record 22168

In "Songs Worth While," T. S. Denison & Company, publishers

Deck the Halls with Boughs of Holly

Old Zip Coon

The Quilting Party

Sleep, Baby, Sleep

Softly Now the Light of Day

NOTE ON DANCES—No directions are given for the dances and the drill since, in most schools, the physical training director usually prefers to direct all such activities. It is essential that the girl who plays Dorabella be a good dancer and the one who plays Edwina, a good singer.

STAGE DIRECTIONS

Up stage means away from footlights; *down stage,* near footlights. In the use of *right* and *left,* the player is supposed to be facing the audience.

THE CHRISTMAS DOLLS' REVUE

SCENE: *One of* SANTA CLAUS'S *stockrooms, early one evening about a week before Christmas. It has two doors at right and left respectively. At center rear is a slightly raised platform, at the back and on opposite ends of which stand two tall, handsomely decorated Christmas trees. Near the platform, a little down left, is a straight-backed chair. Scattered about the front of the stage are a dozen or more similar chairs. Throughout the play, the stage lights are full up.*

At rise of curtain, the dolls NONA, JULIA, PEPITA, BETTY, MOLLY *and* POLLY, AGOONA, MARY JANE, HULDAH, EDWINA, *and* MARIE *are seated on chairs down front. They are all wound up for speaking and are holding an indignation meeting.*

NONA. It's up to us, as self-respecting dolls, to do something about it.

JULIA. Children are not like what they used to be. All they care about today is something that goes fast and makes a big noise.

PEPITA. They do not care for pretty things.

BETTY. Imagine a little girl's not wanting all the dolls she can get!

MOLLY *and* POLLY (*in unison*). Just imagine it!

AGOONA. They like bears better. If they lived in Labrador where I came from, they'd see all the bears they care about.

MARY JANE. Poor Santa gets so discouraged. He used to give a little girl a pretty doll and she was happy; and Santa was happy. Now nobody's happy.

HULDAH. Chemistry sets and cannon and skates and stuff like that! Not that Dutch children don't need skates, but ice skates—not those noisy roller ones that chase you off the sidewalk.

EDWINA. Little girls don't appreciate beauty any more. Santa's very discouraged.

JULIA. So am I. What's the use of being a model if nobody looks at you and says, "Isn't she lovely!"?

MARY JANE. I think the store people are to blame. Why don't they fill their windows with us?

MARIE. It's horrible—little girls playing with trucks and guns!

EDWINA. What can we do about it?

NONA. I don't know, but we've got to do something, Edwina.

MOLLY and POLLY (in unison). Ask Dorabella. She'll know what to do.

EDWINA (crossly). Dorabella won't know any more than the rest of us. Why do you twins, and all the rest of you, think she is so wonderful?

MOLLY and POLLY (in unison). Edwina, you're jealous of Dorabella because she's such a marvelous dancer.

EDWINA. Don't be silly.

MARIE. Don't be jealous. And Dorabella's smart, too.

EDWINA (coldly). Oh, I don't know.

BETTY (looking around). Where is Dorabella?

NONA. Looking for her dancing slippers. She lost them; or somebody took them. All she has to wear now is a pair of black bedroom slippers.

MOLLY and POLLY (in unison). Give us three guesses, Nona, and we'll tell you who took her dancing slippers.

JULIA. Twins, be still, or I'll pull out your keys and let you run down. This is no time for quarrels.

PEPITA. That Molly and Polly, they could talk without being wound up!

MARY JANE. If we could only talk to the store people!

HULDAH. The only way Santa can tell what to take is what the store people say. Maybe you've got something there, Mary Jane.

MARY JANE. I have, but I don't know what to do with it.

AGOONA. Wait till Dorabella comes. She'll know.

EDWINA (*still crossly*). Dorabella! Dorabella! I'm sick of hearing about Dorabella.

MARIE (*looking at* EDWINA). Now I know why children don't like dolls.

DORABELLA *enters at left, wearing her black bedroom slippers.*

DORABELLA. Hello, everybody.

ALL THE OTHERS (*in unison*). Hello, Dorabella.

JULIA. Did you find your slippers?

DORABELLA. No, but Mrs. Santa is going to bring me a new pair in a few minutes. I've been practicing a new dance. I think Santa will like it.

PEPITA. We're having a meeting.

DORABELLA. How nice! Just like people! What about?

NONA. It's very sad, but we dolls aren't as popular as we used to be. Little girls want toys such as their brothers have—you know: noisy things that go bang, bang and jump around.

DORABELLA (*sadly*). Yes, I know.

BETTY. Mary Jane thinks it's the fault of the store people for not showing more dolls.

MARY JANE. And we're going to do something about it.

DORABELLA. Good! What?

AGOONA. We've left that to you.

DORABELLA. To me, Agoona? But I'm a dancing doll, not a—a—decider of what to do about things.

EDWINA (*quickly*). See? I told you she wouldn't know.

DORABELLA. Let's ask Mrs. Santa.

BETTY. That's a good idea. I know she thinks it's a crime for children not to play with dolls any more. (*Looks off left.*) Here she comes now.

Enter MRS. SANTA *at left. She carries a sewing bag.*

MRS. SANTA. Well, well, here you are all wound up. Don't wear out your springs, talking so much.

NONA (*bitterly*). It won't matter if we do. Nobody wants dolls any more.

MRS. SANTA. Now, don't you dolls take things too seriously.

NONA. Santa read in the paper that only one third as many dolls were given for Christmas as used to be. Nobody asks for them.

MRS. SANTA. Don't worry, Nona. Dorabella, here are your new slippers. Please don't lose these, for I haven't time to make any more this year. (*Takes a pair of red dancing slippers from sewing bag and hands them to* DORABELLA.)

DORABELLA. Oh, thank you, Mrs. Santa. They are lovely. (*Examines them admiringly.*)

(EDWINA *watches closely as* DORABELLA *places slippers behind the tree at left.*)

MRS. SANTA. You must show Santa your new dance tomorrow, Dorabella. It's very good.

DORABELLA. I hope he'll like it. Mrs. Santa, before you go, may we ask you a question?

MRS. SANTA. Of course.

DORABELLA. Nona and Mary Jane have a wonderful idea. They say we must do something to make dolls more popular.

MRS. SANTA. What?

DORABELLA. That's what we want to ask you. What can we do—to—to—?

HULDAH (*completing the sentence*). To advertise ourselves.

MRS. SANTA (*flustered*). Dear me! I never do much thinking; Santa attends to all that. We could call him in and ask him what he thinks you should do—but he isn't home. He won't be back till day after tomorrow. (*Struck with an unpleasant thought.*) Oh, my goodness! Tonight the five most important buyers from the five most important stores are coming here to decide what to get from Santa to put in their windows next week. I shall have to talk to them, and I always get so nervous. They're such important people and so smart!

DORABELLA (*excitedly*). Mrs. Santa, did you say, "buyers from big stores"?

MRS. SANTA. Dear me, yes! There will be Miss Lacy, Miss Baks, Miss Hilene, Miss Wields, and Miss Caltman. They are very fussy.

DORABELLA. Mrs. Santa, no matter what they look at or what they order, will you please bring them in here tonight before they go? You can say you want to show them some new dolls.

MRS. SANTA. I can, but what good would it do?

DORABELLA. I'm not sure, but it can't do any harm. We'll put on a show, and if they like us, maybe they'll order dolls for their show windows.

AGOONA. That's a good idea.

HULDAH. It certainly is.

MOLLY *and* POLLY (*in unison*). Didn't we tell you Dorabella would fix things?

MRS. SANTA. All right, Dorabella, but don't tell me any more about it. I get all confused. I'll bring them in here in just two hours. The rest is up to you.

DORABELLA. Thank you, Mrs. Santa.

ALL THE OTHER DOLLS (*in unison*). Thank you, Mrs. Santa.

(MRS. SANTA *goes off at left, leaving her bag hanging on back of chair up left.*)

JULIA. What are we going to do, Dorabella? You may tell me. I can't get more confused than I am now.

DORABELLA. Can't we put on a show for the buyers?

ALL THE OTHERS (*except* EDWINA). Why not?

DORABELLA. Betty, as a mamma doll, you can make the speech. Edwina, you can sing. The rest of you can either sing or dance. Julia, get some more well-dressed dolls and put on a fashion show. That ought to suit anybody.

EDWINA (*sweetly*). Of course, Dorabella, you will dance?

DORABELLA (*apologetically*). Well, there isn't much else I can do.

PEPITA. Of course she'll dance.

NONA. Let's go into the back room before the maids come and take out our keys. We can decide just what to do and then practice. Two hours will be gone before we know it.

MARIE. They certainly will.

Exeunt all the dolls at right except EDWINA. *She waits a moment, then takes the red slippers from behind the tree and puts them back into* MRS. SANTA'S *sewing bag hanging on the chair.* MOLLY *and* POLLY *re-enter at right and see what she is doing.*

MOLLY *and* POLLY (*in amazement*). O-oh!

EDWINA (*hearing them, speaks fiercely*). Listen, you twins! What do you mean by spying on me like this?

MOLLY. What do you mean by stealing Dorabella's new slippers? I'll bet you took the old ones, too.

EDWINA. I'll tell you what I mean. I'm sick and tired of hearing Dorabella praised all the time. No matter what goes on here in Santa land, Dorabella dances. Well, believe me, this is one show in which Dorabella will *not* dance!

MOLLY. But—

EDWINA (*interrupts, taking scissors from sewing bag on chair back*). Do you see these? If either one of you breathes a word about this or tells where the slippers are, I'll cut off your curls. Then who'd want you?

POLLY (*hastily*). Oh, we won't tell, Edwina. You know we won't tell.

EDWINA. They won't be found in here until the show is over. Now, remember: not a whisper.

MOLLY *and* POLLY (*in concert, meekly*). No, Edwina.

SEVERAL DOLLS (*calling from off right*). Edwina! Hey, Edwina! Come on.

Exit EDWINA *at right, leaving the twins standing in scared uncertainty.* NONA *enters at right and stares at them curiously. Then she sees the sewing bag, opens it, takes out the slippers, and holds them up. She carries them to the right-hand tree and puts them in the crotch of a branch high up on the tree. She smiles at the twins and exits at right.*

POLLY. Molly, we've got to tell Edwina. She'll think we did it.

MOLLY. We will *not* tell Edwina. She is a disagreeable, hateful doll, and I wish she'd get the measles or the whooping cough, so she couldn't sing.

POLLY. But she'll cut off our curls. I don't want my curls cut off, Molly.

MOLLY. Polly, I'm ashamed of you.

POLLY. I'm sorry, honest, I am; but I've got to tell Edwina.

(MOLLY, *who is standing back of* POLLY, *suddenly reaches up and pretends to remove the key from* POLLY'S *back, actually taking it out of her own pocket. She holds it up as she walks around* POLLY *and faces her.*)

MOLLY. You won't tell anybody anything until this show is over. (POLLY *tries vainly to speak, but no sound comes from her moving lips.* MOLLY *takes her by the hand.*) Come on; we've got to practice. I'll say you just caught a cold and lost your voice. And don't let me catch you even looking at Edwina. Understand? Look! I'm swallowing the key. (*Pretends to swallow key.*)

(POLLY *nods a forlorn assent, and they exeunt at right.*)

The curtain is lowered for a few minutes to indicate the lapse of two hours. During the interval, the chairs at the

*front of the stage are moved to the sides, where they are
arranged in semicircles, and extra chairs are placed in a
row along the backdrop. When the curtain rises,* MRS.
SANTA *enters at left, followed by the buyers—*MISS LACY,
MISS BAKS, MISS HILENE, MISS WIELDS, *and* MISS CALT-
MAN. MRS. SANTA *waves them to seats.*

MRS. SANTA. Please sit here at the sides, ladies, and
I shall bring out our very newest dolls. I'm sure you will
like them. (*Sees her bag hanging on back of chair.*)
Goodness! There's my sewing bag. I couldn't imagine
where I'd left it. I'm so forgetful. (*Picks up the bag.*)

MISS LACY. You must have a great deal on your mind.

MRS. SANTA (*laughing*). And I haven't much mind,
I'm afraid.

MISS BAKS. I think the nicest things we've seen were
those red fire engines.

MISS HILENE. And the big yellow steam shovels.

MISS WIELDS. I liked the motor boats best.

MISS CALTMAN. It's very kind of you to show us the
dolls, Mrs. Santa, but you must admit they're not very
popular these days. This is a mechanical age.

MRS. SANTA. Well, dolls are mechanical—sort of—
aren't they? Anyway, I'm still old-fashioned enough to
think every little girl should have a doll to love and care
for.

MISS LACY. Oh, dolls are all right, but give me—

MRS. SANTA (*interrupting*). Shh! They're coming.

*To the music of Poldini's "Dancing Doll," the twelve
dolls file on stage at right and take seats along the backdrop
and up left and right.* DORABELLA *is the last to enter and
is in her stocking feet.* EDEWINA *glances at the bag in*
MRS. SANTA'S *lap and smiles complacently.*

MRS. SANTA. These dolls are mechanical. They walk,
talk, sing, dance, and even think, when wound up. They
will give you a little exhibition of what they can do.

MISS WIELDS. How unusual!

Mrs. Santa (*proudly*). They are unusual dolls, Miss Wields. May I introduce them? From left to right—or is it right to left? I always get directions confused—you see Dorabella, our famous dancing doll; Nona, the nurse; Polly and Molly, the twins; Huldah, the Dutch doll; Marie from France; Pepita from Mexico; Agoona from Labrador; Julia, the model doll; Mary Jane, the farmerette; Betty, the mamma doll; and Edwina, who sings. (*Each doll rises and bows as her name is called.*) These dolls have others outside waiting to help them, no doubt. Now all we have to do is just sit back and listen.

(*The buyers applaud politely, but it is plain to see they are bored. All the dolls stand and sing the following "Greeting Song" to the air of "Deck the Halls with Boughs of Holly."*)

GREETING SONG

1.

Ladies, ladies, we've been thinking
    What a jolly Christmas this would be
If a doll were in the stocking
    Of just ev'ry little girl you see.
We can help to make the children
    Much more gentle and more kind.
Why buy skates and guns and trumpets?
    Better far to keep us dolls in mind.

2.

Ladies, ladies, we've been thinking
    You all know it pays to advertise,
So we're asking you to order
    Lot of dolls for Christmas, if you're wise.
In each stocking by the fireplace,
    Hung from mantelshelf above,

One of us should be there waiting
For some happy little girl to love.

(The buyers applaud politely but not enthusiastically, as the dolls sit.)

BETTY *(coming down to center front and addressing the buyers)*. Ladies, as you see, I am a mamma doll. Naturally I feel very much hurt that little girls no longer wish to be mamma to a pretty doll. If this keeps up, all the little girls in the world will be tomboys; and won't that be sad? You ought to do something about it. Fill your windows with pretty dolls and put those noisy toys down cellar where they belong, or give them just to boys. What is Christmas without dolls? Do trucks and fire engines and steam rollers make you think of peace on earth and good will to men? I hope not. Ladies, please think over what I have said before you decide what to put in your windows next week. *(She returns to her seat.)*

(AGOONA, MARIE, HULDAH, and PEPITA march down front, form a line, and in turn address the buyers.)

AGOONA. I am from the far North where the winds blow cold and the snow is deep. I am an Eskimo. My name is Agoona.

MARIE. My home was once in France. All little French girls love dolls. My name is Marie.

HILDA. My name is Hilda, and I come from Holland, the land of tulips and windmills, of storks and canals.

PEPITA. I am from Mexico, the land of cactus plants and high mountains, the land of song and dance. My name is Pepita.

ALL FOUR *(in unison)*. We are your good neighbors. We long to make your children happy. Perhaps through us they may become interested in our countries. Now we shall do an old American dance for you.

(The four do a gay little dance to the music of "Old Zip

Coon" and return to their seats... - The applause is a bit louder than before.)

NONA (*coming down to front*). If any of you needed a nurse's care, I should be glad to give it to you, but you are all looking very well, I am happy to see. May I sing for you? (*The pianist off stage strikes a chord, and* NONA *sings "Beauty Fades" to the air of "The Quilting Party."*)

BEAUTY FADES

1.

There are dolls who dress in velvet;
    There are dolls with golden hair;
There are dolls who dance and sing divinely,
    But, alas, they do not wear.
Chorus
    I'm unbreakable and tough;
    You can treat me very rough.
Beauty fades and dainty limbs are broken;
    I am made of sterner stuff.

(*All the dolls repeat the chorus as follows:*)

    She's unbreakable and tough;
    You can treat her very rough.
Beauty fades and dainty limbs are broken;
    She is made of sterner stuff.

2.

There are dolls just ornamental;
    Every nursery needs a nurse.
There are dolls that cost a lot of money.
    But I'm easy on your purse.

(*The chorus is sung twice as before.* NONA *returns to her seat. The applause is a little louder.*)

MARY JANE (*coming down to front and addressing the buyers*). I am a farmerette. Playing with me may inspire little girls to make gardens. Who knows? And I don't soil easily, and I'm quite unbreakable, too. I'm a good doll for a rough child; I can take it. I am a good example. Every time a little girl looks at me she'll remember that people have to work to raise food for a hungry world. I'll keep her from growing up lazy, I hope. We can't all be beautiful and dance and sing, but we can all work. (*She returns to her chair amid loud applause.*)

MOLLY (*comes down to front, leading* POLLY *by the hand*). Ladies, I'm Molly. I'm sorry to say my twin sister, Polly, has a very bad cold. She's lost her voice. Poor Polly! She has so many things she'd like to say. She can't sing, of course, and she never was a very good dancer, but I'll tell you what we'll do. We're both very athletic, so we'll show you some stunts.

MOLLY *claps her hands, and the two maids,* TESSIE *and* BESSIE, *enter at right, bringing a rubber mat, which they place on the floor at center front. Then they take positions down extreme right.*

MOLLY. Now we'll show you what good muscles we have. Music, please.

(*From off stage comes the music of Jessel's "Parade of the Wooden Soldiers," to which the twins perform handsprings, somersaults, and other stunts commonly done in elementary gymnasium classes. At the end, they bow low to the buyers, while* TESSIE *and* BESSIE *advance, roll up the mat, and carry it off at right. Loud applause.*)

EDWINA (*comes down front with a theatrical air*). My name is Edwina, and it will make me very happy to sing for you. (*As the pianist strikes up the music,* EDWINA *sings "Sleep, Dollies, Sleep" to the air of "Sleep, Baby, Sleep."*)

SLEEP, DOLLIES, SLEEP

1.

Sleep, dollies, sleep,
The shepherd watches his sheep.
The fairies are shaking the dreamland tree,
And down fall dreams upon you and me.
Sleep, dollies, sleep.

2.

Sleep, dollies, sleep.
The bright stars guard will keep.
The moon shines down from the silent sky,
And only Santa is passing by.
Sleep, dollies, sleep.

As EDWINA *returns to her chair, the applause is loud. The music changes to the march from Tschaikovsky's "Nutcracker Suite," while* JULIA *marches down to center front and is joined by an even number of model dolls, half of whom enter at right and the other half at left. They form two horizontal lines behind* JULIA, *facing front.*

JULIA. We are the model dolls, and we are about to give you a fashion show. Watch us closely as we parade before you, and learn what the well-dressed doll will wear.

(*The dolls, led by* JULIA, *parade about the stage, marching to the music, counter-marching, actually doing a drill, but with the outstretched arms and mincing steps of a professional model. They are graceful, but each movement is exaggerated. At the end of the parade, they bow and go off as they entered.* JULIA *acknowledges the loud applause gracefully.*)

DORABELLA (*coming down to front timidly and speaking*

apologetically as the buyers glance curiously at her stocking feet). I am going to dance for you, but I have lost the lovely slippers Mrs. Santa gave me just a few hours ago. Will you forgive me if I dance in my stocking feet?

NONA (quickly). Dorabella, you left your slippers under the tree, didn't you?

DORABELLA. Yes, I did, but they're not there now.

NONA (*pointing*). What's that up in the tree? It looks like a pair of red dancing slippers from where I sit.

(DORABELLA *goes to the tree, looks where* NONA *points, and takes down the slippers. She puts them on, smiling happily.*)

DORABELLA. Thank you, Nona. They're so pretty I guess they thought they belonged on the tree.

(EDWINA *is looking puzzled and angry. She glares at the twins, who look straight ahead. To the music of "The Dancing Doll,"* DORABELLA *does a very pretty dance, which the buyers applaud enthusiastically.*)

MISS BAKS (*as* DORABELLA *goes back to her seat*). Mrs. Santa, we were wrong. You and Santa are right. We do need more dolls for Christmas!

MISS HILENE. We certainly do!

THE OTHER BUYERS (*in unison*). We'll take dolls— lots of dolls.

ALL THE DOLLS (*in concert*). Oh, thank you, ladies.

MISS CALTMAN. It is our duty to prevent little girls from becoming mechanical-minded. They must have dolls.

ALL THE DOLLS (*in concert*). Thank you.

(*The twelve dolls stand in their places and sing "Good Night" to the air of "Softly Now the Light of Day."*)

GOOD NIGHT

1.

Now, good night; our work is done,
And a victory we've won.
Every little girl shall see
One of us upon her tree.

2.

To our friends, both large and small,
Merry Christmas wish we all.
Peace on earth, good will to men
Fill our hearts with joy again.

(*The buyers applaud wildly and start to exeunt at left
with* MRS. SANTA. *As they go, they exchange pleased
comments.*)

MISS LACY. I'll fill all the front windows with dolls.
MRS. SANTA. I'm so glad.
MISS WIELDS. We'd better hurry. There's a lot to do.
(*As the buyers disappear off left,* MOLLY *takes her key
from her pocket and pretends to wind up* POLLY.)
POLLY (*happily*). You—you didn't swallow the key
after all!
MOLLY. What do you think I am? A goat?
NONA. Dorabella, I'm sorry to have to tell you this,
but Edwina hid your slippers in Mrs. Santa's work bag.
I took them out and put them on the tree. The twins
knew about it.
POLLY. Edwina said she'd cut off our curls if we told,
and I was a coward. I was going to tell Edwina what
Nona did, but Molly took out my key and I couldn't talk.
I'm glad she did.
DORABELLA (*puzzled*). But why did you do it, Edwina?
MOLLY. I'll tell you. She's jealous of you. She said

this was one show where Dorabella wouldn't dance. But you did!

NONA. Edwina, unless you promise to stop this foolishness and behave as you should, I shall tell Mrs. Santa.

EDWINA. Please don't do that, Nona. I'm sorry; truly I am, Dorabella. I was jealous of you, but I won't be after this. Please forgive me.

DORABELLA. Of course, Edwina.

EDWINA. I want to give you something for Christmas, Dorabella. Here, take my beads. (*Removes the beads from her neck.*)

MARIE. The beads she's so proud of!

HULDAH. I think she means it!

DORABELLA. Oh, I couldn't take your beads, Edwina.

EDWINA. Please, Dorabella. I want you to have them. Then I'll be sure you've forgiven me. Please, Dorabella.

DORABELLA (*taking the beads and putting them on*). Thank you, Edwina.

BETTY. That's fine.

NONA. Good for you, Edwina.

AGOONA. Let's all sing Edwina's song with her before we go to sleep.

They sit as they did during the show and sing "Sleep, Dollies, Sleep." As the song ends TESSIE *and* BESSIE *enter at right, walk behind dolls and remove imaginary keys from their backs, thus taking away their power to move or speak. They sit motionless, smiling out into space. The maids jingle the keys in their pockets, go front, and look back at the dolls.*

TESSIE. Aren't they pretty, Bessie?

BESSIE. They surely are, Tessie. I'd like to have one of them myself.

(*The maids go off at right. Faint strains of "The Dancing Doll" are heard off stage as—*)

THE CURTAIN FALLS

GRANDMA AND MISTLETOE

A ONE-ACT CHRISTMAS PLAY

By

MARGUERITE KREGER PHILLIPS

PRODUCTION RIGHTS

Copies of this play are available in single pamphlet form. The right to produce this play by one group of amateur players is authorized only by the purchase of four copies (one copy for each speaking part) at the current price of 50c each.

It is dishonest and illegal to copy parts.

GRANDMA AND MISTLETOE

For one man and three women

CHARACTERS

(In the order of their first appearance)

JIM ....*A thief*
MOLLIE ....*The Rogers' maid*
GRANDMA ROGERS.........*More or less of an encumbrance*
MRS. JOHN ROGERS.................*Her daughter-in-law*

TIME—*About ten o'clock on Christmas Eve.*

PLACE—*The suburban home of John Rogers.*

TIME OF PLAYING—*Twenty minutes.*

COSTUMES AND CHARACTERISTICS

Jim is a very young thief, of eighteen or so, with a thin, boyish figure and an undernourished look. He has a shock of rough hair and a pair of sharp eyes, which occasionally betray a keen sense of humor. While pretending to be grandma's granddaughter, he speaks in falsetto, disguising his voice as much as possible, but assuming his own voice when he reveals his identity. He wears a shabby dark suit and overcoat and a well-worn cap pulled down over his eyes.

Mollie is an Irish girl in her middle twenties, good-natured as long as her own comfort is not disturbed and more or less affected by the atmosphere of selfishness that pervades the Rogers household. She wears a plain winter coat over her best dress and has on a winter hat.

Grandma is a sweet little old lady of seventy, pathetically blind and feeble and very sensitive under the isolation of her position, yet uncomplaining. When she moves about, she holds one hand out in front of her gropingly, after the manner of the blind. She is very much dressed up in her best silk, with white lace cap, collar, and cuffs, and wears a modern necklace, old-fashioned bracelets, a diamond ring, and a modern wrist watch.

Mrs. Rogers is a middle-aged matron, cold, calculating, selfish, and completely devoted to fashionable society. She wears an expensive fur coat over a handsome evening gown, also a modish and dressy hat. On her wrist is a costly watch.

PROPERTIES

For Jim, a flashlight. For Grandma, a spray of mistletoe.

STAGE DIRECTIONS

Up stage means away from footlights; *down stage,* near footlights. In the use of *right* and *left,* the actor is supposed to be facing the audience.

GRANDMA AND MISTLETOE

SCENE: GRANDMA ROGERS' *living room in the suburban home of her son John at about ten o'clock on Christmas Eve. The room has three doors: draped double doors up center leading to the reception hall and front door, a door at right leading to the rear of the house, and French doors down left leading out on a side porch. Up extreme left is a window with shade and silken draperies. The room is luxuriously furnished, yet obviously for other eyes than* GRANDMA'S *sightless ones. A decorated Christmas tree hung with electric bulbs is in the upper left corner near the window. Down left is an upholstered armchair, and at right center is a davenport piled with fancy pillows. An ornate table is up extreme right, fitted out with the latest thing in scarfs and the last word in bizarre ornaments. Several straight-backed chairs of a showy pattern are scattered about the room, two on opposite sides of the door up center, another near the table up right, and a fourth near the French doors down left. Half a dozen fancy electric lamps are distributed about the stage: two floor lamps at opposite ends of the davenport, a third just back of the armchair, a fourth near the French doors, a fifth just left of the door up center, and a reading lamp on the table up right. A small stand loaded with bric-a-brac is down right of right door, and a pair of tall urns or vases stand on the floor down extreme right and left respectively. Handsome rugs and pictures complete the furnishings.*

At rise of curtain, the stage is unoccupied and dark, except for a pale blue ray of moonlight entering at the window up left, produced by blue bunch lights above the window off stage. After a brief pause, the French windows are opened slowly from off stage, and JIM, *the thief, enters cautiously, made visible to the audience by the same pale blue light just outside the French doors. He carries a flashlight, which he focuses on various parts of the room for a moment, until the voice of* MOLLIE *is heard off right. He instantly extinguishes the flashlight and goes noiselessly out by way of the French doors, closing them behind him all except a crack, at which he stands listening throughout the ensuing scene, just barely visible to the audience, but unobserved by those on the stage.*

MOLLIE (*speaking loudly, off right*). Sure I will. I'll take you right in there now, even if I am in an awful hurry. You'd be smashin' yersilf ag'inst some of Mrs. Rogers' china, and thin I'd get it—not you. It's a wonder one of thim couldn't take the time to pilot you in here.

MOLLIE *enters at right, dressed for the street, leading* GRANDMA ROGERS, *who fumbles about and holds one hand out protectingly in front of her showing that she is in the habit of finding her way about alone. In the other hand, she holds a spray of mistletoe.* MOLLIE *crosses, leads her down left, and seats her rather hurriedly in the armchair there; then as she talks to* GRANDMA, *she takes a pillow from davenport and adjusts it to* GRANDMA'S *back and also turns on the tree lights and one or two of the many lamps that are about in the room.*

MOLLIE (*good-naturedly*). There, now, you be quiet an' don't move a foot. They've got this place so befuddled wid bric-a-brac an' on top of that, didn't they bring in a whole forest? The missus'll be down soon and read to you. I gotta go. Mike is sore at me, as it is, for stayin' here. He thinks they're a heartless bunch, an' besides I work too hard. Sure that's only his blarney, you understan'. The missus thinks I wint out whin Junior escaped, right after his father, but all me prisints weren't finished.

GRANDMA (*resignedly*). Yes, they all seemed in such a hurry. Christmas Eve should be quiet and peaceful. (*Plead-*

ingly.) You will wait until Mrs. Rogers comes down? I'm lonesome to-night. John will be back soon, but I would like you to wait until some one comes in. I'm afraid.

MOLLIE (*pretending surprise*). Now whativer are you afraid of? Maybe somebody'll get my Mike if I leave him standin' outside too long. He said he'd be waitin' down at the drug store an' help me deliver some packages. You'll be all right. Why, the missus is jist upstairs gettin' dressed.

GRANDMA (*astonished*). Dressed? Why, she was dressed for my party. Why should she dress again?

MOLLIE (*without thinking*). She's goin' out— (*Stops suddenly.*) Glory be! Now, I'll catch it! You weren't to know.

GRANDMA (*startled*). And leave me alone?

MOLLIE (*perfunctorily*). 'Twouldn't be the first time they've left you. Many's the night I come in an' found you holdin' the fort yersilf, an' not a soul in the house. You see, to-morrow is me regular day off but seein' it's Christmas an' there's a big party on here, the missus said to go out to-night. Sure an' there's not even the shank of the evenin' left, but I'm goin', jist the same.

GRANDMA (*catching hold of* MOLLIE'S *clothes blindly and clinging to her*). But Mollie this is my birthday and Christmas Eve! I thought they were all coming in here and have a nice family evening together, after their errands were done.

MOLLIE. Not this family! They had your dinner for you, so they could keep their other dates, an' if it wasn't for deliverin' me own packages, I'd stay wid you mesilf.

GRANDMA (*anxiously*). I heard John say something about burglars in the neighborhood. (*Gasping.*) Perhaps they were looking in at the window when John gave me my watch and necklace.

MOLLIE (*trying to reassure her*). Can you feature that? Now, listen! They's nobody goin' to hurt you. Take my advice. Stop worryin'. It don't get you anywhere at all.

GRANDMA (*tearfully*). But I'll be alone if Mrs. Rogers goes out. Oh, I can't stay alone to-night—I can't!

MOLLIE (*throwing her hands above her head with a despairing gesture*). I'm the dumb-bell! I ain't got no sinse a-tall, to be scarin' you. Why—why—didn't you hear thim say at the table afterwards that the gang was caught? They've caught all the burglars in town, an' there's not a one o' thim left to rob a stockin'. It's true as I'm standin' here beside you. (*Pauses and listens.*) She's comin' downstairs now. Don't let on I told you she was goin' out. An' remimber, to-morrow's Christmas, an' peace be wid you. (*Exit quickly at right.*)

MRS. ROGERS *enters quickly up center, from right. She has her wraps on over her gown, and during the following conversation with* GRANDMA, *she nervously fidgets with her fur coat and glances nervously at her watch from time to time.*

MRS. ROGERS. Heavens! Who turned on all these lamps? The tree is sufficient.

GRANDMA (*meekly*). I guess Mollie did, but I don't really need that. Are you going to read to me for a little, Nellie? Mollie thought you might.

MRS. ROGERS (*sharply*). Mollie never will learn to mind her own business.

GRANDMA (*pretending deafness*). What did you say?

MRS. ROGERS (*sitting on davenport with an exasperated toss of her head*). Did you enjoy your dinner? I thought it was nice having Blanche and Junior with us.

GRANDMA (*pointedly*). Yes, it was nice having the children, for a change.

MRS. ROGERS (*irritated*). You never will get used to these modern young people, mother. You really must not expect too much of their company this Christmas, because I looked over their engagement lists and every waking hour seems taken.

GRANDMA (*pathetically*). Even to-night?

MRS. ROGERS (*proudly*). They could be in sixteen places if they accepted all their invitations.

GRANDMA. Where did I get the idea that you were all coming in here and watch for Christmas morn with me?

MRS. ROGERS (*with sarcasm*). Heaven only knows! But weren't your roses lovely? Oh, of course you couldn't see them.

GRANDMA. I would like them in here, so I might smell them while you are reading to me.

MRS. ROGERS (*sharply*). Reading? I'm sorry, but I couldn't to-night. Blanche borrowed most of your roses.

GRANDMA. Borrowed them?

MRS. ROGERS (*nonchalantly as though they are all used to borrowing* GRANDMA's *things*). Why, yes. I knew you would want to give her that pleasure; you are so unselfish. By the way, did you mention your cake to Mollie? She likes to be praised once in a while, and it does keep her good-natured. She had red candles on it to match your roses.

GRANDMA. I am most awfully sorry, but I neglected to. I would like to have been able to blow out my birthday candles and wish as I used to, but Junior seemed to want to do it.

MRS. ROGERS. Seventy years old, and thinking of such childish things? Junior was too funny! He's as childish as you are, but he did enjoy doing it.

GRANDMA (*unable to resist a little complaining*). I couldn't tell just what all the merriment was about. It's so hard when you can't see and especially when there is a confusion of voices.

(MRS. ROGERS *jumps up with a bored manner and walks nervously toward the door, up center, but comes back again and sits down resignedly.*)

MRS. ROGERS. Yes, yes, I know it is hard for you to make anything out of our conversation at the table, and to-night we were all rather hurried. I am to meet John at the Gordons' for a midnight supper, you know.

GRANDMA (*utterly confounded*). Won't John come back?

MRS. ROGERS (*wearily*). Now, mother, please don't be

unreasonable. You know John has his social obligations, which he cannot shirk—

GRANDMA (*interrupting pleadingly*). But on Christmas Eve and my birthday!

MRS. ROGERS. We had a lovely dinner for you. Why can't you cheer up and think of all the wonderful things you have—all the comforts of the world, besides a loving family around you?

GRANDMA (*utterly crushed*). Yes, I try to count my blessings, but it is hard. And to-night I am so confused because everything has been moved again. Couldn't you ask Mollie to leave the furniture in the same position when she cleans? I am so afraid of breaking one of these lamps.

MRS. ROGERS (*not at all ruffled*). Why, pretty lamps mean so much to a room.

GRANDMA. But I don't need them.

MRS. ROGERS (*ruffled*). You might consider our feelings. When friends stop in to see you, we don't want them to find you in a bare, unfurnished room.

GRANDMA (*on the verge of tears*). Oh, you are good to me, and I am the selfish one. I mustn't expect you to remember not to move things, but I did think when you gave me this room for myself that— Oh, forgive me, Nellie! I am upset to-night but I will try and be more patient. It's just this rushing, rushing you all do that I can't seem to get used to. Even Mollie seemed in a hurry.

MRS. ROGERS. Everyone is busy on Christmas Eve.

GRANDMA (*sadly*). When John was a little boy, his father and I always sat by the tree, after our Santa Claus chores were done, and watched for the dawn of Christmas Day. And then he would lead me under the mistletoe and kiss me. Oh, but those were sentimental days! How I wish some one would kiss me under some mistletoe, now!

MRS. ROGERS (*laughing nervously*). Why, mother, there is still sentiment left in the world, but people just haven't as much time for it as they used to.

GRANDMA. Oh, I'm a foolish old lady! Why should I

expect folks to stop and visit with me on my birthday when they haven't time even to celebrate Christ's birthday?

MRS. ROGERS (*chidingly*). Why, mother, to hear you talk, we are all a lot of heathens.

GRANDMA (*brightening a little*). I've hardly thanked you for everything—this necklace and my watch. John shouldn't have bought it. I can't see it.

MRS. ROGERS. But you can hear it. I'll keep it wound up and then when mine is out of order I shall borrow yours and that will give you a feeling of usefulness. Isn't that what makes you happy? To be useful?

GRANDMA. Yes. If I could just make myself useful—

MRS. ROGERS (*interrupting*). Your necklace is lovely, too. John wants people to know how much we care for you, and of course that is one way of showing it—by giving you pretty things to wear.

GRANDMA. He is so good. But this necklace is really too fine for me. I wish I could see it.

MRS. ROGERS (*stepping close to* GRANDMA). The stones just match Blanche's eyes.

GRANDMA. I do wish the dear child would come into my room more. She is almost a stranger to me. At meal times when she is there, all I hear is an occasional outburst of slang.

MRS. ROGERS. Young people are so busy nowadays, mother, that they have time only for themselves. And as for slang, they all use it, more or less.

GRANDMA. I used to like old ladies when I was a girl. Blanche should have this necklace—

MRS. ROGERS (*interrupting, without thinking*). That's just what I told John—er—er— I mean there is a chance for you to feel that you are doing something useful in this world.

GRANDMA. She shall have it. But can't we have just a little reading? What was that you people were saying about burglaries? It makes me nervous, with all this jewelry on; but it did please John.

MRS. ROGERS. Of course.

GRANDMA. If he could only have stayed!

MRS. ROGERS. Next year we shall celebrate your birthday a day ahead, so it won't conflict with Christmas Eve.

GRANDMA (*deeply hurt*). Oh! I always felt especially blessed having it on Christmas Eve. (*She fondles the mistletoe in her hand gently.*) Poor mistletoe! My hands are withering you. Will you hang it up, Nellie, please?

(*An auto horn is heard off stage.* MRS. ROGERS *starts quickly for the door up center but turns and speaks as she reaches it.*)

MRS. ROGERS. Blanche will do that when she returns. She said she would be back between parties to pick up some gifts. I'll leave a note for her, so she'll surely come in.

GRANDMA (*worried*). Can't you wait a little longer?

MRS. ROGERS (*coldly*).. Mollie will be back at midnight and see you to bed. You said you wanted to sit up, and I'll turn the radio on as I go by.

GRANDMA. No, please! Not that radio!

MRS. ROGERS. As you wish. But the Christmas music is wonderful.

GRANDMA. Not for me when I am alone.

MRS. ROGERS. I'm sorry, mother, but we can't change our plans now. Blanche will run in for a few minutes. Now, try and be sensible and realize that none of us have reached the age when we would be willing to sit still in the gloaming for three hours watching for the dawn. My car is waiting. Good night and merry Christmas! (*Exit quickly, up center, going left.*)

GRANDMA (*rising excitedly to her feet and calling*). Nellie, Nellie, please don't leave me! (*A door slams, off up center.* GRANDMA *calls again.*) Nellie! Nellie! Nellie!

There is no answer. GRANDMA *starts to walk about, stumbles into furniture and finally reaches the curtained doorway up center, just as* JIM *slowly opens the French doors and stands watching her, peering about. curiously, then with determination advances to her side noiselessly.*

JIM (*attempting to disguise his voice*). Here I am.

(GRANDMA *is so startled that she almost falls, but* JIM *catches her.*)

GRANDMA. Oh, thank you, Nellie! You did come back.

JIM (*in disguised voice*). I'm Blanche. I passed mother going out.

GRANDMA. Blanche? Why, you dear child! I didn't expect you so soon. Neither did your mother. I was so upset at being alone, but now you are here, I'm all right. Will you stay a little while?

JIM. Somebody's waitin' for me.

GRANDMA. Your friend won't mind; will he?

JIM (*glancing gloatingly at* GRANDMA'S *jewelry*). He'll wait, but I'm always in a hurry.

GRANDMA. Could you take time to hang my mistletoe?

(*She holds it out towards him.* JIM *hesitates a moment, glancing cautiously around, then, shoving* GRANDMA *rather roughly into a chair, he takes the mistletoe and hangs it on a branch of the Christmas tree.*)

JIM. I'll hang anything once, even my neck.

GRANDMA (*startled by his slang*). What did you say?

JIM (*attempting to make his voice sweeter*). I think your mistletoe is too pretty for words.

GRANDMA. I'm glad you like it. Now, you're sure you won't mind being late for a dance or two at your party?

JIM (*stares at her for a moment as though not comprehending her meaning, then, with a little laugh, replies*). Not me. What's a dance or two in my young life?

GRANDMA. I'll never ask you again, but this is the first time your father hasn't spent the evening with me on Christmas Eve. (*Impulsively.*) Oh, dear child, if you only knew how I have longed to see your face, now that you are grown-up! They tell me you are beautiful.

JIM (*with a startled laugh*). You wouldn't like my face if you seen it.

GRANDMA. How strangely you speak, Blanche!

JIM (*coming close to her and keeping his voice pitched high*). Do I? How does granny like to hear Blanche talk?

(GRANDMA *nervously fingers her necklace, which attracts* JIM'S *attention to it, and he stares spellbound by its beauty.*)

GRANDMA. Well, dear, I so seldom hear you speak and when I do, it's always mixed up with other voices of your friends. Your mother tells me it is the fashion for young ladies now to use slang. When I was a girl, we didn't do it so much. (JIM *tries to touch the jewelry, as though testing its value, and as* GRANDMA'S *hands keep moving nervously as she speaks, he is continuously dodging to avoid contact.*) Your voice seems harder and sharper to-night. Perhaps you go to too many parties. (GRANDMA'S *hand suddenly comes in contact with the thief's arm, and she holds him.*) Forgive me, dear. I don't mean to criticize. It's just that I'm not used to it. You are all such busy people, and when I hear a voice that I haven't heard for some time all alone in this room, it jars a little. Blind people have very sensitive ears, dear.

JIM (*makes an effort to pull away and succeeds*). So long as the jar ain't nothin' more'n my voice, you got nothin' to worry about. (*With a flourish of the arm.*) Howsomever, we'll cut out the rough talk for your benefit and celebrate Christmas.

GRANDMA (*unable to hide her shudder at his abuse of the English language*). I do hope your mother comes in early to-night.

JIM (*glancing nervously about*). Well, I hope she don't. (*Moves back of* GRANDMA, *endeavoring to puzzle out the clasp on the necklace.*)

GRANDMA (*surprised*) You mean you like to stay with me?

JIM. Sure thing!

GRANDMA (*tremulously*). I can hardly believe it. To

think that some one really wants to stay and chat with me! I'm going to cry for joy; I can't help it.

JIM (*now stepping quickly to other side of her*). For gosh sakes, don't! Santy Claus'll hear you!

GRANDMA (*wiping her eyes*). I'll try not to, but what makes your voice move around so much?

JIM (*grins directly at audience*). Got a cold, I guess.

GRANDMA. Then you shouldn't go out at all to-night. Oh, I am so happy with you here! (JIM *covers his mouth to keep from bursting into laughter.*) Do you know, I almost wanted to die to-night when you all rushed from the dining room and left me wandering around alone. If I had waited, your mother would have come back for me, but—

JIM (*interrupting roughly and finishing the sentence*). —when she got darn good an' ready!

GRANDMA. You mustn't talk that way about your mother. I *am* trying at times, and this was such a busy night.

JIM (*pushing back his cuffs as though ready for work*). I'll say it's goin' to be a busy night.

GRANDMA. Slang again! Oh, dear, I don't mind. (*Recklessly.*) Why, you may butcher the King's English all you like, as long as you are willing to stay with me. But come! Tell me about my roses and your dress. I don't smell the roses. Your mother said you used some. Where are they?

JIM (*glancing all around the room then back at* GRANDMA). Roses? I don't see any. You're the only thing that looks rosy to me. An' who wants roses when they got mistletoe?

GRANDMA (*laughing*). Why, Blanche, that is so funny! Your mother must have been mistaken.

JIM. Sure. She gets that way, sometimes.

GRANDMA. Now, Blanche don't let your sense of humor make you disrespectful. You're trying to be funny just to amuse me.

JIM (*looking anxiously around and suddenly growing serious*). You're the one that's funny, an' the laugh may be on me.

GRANDMA. I don't understand what you mean. But no matter. Come and sit down beside me. (JIM *hesitates, then with a shrug of resignation seats himself at her feet and boldly takes hold of her wrist and examines one of the bracelets.*) You won't spoil your dress on the floor?

JIM (*again smiling at the audience as he pats his old coat*). No, madam; not this one!

GRANDMA. Now, first I want to feel your face.

JIM (*starts*). Feel my face? What kind of a game is this?

GRANDMA. Well, faces change. And remember: You were only a baby when I lost my sight. Now, tell me: Whom do you think you look like?

JIM (*nonchalantly*). Like my old man!

GRANDMA (*laughs*). Like John! I can understand that slang even if I don't like it, but John has my features, and now I am happy because you must look like me.

JIM (*scratches his head*). Goll-ee! This is gettin' too hot for me.

GRANDMA (*somewhat hurt*). Don't you want to resemble me? You sound displeased.

JIM (*with sarcasm*). Sure I do, but I got a swell chance —not!

GRANDMA (*blindly feeling for* JIM's *shoulder and fondling him*). Why, you haven't taken off your coat.

JIM (*beginning to enjoy himself as he takes off his coat*). Off she goes. We got to suit the old lady to-night—I mean my dear granny!

GRANDMA. What a precious you are! (JIM *pats himself humorously. Then he turns in his collar, and throws his soft cap on the floor beside him.*) Come close now and put my hand right on your face. (JIM *glances around, then, taking her hand, examines the diamond ring before placing it on his cheek.* GRANDMA *then moves her hand over his face and to his hair.*) Why, where is your hair? Nellie said you had long hair!

JIM (*startled for a moment*). Gee! She forgot to tell

you I had a hair cut last week. Long hair don't go in my business.

GRANDMA. Your business? Nellie didn't tell me you had gone into business. (*Laughs suddenly.*) Now, you're teasing; you mean school. Well, I cannot see it, and I am thankful for my blindness. I don't believe I could bear to see you with short hair.

JIM. I'll say you couldn't!

GRANDMA. I like to think of my son's only daughter with long hair. (*Feels his nose.*) Why, you have a nose just like John, and your cheeks are so soft!

JIM (*pulls away from her*). Sa-a-ay! I'm really a hard guy!

GRANDMA (*really shocked*). Oh, promise me you will never call yourself a guy again. That is one slang word that I just cannot bear. You've made me so happy to-night by staying with me. So you won't mind my asking this one favor?

JIM (*serious for a moment*). I'm glad I've made you happy. It's a long time since anybody ever said I did. Perhaps if you saw me you wouldn't be so happy.

GRANDMA. Nonsense! Would you like to wear my necklace to-night—perhaps keep it?

JIM (*stares unbelievingly for a moment, then remembers what he is there for and jumps to his feet, ready for business*). Oh, boy! Would I?

GRANDMA. Unfasten it, dear, and put it on so I can feel it around your neck.

JIM (*speaks directly to audience as he removes it*). This is too easy!

GRANDMA. Your father did say something about having to take it back to the jeweler and have it tightened. Do you think there is danger of your losing it?

JIM. H'm! Not me! (*Reaches down and places* GRAND-MA'S *hand on the necklace and with his other holds his shirt away so she won't touch that.*)

GRANDMA. Would you like to keep it always? Nellie said the stones just matched your eyes.

JIM (*unable to resist showing his joy at getting the necklace so easily, hops about a little and sings*).

> Christmas comes but once a year
> And when it does, oh, boy! Three cheers!

GRANDMA. If I had known how happy that would make you, it would have been in your stocking for to-morrow.

JIM. I'd rather have it to-night. Thanks just the same. (*Laughs.*)

GRANDMA (*laughs happily*). Now this watch, dear. Wear it, too. (JIM *without hesitation removes it from* GRANDMA'S *wrist and puts it on, gloating over it, while* GRANDMA *runs her hand up and down his arm.*) You are so thin. You should drink lots of milk.

JIM (*thoroughly enjoying himself*). Will that make me fat?

GRANDMA. Of course it will. Now, I want you to humor your old grandma to-night and wear these two bracelets. (*Takes them off.*)

JIM (*grabs them and holds them up to the Christmas tree lights*). Solid stuff! (*Puts them quickly in his pocket, then gazes almost raptly into* GRANDMA'S *face as she continues.*)

GRANDMA. When you are dancing to-night, just pretend you are I, and as I sit here alone, I will try and imagine myself in your place, having a lovely Christmas party.

JIM (*rapturously*). Won't that be swell?

GRANDMA (*dreamily*). You see, you all ate dinner so fast to-night and seemed in such a rush—even your father—that I really did not have as long a party as I wanted. Would you believe that I used to be a very nice dancer?

JIM (*with absolute seriousness*). I'd believe anything you told me, granny.

GRANDMA (*wiping her eyes*). Oh, you blessed child! You don't mind my calling you a child? Nellie tells me you are quite grown up for eighteen. It is so hard to think that· I shall never see you. (*Begins to weep.*)

JIM (*terribly distressed*). Here, here, old lady, don't do that! I mean—granny, gosh! Don't get the weeps. I'm here, you know. (*Suddenly gets hold of himself and is back on the job of thieving.*) That's a good-looking ring you got on.

GRANDMA (*wiping her eyes*). I'm a foolish old woman for crying, when we were having such a good time. Why, I haven't been so happy in years. I almost spoiled it all by crying.

JIM. I'll say you did.

GRANDMA (*determinedly*). Blanche, I won't cry any more. I don't want to spoil one minute of this happy time. Would you like to wear my ring, too? (*Removes it and holds it out to* JIM, *who grabs it.*)

JIM. Three rocks!

GRANDMA. No, dear, not rocks! Those are full carat diamonds. Your dear grandfather gave me that the year he died, just ten years ago; and I've never seen it. (*A sob breaks her voice.*)

(JIM *stops gazing at the ring and stares at* GRANDMA, *then shudders, and it is plain to see that* GRANDMA'S *helplessness is at last taking hold of his heart.*)

JIM. Ten years you've had it an' never seen it. Ten years is a long time. I almost got put in the stir for that time, but the judge said I was too young, an' he let me off with the reform school.

GRANDMA (*astonished at his words*). What are you saying, Blanche? You—you— Why, there's something wrong!

JIM (*as though convincing himself*). Aw! I can't pull this job off. Hell! It's this Christmas stuff, an' you're blind—

GRANDMA (*interrupting with anxiety in her voice*). Please, please! What are you talking about?

JIM. I said I couldn't rob a blind woman.

GRANDMA (*astounded*). Rob me? I'm giving you those. They are Christmas presents. Why, you've given me the happiest night I've had in years. It's been such fun to sit here, with you so close. My son's daughter— (JIM *drops his hands dejectedly at his side and hangs his head.*) **Dear** child, don't make me unhappy after this jolly time. Tell me: What you mean by talking about robbing?

(*With determination* JIM *steps to her side and speaks in husky tones in his own voice.*)

JIM. Get this straight now, granny. I've had a swell time, too, but I'm not your Blanche. I'm a— Well, I'm a thief.

GRANDMA (*unbelieving*). A thief? Blanche, don't treat such a serious matter lightly. How could you be a thief?

JIM (*brokenly*). But I'm not your Blanche. I came here to rob this house to-night. The gang said it was·a cinch 'cause nothin' but an old woman was on guard most o' the time. I saw the light upstairs from the road, then a couple of cars drove away, an' I hung aroun' a little longer thinkin' you was upstairs. Then jes' as I got inside that door off the porch, the dame brings you in. Then the other one comes in—the one that browbeat you an' wouldn't read to you—an' then lit out an' left you alone. Well, I thought it was goin' to be a pipe until your blindness got me. (*Unclasps the necklace and dangles it about in his fingers.*)

GRANDMA (*remarkably calm*). You mean I am alone with a thief? You have been pretending all this time? Nellie went out and Blanche never came in? But your voice—

JIM. You almost caught me with that, but I'm a pretty good actor.

GRANDMA (*hurt*). It's hard to believe it of you. I don't want to believe it. Why, we've had such a jolly Christmas Eve, and you hung up my mistletoe for me!

JIM (*very much touched by her distress*). Gosh! Granny, I hate like the devil to gum up the works, but I draw the line at dirty work to an old blind woman. (*Disgusted.*) I'm soft.

GRANDMA (*trying to make herself understand the situation*). I'm alone with a thief? Why—why, I just can't believe it! I'm not afraid—not in the least.

JIM (*with feeling*). D'ye know why? 'Cause you're so

good that nothin' could hurt you—nothin' but that bunch you live with. Say, that skirt that was in here is about the meanest I ever see. The wise way she got you to promise all your jewelry! I ought to lay for her. (*Menacingly.*)

GRANDMA (*frightened by the menace in his voice*). Oh, no, no, no! They all mean to be kind. It's just—just thoughtlessness!

JIM. Say, they ain't got a thought in their heads but for themselves. Didn't I hear her? Don't you s'pose I know square shooters? Any bunch that'ud go an' leave a jolly old granny like you alone oughta be kicked! (*Suddenly surprised at himself.*) Gee! Listen t' me! I'm turnin' into a preacher.

GRANDMA (*her voice trembling as she holds out her hands to him blindly*). You are too nice to be a thief.

JIM (*laughs*). The gang should hear you! I gotta beat it now an' make a haul somewhere else, to make up for fallin' down on this job.

GRANDMA (*pleadingly*). Don't go! Tell me your name. Will they hurt you if you don't steal something?

(JIM *glances at her with a longing sigh and looks about the comfortable room, picks up his hat and coat and puts them on, then steps to her side and dumps all the jewelry into her lap, while he speaks with a nonchalant air.*)

JIM. Here's your junk. The gang calls me Speedy, but I'll be Soft Soap Sam after to-night. (*Bends close to her.*) My real name's Jim.

GRANDMA (*delighted*). Jim? Why, that was my dear husband's name. Oh, Jim, must you go back to this gang?

JIM. Say, they treat me better than your gang does you. Why, d'ye think they'd desert me if I was blind? Not much!

GRANDMA. But they make you steal, and you're so young; at least your voice is.

JIM. I'm old at this game.

GRANDMA. It's stealing!

JIM. So does your gang steal. They steal from you.

They steal your laughs. Why, a blind fellow can't get much out o' life but a few laughs. Didn't you tell me that I gave you the first laughs you've had in years? Where are your laughs? They got 'em. That old hen steals 'em every time she won't read t' you! (*He wipes his forehead with his coat sleeve, as though quite exhausted with his own feelings.*)

GRANDMA. I wonder if you are right about this, Jim. Can there be more than one kind of stealing?

JIM. Stealin's stealin', whether it's cold cash or laughs.

GRANDMA (*suddenly tense with emotion*). Jim, let me hold your hand! (JIM *hesitates, taking a cautious look about, listens for footsteps, then, with a grin, places his hand in hers.*) Would you come here every night and make me laugh?

JIM (*surprised at her lack of common sense*). An' let that bunch o' crook relatives o' yourn nab me an' call a cop? Not much!

GRANDMA. I wouldn't let them. I'd send them all out. They'd be glad to go.

JIM. Sa-a-ay! I wouldn't trust that bunch for a thousand bucks! (*A door slams, off up center, and* JIM *starts for the French doors on the run.*) They're comin', granny. I'm beatin' it.

GRANDMA (*half rising*). Jim, please wait! They won't come in right away. Please take my bracelets, so your gang won't be cross with you. Take them, Jim, for a Christmas present, and come back some night and make me laugh again!

(JIM *hesitates a second, then steps quickly to the tree, picks off the piece of mistletoe and, stepping to her side, holds it over her head, then with a chuckle bends down and kisses her.*)

JIM. Merry Christmas, granny! (*Exit quickly by French doors, leaving her gasping.*)

CURTAIN

CHRISTMAS STORY

A CHRISTMAS PLAY IN ONE ACT

By

LEONORA SILL ASHTON

PRODUCTION RIGHTS

Copies of this play are available in single pamphlet form. The right to produce this play by one group of amateur players is authorized only by the purchase of five copies (one copy for each speaking part) at the current price of 50c each.

It is dishonest and illegal to copy parts.

CHRISTMAS STORY

For four boys and three girls

CHARACTERS

RALPH ....boy who reads the story. Aged twelve.
Dressed in school clothes.

JEAN......................sister of Ralph, who listens to the story.
Aged ten. School clothes.

CHARACTERS IN THE STORY

MEG—Aged ten. Dressed for out of doors in a warm coat and cap.

DICK—Aged twelve. Dressed in a warm overcoat and cap.

JACK—Aged fourteen. Wears an overcoat. No cap.

SHEPHERD BOY—Aged twelve. Wears a rough burlap tunic with a rope knotted around the waist. A pouch made of rough material hangs at his side from a cord slung over his shoulder.

THE VIRGIN MARY—A girl of fourteen. Wears a blue dress, and a long white veil draped over her head and falling down over her shoulders and dress.

TIME: The present, at Christmas.

SCENE OF THE STORY: A wooded field.

Supplementary parts are played before the curtain.

Prologue

Before the curtain opens, RALPH and JEAN come in from the right and stand near the center of the stage. RALPH holds an open book and together they sing to the tune, "Christmas," by Handel:

"While shepherds watched their flocks by night
  All seated on the ground,
The Angel of the Lord came down
  And glory shone around.

" 'Fear not,' said he, for mighty dread
  Had seized their troubled mind,
'Glad tidings of great joy I bring
  To you and all mankind.'

" 'To you in David's town this day
  Is born of David's line
The Savior who is Christ the Lord
  And this shall be the sign.'

" 'The heavenly Babe you there shall find
  To human view displayed,
All meanly wrapped in swathing bands
  And in a manger laid.'

"Thus spake the seraph and forthwith
  Appeared a shining throng
Of angels praising God, who thus
  Addressed their joyful song.

" 'All glory be to God on high
  And to the earth be peace
Good-will henceforth from heaven to men
  Begin and never cease.' "

JEAN *(As they finish singing.)* That's my favorite Christmas carol. What's the next one in the book?

RALPH *(Turns the page.)* The next one's "Silent Night" but in between the carols there's a story.

JEAN. What's it called?

RALPH *(Scans the page as though he were reading ahead.)* It's called "Christmas Story."

JEAN. What's it about?

RALPH. It's about a boy named Dick, and a girl named Meg, and . . .

JEAN *(Clapping her hands.)* ·Read it, Ralph. Read it out loud, and then we'll sing the next carol. *(The two walk over to the right corner of the stage outside the curtain and seating themselves on a bench they remain there during the play.)* Please begin, Ralph. Don't wait.

RALPH *(Reading.)* "It was Christmas Eve, and Dick and his sister, Meg, were on their way home from Ned Dalton's party. Suddenly Meg stopped and said . . . *(Here the curtain opens. As it is drawn, RALPH stops reading and the play begins. MEG taking up the words as RALPH'S voice ceases.)*

CHRISTMAS STORY

AT THE RISE OF THE CURTAIN: *The stage scene represents a field in winter. Bare branches of trees and shrubs of different heights stand at the rear of the stage against a background of neutral color, giving the impression of a fringe of woods on the edge of the field. An opening in the bushes coincides with the overlapping parts of the curtain or background, and forms an extra exit and entrance near the center of the stage. Above the bushes is stretched a piece of dark blue muslin, large enough to overarch the entire stage. Openings in the shape of stars are cut at irregular intervals in the muslin and are lighted from behind the scene by electric bulbs. At the upper left of the blue curtain is cut a large star opening with a clear glass electric bulb placed behind it. This should be so powerful that at the proper instant it will throw a dazzling light through the opening. Until this time arrives, the large star opening is concealed with several layers of the blue material placed over it. Directly below the large star, at the left rear of the stage stands a rough shed with a manger. This is best made by slanting some rough boards on a light trellis to give the effect of an overhanging shed of a building. The sides are obscured with the bare branches clustered closely around them. The ground beneath the shed is covered with straw, and the manger is filled with hay. Until the final scene, this corner of the stage is curtained off with material corresponding to that of the neutral background. Twigs and pieces of broken branches lie on the ground at the rear of the stage. Near the center, three red electric bulbs are set in an irregular group, and concealed with gray cellophane, giving the impression of a stone on the ground. When the time for building a fire comes and sticks and twigs are placed over the bulbs, and the lights are snapped on, the cellophane is easily removed as this takes place. The small stars burn throughout the play. Blue footlights supplement these. As the curtain opens,* DICK *and* MEG *come in. Each one carries a package loosely wrapped in bright colored Christmas paper, and tied carelessly with bright ribbons as though they had been opened and hurriedly wrapped again. The two walk slowly as though they were tired.*

MEG. I think this is a long way home.

DICK. So do I, and I thought it was going to be short. Oh, well . . . *(Changing his tone.)* Ned had nice presents on his tree, didn't he?

MEG. I should say he did. *(Stops and wraps her package more securely.)* I just hope I don't drop mine.

DICK. What is yours? I didn't see it.

MEG. It's a jig saw puzzle with three hundred pieces, and if I lost one it would be spoiled. What did you have?

DICK *(Enthusiastically.)* A flashlight, and it's the best I ever saw. Look! *(He unwraps an electric torch and flashes it along the ground and on the bushes.)*

MEG *(Delighted.)* It's a beauty! *(Turns to watch the light—then stops suddenly and looks around with a startled expression on her face.)* Dick! I never saw these woods before! Where are we?

DICK *(Turning the light slowly around.)* I don't—know just—where we are—but . . .

MEG *(Very much frightened.)* How far is it from home?

DICK. I don't know, but it can't be far. *(He steps forward a little, flashing the light in front of him and peers ahead, then shakes his head.)* No—that isn't the way.

MEG. But which *is* the way?

DICK. That's what I'm trying to find out. *(He flashes the light in another spot, but turns away disappointed.)*

MEG. Dick! We're lost! We're lost! And it's Christmas

Eve, and we haven't hung up the stockings, and Mother will be watching, and . . .

DICK. Now don't get scared. We'll find the way home. *(He flashes the light this time to the opening in the curtain. Just as he does this the* SHEPHERD BOY *comes through the curtains.)*

DICK. I'm glad to see someone! Which way are you going?

SHEPHERD BOY *(Stepping into full view.)* I am going over towards the town.

DICK. Good. So are we. Then you know the way?

SHEPHERD BOY. I know all the ways around here. I've lived here ever since I was born. Which one do you want to take?

DICK. The shortest one back to town. I thought we had taken it when we left the road, but we must have gone by it in the dark. *(He starts back towards the back entrance.)*

SHEPHERD BOY. No. That is not the way. *(He points to Left.)* This is the way I am going.

DICK. Well, we'll follow you. I'm all turned around. We never came this way before, and we were talking about the party, and . . . *(He breaks off and looks at the* SHEPHERD BOY *carefully.)* Have you been to a party, too?

SHEPHERD BOY *(Puzzled.)* I do not know what you mean.

DICK. Why, I mean just that. Have you been to a Christmas party? *(*SHEPHERD BOY *looks at* DICK *puzzled and amazed.)* It must have been a costume party because you're dressed like a shepherd.

MEG *(Darting up to the two.)* Don't ask him, Dick. He's probably going to surprise someone, by singing Christmas carols.

SHEPHERD BOY *(Looking from one to the other.)* I do not know what you mean by a Christmas party or a Christmas carol.

DICK *(Also very much puzzled.)* Where have you been all this time?

SHEPHERD BOY *(Pointing to bushes.)* Over in the fields beyond the forest.

DICK *(In surprise.)* What were you doing there on Christmas Eve?

SHEPHERD BOY. I do not know what you mean by Christmas Eve, but I was over there with the other shepherds watching the sheep.

DICK. Where are the other shepherds now?

SHEPHERD BOY *(Eagerly.)* They have gone to Bethlehem to see the Wonderful Thing—the . . .

DICK *(Interrupting.)* To Bethlehem? You must be the one that's lost. I've lived here all my life too, and I don't know any place around here called Bethlehem.

SHEPHERD BOY. Oh, yes, there is! And it isn't far. Come with me—both of you. We will go together and see the wonderful . . .

MEG *(Hastily.)* No! No! We mustn't go anywhere but home. It's very nice of you to ask us, but we've been away a long time, and we haven't hung up our stockings yet, and Mother will be watching and she'll wonder . . .

DICK *(Decidedly.)* Mother won't be wondering, and if it's very late she'll have the stockings all ready for us. She knows it's Christmas Eve, and she knows what Christmas parties are. Everybody does.

SHEPHERD BOY. I don't know about Christmas parties or Christmas Eve. And I wish you would tell me.

DICK *(More and more puzzled.)* Well—I'll try to explain. A party is when you have cake and ice cream and play games. When it's a Christmas party, the one who gives it has a Christmas Tree and presents.

SHEPHERD BOY *(Intensely interested.)* What kind of a tree is a Christmas Tree?

DICK. A Christmas Tree is an evergreen, and it's trimmed with all sorts of bright things, and it has lights in its branches.

SHEPHERD BOY *(Eagerly.)* I know now! I know what a Christmas Tree is. I've seen one of those, with snow and frost sparkling on the needles, and when the stars shone through the branches, it looked as if they were on them.

DICK. No. You don't understand. That isn't what I mean. Real stars don't shine through the branches I mean, because a Christmas Tree is in the house.

SHEPHERD BOY. A real tree in a house?

DICK *(Earnestly.)* Yes—a real tree. You cut one down in the woods, and stand it up in a room and hang bright ornaments on it. The lights are little colored electric bulbs on a string that's connected with a switch and you snap them on, like this. *(He snaps on his flashlight and circles it over the ground.)*

SHEPHERD BOY *(Delighted.)* That is wonderful!

DICK *(Proudly.)* That's the present I had at the party. You snap the Christmas Tree lights on just like that. *(*SHEPHERD BOY *shakes his head.* DICK *looks at him questioningly.)* Don't you really know about Christmas? . . . The Christmas that will be here tomorrow?

SHEPHERD BOY. Not yet. I wish you would tell me more.

DICK. I will . . .

MEG *(Shivering.)* I'm cold. I'm dreadfully cold.

DICK *(To the* SHEPHERD BOY.*)* Wait—we'll build a fire. Then we can talk. *(The three children gather twigs and branches from the ground and pile them above and around the stone.)*

DICK *(Standing up in dismay.)* But how are we going to light it? I haven't any matches, and there isn't . . .

SHEPHERD BOY *(Quickly.)* I'll light it! *(He takes a small stone from his pouch, picks up a pebble, and holding the two behind the pile of sticks appears to strike a spark when he really snaps on the light in one bulb.* DICK, *bending over, appears to be re-arranging the twigs, and snaps on a second, then a third, so a bright glow appears.)*

MEG *(Kneeling down and spreading out her hands over the twigs.)* You can kindle a grand fire, Shepherd Boy.

SHEPHERD BOY. I should know how. *(He and* DICK *sit down beside the fire facing the audience.)* Every night when the air grows cold I gather wood like this and build a fire. Then when the sheep are quiet for the night, we shepherds watch them and we are warm and comfortable, all seated on the ground.

MEG. Why! That's part of the Christmas carol.

SHEPHERD BOY *(Turning to* DICK.*)* You said you would tell me about the Christmas carol.

DICK. A Christmas carol is a hymn about what happened the first Christmas night, nearly two thousand years ago.

SHEPHERD BOY. Two thousand years ago?

DICK. Yes, and it must have been a night just like this, with the stars shining. Some shepherds were out in the fields . . . *(He stops and looks at the* SHEPHERD BOY *puzzled.)* I never saw any sheep around here.

SHEPHERD BOY. Oh, there are great many, and our flock is one of the largest of all. And they were quiet as they could be tonight—only one strayed away—a little lamb— but I stayed and found it and took it back to its mother. They were quiet then, as quiet as they were when the Angel came, and the glory shone around.

MEG *(Softly as though to herself.)* That is what the carol says again.

DICK *(Speaking slowly and trying to choose his words with great care.)* Every year at this time, we sing Christmas carols, and every year on the twenty-fifth of December we keep Christmas because it is the birthday of the Christ Child who was born in a cattle shed where his Mother laid him in a manger because there was no room for them in the Inn at Bethlehem . . . *(He pauses.)* You spoke of going to Bethlehem?

SHEPHERD BOY. Yes, I live near Bethlehem. But tell me more about Christmas.

DICK *(As though he had not been interrupted.)* And you spoke too about something wonderful. You tell what happened to you, and then I will tell more about Christmas.

SHEPHERD BOY. It happened just a little while ago. The

sky was sparkling with stars, when suddenly a Great Star appeared, that made a light all around. I was frightened, and my father and the other shepherds were frightened too, until the Angel came, and he said . . . "Fear not! For behold I bring you good tidings of great joy which shall be to you and all people, for unto you is born this day in the City of David, a Savior which is Christ the Lord. And this shall be a sign unto you. You shall find the Babe wrapped in swaddling clothes, lying in a manger." And suddenly there was with the Angel a multitude of the heavenly host, praising God and saying, "Glory to God in the highest, and on earth peace, good will to men."

MEG *(In an awe-stricken little voice.)* Then you are one of the shepherds in the carol.

DICK *(Thoughtfully.)* That is the Christmas Story. That is what we sing about in the Christmas carols. Christmas is remembering all those things . . . but it happened a long time ago. We think about it—and you talk as if it happened tonight—you sound as if you knew about the real Christmas . . .

MEG. Isn't Christmas always real? *(DICK and the SHEP-HERD BOY look at MEG without speaking. In the silence there comes the sound of a rustling in the bushes. MEG looks up startled. The two boys turn to see. The bushes part and JACK steps out. He stands looking at the group, then turns to go back.)*

DICK *(Hurrying over to him.)* Wait. Don't go. Aren't you Jack Norton? *(During the conversation that follows, the SHEPHERD BOY stands back a little away from the fire.)*

JACK. That's my name. *(He comes forward a little.)*

DICK. I thought so. You live in the bungalow over at the foot of the hill.

JACK. That's it.

MEG. And your father is a writer. I know. My father said he was.

JACK *(In a dubious tone.)* He's a writer when he hasn't got a broken wrist.

MEG. Oh, I'm sorry he's hurt.

DICK. I suppose that's why you didn't come to the party tonight. Ned was looking for you.

JACK *(Shrugs his shoulders.)* No—that wasn't the reason. I just didn't think anything about going. I guess Dad and I are pretty much alike—keeping to ourselves.

MEG. Do you write stories, too?

JACK. Not I! I haven't any imagination. I like real things. And if they're not real—I can't make them so. *(Disdainfully.)* I've found that out tonight.

MEG. What did you find out?

JACK *(Smiling faintly at her.)* You wouldn't understand.

DICK. What's on your mind, Jack? Why do you act like that on Christmas Eve instead of going to a perfectly good party? Why did you come out here alone?

JACK. To look for something I didn't find.

MEG *(Eagerly.)* What was it? I'll help look.

DICK. I will too. See! *(He flashes his electric torch.)* Guess I could find anything with that, if I looked long enough. *(He holds the torch out for JACK to see.)*

JACK *(Looking admiringly.)* That's great. It's a beauty. I had one, but the bulb's burned out, and with Dad so he can't drive the car I'll have to wait till we can go to town to get one.

DICK. Well, come on. Use mine tonight. Tell what you lost, Jack, and we'll hunt for it.

MEG. Yes! Please tell.

JACK *(Rather shamefaced.)* I just had the crazy idea, I'd come out here and see if I could feel the way I did when I was a kid, looking at the stars shining on Christmas Eve—and all the time—thinking of the tree in the house and all of us singing Christmas carols, and having presents.

MEG. Don't you have presents now?

JACK. Sure. Dad and I give each other things, but—you know what I told you about his not being able to drive the car, and I can't get a license yet. We'll have something when we can get into town.

MEG. But it won't be Christmas then.

JACK. You're right, but that won't make any difference. There isn't any real Christmas at our house anymore.

MEG *(Impulsively puts her package in* JACK's *hand.)* Here's some real Christmas—it's for your father. It's a puzzle and he can make it with his left hand.

JACK *(Smiling but remonstrating.)* See here. I can't take your present. I wouldn't take it from you for anything.

MEG *(Drawing away, as* JACK *holds the package out to her.)* Yes, you must. I'll have lots more presents tomorrow.

JACK *(Smiling and yielding.)* Well—say I just borrowed it. Dad will be tickled to pieces to work on this—and he'll like these trappings too. *(He flicks the brightly colored papers in which the puzzle is wrapped.)*

DICK *(Holding out the torch.)* And take the flashlight too—that is, till you get to town.

JACK. Oh, no.

DICK *(Insisting.)* Yes. Go on—take it. That's a dark lane where you live . . . *(He holds it out again.)*

JACK. Well, it will be fine to have it for a day or two. *(Takes the light.)*

DICK. And say—come over to our house tomorrow. We've got a tree and presents and everything.

MEG *(Clapping her hands.)* Yes, come. Please come!

JACK *(Happily.)* Sure I will. I'd like to. *(He flashes the torch here and there, till it points to the spot at the left hand corner of the stage where the great star opening is.)* You two make it seem like real Christmas again. *(As the arc of light from the electric torch reaches the spot of the opening of the large star, the brilliant, almost blinding, light streams through the opening.)*

SHEPHERD BOY *(Breathlessly.)* The light from your torch is like that from the Great Star! *(He moves forward slowly, with wonder and reverence.* DICK, MEG *and* JACK *stand looking up in amazement. The curtain across the corner of the stage is drawn showing the manger scene.*

SHEPHERD BOY *falls on his knees.* DICK *and* JACK *stand speechless.)*

MEG *(Clasping her hands.)* It's here tonight—the real Christmas . . .

DICK *(Wonderingly.)* That came two thousand years ago. *(The main curtain falls slowly on the scene, as* RALPH *and* JEAN *sing:)*

"Silent Night. Holy Night.
All is dark, all is bright
Round yon Virgin, Mother and Child,
Holy Infant so tender and mild,
Sleep in heavenly peace,
Sleep in heavenly peace."

CURTAIN

CHRISTMAS FOR CINDERELLA

A COMEDY IN ONE ACT

By

LINDSEY BARBEE

PRODUCTION RIGHTS

Copies of this play are available in single pamphlet form. The right to produce this play by one group of amateur players is authorized only by the purchase of six copies (one copy for each speaking part) at the current price of 50c each.

It is dishonest and illegal to copy parts.

CAST OF CHARACTERS

For seven women

JOAN HOLLISTER..one of the cousins

SUSAN HOLLISTER...another cousin

MARY ANN BAXTER..the third cousin

LOUISE HOLLISTER...last to arrive

JANE HOLLISTER GORDON....The elusive and mysterious hostess

KITTY...a maid

MRS. KELLY...the housekeeper

TIME: *The present. Christmas Eve.*

PLACE: *Living room in* MRS. GORDON'S *home.*

TIME OF PLAYING: *Approximately thirty minutes. (The curtain is lowered for a moment during the play to indicate the passage of a few hours.)*

CHARACTERS AND COSTUMES

Joan and Susan are charming and poised with a definite air of self-reliance. In contrast, Mary Ann is impulsive and a bit provincial. Louise is stately, impressive and somewhat reserved. Mrs. Gordon is sophisticated and delightful. Kitty makes a demure maid and changes into a gay and sparkling daughter. Mrs. Kelly is staid and impassive.

Joan and Susan are in simple, modish gowns. Mary Ann (appearing in shabby coat and hat) changes her unattractive dress to a gown similar to that of the other girls. Louise is in a long black gown with beautiful lace fichu and old-fashioned brooch. Kitty, at first, wears a maid's dress with a sheer cap, apron, collar and cuffs; later on, a pretty afternoon dress. Mrs. Gordon is in a very lovely afternoon gown.

CHRISTMAS FOR CINDERELLA

AT THE RISE OF THE CURTAIN: *We see a charming and home-like room with a door down Left and a wide door or archway up Left Center. Soft, heavy curtains at this archway hide the hall beyond. Down Left is a handsome settee, and in front of it a low coffee table. Large chairs are at Left Center, one near the upper end of the table, the other at the lower end. Another large chair is at Right Center. Right of the archway is a large window with colorful draperies. Up Right is a small table with a telephone, paper and pencils with a telephone chair nearby. Down Right is a mantel with andirons on the hearth and brass candlesticks on the mantel. In the fireplace a merry fire is burning, and above the mantel hangs the imposing portrait of an ancestor. Left of the fireplace and at right angles is a small settee, and in front of it a hassock.*

JOAN is sitting stiffly on the fireside settee, and from time to time she gazes nervously around her. The curtains of the archway move, and a hand belonging to an unseen person pushes them aside. JOAN, turning in time to see this, rises hastily; but the curtain has fallen into place. For a moment she hesitates, then crosses, pushes aside the curtains, and looks out. In a moment she turns, and with a puzzled air goes slowly back to the settee.

Suddenly the door at Left opens and SUSAN stands on the threshold. For a moment the two girls gaze at each other, then SUSAN smiles and advances with an outstretched hand.

SUSAN. I'm Susan Hollister, and I teach English in a girls' school.

JOAN *(Greeting her.)* And I'm Joan Hollister. I model gowns in one of the exclusive city shops. *(Draws SUSAN to the settee.)*

SUSAN. Of course you're an orphan.

JOAN. Of course. That was the particular stipulation in that very amazing letter.

SUSAN. Exactly. Something like this, wasn't it? *(Pauses.)* "I am celebrating Christmas with a house party for all my young cousins no matter how distantly connected they may be. You are among the number, and the fact that you are an orphan makes you eligible for the gathering."

JOAN. My letter is just like that.

SUSAN *(Laughing.)* And I suppose the check for expenses was enclosed.

JOAN. It was. Otherwise, I shouldn't have been here.

SUSAN. Nor I. *(Pauses.)* It sounds strange to me — very strange.

JOAN. As a rule, wealthy relatives do not materialize all of a sudden. *(Looks around.)* And she must be wealthy.

SUSAN. At first, I thought I'd refuse, for it didn't seem wise to agree to anything so unusual. *(Pauses.)* And then . . .

JOAN *(Eagerly.)* Yes?

SUSAN. I couldn't stand the thought of a Christmas—alone —in a deserted school.

JOAN. I know. *(Pauses.)* My Christmas in a boarding house would have been ghastly.

SUSAN. So we both decided to face the unknown.

JOAN. And to have an adventure.

SUSAN. Have you ever heard of this Jane Hollister Gordon—our hostess?

JOAN. Never.

SUSAN. Nor have I. My branch of the family must have been so far removed that all communication ceased.

JOAN. If it ever had existed. *(Pauses.)* I can't find a thing in the family Bible.

SUSAN. My father died years ago. Mother and I struggled along until I finished my education. After her death I found this place in a girls' school.

JOAN. My mother and father were killed in a motor accident.

SUSAN. Oh—my dear! *(JOAN rises and stands in front of the fireplace.)*

JOAN. There was enough money to educate me, and I lived with my mother's sister until . . .

SUSAN. Yes?

JOAN. I found this position. That's all.

SUSAN. When did you arrive?

JOAN. Early this afternoon.

SUSAN. I came in on a bus about a half hour ago.

JOAN. Are there any more of us?

SUSAN. I don't know. *(Pauses.)* In fact, I don't know anything.

JOAN. Isn't it rather—strange—that Mrs. Gordon hasn't welcomed us?

SUSAN. The maid informed me that Mrs. Gordon has a severe cold.

JOAN. And will be with us tonight? *(As* SUSAN *nods.)* So you've heard the same story.

SUSAN. I have, indeed.

JOAN. I must be back on my job by Monday. How long will you stay?

SUSAN. Only until after Christmas—here.

JOAN. And then?

SUSAN. Back to the school. *(Laughs.)* Oh, well, the Christmas celebration should last me for the rest of the vacation.

JOAN *(In a lowered tone.)* Susan, don't turn.

SUSAN. Why?

JOAN. Someone has moved those curtains.

SUSAN. Then someone has been listening to everything we've been saying.

JOAN. The same thing happened just before you came in. *(Pauses.)* Only I saw a hand.

SUSAN. Something happened in my room, too.

JOAN. Tell me.

SUSAN. While I was unpacking my bag, I had a strange feeling that someone was watching me. I turned quickly—and the door was closing.

JOAN. Someone *had* been watching you.

SUSAN. Exactly.

JOAN. It's all a bit frightening.

SUSAN. But we have each other.

JOAN. And just meeting you is worth the risk of a Christmas party in an unknown house with an unknown hostess.

SUSAN *(Standing by* JOAN.*)* I feel the same way. *(And even as they speak,* MRS. KELLY's *dictatorial tones come from back of the curtain.)*

MRS. KELLY. Push back the curtains, Kitty. *(Whereupon,* KITTY, *the pretty maid, pushes back the curtains, allowing* MRS. KELLY *to advance majestically, bearing a tray with coffee service, cups and plates.)*

383

KITTY *(Crossing to the settee.)* Over here, Mrs. Kelly?

MRS. KELLY *(Nodding at the coffee table.)* Over there. *(As* KITTY *adjusts the table, she places the tray upon it.)* It's a cold day, young ladies, and Mrs. Gordon feels that a little coffee and some cakes will be welcome.

JOAN. That's very thoughtful of her.

KITTY. I'll bring the cakes. *(Hurries out at the hall.)*

SUSAN. Is Mrs. Gordon feeling better?

MRS. KELLY. She hopes to be with you for the Christmas tree tonight. *(Pauses.)* Mrs. Gordon wishes you to call her cousin Jane. *(*SUSAN *and* JOAN *cross to the settee as* MRS. KELLY *goes to the hall.)* I am Mrs. Kelly, the housekeeper, and should you wish anything else . . .

JOAN. There will be nothing else, Mrs. Kelly.

SUSAN. And thank you. *(*MRS. KELLY *goes out.)*

JOAN. Even if we can't have a hostess, we can have coffee.

SUSAN. Let's hope that it isn't drugged.

JOAN. Susan! *(Suddenly.)* Oh, Kitty, you startled me! *(For* KITTY *has suddenly appeared in the hall.)*

KITTY. I'm sorry, Miss. *(Crosses.)* Here are some little cakes right out of the oven.

SUSAN. They look delicious.

KITTY. I'll be coming back in a little while with some more. *(Goes into the hall and draws the curtains behind her.)*

SUSAN. Pour, Joan. You look as if you belonged at a coffee table.

JOAN. Just as you say. *(The girls take their coffee and help themselves to cakes.)*

SUSAN. My, but these cakes are good!

JOAN. And it's fun to live this way—even for a few days.

SUSAN. And then back to the old routine.

JOAN. How I wish for enough money to take a course in design. I love to plan clothes—and I'd make a success of it.

SUSAN. I'm sure you would. *(Pauses.)* You—and your clothes—are just right.

JOAN. Thanks for that.

SUSAN. And how I'd like to finish my education in the way I've planned and wanted. *(Sighs.)* I have brains even if I do say it as I shouldn't.

JOAN. Well, I *know* you have.

SUSAN *(In a whisper.)* Go on talking, but notice the curtain. It's been moving.

JOAN *(Also in a whisper.)* Someone has been listening again.

SUSAN *(In her ordinary tone.)* I'm wondering just why Mrs. Gordon after all these years wanted to hunt up all the far-away relatives.

JOAN. And maybe some of us aren't even relatives. *(At this point, the door at Left opens suddenly, and* MARY ANN *precipitates herself. Down she goes with the big bag that she carries, opening, and thereby spilling various articles of apparel.* MARY ANN *wears an impossible hat upon a disordered coiffure. Her coat is too long and her dress provincial.)*

MARY ANN. Oh, dear—oh, dear—oh, dear!

SUSAN. What *is* the matter? *(Helps her to rise.)*

JOAN. I'll pick up your things. *(Quickly she places the various articles in the bag and fastens it.)*

MARY ANN. I was running away.

SUSAN. Well, run over here and take a bit of coffee to boost your morale. *(*MARY ANN *sits between* SUSAN *and* JOAN *on the settee.* JOAN *pours the coffee.)*

MARY ANN. *(In an awe-struck tone.)* Are—you—the—cousins?

JOAN. Two of them.

MARY ANN *(After a moment.)* You're perfectly wonderful —both of you.

SUSAN. That helps. I'm Susan Hollister and this is Joan Hollister.

MARY ANN. Sisters?

SUSAN. Never saw each other until a half hour ago.

MARY ANN *(Wildly.)* What's it all about?

SUSAN. Ask me something easy.

MARY ANN. I'm Mary Ann Baxter and my mother's name was Hollister.

JOAN. Well, here we are — three of the lost and strayed Hollisters.

MARY ANN. I don't look like you. Why, I—I . . .

JOAN *(Trying not to shudder.)* Let's take off the hat. *(*MARY ANN *removes the offending member.)*

SUSAN. And the coat. *(*MARY ANN *stands up obediently as* SUSAN *helps her out of her coat.)* Now we'll put the hat and coat and bag over here by the fireplace. *(Which she proceeds to do.)*

JOAN. Shut the door, Susan, so that Mary Ann can't run away again.

MARY ANN. I don't want to run away—now.

SUSAN *(Closing the door and sitting once more on the settee with* MARY ANN *and* JOAN.) Just why *were* you running away?

MARY ANN. Because everything is—queer.

JOAN. It is, indeed.

MARY ANN. All the time I was in my room I had a funny feeling—just as if somebody was watching me. *(Unseen by the girls, the door at Left opens slowly and slightly.)*

SUSAN. I know just what you mean.

MARY ANN. And I told myself all along that I shouldn't be a bit afraid because my room is right across from Mrs. Gordon.

JOAN. How do you know?

MARY ANN. That Kitty said so.

JOAN. Mrs. Gordon is sick.

MARY ANN. Is she?

JOAN. Didn't Kitty tell you?

MARY ANN. Yes, she did—but—but . . .

SUSAN. But what?

MARY ANN. It isn't so.

SUSAN. Mary Ann!

MARY ANN. She would be in her room if she were sick, wouldn't she?

SUSAN. Why, of course.

MARY ANN. Well, she *isn't* there.

JOAN. How do you know?

MARY ANN. Because I've been in her room.

SUSAN. But how—why . . . ?

MARY ANN. Something frightened me, and without thinking, I ran right across the hall and into that room.

JOAN. *Oh!*

MARY ANN. And—she—wasn't there.

SUSAN. I don't understand.

JOAN. Maybe there's no such person.

MARY ANN. Is she—young? Mrs. Gordon, I mean.

SUSAN. How do *we* know?

MARY ANN. Well, this room didn't look as if it belonged to any old lady.

JOAN. How could you tell?

MARY ANN *(Gesticulating wildly.)* Pink underthings—*you know*—just everywhere. All pretty and lacy. Little pink slippers—and a lovely pink bathrobe.

JOAN *(Breathlessly.)* Anything else?

MARY ANN. Lovely things all around. Gold things—*young things.*

SUSAN. Kitty told you the wrong room.

JOAN. What frightened you so much that you ran out of your own room?

MARY ANN *(Dramatically.)* I saw somebody—all wrapped up — getting into a car at the side of the house — and that housekeeper was helping her.

SUSAN *(Excitedly.)* You mean . . . ?

MARY ANN. Maybe it was Mrs. Gordon.

SUSAN. But—why . . . ?

JOAN. Why—*anything?* *(Pauses.)* Oh, dear! I wonder if we should have come.

SUSAN. I'm enjoying myself.

MARY ANN. I ran away from home, too.

JOAN. And here you were running back.

MARY ANN. Aunt Frances didn't want me to come.

JOAN. Aunt Frances?

MARY ANN. She's my father's sister. I've lived with her since my parents died.

SUSAN. Is she good to you?

MARY ANN. Oh, yes—yes, indeed. I wouldn't say *anything* against Aunt Frances.

JOAN. Pretty strict?

MARY ANN. Well, she doesn't like me to go out with other young people and she won't let me wear anything but practical clothes.

JOAN. That's enough, Mary Ann. I have a perfectly good mental picture of Aunt Frances. *(KITTY enters from back of the curtains, carrying a plate of cakes.)*

KITTY. I thought you'd be wanting some hot cookies.

JOAN. Oh, how nice of you, Kitty.

SUSAN. They're delicious.

KITTY. Why, Miss Mary Ann! I thought you were in your room.

MARY ANN. I wanted to meet my cousins. *(KITTY crosses to the window and looks out.)*

KITTY. It's beginning to snow. *(SUSAN joins her.)*

SUSAN. Then it will be a real Christmas.

KITTY. Why—why—I wonder who *that* is.

SUSAN. She's coming here.

KITTY. I believe it must be—Miss Louise Hollister.

SUSAN. Another cousin, I presume.

KITTY. Oh, yes. *(Turns.)* Oh, I must hurry out to her. *(Goes out through the hall.)*

JOAN. How does the new cousin impress you?

SUSAN. Couldn't see her very well, but she's rather distinguished in appearance.

MARY ANN *(Wailing.)* Oh, dear—oh dear!

SUSAN. What's the matter now?

MARY ANN. If she's — distinguished — I'll look perfectly awful by the side of you three.

SUSAN. No such thing. You're pretty.

MARY ANN. But I haven't the—something—that you people have. Oh, you know what I mean.

JOAN *(Rising.)* Then we're going to get it right away.

MARY ANN. What do you mean?

JOAN. I'm going to turn you into another person.

MARY ANN. *Joan!*

SUSAN. And since Joan models clothes and knows all about what's what she'll make you over in no time.

MARY ANN *(Rising.)* Oh, let's hurry—hurry.

JOAN. I'll take your coat and hat and you bring the bag. *(Crosses to Right, followed by MARY ANN.)*

MARY ANN. Oh, that will be—wonderful! *(The two turn and come back to the door at Left.)*

JOAN. *Susan!*

SUSAN. What's the matter?

JOAN. That door is open.

SUSAN. I closed it. I certainly did.

JOAN. Then something else is happening.

SUSAN. And somebody's listening.

JOAN. Come along, Mary Ann.

SUSAN. And don't stay too long. Remember, I'll be entertaining the other cousin.

JOAN. We'll speed up. *(MARY ANN and JOAN go off at Left. SUSAN, left to herself, walks idly around the room and finally stops before the fireplace where she thoughtfully regards the portrait hanging above the mantel. LOUISE, appearing in the archway, stands there for a moment watching SUSAN. She is distinguished in appearance—tall, with white hair, in a black gown, with a lace collar and a beautiful old brooch. She uses a cane.)*

LOUISE. Handsome old fellow, wasn't he? And one of the worst old scoundrels in the country.

SUSAN *(Turning suddenly.)* Oh! *(After a moment.)* Are you one of the cousins?

LOUISE. I am Louise Hollister, if that answers your question.

SUSAN. Then that makes four of us.

LOUISE. *Four?*

SUSAN. I'm Susan Hollister and there's also Joan Hollister—to say nothing of Mary Ann Baxter whose mother was a Hollister.

LOUISE. Just how are we all related?

SUSAN. We don't know.

LOUISE. It's just like Jane to concoct such a wild scheme as a homecoming for lost and strayed relatives.

SUSAN. Jane! *Jane!* Then there is such a person!

LOUISE. Of course there's such a person.

SUSAN. We had begun to wonder about it.

LOUISE. When she had invited you here?

SUSAN. But nobody's had a glimpse of her—and—and . . .

LOUISE. And what?

SUSAN. Strange things happen—at least, they seem strange to us.

LOUISE *(Sighing.)* I'm tired—all of a sudden.

SUSAN. Oh, I've been so thoughtless! Here. *(And she draws out the chair at Right Center.)*

LOUISE *(As she sits.)* I forgot that I can't do what I once did.

SUSAN. Perhaps, some coffee . . .

LOUISE. No—no. I'm quite all right. *(*SUSAN *sits on the hassock.)*

SUSAN. You *know* Mrs. Gordon?

LOUISE. Why, of course I know her.

SUSAN. Some way or other—she doesn't seem real.

LOUISE. She's very real—and when she was Jane Holliste I saw much of her.

SUSAN. You haven't been with her lately?

LOUISE. Not for years. *(Pauses.)* After her marriage she lived abroad.

SUSAN. Oh, tell me about her.

LOUISE. Of course you know that she was an actress.

SUSAN. An actress! How—wonderful!

LOUISE. More or less successful, too. Gave it all up when she married John Gordon.

SUSAN. He must have been wealthy.

LOUISE. Jane did pretty well for herself. *(Bitterly.)* Some people have everything—and others, nothing.

SUSAN. But she's a very generous person. Think of giving us this wonderful Christmas celebration.

LOUISE. We're poor—all of us. At least, I suppose we are.

SUSAN. I teach school—Joan models gowns—and Mary Ann is under the sway of a very dictatorial aunt. *(Suddenly the door at Left opens and MARY ANN rushes in, followed by JOAN. A transformed MARY ANN — for the unruly hair has been brought into bounds and a smart gown has taken the place of the plain little dress.)*

MARY ANN. Oh, Susan—Susan! Look at me.

JOAN *(Almost as excitedly.)* I had an extra dress with me— and . . .

SUSAN. Mary Ann, you're lovely.

MARY ANN. And I feel as if I'm in another world.

JOAN. Aren't you glad that you didn't run away?

SUSAN. Girls! This is Miss Hollister.

LOUISE. Why not Cousin Louise since we're resurrecting the family?

JOAN *(Laughing.)* I'm Cousin Joan.

MARY ANN. I'm Cousin Mary Ann.

LOUISE. And already I'm on intimate terms with Cousin Susan.

MARY ANN. Oh, this *is* fun!

LOUISE. I feel now that a cup of coffee would be just right.

SUSAN. Of course it would. *(JOAN runs to the coffee table and pours the coffee. MARY ANN carefully escorts LOUISE to the chair near the settee and SUSAN carries her the coffee.)*

JOAN *(Anxiously.)* Is it warm enough?

LOUISE *(Sipping.)* Quite.

SUSAN. Girls! What do you think? *(Sits on the settee.)*

JOAN *(Laughing.)* Lots of things. *(Sits by SUSAN.)*

SUSAN. Mrs. Gordon—I mean Cousin Jane—used to be an actress.

JOAN. Really?

SUSAN. And she left the stage when she married Mr. Gordon.

MARY ANN. Oh—how—romantic! *(Walks to the window.)*

LOUISE *(Looking around.)* After his death she came here to live. *(Pauses.)* Did pretty well for herself, didn't she?

JOAN. But she's generous—oh, so generous! If it hadn't been for her, I'd be—alone—in a boarding house.

SUSAN. If it hadn't been for her, I'd be in a dreary school.

MARY ANN. It's snowing—oh, so hard. *(And, in spite of herself, she sobs.)*

JOAN. Mary Ann, what *is* it? *(Hurries to her.)*

MARY ANN. I'm thinking of Joe.

JOAN. *Joe?*

MARY ANN. Joe Burns. I'm in love with him and he's in love with me.

JOAN. That's nothing to cry about.

MARY ANN. But Aunt Frances won't let me marry him.

SUSAN. Why?

MARY. She just doesn't believe in anybody's marrying anybody else.

LOUISE. Perhaps she thinks he isn't good enough for you or isn't able to take care of you.

MARY ANN *(Indignantly.)* Joe is perfectly splendid and he has a fine position at the bank. *(Turns back.)* Oh — dear! *(Sobs again.)*

JOAN. I'm a bit depressed myself. *(Pauses.)* I'll soon be back in the boarding house.

SUSAN. And I'll soon be one of the few left in school during the holidays.

LOUISE. You at least have youth. I can think tonight only of bitterness in the past.

JOAN. I wish I hadn't come.

SUSAN. I'm not so—happy—myself. *(And* MARY ANN'S *sobs show just how she is feeling. Suddenly* MRS. KELLY *appears from the hall.)*

MRS. KELLY. I shall remove the tray if everyone has finished. *(Looks at* LOUISE *who still holds her cup.)*

LOUISE. I've quite finished.

MRS. KELLY. Mrs. Gordon suggests that you rest a bit, Miss Hollister.

LOUISE *(Sharply.)* I'll rest when I need it.

JOAN. Aren't we going to see Mrs. Gordon—I mean, Cousin Jane?

MRS. KELLY *(Stiffly.)* Mrs. Gordon has been ill with a cold as I told you.

JOAN. That isn't answering my question.

MRS. KELLY. Mrs. Gordon will be with you after dinner. The tree will be there. *(Points to the archway.* MRS. KELLY *gathers up the tray, cups and plates and sweeps out majestically.)*

JOAN. And that's that. *(Sits on the hassock, as* MARY ANN *sinks into the telephone chair.)*

SUSAN. I know what we need.

LOUISE. Could you be suggesting a hostess?

SUSAN. Well, of course we'd like to have her but I was thinking of something else.

JOAN. Let's have it.

SUSAN. We need cheering up.

LOUISE. I quite agree with you.

SUSAN. And I have an idea.

LOUISE. Out with it.

SUSAN. We're all Cinderellas, aren't we?

MARY ANN. *Cinderellas?*

SUSAN. Figuratively speaking, we've all sat in the chimney corner.

JOAN. Until the fairy godmother appeared upon the scene.

LOUISE. You can look upon it in that light if you wish—but . . .

SUSAN. You'll remember that the fairy godmother asked Cinderella just what she wanted.

JOAN. And the short-sighted Cinderella couldn't think of anything but a ball.

SUSAN. Well, we can make better wishes than that.

MARY ANN. What do you mean?

SUSAN. I'll write a rhyme for each of you which you will put in one of your slippers. Cinderella's slipper, we'll call it.

LOUISE. Foolish, my dear, foolish.

JOAN. But it will be fun just the same.

MARY ANN. Tell me again.

SUSAN. I'll make a rhyme which tells what each one of you wishes—way down in her heart.

JOAN. I'll write one for *you.*

SUSAN. Fine!

LOUISE. And we're to put our respective wishes in our respective shoes? I won't do it.

SUSAN. Oh, yes, you will, Cousin Louise, for it will be fun.

JOAN. And if the wish is in Cinderella's slipper it's bound to come true.

LOUISE. Well, if you put it that way . . .

SUSAN. Please.

LOUISE. It will at least give us something to do.

SUSAN. Now, wait just a moment. Where will I find some paper?

MARY ANN. Here. There are pencils, too.

SUSAN. Change places with me. (MARY ANN *crosses to the settee, and* SUSAN *sits at the telephone table.*)

JOAN. Give *me* a pencil and some paper.

SUSAN. Help yourself. (JOAN *takes the pencil and paper and seats herself at Right Center.*) Remember—we must tell the slipper just what to do.

JOAN. I understand. (*For a moment the two are busily thinking and writing.* MARY ANN, *quite fascinated, watches them, and* LOUISE, *in deep thought, leans her head on her hand.*)

JOAN. Here's yours, Susan.

SUSAN. Read it to me.

JOAN (*Reading.*)
      Take me along to a cap and gown,
      Show me the way to a laurel crown

SUSAN. That's—perfectly—splendid.

JOAN. Now, read mine.

SUSAN (*Reading.*)
      I'll follow you gladly—I'll never tire —
      If you lead me straight to my heart's desire.

LOUISE. What is your heart's desire?

JOAN. Training in the work I love.

SUSAN. Here's yours, Cousin Louise. (*Reads.*)
      Take me along the rainbow ways.
      That lead to my happy golden days.

LOUISE. That's lovely and comforting, my dear. I'll not forget it.

MARY ANN. What about me?

SUSAN (*Reading.*)
      Heel and toe—heel and toe—
      Carry me straightway back to Joe.

MARY ANN (*Again weeping.*) I wish it were true—oh, how I wish it!

SUSAN. Now to business — each one of you. Take off a slipper . . .

LOUISE. I feel foolish, Susan.

SUSAN. Well, you needn't. (*Pauses.*) All set?

JOAN (*Gayly.*) All set.

SUSAN. Hide your little paper in your slipper. (*Distributes the papers.*) There! Now, we'll put the slippers in a row—here by the curtain at the foot of the Christmas tree that's supposed to materialize.

JOAN. I'll take yours, Cousin Louise. (*Very gayly, the four slippers are placed in a row by the hall door.*)

MARY ANN (*Limping around.*) There are my only slippers. What shall I do?

JOAN. I have an extra pair.

SUSAN. And so have I.

JOAN. Cinderella parted with her slipper—and it brought her luck.

LOUISE (*Pounding with her cane.*) Christmas for Cinderella! (*The stage is dark for a moment or so to indicate the lapse of a few hours. When it becomes light again, the room is clear. In a moment, SUSAN, followed by JOAN, rushes from the door at Left and takes up the receiver of the telephone. As she dials, she listens, evidently without results, then tries again. Finally she replaces the receiver and turns slowly.*)

JOAN. What's the matter?

SUSAN. The line is dead.

JOAN. You mean . . . ?

SUSAN. There's no response.

JOAN. Try again. (*Which SUSAN proceeds to do.*)

SUSAN. No use. (*Replaces the receiver.*)

JOAN. But what are we to do?

SUSAN. You're sure that Cousin Louise isn't here?

JOAN. Of course I'm sure.

SUSAN. Tell me about it again.

JOAN. After dinner, I promised to call for her before we came down here.

SUSAN. Yes?

JOAN. I knocked, and there was no answer. I opened the door—and she wasn't there.

SUSAN. She may have gone out for just a moment.

JOAN. Her lovely brooch was on the dressing table and her cane . . .

SUSAN. She couldn't have gone far without that cane.

JOAN. And her traveling bag was there.

SUSAN. She's somewhere in the house.

JOAN. Her coat and hat were in the closet.

SUSAN. Then, of course she's here. *(MARY ANN rushes in from Left.)*

JOAN. Did you find her, Mary Ann?

MARY ANN. Mrs. Kelly hasn't seen her, and Kitty says that she hasn't gone out.

JOAN. Then something's happened.

SUSAN. Something very serious has happened.

MARY ANN. You mean . . . ?

SUSAN. She's hidden in this house. She must be.

MARY ANN. But who would hide her?

SUSAN. I wonder.

MARY ANN. You mean . . . ?

SUSAN. *Hush.* Don't say it.

MARY ANN. Oh, I want to go home.

SUSAN. So do all of us. But we can't make it.

MARY ANN. What do you mean?

SUSAN. I came in here to find out about trains.

MARY. When can we leave?

SUSAN. We can't leave.

MARY ANN. Why?

SUSAN. The telephone won't work.

MARY ANN. It can't be.

SUSAN. Just try.

MARY ANN. But as I came along the upstairs hall I heard the telephone ring.

JOAN. You imagined it.

MARY ANN. I didn't imagine it. What's more, somebody took down the receiver and began talking.

SUSAN. Then I'll try again. *(She dials—no response.)* It just won't work. *(MARY ANN and JOAN are standing close by and they do not see the door at Left open. MRS. GORDON enters, very charming in her lovely gown, her hair just touched with gray.)*

MRS. GORDON. Girls! *(They turn, but nobody speaks.* Can't you guess who I am? *(Laughs.)* I'm cousin Jane.

MARY ANN. Cousin Jane! *(In awe.)* You're really a per-son. *(Comes slowly toward her.)*

MRS. GORDON. Very much of a person, Mary Ann.

MARY ANN. How do you know my name?

MRS. GORDON. I know a lot of things, my dear. *(Holds out her hand.)* Susan?

SUSAN *(Taking her hand.)* Good guess, Cousin Jane. *(Laughs.)* I am Susan.

MRS. GORDON. Of course you're Susan. *(Holding out her hand.)* And Joan.

JOAN. By process of elimination.

MRS. GORDON. By process of second sight.

MARY ANN. Why—why—it's hard to think of you as—real.

MRS. GORDON. I've been a very elusive hostess—and I'm sorry.

JOAN. I hope the cold is better.

MRS. GORDON. I never had a cold.

JOAN. But . . .

MRS. GORDON. I've been doing a bit of play acting, my dear. I used to be an actress, you know.

JOAN. Yes—but . . .

MRS. GORDON. I decided that I wanted to know you in my own way, so I kept in the background. *(Motions to the settee as she seats herself right of the settee.)*

SUSAN *(As the three girls sit on the settee.)* You managed it very cleverly.

MRS. GORDON. Later on, I'll tell you just how.

JOAN *(Suddenly rising.)* Girls! We're forgetting Cousin Louise.

MRS. GORDON *(Puzzled.)* Cousin Louise?

JOAN. She's gone and we can't find her.

SUSAN. Her cane is here—her bag—her hat—and coat . . .

JOAN. How could we forget!

MARY ANN. And until we find Cousin Louise we must not think of another thing.

SUSAN. She's such a dear.

JOAN. She's one of us.

MARY ANN. And I just love her.

MRS. GORDON. It makes Cousin Louise very happy to hear all that, my dears.

MARY ANN *(Suddenly.)* Oh!

MRS. GORDON. You begin to understand, Mary Ann, don't you?

MARY ANN. *Girls!* Cousin Louise is really Cousin Jane.

SUSAN. Of course she is.

JOAN. And to think that we never even guessed it.

MRS. GORDON. I used to be an actress, you know.

SUSAN. How stupid of us not to see.

MRS. GORDON *(Laughingly.)* Mary Ann has sharp eyes. MARY ANN *sits on the arm of* MRS. GORDON's *chair.)*

JOAN *(Sitting.)* We should have known.

MRS. GORDON. I thought that the characterization of Cousin Louise would bring me all I wanted to know.

SUSAN. It did.

MARY ANN. Was it—you—who was being helped into the car?

MRS. GORDON. It was, indeed. I drove around until time. for Cousin Louise to make a proper entrance through the front door.

JOAN. You didn't neglect details.

MRS. GORDON. Hardly—having been an actress.

MARY ANN. And was it — really — your room across from me?

MRS. GORDON. With all the pink slippers and negligees? Hardly. All that belongs to Kitty.

MARY ANN. *Kitty?*

MRS. GORDON. She happens to be my daughter.

JOAN. And she's a pretty good actress, all by herself.

SUSAN. Just how did you happen to think of us?

MRS. GORDON. Family interest after I came back here to live after my husband's death—and the desire to help any relative however distant . . .

JOAN *(Softly.)* Who needed help.

MRS. GORDON. My lawyer investigated.

SUSAN. It was wonderful of you to do it.

MRS. GORDON. It has brought results far greater than my expectations.

SUSAN. I'm glad of that. *(From back of the curtains comes a laugh, followed by a voice.)*

KITTY. Is it my cue to enter?

MRS. GORDON. The right cue. *(*KITTY, *in the most charming of gowns, enters from behind the curtains. She rushes to each girl, embracing her.)*

KITTY. Oh, but it's been fun!

JOAN. And fun for us.

SUSAN. With this wonderful surprise ending.

MARY ANN. Oh, *Kitty!*

MRS. GORDON. Throw back the curtains, my dear. *(*KITTY *obeys, revealing a very beautiful Christmas tree with gay packages around the base.)*

MARY ANN. Oh, how beautiful! How — very — beautiful! *(Stands close to the tree.)*

SUSAN *(Tremulously.)* It's the first Christmas tree I've seen —since mother went. *(Stands at right of the archway.)*

JOAN. It brings back—oh, so many things! *(Stands by* SUSAN.*)*

KITTY. Here are the slippers.

MRS. GORDON. All for our Cinderellas.

SUSAN. That was my silly idea.

KITTY. It wasn't silly.

JOAN. And you must have thought us very presuming, Cousin Jane.

MRS. GORDON. I loved every moment of it.

KITTY *(Impatiently.)* Hurry. Hurry. Take your slippers. Here, Susan. *(As* SUSAN *takes it.)* Look inside.

SUSAN *(As she draws out a folded piece of paper and opens it.)* Oh!

MRS. GORDON. If that check doesn't cover all expenses, Susan, more will be coming your way.

SUSAN. Oh—Cousin—Jane!

KITTY. Here, Joan. *(*JOAN *takes the slipper and draws out the paper.)*

MRS. GORDON. That will send you to the best school of design in the country.

JOAN *(Tremulously.)* Oh—I can't speak—for joy.

KITTY. Don't try to. Here, Mary Ann.

MARY ANN *(As she draws out the paper.)* Oh—Cousin—Jane! I've never had so much money in all my life.

MRS. GORDON. It's for the trousseau.

MARY ANN *(Wildly.)* Trousseau?

MRS. GORDON *(At Center.)* We're about to have a wedding, girls—right here.

JOAN. Oh, what *do* you mean?

MRS. GORDON. I've been talking to Joe long distance and he can reach us by Wednesday.

MARY ANN. Joe? *Joe?* *(Runs to* MRS. GORDON.*)*

MRS. GORDON. I like him very much, Mary Ann.

MARY ANN. But—I—don't—understand.

MRS. GORDON. You're to be married right here with Joan and Susan and Kitty as bridesmaids.

MARY ANN. But—Aunt—Frances . . .

MRS. GORDON. I have also talked with Aunt Frances. *(Grimly.)* She'll remember the talk for quite a while, I fancy.

SUSAN. Oh, Cousin Jane, it's just — heavenly — but my school . . .

MRS. GORDON. The school is a thing of the past, my ·dear— nor is Joan going back.

JOAN. But . . .

MRS. GORDON. I've attended to everything.

SUSAN. Could anybody be so absolutely happy as we?

JOAN. I doubt it.

MARY ANN. But how could you reach Joe, Cousin Jane? The telephone is out of order.

MRS. GORDON. I used my own line upstairs. Much more satisfactory.

KITTY *(Laughing.)* We disconnected this one because we were afraid you'd try to get away.

MRS. GORDON. There were mysterious noises and listenings, you know.

KITTY. Oh, let's distribute the gifts, Mother. I'm getting impatient.

MRS. GORDON. I haven't Cousin Louise's cane, my dears, but I can pretend to pound it. *(Which she does.)*

KITTY *(With her arms full of packages.)* Merry Christmas!

MRS. GORDON *(Laughing.)* Christmas for Cinderella!

PROPERTIES

Candlesticks for mantel and andirons for hearth. Curtains for archway and draperies for the window. Table for the telephone, with paper and pencils on the table. Telephone chair. Small fireside settee. Hassock. Large settee with a low coffee table. Three chairs. Traveling bag with contents for Mary Ann. Cane for Louise. Tray with coffee pot, plates, cups, etc., for Mrs. Kelly. Plate of small cakes for Kitty. Elaborate Christmas tree. Gayly-tied packages for the base of the tree. Checks for the toes of the slippers.

CHRISTMAS IN HER EYES

A CHRISTMAS PLAY IN ONE ACT

By

MABEL CROUCH

PRODUCTION RIGHTS

Copies of this play are available in single pamphlet form. The right to produce this play by one group of amateur players is authorized only by the purchase of six copies (one copy for each speaking part) at the current price of 50c each.

It is dishonest and illegal to copy parts.

CAST OF CHARACTERS

For seven women

GRANDMA WILLARD
  a lovable old lady with Christmas in her eyes.

JUDY WILLARD ....her granddaughter.

ELLEN SCOTT ....⎤

KATE MILLER ....⎥

                          ⎬ former school friends of Judy's.

FREDA DELL ....⎥

CLARE PENDLETON ....⎦

GLORIA ROSS ....a snob who comes home with Judy.

CHARACTERISTICS AND COSTUMES

GRANDMA WILLARD—should be small—wear a white wig and have a clear, pleasant voice. In the opening of the play she wears a dark coat and frock and has adorned herself with mistletoe. Mistletoe on her hat, a sprig on her coat and a gay bit tucked through the belt of her dress. Her eyes should dance like a child's with thoughts of Christmas. About 65.

JUDY—proud of her success in New York, is a little high-hat on her arrival. Should be pretty, and smartly clad in street frock, wraps, etc.

KATE, ELLEN, FREDA, CLARE—the four home town girls. Should wear outdoor togs over their girlish frocks. They're gay—full of pep and eager to keep that Christmas in Grandma Willard's eyes.

GLORIA—Judy's city guest, is snobbish and unkind. Smartly clad in street frock, coat, etc.

CHRISTMAS IN HER EYES

SCENE: GRANDMA WILLARD'S *comfortable living room. There's a pile of Christmas decorations on the table. Some tree ornaments on a chair. Christmas do-dads scattered everywhere.*

PLACE: *Jonesville.*

TIME: *Early one evening—three weeks before Christmas.*

AT THE RISE OF THE CURTAIN: KATE, ELLEN, FREDA *and* CLARE *rush in Right. They are laughing and talking enthusiastically.*

FREDA *(Calling.)* Oh, Grandma Willard, are you home?
CLARE *(Peeking out Left.)* She isn't in the kitchen.
KATE *(Peeking out Center.)* Nor the bedroom.
ELLEN *(Glancing about in a puzzled manner.)* But where can she be? I wouldn't think Grandma would go calling when she's looking for Judy.
CLARE *(Peeping into kitchen again.)* Say, the table in the dinette is set for seven. Wonder who else she's expecting? *(Cries out in admiration.)* Come girls, take a peek. *(The other girls rush over to* CLARE *and shove a little to see over* CLARE'S *shoulder.)*
ELLEN *(Awed tone.)* Look—the red and white linen cloth. The red-handled knives and forks. The red-rimmed plates and cups. *(Claps hands.)* There's a white sleigh and quaint little reindeer for a centerpiece.
KATE. Isn't that just like Grandma Willard.

CLARE *(Breathlessly.)* Her poinsettia has five blooms. If I were a Christmas flower I'd like blooming for dear old Grandma, too.

FREDA. She is a swell person.

KATE *(Leaning sidewise and looking wistfully at something.)* Fruit cake. My, it makes me hungry to look at it.

FREDA *(Catching hold of* KATE's *arm and pulling her back.)* Hey, you can't walk off with a slice of Grandma's cake. *(The girls move away from Left entrance.* CLARE *walks over to the window and stands staring out. The other girls move about restlessly.)*

KATE *(Thoughtfully.)* Maybe Grandma has forgotten Judy is due on the first bus. You know, she does get a little confused about things at times.

FREDA. Oh, she'll be here any minute. And we're all dying to stay and say hello to Judy.

ELLEN. And ask her if she'll be in our Christmas play.

CLARE *(Drawing a deep breath.)* I wonder if she'll take a part? *(Shakes head thoughtfully.)* I don't know what to think of Judy. When she first left Jonesville she wrote us regularly. Then, this summer she got that position directing a small production company and none of us have heard from her since.

FREDA *(Nods.)* It is strange—so unlike Judy.

ELLEN *(Shrugs and throws out hands.)* Do you suppose she's gone high-brow on us?

KATE *(Trying to be reassuring.)* Of course not. Grandma says she's awfully busy these days.

CLARE *(Shrugs and moves about.)* Well, just the same I feel Judy could find time to write if she wished.

KATE. Let's just pass over her negligence. Make her homecoming like old times when we all went to school together.

ELLEN. We'll tell her about the play—that we're giving her the lead . . .

CLARE. And she may tell us to go jump in the lake.

ELLEN *(Giggling.)* We couldn't—it's frozen over.

KATE. There's one thing sure. If Judy is the star we'll sell more tickets. Because she really can act.

ELLEN. And the more tickets we sell the more money we'll get for the P.T.A.'s Christmas fund.

KATE *(With enthusiasm.)* And say—let's give Judy a party. A skating party.

ELLEN *(Claps hands.)* Fine. I'll furnish the marsh-mallows.

CLARE. If she agrees to go I'll furnish the hot lunch.

FREDA *(Grinning.)* It would be fun—getting the old crowd together—skating and talking about our school days.

CLARE *(Glancing out window.)* Here comes Grandma Willard now, her arms full of packages and Christmas in her eyes. *(Enter GRANDMA WILLARD Right. She is carrying a number of packages, 'her eyes are bright and she's humming a Christmas tune.)*

ELLEN *(Rushing forward and relieving GRANDMA of the packages.)* Grandma, we came over to say hello to Judy when she gets here. Do you mind?

GRANDMA. Mind? Why, kids, I was looking for you. I even set some extra plates.

ELLEN *(Putting packages on table and giving GRANDMA a quick hug.)* Why, bless your heart, Grandma.

CLARE. We'll all love staying.

KATE. Umm! Umm! Are you serving fruit-cake to-night, Grandma?

GRANDMA *(Gives KATE a hug.)* You bet, honey.

FREDA. And we can all help you.

GRANDMA *(Laughing.)* Oh, no you can't—I want the kitchen all to myself.

FREDA *(Grabbing KATE by the arm.)* Come on, darling, let's shed these coats. It looks like there's quite a little decorating to be done around here. *(Exit FREDA and KATE Center.)*

GRANDMA *(Calling after KATE and FREDA.)* Girls, we aren't doing one bit of decorating until Judy gets here. She always got such a kick out of hanging holly and mistletoe. *(Softly.)* Just think! She'll be here any minute now—my only granddaughter.

ELLEN *(Placing a hand on* GRANDMA'S *arm.)* Grandma, we've got such nice plans for Judy. We're going to give her the lead in the play—and we thought she'd like a skating party.

GRANDMA *(Smiles at* ELLEN, *then* CLARE.*)* She'll love that, girls. *(Dreamily.)* Just think, she'll be here three whole weeks. Soon as I knew she was having three weeks at Christmas I wanted to shout—I was that happy.

ELLEN *(Smiling softly.)* Yes, Grandma, we understand.

GRANDMA *(Commanding with a pleasant laugh.)* You girls get out of those wraps—hear me? *(*ELLEN *and* CLARE *slide out of their wraps as they rush out Center. Their laughter floats back.* GRANDMA *looks at clock and gasps in amazement. Rushing about.)* Where's my apron? I must finish up the dinner quick. *(Throws hat and coat aside, rushes out Left. Enter* JUDY *and* GLORIA *Right. They pause near entrance.* JUDY *puts the bag she is carrying down with a thud.* FREDA *and* KATE *appear at Center entrance; they move back partially concealed by curtains.)*

JUDY. Why did I ever consent to come back to this dull dead town for Christmas?

GLORIA *(Shrugs.)* Don't ask me. I begged you to stay in New York for Polly's house-party. They'll have real fun.

JUDY *(Sighing.)* So I'm beginning to realize.

GLORIA. Think of the interesting people we would have met. *(*ELLEN *and* CLARE *join* FREDA *and* KATE—*the four girls listen in amazement.)*

JUDY *(Coming forward slowly.)* Imagine Christmas in Jonesville?

GLORIA *(Sarcastically.)* Where they think a pie social and a Christmas program is an event.

JUDY *(Wails.)* How did I ever live here!

GLORIA *(Walking up to* JUDY *and touching her on arm.)* We could leave in the morning, Judy.

JUDY *(Excitedly.)* That's what we'll do. I'll tell Grandma that I just can't stay the three weeks—that I have work to do. *(Home town girls look horrified.)*

GRANDMA *(Offstage.)* Judy—do I hear your voice? Come in here, honey. I've got my hands in some dough. Oh, you sweet child, hurry.

JUDY *(Moving toward Left.)* Come on, Gloria, we might as well get it over with. But don't be surprised if she gushes a lot about Christmas. She still goes in for that. *(The home town girls stare with mouths wide open.)*

GLORIA *(Lifting both eyebrows slowly.)* Really? Isn't it strange how some people cling to sentiment—even in this whirlwind age? It's more than I can understand.

JUDY *(Nods.)* You're right, Gloria; we don't need so much sentiment.

GRANDMA *(From offstage.)* Come on—honey—I want to look at you—to see if you've changed. You can talk to the girls later. *(Home town girls dart back out of sight.* JUDY *glances around puzzled.)*

JUDY *(To* GLORIA.*)* What girls? What is she talking about? *(Sighs.)* Come on, Gloria. We'll run in and say hello; then shed our wraps. *(Exit* GLORIA *and* JUDY *Left. Enter* ELLEN, CLARE, KATE *and* FREDA *Center. Home town girls look worried and troubled.)*

FREDA *(Shakes head sadly.)* So that's the sort of girl Judy is now. Oh, dear, let's go home. I don't think I care to stay and talk to her.

KATE *(Walking back and forth with hands behind her.)* Imagine Judy going high-hat.

ELLEN *(Sits down and groans.)* Well, she'll never be in our play now.

KATE. Oh—dear . . . *(Gripping hands together.)* Oh—dear.

CLARE *(Tossing head.)* And would she go to one of our skating parties? *(Sniffs disgustedly.)* Not her.

FREDA *(Moving toward Center.)* Let's get our wraps and go home. I'm so disappointed . . . *(Breaks off with a sob.)*

ELLEN *(Jumping up and rushing after* FREDA, *drawing her back.)* Freda, we can't run away and leave Grandma.

KATE *(Coming up to* ELLEN *and* FREDA.*)* That's right. Grandma needs us now.

CLARE *(Throws out hands helplesly.)* But what can we do?

KATE. We might be around when Judy tells her the bad bad news—about leaving in the morning.

ELLEN *(Gripping hands together dramatically.)* And see the Christmas go out of her eyes.

KATE. Her heart will be desolate, too. Oh, she'd go on doing for others. Making others happy but she would be so hurt—so lonely way down deep—and we don't want it to end like that.

FREDA *(Throws out hands helplessly.)* But, girls, what can we do? We can't walk up to Judy and say, "Look here, beautiful, you've got to tell Grandma you'll stay for Christmas." *(Sighs and shrugs.)* You know how people are when you tell them *they've got* to do a certain thing.

ELLEN *(Moves about restlessly.)* We have a problem on our hands all right.

CLARE *(Nods.)* It'll be no small task to save Grandma's Christmas happiness.

FREDA *(Touching first one girl then another on the arm.)* Listen, kids, I want to tell you something that happened when we were in the fifth grade. Remember the airs Mrs. Doran had?

CLARE *(Thoughtfully.)* Mrs. Doran?

FREDA. Yes, you know she lived here for two years in that big stone house on the edge of town.

CLARE *(Sitting down and looking up at* FREDA.*)* Yes, I remember now.

FREDA. Well, I remember Judy saying once if she ever got the big-head like that woman she hoped someone would scrub her face with snow.

CLARE *(Laughing.)* Hmm—there's plenty of snow outside.

ELLEN *(Grabs* FREDA'S *arm.)* You wouldn't dare.

KATE *(Grabs* FREDA'S *other arm.)* Don't be absurd.

FREDA *(Frowning at first* ELLEN *then* KATE.*)* Just the same she needs it scrubbed.

KATE *(Shaking* FREDA *a little.)* It wouldn't do at all.

ELLEN. Of course not. Why, it would make her furious.

KATE *(Pulling* CLARE *from chair and drawing the girls together.)* Come on, let's go into a huddle and decide how to bring Christmas back to Judy.

ELLEN. And Grandma. For her we'd make any sacrifice. *(The girls crowd close together, talking in an undertone.)*

KATE *(With an arm about* ELLEN.*)* I've got it. Let's go ahead as if nothing had happened. Let's keep sweet . . .

ELLEN *(Interrupts.)* I see—sort of innocent like.

KATE. We'll still ask her to be in our play.

ELLEN. And invite her to our skating party—Gloria, too, of course.

FREDA *(Grins impishly.)* The easier way would be washing Judy's face with snow.

ELLEN *(Shakes head reprovingly.)* Freda, will you get that off of your mind?

KATE *(Glancing from one to the other.)* Tell you what— I'll run over home and get a copy of our Christmas play.

FREDA. What if Judy doesn't even look at it? *(Sighs.)* I think we're wasting time on that girl. *(Walks over to window and stares out.)* I always was good at washing faces.

ELLEN. I'll say you were. *(To* KATE.*)* Thought you were going after a copy of that play, darling.

KATE *(Rushing toward Right.)* On my way—I don't need a wrap that short distance. *(Exit Right.)*

ELLEN. How Judy could have the heart to make her own grandmother unhappy, I don't know.

FREDA *(Hand on* ELLEN'S *arm.)* Shh! I hear Judy and her friend coming back.

GRANDMA *(Offstage.)* Yes, the girls are around somewhere. They came over to welcome you home, Judy. Now

409

you young folks go on and have a good time together. Being it's so near Christmas I know you have lots to talk about. *(Enter* JUDY *and* GLORIA *Left.* GLORIA *and* JUDY *stand near the entrance talking.)*

JUDY *(Shrugging.)* My school-mates. Can't Grandma see I've outgrown them? I'm holding an important position.

GLORIA. You should have told her—your grandmother— right then—about us going back in the morning.

JUDY *(Making a wry face.)* She said the girls had plans and . . . *(Notes* FREDA, ELLEN *and* CLARE *and gives a little startled gasp.* ELLEN *comes forward, hands outstretched and a warm smile on her lips.* FREDA *stands with mouth wide open for a minute.* CLARE *frowns.* ELLEN *shows she is going to ignore what she has just overheard.* FREDA *and* ELLEN *look at each other and shrug, then move to follow* ELLEN, *a little reluctantly.)*

ELLEN *(Flings an arm around* JUDY'S *neck and kisses her fondly.)* Judy, it's so good to see you. *(Holding on to* JUDY'S *hands and leaning back.)* Let me look at you—let me look at you—our pretty Judy. You always were the prettiest girl in Jonesville.

JUDY *(Showing surprise.)* Why—why—Ellen—I . . .

FREDA *(Forcing a pleasant smile.)* Hello, Judy.

JUDY *(Regaining composure and speaking cooly.)* Oh, it's you, Freda. Are you still in Jonesville?

FREDA *(Laughs shortly.)* Why not? It's good to me.

JUDY *(Introducing* GLORIA.) Gloria Ross, girls. And Gloria meet Freda Dell, Clare Pendleton and Ellen Scott. *(The girls all nod and smile, including* GLORIA.)

ELLEN *(Sweetly.)* We're always glad to know Judy's friends. *(Assisting* GLORIA *out of hat and coat.)* I'll take your things for you.

GLORIA *(Cooly.)* Thank you.

CLARE *(Taking* JUDY'S *wraps and tossing them on* FREDA'S *arm.)* Make yourself useful, darling, while I get the bag. *(Rushes over to Right and picks up bag.* JUDY *notes deco-*

rations on a chair. She picks them up and tosses on table peevishly. FREDA *looks at* ELLEN *and shrugs.* JUDY *offers chair to* GLORIA. GLORIA *sits down.* FREDA, ELLEN *and* CLARE *move toward Center.)*

FREDA *(Crossly.)* I still think . . .

ELLEN. Ssh—put yourself out a little. Remember, we want to keep Christmas in Grandma's eyes. *(Exit* FREDA, ELLEN *and* CLARE *Center.)*

GLORIA *(Staring after* KATE *and* FREDA.*)* What were those girls mumbling about?

JUDY *(Sitting down near* GLORIA.*)* Something about Christmas in somebody's eyes. Those girls—always going in for Christmas. I'll admit I used to be interested. I was in all the entertainments and plays—I sold seals and—oh, you know.

GLORIA *(Yawning.)* How boring. *(Enter* KATE *Right. She is carrying several play books. Pauses breathlessly near the entrance for a moment, eyeing the other two girls thoughtfully.)*

JUDY *(Glancing at the various decorations and shrugging.)* I wonder if Grandma thinks I'll put those up.

GLORIA *(Shrugs.)* Such a clutter. *(Dreamily.)* Don't you wish you were at Polly's?

JUDY *(Nods.)* It would be nice. *(*KATE *comes forward and the other two girls rise.)*

JUDY *(To* GLORIA.*)* Gloria, this is Kate Miller. Gloria Ross, Kate. *(*GLORIA *and* KATE *acknowledge the introduction. Enter* CLARE, FREDA *and* ELLEN *Center. The girls have disposed of the wraps.)*

KATE *(Gives* JUDY *a quick hug.)* We're so glad you're home, honey. To be with Grandma for Christmas. We have some of the nicest plans.

JUDY *(Coldly.)* I—I—don't think . . .

ELLEN *(With girlish eagerness.)* Judy, you will take a part in our play—won't you?

JUDY *(Crossly.)* Now—Listen . . . *(*GLORIA *looks on amused.)*

KATE *(Showing* JUDY *one of the play book: hurriedly.)* You'd like this—and we're giving you the lead.

JUDY *(Pushes the book away and glares at* KATE.*)* I couldn't possibly . . .

FREDA *(Interrupting* JUDY.*)* We just knev you'd help, Judy, for old times sake.

JUDY *(Peevishly.)* Don't remind me of old times. *(The hometown girls ignore* JUDY's *rudeness.* GLORIA *tries to frown them down but the girls go right on smiling.* JUDY *moves about nervously.)*

ELLEN *(Following* JUDY *and tucking a hand through her arm.)* Remember what fun we used to have?

KATE *(Sitting on edge of table and grinning at* JUDY.*)* There's something else, Judy. We've planned a skating party. The lake is just right. What night would suit you best?

JUDY *(Frees self from* ELLEN *and whirls on* KATE.*)* I don't think . . .

KATE *(Jumping down from the table and giving* JUDY *a hug.)* Judy, we're inviting the old crowd. You couldn't miss it.

JUDY *(Turning to* KATE.*)* Listen, Kate, I've been trying to tell you that . . .

KATE *(Dancing about.)* You'll like the part we gave you in the play. *(Places play books on table.* JUDY *sighs worriedly. Walks over to table, pauses for a moment.* JUDY *shrugs, glances toward the hometown girl and shrugs again.)*

FREDA *(Gritting teeth and speaking to* CLARE *in an undertone.)* Oh, what I couldn't do with two hands full of snow.

CLARE *(Whispers loudly near* FREDA's *ear.)* And I could help you.

KATE *(Smiling at* JUDY.*)* We need you, Judy, to help us make money. People in this town know how well you can act and they'll come out to see you. Judy, can't you see?

Judy. Yes, I see. *(Boastingly.)* And I can act—I know it—but just the same . . .

Clare *(Shakes head smilingly.)* Think it over—Judy—please honey—we won't let you say no.

Gloria *(Laughs at Judy.)* They won't let you? That's good. *(All but Freda looks at Gloria and smile. Gloria shrugs and looks bored.)*

Judy. I won't be here long, girls, and . . .

Ellen *(Clinging to Judy's arm.)* But of course you'll stay the three weeks, Judy. You know how much it means to Grandma.

Judy *(Glancing at first to one hometown girl then to another.)* You girls have lived in Jonesville so long that you're still smalltown. *(Shrugging.)* You don't realize I see things differently.

Freda *(Flies off handle unexpectedly.)* All right, be different. *(Moves toward Judy with hands clenched at sides and eyes flashing.)* You told me once that if you ever got the big head to wash your face with snow. Well, when I saw the snob you'd become I wanted to do it. *(Shrugs in direction of hometown girls.)* Oh—no—they wouldn't let me. They said that no matter what you did, to be nice—to carry you around on a silver chip. *(Judy is so amazed she is speechless. The hometown girls are frowning at Freda, trying to keep her from saying anything else.)*

Gloria *(Shouts at Judy.)* Judy, you don't have to stand there and be insulted. Come on, let's go somewhere else and talk.

Judy. All right. *(Staring at Freda over shoulder and moving toward Center.)* This way, Gloria. *(Exit Gloria and Judy Center.)*

Ellen *(Coming up to Freda and shaking her reprovingly.)* Now you've done it, little Miss Fly-off-the-handle. You've spoiled everything we tried to do.

Freda *(Trembling all over, she sits down on lounge, looking up at the others woefully.)* D-Do you suppose I have? Oh, dear, maybe I did speak out of turn. *(Grips hands worriedly.)* What am I going to do now? *(The other girls move about, sighing a little. Enter* GRANDMA *Left.)*

GRANDMA *(Beaming happily.)* Well, dinner is almost ready. Whatever became of Judy and her guest?

KATE *(Facing* GRANDMA *and forcing a smile.)* I think you'll find them in the guest room. *(The other girls face each other moodily.* GRANDMA *catches that look and is suddenly thoughtful.)*

GRANDMA *(Puzzled tone.)* What is wrong, girls? You act as if you were upset about something. *(Laughing.)* Don't tell me you're going to wear those long faces for Christmas.

KATE *(Nudging* CLARE *and smiling.)* Clare—please . . .

CLARA *(Gulps and smiles.)* Grandma, it's just . . . *(Breaks off with a gulp.)*

KATE *(Nudging* ELLEN *and speaking reprovingly.)* Ellen!

ELLEN *(Gulps and smiles, too.)* Okay. *(Even* FREDA *manages a smile after a moment. All the girls watch* GRANDMA *as she picks up a few decorations, her face crinkling up merrily.)*

GRANDMA *(Putting decorations down.)* These colorful bits get my head as every yuletide comes around. I know Judy can hardly wait to pitch in. *(Eyes sweeping decorations again. The girls all look at* GRANDMA *with sick eyes.* ELLEN *grips her hands together.* KATE *draws a deep sigh.* FREDA *gulps painfully.* CLARE *starts biting her fingernails.* GRANDMA *turns, searching their faces for a moment.)* Girls, I still think you're worried about something. *(Eyes slightly troubled for a moment.)* And there's something else—have you all sensed a change in Judy?

ELLEN *(Walking up to* GRANDMA *and floundering for words.)* Why—why—what made you think that, Grandma? *(Enter* JUDY *Center. She stands there listening, face thoughtful.)*

GRANDMA *(Frowning.)* Oh, I don't know—her voice seemed different. *(Quavering voice.)* She seemed amazed that I had decorated the table in a Christmasy fashion— several weeks ahead of time. Why, when she was a little girl she dragged the decorations out before Thanksgiving and demanded I put them up.

KATE *(Nods.)* Uhuh!

ELLEN *(Tucking a hand through* GRANDMA'S *arm.)* Don't you let a bad old imagination spoil your Christmas.

GRANDMA *(Thoughtfully without looking at* ELLEN.*)* Maybe she's outgrown decorations. *(Glancing about worriedly.)* I don't want to displease Judy. *(*GLORIA *is looking over* JUDY's *shoulder.)*

KATE *(Rushes over to* GRANDMA *and throws both arms about her neck.)* Of course Judy will want to decorate. And, anyway, would you want to disappoint Ellen, Freda, Clare and myself? *(Throwing head back and laughing.)* Why—we like our Christmas early.

GRANDMA *(Eyes twinkling again.)* My, my, you girls are sweet—like very own grandbiddies. *(Gasps.)* Land sakes, I must get back to that dinner.

ELLEN *(Laughing gaily.)* We'll carry you. *(Laughing happily the home town girls carry* GRANDMA *out Left.* GLORIA *and* JUDY *move forward.* JUDY *sinks down on the couch seemingly disturbed.* GLORIA *glancing toward Left and laughing sarcastically.)*

JUDY *(Cries out.)* Stop that!

GLORIA *(Looks amazed for a minute.)* There—there, Judy . . . *(Searching* JUDY's *face.)* I know you've had enough to make you jittery in this crazy house.

JUDY *(Frowns.)* Remember, *this is* my home town, Gloria.

GLORIA. But surely you aren't going to let your little old home town make you sentimental?

JUDY *(Brushing fingertips of one hand across forehead.)* Well, at Christmas . . .

GLORIA *(Scoffs.)* Christmas—Come, let's get the late bus back for New York—we can barge in on Polly about four in the morning. *(Shrugs.)* You can leave a note for your grandmama . . . *(Throws out hands.)* She doesn't need you—she has all of those other girls. *(Girls heard offstage*

—*laughing and singing. Hatefully.)* Listen to them. They are having a good time without you.

JUDY *(Moodily.)* Yes, it looks like they are.

GLORIA *(Leaning toward* JUDY *and insisting.)* And it's as I say—they'll take good care of your grandma . . .

JUDY *(Buries face in hands.)* If I go away it would be the first Christmas away from Jonesville.

GLORIA *(Angrily.)* Oh, you baby.

JUDY. Maybe I should stay with Grandma these three weeks.

GLORIA *(Snorts and snaps fingers.)* Those girls! Come on, Judy, run away before you are buried in smalltown Christmas sentiment. *(Noise and laughter heard offstage. Enter the hometown girls. They look startled when they note* JUDY'S *expression.)*

KATE *(Coming up behind* JUDY *and bending over her.)* Judy, you will help with those decorations, won't you? For Grandma's sake?

GLORIA *(Sniffs and glares at hometown girls.)* So you think Judy wants to decorate? *(Enter* GRANDMA *Left.)*

GRANDMA *(Voice quavering.)* D-Did I hear you talking about decorations?

JUDY *(Rising and nodding.)* Yes, Grandma. *(Walking up to* GRANDMA *and catching one of her hands.)* It was swell of you to wait for me . . .

HOMETOWN GIRLS *(Delightedly.)* Oh, Judy—Judy! *(Eyes bright as they look at* JUDY.)

GLORIA *(To* GRANDMA.) I'm sorry but I find I must leave on the next bus.

GRANDMA *(Horrified.)* But we haven't had dinner and everything is fixed up so pretty.

GLORIA. I'm sorry—but I must leave . . . *(Exit Center.)*

JUDY *(Moving toward Center.)* I'll help Gloria with her wraps. *(Exit Center.)*

KATE. Well, what do you know about that!

GRANDMA *(Worried.)* Wonder why she came if she isn't going to stay?

FREDA *(Wide-eyed.)* Girls, do you suppose Judy *will* help with that play?

KATE. I wouldn't be surprised. *(GLORIA rushes in Center. She is putting on her coat, jamming on her hat. JUDY rushes in after GLORIA.)*

JUDY. Gloria, I wish . . .

GLORIA *(Snaps over shoulder.)* I don't need any help. And the only thing I have to say is—goodbye! *(Exit Right.)*

GRANDMA *(Moving over to Right and staring out.)* Oh, dear, she really did go.

JUDY *(Smiling at first one then another.)* She hasn't lived in Jonesville. She doesn't know it will get you once you come back. *(Softly.)* Especially at Christmas time.

ELLEN *(Rushes up to JUDY.)* And you'll be in the Christmas play?

JUDY *(Hugs ELLEN.)* You bet.

KATE *(Eyes shining.)* And go skating?

FREDA *(Coming forward.)* Will you forgive me, Judy, for what I said?

JUDY *(Grins at KATE.)* I'd love to go skating. *(Turns to FREDA.)* And there's nothing to forgive, honey. I'll always be grateful—grateful to all you girls—you prevented me from making a terrible mistake.

GRANDMA. What mistake, Judy? *(GRANDMA's face is shining, eyes are deeply happy. All hometown girls wink warningly at JUDY. JUDY winks back at them.)*

JUDY *(Giving GRANDMA a little squeeze.)* Must you know, Grandma? It's sort of a secret between the girls and myself.

GRANDMA *(Grinning.)* I declare, that sounds like old times, Judy. Secrets with your girl friends—oh, but it's good to have you home again.

JUDY *(Brushing GRANDMA's cheek with her lips.)* And I'm happy, too—now that I have arrived.

GRANDMA *(Staring toward Right absently.)* The only thing—I can't get that girl off my mind—why she looked as if—as—if . . . *(Breaks off sadly.)*

HOMETOWN GIRLS. There was no Christmas in her eyes.

CURTAIN

STAR OF WONDER

A CHRISTMAS PLAY IN ONE ACT

By

EFFA E. PRESTON

PRODUCTION RIGHTS

Copies of this play are available in single pamphlet form. The right to produce this play by one group of amateur players is authorized only by the purchase of eight copies (one copy for each speaking part) at the current price of 50c each.

It is dishonest and illegal to copy parts.

CAST OF CHARACTERS

For eight men, eight women, and one boy
(In the order of their first appearance)

MRS. ELSA CLARK
MR. GERALD CLARK } *a couple of dissatisfied travelers*

MISS MARY PRUETT .... *the station agent*

JOEY MARCH .... *a lonely orphan*

JOSEPH
MARY } .... *the parents of Christ*

FIRST SHEPHERD

SECOND SHEPHERD

MELCHIOR
BALTHASAR } .... *the Wise Men*
CASPAR

INNKEEPER

HIS WIFE

FIRST ANGEL

SECOND ANGEL

THIRD ANGEL

FOURTH ANGEL

TIME: *Christmas Eve of today.*
PLACE: *Waiting room of a small town railway station.*
TIME OF PLAYING: *Thirty minutes.*

COSTUMES AND CHARACTERISTICS

Mrs. Clark is an attractive young woman with a disagreeably superior manner. After seeing the vision, her attitude changes, and she is first frightened, then ashamed. She wears a fur coat and an expensive-looking hat.

Mr. Clark is a prosperous-looking man of about thirty-five with a superior air and a bored and condescending manner of speaking. After seeing the vision, he acts bewildered and worried. He wears an expensive, well-cut dark business suit and hat, and an overcoat with a fur collar.

Miss Pruett is plump, middle-aged, and wholesome-looking, with an emphatic and rather snappy way of speaking. All who meet her, however, are impressed by her kindness and sincerity. Her manner to Joey is affectionate and sympathetic, but not sentimental. She wears a dark dress, with a sprig of holly pinned on the waist, and when she goes out, she dons a man's cap and a plain black coat.

Joey is a thin, sad-looking boy of nine, who is so lonesome that he tries to make friends with everybody. He is always very polite. He has a good singing voice. He wears a shabby suit, a ragged overcoat, a knitted red cap rather the worse for wear, and red mittens. The role may be played by a teen-aged boy of small stature.

Joseph is a tall, dark-haired man just entering middle age, with a dark beard, if desired. He has a calm, judicial temperament, and his manner to his wife is soothing and reassuring. He wears a brown robe and mantle, with brown sandals. A lounging robe may be used.

Mary is a sweet-faced young woman with a pleasant voice. She looks tired and anxious. She wears a dark red dress with a long, full skirt and a tight, long sleeved waist, a dark blue mantle reaching the floor, black sandals, and a white scarf covering her brown hair.

The two shepherds are burly, muscular men in their thirties and forties, with harsh, loud voices. They are excited, but sincere in their belief in the star. They wear costumes consisting of a blouse and trousers made of burlap sacking and brown sandals.

The Wise Men—Caspar, Melchior, and Belthasar—are tall, gray-haired, and dignified. They wear long, flowing robes, Caspar's being purple, Melchior's dark green, and Belthasar's crimson, together with black sandals and turbans made of the same materials as their respective robes. Pictures of their costumes may be seen on Christmas cards or in books of Bible stories.

The Innkeeper is a burly man in his late thirties, with a loud voice and a confident manner. He wears black, knee-length trousers, white blouse, white stockings, and black sandals.

The Innkeeper's wife is a comely woman a few years younger than her husband with a nervous manner and a worried way of speaking. She wears a dark blue dress made with a tightly-fitting waist and a long, full skirt, together with black sandals and a blue scarf wound around her head.

The Four Angels are fair-haired young girls with low-pitched, sweet voices. Their costume is a flowing white robe with long, wide flowing sleeves, wired wings of the same material as the robe and trimmed with silver tinsel, a tinsel band around the forehead, and white or silver sandals.

PROPERTIES

Several wooden benches; window shade; painted canvas with small stars cut in it, also one large star with the opening covered with pale yellow or white transparent paper; a few railway tickets; a large, old-fashioned clock; a dozen or more wreaths of pine and holly; a train whistle; a motor horn. *Personal*: For Mrs. Clark, a large box of candy gift-wrapped with red ribbon. For Mr. Clark, two small traveling bags. For Miss Pruett, box of lunch. For Joseph, a staff. For each shepherd, a crook and a dark blanket. For Caspar, a brass vase. For Melchior, a brass bowl. For Balthasar, a small metal chest.

MUSIC

The Christmas songs used in the play will be found in *"Denison's Christmas Songs and Carols,"* which may be obtained from the publishers for the price of 50 cents, postpaid.

STAGE DIRECTIONS

Up stage means away from footlights; *down stage,* near footlights. In the use of *right* and *left,* the actor is supposed to be facing the audience.

STAR OF WONDER

SCENE: *Waiting room of the railway station in the village of Greystone at about seven o'clock on Christmas Eve. The room has three doors—one in the center of the left wall leading to the station yard, another down right leading to the street, and a third up extreme right leading from the rear of the ticket office to a small room back of it. This office is a closet-like affair up right, made of screens, with an opening in the center of its front wall for a window, back of which is a shelf. The office has a door in its up-stage wall, used solely by the agent. In the wall up left is an outer window nearly covered by a dark shade, which has been pulled down to within a foot of the bottom of the window. Off stage back of the window is a painted scene of the sky done on canvas and fastened to the window frame. On the canvas a number of small stars are cut out, also a large star—the star of wonder—whose opening is covered with pale yellow or white transparent paper. Behind this opening is placed a spotlight or powerful electric bulb, which shines through the paper when the shade is raised. A few wooden benches stand down right, extending from the ticket office almost to the footlights. A large, old-fashioned clock hangs on the wall up center. The walls and doors are lavishly trimmed with wreaths of pine and holly as if for a party. There are several bracket lights on each side wall, all of which burn dimly. On the shelf of the ticket office several railway tickets are lying. The footlights and borders are halfway up throughout the play.*

AT THE RISE OF THE CURTAIN: *A train whistle sounds off left as if a train was pulling out of the station. MISS PRUETT stands inside the ticket office looking through the window at the office. In a minute or two MR. and MRS. CLARK enter at left. MR. CLARK carries two small traveling*

bags and MRS. CLARK *carries a gift-wrapped box of candy.*
MR. CLARK *sets the bags on the floor, and the couple look
about the room in bored annoyance.*

MRS. CLARK *(To her husband.)* I simply can't understand
it. I never knew Dora Madison to be so thoughtless.

MR. CLARK. Here we are, stranded in the wilderness on
Christmas Eve. Dinner at eight and no one to meet us.

MRS. CLARK. Serves us right for coming to the wilderness.

MISS PRUETT *(Dryly.)* Well, I suppose Nazareth wasn't
exactly an aristocratic town.

MR. CLARK *(To his wife, ignoring the remark.)* We may
as well sit down and be comfortable, if possible.

MRS. CLARK *(Softly.)* What did she mean about Nazareth?

MR. CLARK. I don't know. I've never been here before.

MRS. CLARK *(Glancing around at the Christmas decorations.)* Just look at the trimmings. Why anyone should
decorate a two-by four station out in the country I can't see.

(They seat themselves on one of the benches at right.
MISS PRUETT *comes out from the door of the ticket office
and faces them.)*

MISS PRUETT. I'll tell you why we decorate what is, as
you say, a two-by-four station out in the country. Quite a
number of people pass through here every day, especially
at this time of the year. Many of them have to wait between trains because, as you probably have guessed, the
service is none too good. Why not make the room look attractive? Even out here in the wilderness we try to have
the Christmas spirit.

MRS. CLARK *(Languidly.)* Quite an idea, Mrs.—Mrs.—

MISS PRUETT *(Supplying the name promptly.)* Pruett,
Miss Mary Pruett, station agent here for twenty years.

MRS. CLARK *(Yawning.)* What a life!

MISS PRUETT. What a fine life! I meet all sorts of people.
I'll bet I know more about human nature than any psycholo-
gist or psychiatrist you could name. And I got my knowledge from experience, not from books.

MR. CLARK. How—er—unusual! Don't you ever get tired of staying here?

MISS PRUETT *(Enthusiastically.)* Never, and at Christmas time it's very exciting, and I'm very happy. Did you ever realize that the more you understand about Christmas the happier you are?

MRS. CLARK *(Peevishly.)* Well, my Christmas is ruined already. I buy Dora an expensive gift, and she can't even meet me on time. Yes, my Christmas is spoiled.

MISS PRUETT. It's too bad if we let a few minutes' delay or anything spoil Christmas.

MRS. CLARK. But all that stuff about Bethlehem and the star seems so far away now . . . just an old-fashioned legend.

MISS PRUETT. Old-fashioned maybe. I never heard it was stylish to be born in a manger. But don't say Christmas is a legend. It's just something far away and long ago. It isn't far to Bethlehem town. It's anywhere people live and love and help each other. Why, the road may run right past your house and mine, or this little railroad station, if we just remember the teachings of the Christ child. Our pastor says all things give God glory if we mean they should.

MRS. CLARK *(Coldly.)* A very pretty idea, but I'm really not interested. Gerald, look out the window and see if the car is coming.

MISS PRUETT. Oh, dear me! Here I've been talking and quite forgetting I'm a station agent and not a missionary. Are you the folks going to the Madisons? Are you Mr. and Mrs. Clark?

MR. CLARK *(With condescension.)* We are.

MISS PRUETT. The car won't be here for at least half an hour yet. Mrs. Madison called me up just before train time. You see the station wagon is the only car that's running, and there's something wrong with that. But don't worry. It's being fixed. Their chauffeur is a good mechanic.

MRS. CLARK *(Exasperated.)* Another half hour!

JOEY *enters down right slowly as if frightened.*

MISS PRUETT. Well, Joey, so you're really going.

JOEY. Yes, Miss Pruett.

MISS PRUETT *(In a kindly tone.)* Come in and sit down, dear. The train won't be along for quite some time. *(Goes to ticket window, takes a ticket from off the shelf, and hands it to JOEY.)* Here's your ticket. Put it in your pocket so you won't lose it.

JOEY. Aunt Julia˙ sent me money to pay for it.

MISS PRUETT. You keep your money, Joey. I bought this ticket, from me as a Christmas gift to you.

JOEY *(Putting the ticket into his pocket.)* Thank you, Miss Pruett. I'm to stay a week, Aunt Julia says. Then she'll take me to the home.

MISS PRUETT. Now don't you feel sad, Joey. That home is a fine place. I have two young friends there now, and after next week there'll be three of you. As often as I can, I'll come to visit you.

JOEY *(Choking back his tears.)* Th—thank you, Miss Pruett.

MISS PRUETT *(Glancing at the clock on the wall.)* Good gracious! It's time I went and got my supper. *(To MR. and MRS. CLARK.)* You folks just make yourselves comfortable. I'll be back in a few minutes. Joey, I'll bring you some sandwiches and cookies to take on the train. You come along in the back room and take a nap while I'm gone.

(MISS PRUETT takes JOEY off up right into the room back of the ticket office. The Clarks gaze at each other in disgust. In a moment MISS PRHETT returns, donning her coat and a man's cap.)

MR. CLARK. Suppose the telephone rings while you're gone.

MISS PRUETT. It won't. Poor little Joey! He's an orphan. His father and mother were both killed in an accident a month ago. He's been staying at the Smiths' till they could get him into the home.

MRS. CLARK. Why doesn't his aunt keep him?

MISS PRUETT. The poor woman would like nothing better,

but she's a widow with three small children of her own. It's all she can do to support them.

MRS. CLARK *(Indifferently.)* Oh!

MISS PRUETT. I'll be back soon. Keep an eye on Joey, will you, while I am gone? *(Exits down right.)*

MRS. CLARK. It's a good thing Jane isn't here. I never had a housekeeper who was so absurdly fond of children, and I've had plenty of housekeepers.

MR. CLARK. If she could get a job in a family with a lot of noisy children running all over the place, she'd leave us in a flash.

MRS. CLARK. She's always talking about the little boy next door and giving him cookies. Not that I care about the cookies, but I'm sure he tracks in dirt.

MR. CLARK *(Carelessly.)* Oh, well, Jane cleans it up if he does.

MRS. CLARK *(Pettishly.)* What a way to spend the evening! I wish we'd stayed at home. This Christmas idea is really overdone. We could have gone to Dora's some other time.

MR. CLARK. But I don't want to offend Richard. He's very useful to me as a reference in my business. After all, there's no good in having friends that aren't of use to you.

MR. CLARK. I often wonder why Dora married him, aside from his money. And you'd never know they're rich by the way they live.

MR. CLARK. Such people shouldn't have money. Where's that box of candy? I'm hungry.

MRS. CLARK. Right here, but I won't open it. Dora is very fond of chocolate nuts, and I hunted all over for this assortment.

MR. CLARK *(With a martyred air.)* O.K. I'll just starve quietly.

(JOEY enters softly up right, comes through the door of the ticket office opening into the waiting room, and stands looking at MR. and MRS. CLARK.)

JOEY *(Timidly.)* I got sorta lonesome in there.

MR. CLARK. All right. Sit down.

JOEY *(Sitting on the bench farthest from the couple.)* I'm nine years old. I'm in the third grade.

MRS. CLARK *(Yawning.)* Really?

JOEY *(After a moment's silence.)* Have you any little boys or girls?

MRS. CLARK. No.

JOEY *(Sympathetically.)* Oh, that's too bad. You must get awful lonesome.

MRS. CLARK *(Perversely.)* We like to be lonesome.

JOEY *(Amazed.)* On Christmas Eve?

MR. CLARK. Even on Christmas Eve.

JOEY. I don't.

MRS. CLARK *(Bored.)* Christmas may be all right for children, but it doesn't interest me.

JOEY *(With enthusiasm.)* I love it. Our teacher read us a poem last week, something about the silence in the starry sky and sleep on the lonely hills. It was beautiful. Shall I say it for you? I know most of it.

MRS. CLARK. No, thank you. Don't bother.

JOEY. And there was something about "I found Him in the shining of the stars." I always used to say poems to my mother and father. I know. I'll say the poem tonight when I go to bed. Maybe they'll hear it up in heaven.

MRS. CLARK. Maybe. *(Speaks abruptly as if trying to conceal pity.)*

(For a moment all is silence. Then JOEY can keep still no longer.)

JOEY. I could sing "Jingle, Bells." Maybe that would cheer us up.

MR. CLARK *(Greatly annoyed.)* No.

JOEY. I'm sorry if I made you cross. I just wanted to be friendly. It seems as if everybody ought to be friendly at Christmas. Miss Pruett, she's friendly all the time. She says every day can be Christmas if we make it so. *(He waits for an answer but receives none. He continues timidly.)* I wouldn't mind the back room if there was a light in it, even a candle. I know a song, "I can light a candle; God can light a star." *(Still no one answers him. He makes one last effort.)* Do you mind if I take a nap on that back bench? I'd go to the back room again, but it's lonesome with Miss Pruett gone. It's so quiet.

MR. CLARK *(Impatiently.)* All right. Lie down and go to sleep. I wish I could.

JOEY. Thank you. *(Goes to last bench at back, lies down, and is soon asleep.)*

MRS. CLARK *(Exasperated.)* If that station wagon isn't here soon, I shall have a nervous headache.

MR. CLARK *(Holding his head.)* I have one now.

MRS. CLARK *(Reflectively.)* You know, that Joey is sort of cute in an annoying way. Wouldn't Jane just love him!

MR. CLARK. Thank heaven she isn't with us.

MRS. CLARK. He's lucky to get into a good home. I suppose it will seem a little lonesome to him at first, but he'll soon get used to it.

MR. CLARK. Sure. *(Looking back at JOEY.)* He's sound asleep already.

(The lights in the waiting room have been slowly growing dimmer during the conversation.)

MRS. CLARK. Am I imagining it, or are the lights dimmer than they were? It seems gloomier than ever.

MR. CLARK. It certainly does. I wonder why. Oh, I suppose the power is weak in Graystone or whatever this place is called.

MRS. CLARK *(Disgusted.)* That's the country for you. Christmas in the sticks! Never again.

MR. CLARK. They have a lot of stars out here, anyway.

MRS. CLARK. Raise that shade, Gerald, all the way to the top. Let's have all the starlight there is.

(MR. CLARK goes to the window up left and raises the shade to the very top. The room lights gradually go out. Through the window the bright blue sky, many little stars, and one huge bright one appear.)

MR. CLARK *(Indicating the large star.)* Look at that star! I suppose that's like the star of Bethlehem they talk so much about.

MRS. CLARK *(Slowly.)* I'm beginning to understand why that old carol called it star of wonder. When I was a little girl I belonged to the Carollers, and every Christmas we went around singing.

MR. CLARK *(Disparagingly.)* I can't imagine you singing Christmas carols.

MRS. CLARK *(Offended.)* Well, I might never have made the opera, but when I was fourteen I had a very nice voice.

MR. CLARK *(Impatiently.)* O.K. You had a nice voice! *(Sits as before.)*

MRS. CLARK. What was that Joey said? "We can light a candle; God can light a star." *(Nervously.)* I wish the car would come. I don't like the dark, and the star gives me a queer feeling. I even wish Miss Pruett would come back. I feel afraid.

MR. CLARK *(Inagitation.)* Shh! Don't talk. I . . . I feel as if something is about to happen.

(All is quiet for a long moment. The small stars fade and the large one grows brighter and brighter. The stage is now dark except for the starlight. The music of "O Little Town of Bethlehem" is played softly off stage as JOSEPH *and* MARY *enter at left, walking slowly as if very tired. They cross to center, where they halt in the starlight. The music continues pianissimo throughout the ensuing dialogue.)*

JOSEPH. Soon we shall reach the inn door, Mary. Rest a moment and gaze at the star. It is beautiful.

MARY. Joseph, will our poor donkey be safe alone by the barn? He is so kind and gentle I could not bear aught to happen to him.

JOSEPH *(Gently.)* Fear not, Mary. Tonight is the time foretold by our Creator. All will be well. Have no doubts. Remember the star of Bethlehem is shining as a messenger of peace and great joy. It has guided us on our way. All the world should be glad tonight. On earth there is surely peace to all men of good will.

MARY. You are right, Joseph, and I am foolish to be worried. The innkeeper will receive us kindly, I am sure, though we seem poor and unimportant. I have no fear now, Joseph. The starry heavens fill me with peace. *(She smiles up at the star.)*

JOSEPH. And the star of Bethlehem shall be a sign of peace through all the ages to come.

(JOSEPH and MARY cross to the door down right and exeunt, while the music swells louder, then dies away. MR. and MRS. CLARK are absolutely motionless, and JOEY is asleep. The music of "While Shepherds Watched Their Flocks by Night" begins softly off stage. As it ends, FIRST SHEPHERD and SECOND SHEPHERD enter at left, cross to center, pause, and look up at the star in amazed excitement.)

FIRST SHEPHERD. It happened! It really happened! The heavens opened; throngs of angels appeared singing.

SECOND SHEPHERD. They sang, "Glory to God in the highest and on earth peace to men of good will."

FIRST SHEPHERD. And three Wise Men—the Magi—came out of the East and asked us the way to Bethlehem. They had gifts for the babe—gold, frankincense, and myrrh.

SECOND SHEPHERD. And the angel spoke to all us poor shepherds. She said, "Fear not, for behold I bring you good tidings of great joy that shall be to all people. For this day is born to you a Saviour and this shall be a sign unto you. You will find the infant wrapped in swaddling clothes and laid in a manger."

FIRST SHEPHERD. The angel told the Wise Men, too. Their guide was a star, just as ours is. And the sheep all stood up when they saw the star, their heads turned to the east.

SECOND SHEPHERD. The star of Bethlehem, star of wonder.

FIRST SHEPHERD. This night will live forever.

SECOND SHEPHERD. All the other shepherds said as we

did, "Let us go to Bethlehem and see this word that is come to pass." Shall we wait for the others?

FIRST SHEPHERD. No. Let us find the manger at once. Let us be the first to adore Him.

(The two shepherds cross and exeunt down right, as the same music again is heard off stage, soon to die away. MR. and MRS. CLARK remain motionless, and JOEY is still asleep. The music changes to "We Three Kings of Orient Are," during which CASPAR, MELCHIOR, and BALTHASAR enter at left. CASPAR is carrying a brass vase, MELCHIOR a brass bowl, and BALTHASAR a small metal chest. They cross to center and, standing in the light, gaze up at the star. The music continues very softly throughout the ensuing dialogue.)

CASPAR. We must find Him. We have seen His star in the East and we must now hasten to adore Him.

MELCHIOR. Our gifts of gold, frankincense, and myrrh will, I hope, be pleasing to Him.

BALTHASAR. To think that the Saviour of mankind was born here in a stable! Great are the ways of the Almighty —great and mysterious!

CASPAR. The greatest thing in the history of the world has happened here in Bethlehem—an event that will determine the destiny of all mankind, now and to come. The stable has become a shrine, and countless generations will worship here.

MELCHIOR. See how the star shines down upon the waiting earth.

BALTHASAR. The star of Bethlehem has brought salvation to all the world.

CASPAR. And may mankind never forget what happened this sacred night!

MELCHIOR. Come. Let us make haste to the manger where lies the little Lord Jesus, a babe beside whom a king must fall in adoration.

BALTHASAR. The whole of the world will bow before Him.

(The three Wise Men cross and go off down right. The music changes to "Luther's Cradle Hymn," which is played

through once off stage very softly. As it ends, the Innkeeper and his wife enter at left and cross to center, where they pause. But they do not look at the star.)

WIFE. I can bear to remain in the inn no longer. My husband, we have sinned grievously.

INNKEEPER *(Uneasily.)* Nonsense, Martha! I was just a trifle selfish perhaps.

WIFE. Is there in all the world no one who is truly unselfish? No one, my husband?

INNKEEPER. I am but a poor innkeeper. How many of us can afford to be truly unselfish? Certainly not I. Even the mighty King Herod never forgets that wealth is power. As for giving those two a room . . .

WIFE *(Interrupts sorrowfully.)* We could have given them a room. That poor woman!

INNKEEPER. They and their miserable donkey are perfectly comfortable in the stable. The straw is clean and soft.

WIFE. You do not know that. You have not been there to see. My husband, do you remember the prophecy?

INNKEEPER. Prophecy? What prophecy?

WIFE. That the King of Kings was to be born . . .

INNKEEPER *(Interrupting.)* Martha, you certainly do not think those beggars have any connection with the prophecy!

WIFE. Maybe they are not beggars after all. At any rate, rich or poor, we should have let them in. I am ashamed.

INNKEEPER *(Worried.)* Do not blame yourself, wife. The fault, if any, is none but mine. I still cannot believe they have aught to do with the prophecy—a poor carpenter and his wife come from Nazareth!

WIFE. And can no good come out of Nazareth?

INNKEEPER *(Troubled.)* I wonder . . . could the infant be the Messiah? There was no room, it is true, but my door should not have been the one to shut out Mary and her child.

WIFE *(Taking his arm and urging him forward.)* Come.

Let us hasten to the stable and try to make amends for our fault. Let us bow before the Messiah.

(While the same music is played again, they cross and go off down right. The music changes to "Hark! the Herald Angels Sing," at the end of which "Silent Night" is softly played while FIRST, SECOND, THIRD, *and* FOURTH ANGELS *enter at left, cross to center, and face the audience. The music continues pianissimo as the angels speak.)*

FIRST ANGEL.
> The world lay silent and still.
>> We descended to earth.
> We played on our harps of gold
>> And told the shepherds,
> As they watched their flocks in the night,
>> That glory would shine
> And Christ the Saviour be born.

SECOND ANGEL.
> We counselled the Magi
> And bade them follow the star
> To the manger in Bethlehem
>> Where the young child lay.
> Our music shall float through the years
>> O'er a sad and weary world,
> But triumphant and joyful still
>> Will our song remain.

THIRD ANGEL.
> Through the dark streets
>> Our light shall shine,
> And the world will rejoice
>> When the star of wonder they see,
> And think of the child
>> Who was born in a manger,
> Our Saviour to be,
>> And the hope of the world.

FOURTH ANGEL.
> Oh, come, all ye faithful, and rejoice;
>> The Christ child is born.

Praise God for His gift to the world
    And follow the star.
(The four angels cross and go off down right, while the music swells loudly, then dies away. The stage lights come up slowly, making the stage brighter, while the starlight fades. After a moment's silence, MR. and MRS. CLARK stir and seem to waken from sleep. They look at each other and then up at the starry sky in silence.)

MRS. CLARK *(Rousing herself with an effort.)* Funny! I must have been asleep.

MR. CLARK. Why, so was I.

MRS. CLARK. I had a dream, sad but beautiful. It must have been a dream.

MR. CLARK *(Wonderingly.)* A dream? Elsa, did you hear sweet music? Did you see . . . ?

MRS. CLARK *(Interrupting eagerly.)* Wait. Don't say it. Let me tell you what I dreamed. The starlight grew brighter and brighter. And in it I saw Mary and Joseph. I saw the shepherds and the three Wise Men. I saw the innkeeper and his wife. I saw angels. Did you?

MR. CLARK *(Softly, in bewilderment.)* I did. Now let's be sensible about this. We couldn't both have the same dream.

MRS. CLARK. I know we couldn't, but we did. There are more things in heaven and earth . . .

MR. CLARK *(Interrupting impatiently.)* Don't quote Shakespeare to me. Maybe we looked so long and so hard at the star that it hypnotized us.

MRS. CLARK *(Humbly.)* It made me wonder if I'd ever appreciated Christmas and what it stands for. Maybe I was wrong. Maybe Christmas in the country is nice. After all, Bethlehem was country, wasn't it? Stables and fields and sheep and things?

MR. CLARK. I suppose it was.

(MISS PRUETT enters down right, wearing cap and coat and carrying a box containing JOEY'S lunch. She goes up right to the ticket office.)

MISS PRUETT. I'm sorry, folks. I didn't mean to be so long. Where's Joey? *(Turns front and looks around the room.)*

MR. CLARK. Asleep back here. He—er—got lonesome in the back room.

MRS. CLARK *(Abruptly.)* Miss Pruett, is this station haunted?

MISS PRUETT. Goodness, no! Have you been seeing ghosts? *(Looks at her keenly.)*

MRS. CLARK. First the lights grew dim. They almost went out. After a while they did.

MISS PRUETT. Power's low early in the evening.

MR. CLARK. Just what I said.

MRS. CLARK. We both evidently went to sleep.

MISS PRUETT. That's nice.

MR. CLARK. But, admitting that we were asleep, we both had the same dream.

MISS PRUETT *(Astonished.)* You—you what?

MRS. CLARK. He's right. We both had the same dream.

MISS PRUETT. But you couldn't.

MR. CLARK. Miss Pruett, I know it sounds crazy, but it happened. The star shone so bright it dazzled us. Then we saw angels and shepherds and the Magi and Joseph and Mary . . .

MRS. CLARK *(Interrupts.)* . . . and the innkeeper and his wife.

MISS PRUETT *(Slowly, as the two watch her eagerly.)* Then that old story must be true.

MR. AND MRS. CLARK *(In concert.)* What story?

(MISS PRUETT looks at them thoughtfully as if in doubt whether to tell them or not. At last she sits on the bench beside them and speaks.)

MISS PRUETT. I've heard my father tell it. Years and years ago the station master here was a mean, stingy man. I won't tell you his name. It should be forgotten. His wife, Martha, meant well, but she was a weak little thing. The man didn't believe in Christmas; he didn't believe in charity; he didn't believe in anything. One Christmas Eve, so the story goes, it was wild and snowy. A young man and his wife stopped here at the station. They wanted to get the train to Havensville. They didn't have any money. The begged the station master to let them have tickets and promised to bring him the money for them the very next day. He refused.

MR. CLARK. He couldn't give people tickets. That wouldn't do. But you did. Didn't you?

MISS PRUETT *(Ignoring the question.)* Then they asked if they might stay in the station all night or until a cousin came for them. But they hadn't even a dime to pay the telephone charges to call up the cousin. When the station master got ready to close up, he sent them out into the snow.

MR. CLARK. He could have loaned them a dime, anyway.

MRS. CLARK. They might have frozen to death in the snow.

MISS PRUETT. Luckily a farmer picked them up in his sled and took them where they wished to go. But the station master never knew or cared what happened to them.

MRS. CLARK. How does that story explain our dream?

MISS PRUETT. I'm coming to that. Before he went home that Christmas Eve, the station master put up the shade at that window. He felt for some reason, so he said afterward, that he had to look at the sky. He said the station lights grew dim and the star in the east grew dazzlingly bright.

MRS. CLARK. So it did tonight.

MISS PRUETT. He stood there, unable to move, and in the beam of light from the star he saw Joseph and Mary, the shepherds, the Magi, the innkeeper and his wife and the angels. They talked, and he heard sweet music.

MR. CLARK. So did we.

MISS PRUETT. Then the man did tell the truth. Everyone thought he'd had a dream. After that, he became a much kinder man. Still, why should you two dream that dream?

MRS. CLARK. Yes, why? We didn't turn anyone out into the snow.

MR. CLARK. But we didn't show much Christmas spirit. Did we?

MRS. CLARK. And we weren't kind to that lonesome little boy. Maybe that's it. Miss Pruett, I feel awfully strange saying this, but when Joey comes back from his aunt's, could he visit us before he goes to that home? About a month, say? It would please Jane very much.

MR. CLARK. Our housekeeper just loves children.

MISS PRUETT *(Gives him a penetrating look.)* And you?

MRS. CLARK. Well, to tell the truth, we never did before, but somehow things seem different since the dream.

MR. CLARK. We can give you references. We have plenty of money and a nice home.

MISS PRUETT. A man's wealth is the good he does in the world, Mr. Clark.

MRS. CLARK. Jane might be appointed his guardian. We'd help her support him.

MR. CLARK. A boy needs a man to look after him.

MISS PRUETT. You go to the home. It's in Waynesburg. Talk to the trustees, but first see Joey's aunt. You will make her very happy. My friends, you did see the vision. You found Him in the shining of the stars.

MRS. CLARK. *(Softly.)* Yes, we did.

MR. CLARK. And we found Joey in a little country railroad station.

(From off right comes the sound of a motor horn.)

MISS PRUETT. Your station wagon.

MR. CLARK. Shall we wake Joey and tell him?

MISS PRUETT. No, I wouldn't. Wait till you go to his aunt's.

*(*MRS. CLARK *takes her box of candy and puts it on the bench by* JOEY.*)*

MR. AND MRS. CLARK *(In confused chorus.)* Good night, Joey. Merry Christmas! Miss Pruett, Merry Christmas!

MR. CLARK. I'll see you soon. I'd like you to go with me to see Joey's aunt.

MISS PRUETT. Good night, my friends. I know yours will

be a merry Christmas. (MR. *and* MRS. CLARK *go off down right. A moment later there is the. sound of a car driving away.* MISS PRUETT *gently hums the refrain of "We Three Kings of Orient Are." Then she wakes* JOEY.) Nearly train time, Joey. Here's your lunch to eat on the train, and here's a beautiful box of candy the kind people left for you.

JOEY *(Surprised.)* Oh! I didn't think they liked me. *(Takes the box.)*

MISS PRUETT. They like you very much, Joey. They just didn't know it at first.

JOEY *(Coming to center of room.)* It's nice to have friends at Christmas.

MISS PRUETT. Yes, Joey, very nice.

JOEY. I'll give my aunt this box of candy. I didn't have any present to take her, and it made me sad, sort of, because everybody gives presents at Christmas. *(Holds the box closely against his breast.)*

MISS PRUETT. Yes, Joey, they all brought gifts to Him.

JOEY. *(As* MISS PRUETT *fastens his coat.)* It's nice to have friends all the year round, too.

MISS PRUETT. You'll always have friends, Joey. And never forget to keep the Christmas spirit in your heart always.

(The lights grow dim, and the star shines more brightly again. JOEY *looks up at it with awed interest.)*

JOEY. Isn't that star bright!

MISS PRUETT. It's the star of wonder, Joey.

JOEY *(In solemn joy.)* Star of wonder!

(In a sweet, clear little voice he sings the chorus of the carol, or hums it, if preferred. A train whistle is heard in the distance. JOEY, *holding his lunch and the box of candy, turns to go off right. Then loud music, "We Three Kings of Orient Are," is played off stage.)*

CURTAIN

THE CHRISTMAS EVE VISITOR

A BIBLICAL PAGEANT-PLAY FOR CHILDREN

By

RENETTA BADEN

PRODUCTION RIGHTS

Copies of this play are available in single pamphlet form. The right to produce this play by one group of amateur players is authorized only by the purchase of ten copies (one copy for each speaking part) at the current price of 50c each.

CAST OF CHARACTERS

TOMMY .... Modern young boy
SUSAN .... Modern young girl
STRANGER .... Boy dressed as in Christ's time
MARY .... Mother of Jesus
JOHANNA .... Maid of Nazareth
ANGEL (unseen)
10 LITTLE ANGELS .... Small tots
ALMON .... Wealthy young man of Palestine
ENOS .... Ordinary young man of Palestine
DAVID .... In love with Rebecca
REBECCA ....Maid of Bethlehem. Distracted
OLD MAN
JAKIM .... Excited grandson of Old Man
PEOPLE OF BETHLEHEM .... (Any number)
BEN JUDA .... Shepherd
ADAN .... Shepherd
DAN .... Shepherd
BENJAMIN .... Shepherd
JONATHAN .... Shepherd
SAMUEL .... Shepherd (old)
ANGEL
ANGEL CHOIR
BALTHASAR .... Wise Man
MELCHIOR .... Wise Man
CASPAR .... Wise Man
MARCUS .... Roman Guard
CLAUDIUS .... Roman Guard
GLADDIUS .... Roman Guard
2 PRIVATE GUARDS
KING HEROD
JOSEPH .... Mary's husband
1ST WOMAN ....,........................ Haughty. Rejects Christ
2ND WOMAN .... Humble maid.

SPECIAL COSTUME SUGGESTIONS

TOMMY—Wears modern bath robe.

SUSAN—Wears modern house coat.

STRANGER—Costume of boy in Christ's time.

MARY—Subdued costume—gown and shawl.

10 LITTLE ANGELS—Wear white robes (or pastels), wings and halos. Make halos from strips of string tinsel. Wings can be made by covering wire frames with cheesecloth.

ALMON—Wears rich-colored costume.

DAVID—Ordinary costume. (gown, sash, and shawl)

REBECCA—Ordinary costume. (gown, sash, and head shawl)

OLD MAN—Wears a white beard. May carry a stick.

PEOPLE OF BETHLEHEM—(Any number) May wear bathrobes and shawls. Suggest they wear bedroom slippers to eliminate noise.

SHEPHERDS—Wear short gowns or robes tied at the waist with a cord or drab sash. Invert sheepskin-lined jackets and throw over shoulders, or use shawls. Carry crooks.

ANGELS—White robes, wings and halos. Effective halos for older children: Make wire frame of two connected circles several inches apart. On top circle wind Christmas tree string tinsel.

WISE MEN—Costumes and turbans of rich hues.

ROMAN GUARDS—Skirts about knee-length. Breast shields can easily be made from aluminum foil backed by pliable cardboard. Shin shields can also be made thus. Mantles can be thrown over their shoulders. Spears can be made from wood covered with silver paint.

KING HEROD—Dressed in brilliant colors. Black beard. Make crown of silver paper, add jewel or two.

JOSEPH—Dressed quietly. Brown beard.

1ST WOMAN—Haughty and richly dressed.

2ND WOMAN—Inconspicuous costume.

THE CHRISTMAS EVE VISITOR

SCENE I

FIREPLACE SCENE: TOMMY *and* SUSAN *enter from Left, preferably from a door directly onto the front stage, if there is one. They tiptoe in in their pajamas and robes.*

SUSAN. We really shouldn't be doing this . . .

TOMMY. Aw . . . *(Loudly.)*

SUSAN. Shh! We don't want Mommy and Daddy to hear us! *(Both sit by the fireplace.)* Let's wait for Santa Claus right here!

TOMMY. Do you really think he'll come down the chimney?

SUSAN. Well . . . Oh, Tommy, just wait till I get that little red purse and the beautiful blue mittens, and . . .

TOMMY. And my yoyo. And I can't wait till I get my football! *(Yawns. Then more slowly.)* Of course, the best will be the toy train . . . and the leather jacket!

SUSAN. Umm. *(Yawns.)* Sure is quiet, isn't it? Say, I hear some carolers. Let's go to the window.

TOMMY. No, Susan, you're not supposed to. You're supposed to just sit and listen!

CAROLERS *(Go by.) Children may either just stand in the auditorium or a group may wander past the fireplace scene. Sing "The First Noel" and "Hark, The Herald Angels Sing."*

SUSAN *(Sighs.)* Christmas Eve is awfully nice.

TOMMY. Yes, it is. Maybe it's because we go to church.

SUSAN. You know, in church tonight *(Slowly.)* I was just thinking . . .

TOMMY. About what?

SUSAN. I was thinking about Jesus. I wonder how He feels tonight. *(*STRANGER *enters (little boy) quietly, un-noticed.)*

TOMMY. I never thought of that. I guess I was thinking about the leather jacket I'm getting, and the train . . .

SUSAN. Did you hear Pastor ————— say that Jesus comes to us again tonight? Tommy, do you really suppose He could?

STRANGER. He could if people would let Him. *(*TOMMY *and* SUSAN, *startled, jump up.)*

SUSAN. Where did you come from?

TOMMY. What queer looking clothes!

SUSAN. And you're not dressed very warmly. You came in the snow, like that?

STRANGER. Clothes don't matter so much, really. The important thing is that you're warm inside.

SUSAN. But why did you come here?

STRANGER. I heard you talking about Christmas gifts and I came to tell you the story of a really wonderful gift.

TOMMY and SUSAN. Oh, good!

STRANGER. Long ago, and yet not so long ago, when God's chosen people had looked for the Messiah for a long time, times became hard and many people suffered under the government of Rome. They looked and longed for the Messiah to come and help them. For many years the prophets had promised His coming. In their hearts the people cried to God that He soon would come. Then, when the fullness of time was come, a certain virgin, named Mary, a maid of Nazareth, was sitting one day by the window, where the fig tree trembles in the gentle south wind . . . *(This speech may have to be cut down, depending on ability and age of boy taking the part.* TOMMY, SUSAN *and* STRANGER *leave as inconspicuously as possible.)*

Curtain opens to SCENE II

SCENE II

ANNUNCIATION SCENE: *Curtain opens only in center, showing* MARY *sitting, weaving a basket. She looks up when she hears someone approaching.*

JOHANNA *(Enters.)* Peace to thee, Mary, in the name of our gracious God.

MARY. Peace to thee, Johanna. May you and your family be forever blessed.

JOHANNA. You are always busy at work. Do you never tire of it?

MARY. Indeed, no. Busy hands bring peace of mind. But, Johanna, how is your mother feeling?

JOHANNA. Oh, not so good, I fear.

MARY. I must come to see her again. It is good to see her face light up when she has a visitor.

JOHANNA. Oh, Mary, it is such a tiresome journey! And you have been there so many times. It is so good of you, but . . .

MARY. Your mother is a very sweet woman, and time lies heavy on her hands.

JOHANNA. I really must go. I just wanted to stop and give you my greetings. *(As* MARY *begins to rise.)* No, no, do not rise. I will let myself out. Peace be with you.

MARY. Peace. *(Smiles and works on. Suddenly a bright light appears.* MARY *gasps and falls to her knees, her side to the audience.)*

ANGEL *(Behind the scenes.)* Hail, thou that art highly favoured, the Lord is with thee; blessed art thou among women. Fear not, Mary: for thou hast found favor with God. Behold, thou shalt conceive and bring forth a son, and thou shalt call his name Jesus. He shall be great, and shall be called the Son of the Highest: and the Lord God shall give unto him the throne of his father David. And he shall reign over the house of Jacob forever; and of his kingdom there shall be no end.

MARY. How shall this be, seeing I know not a man?

ANGEL. The Holy Ghost shall come upon thee, and the power of the Highest shall overshadow thee; therefore also that holy thing which shall be born of thee shall be called the Son of God.

MARY. Behold I am the handmaid of the Lord; let it be to me according to your word. (ANGEL *disappears as the curtain closes. Music.)*

SCENE III

SCENE OF HEAVENLY ANGELS (5 or 6-year olds.)

ANGEL No. 1. Have you noticed anything strange in heaven?

ANGEL No. 2. What is it, loving angel?

ANGEL No. 1. Jesus, the Son of God, wants to leave His heaven.

ALL. Ohh!

ANGEL No. 3. But where does He want to go?

ANGEL No. 4. I heard He wants to go to the earth.

ANGEL No. 2. But the earth is a vale of tears where God is often forgotten.

ANGEL No. 1. The people there are very bad sometimes and He wants to save them.

ANGEL No. 2. Are you sure of this?

ANGEL No. 1. I heard it from Gabriel who stands in the very presence of God.

ANGEL No. 5. I heard He wants the heavenly host to go with Him and sing.

ANGEL No. 6. Won't that be glorious?

ANGEL No. 5. But He isn't going in glory. He is to be born a poor, poor baby—in a manger!

ANGEL No. 7. God is very wise!

ANGEL No. 8. He wants to live with men and tell them of God. He will also die for them and then return to heaven.

ANGEL No. 9. How wonderful God's love is!

ANGEL No. 10. I hope every boy and girl, and every grown-up, too, will hear of Jesus and love Him. Let's sing!

ALL (Sing "Silent Night.")

CURTAIN

SCENE IV

Chorus, duet, or solo: "O Little Town of Bethlehem"

SCENE OF STREET IN BETHLEHEM: *Throughout the scene, people are milling back and forth, as many as available or desirable.* SEPHORA *and* ALMON *cross from Left.* SUSANNA *and* ENOS *cross from Right. They pass each other. Suddenly* ALMON *stops short, turns and calls.)*

ALMON. Enos?

ENOS *(Turns and looks questioningly.)*

ALMON. Enos! You do not remember me? I am Almon. We used to tend sheep together. *(The women talk in low voices.)*

ENOS. Almon, of course! What brings you here to this ugly little town? But, of course—the taxing!

ALMON. Yes, the taxing. It is a nuisance, but I have seen many old friends. And that makes up for it.

ENOS. I'll be glad to leave this wretched place. Even my donkey was stubborn in coming. *(Shakes his head.)* A peculiar thing happened just a little bit ago. The donkey had aggravated me all day. Then when I was at my wits' end, I raised my hand to strike him a good one, when just like that my hand was frozen in mid-air. Somehow I couldn't strike. *(Shakes his head again.)* Well, perhaps we will see each other again before we leave.

ALMON. Yes, perhaps we shall. But it's getting late. Peace to you and your wife. *(Both couples move slowly offstage.* DAVID *has entered from Left.* REBECCA *enters from Right. They meet a little to right of Center.)*

DAVID. The peace of God to you, Rebecca. You look doubly sweet tonight.

REBECCA. Peace to you, David. I cannot tarry. We are very busy at the Inn tonight. We have more people than we can take care of.

DAVID. The town is certainly brimming with excitement. May I see you tomorrow?

REBECCA. Why, yes, I believe so.

DAVID. What is troubling you, Rebecca?

REBECCA. Oh, nothing really. But yes, there is. I suppose it really is nothing, but I cannot put it from my mind. Tonight, not so long ago, a man and a young woman came seeking shelter. She looked so tired. They had looked everywhere and could find no place to stay. When they came to our Inn, the Innkeeper just had to tell them there was no room. But he felt sorry for them and told them they were very welcome to rest on the straw in the stable, which they seemed glad enough to do.

DAVID. And their sleeping on the straw bothers you so?

REBECCA. Well . . . I have not been able to put it out of my mind. Then just a little bit ago a beggar came to the door. The Innkeeper, being a little short of temper at this hour, raised his hand against him, and somehow his hand was caught in the air and for an instant he could not move. He looked very astonished and I too could scarcely breathe. It was as if the whole earth trembled and stopped breathing.

DAVID. What could it mean?

REBECCA. I don't know. It was a moment I shall never forget. Not a leaf stirred in the myrtle tree. The cattle ceased their lowing, the breeze stopped short—only the stars twinkled brightly. And there was one star, a very large one, that seemed all of a sudden to sweep into view. *(Rubs her eyes.)* It was all very mysterious, and a little frightening.

DAVID. Come, I will walk back to the Inn with you. *(Exit off Right.* OLD MAN *and boy* JAKIM *come slowly from Right.)*

OLD MAN. My little Jakim, it is getting late; we must get you to bed.

JAKIM. But, Grandfather, this is all so exciting, being in Bethlehem, the town of all our great forefathers.

OLD MAN. Yes, yes, I suppose it is. *(Sighs and shakes his head.)* "But thou, Bethlehem Ephratah, though thou be little among the thousands of Judah, yet out of thee shall he come forth unto me that is to be ruler in Israel; whose goings forth have been from of old, from everlasting."

JAKIM. What is that, Grandfather?

OLD MAN. That, my boy, was written by the prophet Micah many, many years ago.

JAKIM. What does it mean?

OLD MAN. It means that a great ruler shall come out of this very little town. I have thought much upon it and studied many hours and many days and I am convinced that it will be the Messiah. Just think, from this very town!

JAKIM. Oh, Grandfather, what if it should happen tonight while we are here!

OLD MAN *(Smiles and shakes his head.)* Ah, it is not likely. Our people have waited for Him for hundreds of years. *(Shakes his head thoughtfully.)* Yet, who can tell? I have had strange forebodings tonight.

JAKIM. What are forebodings?

OLD MAN. Somehow this night seems different. Remember that beggar we passed a few minutes ago? I wasn't going to give him anything because our money is running very short. But somehow my hand went into my purse quite against my will and I thrust into his hand a large coin. But just as I reached my hand forward, everything seemed suddenly to stand still—as if all breath and motion had stopped. And in the eyes of the beggar I saw a light such as I have never seen before. It . . . it wasn't . . . natural! *(Rubs his hands over his eyes.)*

JAKIM. Was it like when I was chasing the cat? That was when you gave the money to the beggar. I picked up a stone to throw at the cat and for a minute I thought I couldn't move. Then I didn't want to throw it at all. *(*OLD MAN *looks at boy, startled. Shakes his head. He and boy start to walk slowly offstage.)*

OLD MAN. It is very strange, indeed.

JAKIM. Grandfather, that star—was it there before? It's so bright!

OLD MAN. No, I don't believe it was. Strangely bright. *(Hesitates.)* I'm trying to remember something about a star. It's as if someone is whispering something, but I can't quite hear. Very strange, indeed. *(Both walk offstage at Left.)*

SCENE V

SHEPHERDS

MUSIC: *"While Shepherds Watched Their Flocks" sung if possible by one or two of the costumed shepherds.*

BEN JUDA *(Rubbing his hands.)* These nights are getting uncomfortably cool here on the hill.

ADAN. Yes, but they are clear and bright from the stars. At least we can see the lion when he comes near our sheep.

BEN JUDA. True. Would that we could have seen him two nights ago! We would have six more sheep!

ADAN. Look at Samuel! He is at his dreaming again.

BEN JUDA. Ah, if dreaming could make me as wise, then would that I should dream all the time!

ADAN. I wonder what is keeping Jonathan. It seems he should have been back long ago.

DAN. Remember, Bethlehem is full of strangers and travelers. Everyone of the house of David has come to Bethlehem to be taxed. Caesar Augustus has so decreed, then so it must be. *(Shrugs his shoulders.)*

BENJAMIN *(Scornfully.)* Caesar Augustus says *"Go to Bethlehem,"* then we go to Bethlehem. Caesar Augustus says "Pay money," we pay money. If Caesar Augustus says "Drink the ocean," we would have to drink the ocean!

SAMUEL *(Old. Stirs.)* Now Benjamin, it has not quite come to that.

BENJAMIN. And Herod! What kind of ruler can he be when he is a stranger to the house of Israel?

SAMUEL. Aye, a stranger he may be and very cruel. But in a few respects he is a good king. Somehow I feel that God will use him to accomplish His purpose. The ways of God are marvellous beyond reason.

BENJAMIN. What do you mean—His purpose?

SAMUEL. I am almost afraid of putting words together tonight. The thoughts that have troubled me tonight are almost beyond putting into words.

BEN JUDA. Why, Samuel! I have never known you to be without words!

SAMUEL. It is no jest, my son. Let us stop and reason for a moment. The temple is more beautiful now than ever— and we *can* thank Herod for that. Our people have grown in numbers in spite of oppression. And we have had comparative peace for quite a long time now. Sometimes I think that the time is close at hand when the promises of the prophets shall be fulfilled.

BEN JUDA. You mean that the Messiah shall come soon?

SAMUEL *(Smiling.)* There! It takes a youth to come out with it, straightforward. That is exactly what I mean. Is it not strange that on this very night all the descendants of David, if there be many left, are in Bethlehem by the decree of Caesar Augustus? And if we put two and two together . . . Ah, how I have studied upon it. The prophets spoke of the Messiah as the Son of David and also that He should come forth out of . . . Bethlehem!

BEN JUDA. Yes, yes, I see. Truly the ways of God are past finding out.

BENJAMIN. I should be thankful to God the rest of my days if He should send us the Messiah now. Our people need Him sorely.

SAMUEL *(Shaking his head.)* Benjamin, you are kind and thoughtful, although a little too hot-headed maybe. But if we search the Scripture, we find that the prophets do not actually refer to the Messiah as an earthly king.

BENJAMIN. What other kind of ruler could we have here in Judea?

DAN. Look, here comes Jonathan, running as if someone were about to take his life.

SAMUEL. Your eyes are sharp, Dan. You say he is running?

DAN. Yes, and it is not like him to run so at night when the path is a bit treacherous. Here he comes now.

JONATHAN *(Panting.)* Peace to you all.

ALL. Peace.

JONATHAN. Samuel, I could not wait to talk to you.

SAMUEL. What is it, my son? What has put this excitement into your voice?

JONATHAN. Tonight in Bethlehem I was stopped by a man and his young wife. They both looked so tired, especially the wife. I feared lest she would fall off the donkey. They asked directions to the Inn and when I told her she smiled at me, and when she did so it was almost as if Heaven itself bent down to thank me.

ADAN (Good-naturedly.) And the woman's smile did this to you?

JONATHAN. Oh, no, of course not. But then later I happened by the Inn and overheard the keeper tell this same pair that they had no more room. And then! Then he invited them to stay in the stable. And they went! And Samuel, she is going to have a child. It set me to thinking . . . Could it be . . . I mean, couldn't it be possible that . . . ?

SAMUEL. Say it, Jonathan, say it.

BENJAMIN. Now, Jonathan, if you are suggesting that this great ruler is to be born a lowly baby—in a *stable!*

SAMUEL (Excitedly.) Go on, Jonathan, go on. What more?

JONATHAN. I was so troubled by these thoughts as I was coming up the hill that I didn't notice the lion. Suddenly I stopped in my tracks. It took me so by surprise that all I could do was to raise my staff. And before I could strike, it was as if suddenly all life were gone from me. The lion, too, seemed almost paused in mid-air. There was a hush such as I have never experienced before. And again it was as if heaven were bending close! Then just as suddenly as it had come, the feeling was gone, and would you believe it! . . . The lion turned around and walked away as if it were a mild little lamb.

SAMUEL. Glory be to God if these things are signs. All evening I have felt a strangeness about the night. Oh, if the holy and just God would only let me live to see the day when the Messiah comes! For that I have prayed as long as I can remember. (Shakes his head.) These things are too deep for thought.

BEN JUDA. I have been watching our sheep. They are behaving very strangely. They have stopped eating and almost seem to be listening for something.

SAMUEL. This is strange indeed. *(Suddenly the* ANGEL *appears and the angel host. All gasp and fall on their knees.)*

SAMUEL. The holy angels of God Himself!

ANGEL. Fear not, for behold, I bring you good tidings of great joy, which shall be to all people. For unto you is born this day in the city of David a Savior, which is Christ the Lord. And this shall be a sign unto you; ye shall find the babe wrapped in swaddling clothes, lying in a manger.

ANGELS *(Sing "Gloria." Disappear. Silence for a moment. Then slowly the shepherds raise their heads and look around. All is quiet in the night. They rise and look at one another. Finally* SAMUEL *speaks.)*

SAMUEL. Come, let us go to Bethlehem right now and see this thing that has come to pass which the Lord has made known to us.

JONATHAN. Samuel, can it be that we are the first to know? Bethlehem seems quiet and asleep except for . . . except for that star that shines directly down on it.

SAMUEL. Come, let us not tarry a minute. Oh, may God be praised! *(All hurry offstage.)*

CURTAIN

SCENE VI

THE THREE WISE MEN

MUSIC. *"We Three Kings"*

THREE WISE MEN *step out in front of the curtain.*

BALTHASAR. Come, let's have our camels rest a moment.

MELCHIOR. Indeed, it feels good to stand on my own two feet again.

BALTHASAR. What a gloriously beautiful night! This wonderful creation of God's!

MELCHIOR. Tell me again, how does it happen that you know about this God of Israel?

BALTHASAR. King Nebuchadnezzar brought the people of Israel to Babylon when he made conquest of Jerusalem. It was in the city of Babylon that these people told me about their God. But too many of them have forgotten Him since! And what a holy religion. Not the human sacrifices and the shameless rites that my former religion taught.

MELCHIOR. What, then, does their religion offer?

BALTHASAR. Peace of heart and hope.

CASPAR. Then I want to hear more of it. My religion has left despair in my heart.

MELCHIOR. Tell me again, how did you interpret this new star?

BALTHASAR. In the writings of the people of Israel a star is mentioned. A great Star of Jacob sent from God that shall rise to save His people—not so much from worldly oppression, but from sin itself.

CASPAR. What a marvellous God to be so concerned about His people!

BALTHASAR. And this star that we see, if my calculations are correct, and yours too, must lead us to Jerusalem in Palestine.

MELCHIOR. Then let us hurry on. That is not so far distant!

BALTHASAR. Look, the star is suddenly brighter than ever. Come! Back to our camels. *(The three go off.)*

SCENE VII

KING HEROD

MILITARY MUSIC

A Roman guard steps out of the door on the left of the stage and one from the door at the right of the stage. If no door, from behind the curtain. They march stiffly to opposite edges of the stage and stand at attention. Curtain is closed.

MARCUS *(At Left. Looks cautiously around.)* Good Claudius, is no one around?

CLAUDIUS. I think not. What is it?.

MARCUS. Have you heard the strange news tonight?

CLAUDIUS. No. What news?

MARCUS. Good Marcellus just came through Bethlehem on his way back from his long journey. And as he passed through, he met some shepherds who were jubilant and almost beside themselves with joy. They were shouting, "God be praised, our King has come."

CLAUDIUS. No! What king?

MARCUS. I have no idea. But you know these Judeans. They have tried to make trouble before.

CLAUDIUS *(Whistles softly.)* If King Herod finds this out there will be bloodshed, I'll wager.

MARCUS *(Chuckles.)* Can't you see the expression on his face? *(Mimics.)* A new king? Incredible! Impossible! By all the thunder in Rome, there'd better not be!

CLAUDIUS. Even his wine wouldn't help him much.

MARCUS. Shh. Someone is coming.

GLADDIUS *(Enters through the Right door, or from behind the curtain. Stiffly calls out.)* A message for his majesty, King Herod.

CURTAIN: *Opens at Center, showing* HEROD, *and a guard on either side of the throne.*

GLADDIUS *(Marches before* HEROD *and bows slightly.)* Your majesty, three men of royalty are awaiting your audience.

HEROD. What is their business?

GLADDIUS. They . . . your Honor . . . they . . . are from the far East.

HEROD. I asked you, "What is their business?" Don't you know I am a busy man? Speak up!

GLADDIUS. They are here to find . . . the new King.

HEROD. What! A new king? Incredible! Impossible! By all the thunder in Rome, there'd better not be! *(GUARDS exchange quick glances.)*

GLADDIUS. What shall I tell them, good sir?

HEROD. Send them away! Such impudence! No, bring them in. I would hear more of this new King.

GLADDIUS. Very well, your highness. *(Goes out through the right door.)*

HEROD. A new king? Should I not hear it from Caesar himself? *(GLADDIUS enters with Three Wise Men. They come before HEROD and bow low.)* Rise. *(Speaks calmer.)* Now, who are you?

BALTHASAR. We have come from the far East where we first saw His star.

HEROD. What star? What are you prattling about?

BALTHASAR. From the writings of the people of Israel, we know that the star we saw betokens the arrival of a new King.

HEROD. Gladdius, go consult with the scribes and the pharisees to see where this . . . this King should come from. And hurry. They are gathered in the palace this night. *(Turning to the Wise Men.)* And how did you first perceive this star?

BALTHASAR. We are magi. One evening we were studying the stars and even then we were speaking of the promise of a Messiah to the people of Israel. Suddenly this brilliant new star came into view, even as we were watching. We knew then that the time had come and that the God of Israel took this form of announcing it. We have come to worship Him.

HEROD. Just figments of imagination! These Hebrew people are well noted for it. *(GLADDIUS enters and comes before HEROD.)* Well, what did you find out?

GLADDIUS. Good sir, the pharisees and the scribes say that the King will come from Bethlehem.

HEROD. Bethlehem, is it? A king from Bethlehem? Impossible! *(Turning to Magi.)* But perhaps this is so. Now go on your way, and when you find this King, return to me and tell *me* where to find Him, so that I may go and worship Him also.

BALTHASAR. You are very kind.

CASPAR *and* MELCHIOR. Thank you, good sir. *(All three bow low, and follow* GLADDIUS *out at Right.)*

HEROD. A king, indeed! *(The guards exit by the side doors or the curtain.)*

CURTAIN

SCENE VIII

STABLE

MUSIC: *Suggested, choir backstage singing "O Holy Night."*

SCENE *opens with* MARY, JOSEPH, *and* BABY, *with angel choir hovering in the background.*

JOSEPH *and* MARY *gaze intently at the Baby. (The light in the manger is more effective than a doll.)*

MARY *(Slowly, still gazing at Baby.)* Truly my heart is too full to speak. *(*JOSEPH *merely nods.* SHEPHERDS *come from Right. Fall on their knees before the crib.)*

SAMUEL. May the God of our forefathers be praised from this time forth and forevermore.

JONATHAN. Honor to the new King!

SAMUEL. We are poor, humble shepherds with nothing to bring except our hearts and our faith in You. Accept these poor gifts as they are given, in great hope.

MARY. Arise, good shepherds. *(*SHEPHERDS *rise.)* How is it that you have come here?

JONATHAN *(Excitedly.)* All evening I had sensed something most unusual about to happen. When I returned to the hill we were even then talking about the promised Messiah and how according to the prophets He would come out of Bethlehem, when suddenly an angel appeared in all the splendor of heaven and announced to us that the time had come. "For unto you is born," he said, "in the city of David a Savior, which is Christ the Lord."

BEN JUDA. And then he said, "And this shall be a sign unto you, ye shall find the Babe wrapped in swaddling clothes, lying in a manger."

DAN. The Star, too, shone over this stable.

SAMUEL. And so, by the very hand of God Himself, we have first found the Messiah—the Son of God and Son of Man! Oh, now I am happy for I have seen the prophesies come true! (MARY and JOSEPH *look at each other as if hardly able to believe their ears.* SHEPHERDS *bow low again and begin to depart.)*

WOMAN (*Comes from the door, or curtain, at Left, a passer-by. Halts momentarily as* SHEPHERDS *begin to leave. Front stage is to represent a street throughout.)*

SAMUEL. Most noble lady! See! Good news! Our Messiah has come. (*Points to the manger.)*

WOMAN. Messiah? Here? This child in the stable? (*Laughs and shrugs her shoulders and moves on. A* SECOND WOMAN *enters, passer-by, from the door at Right. She is carrying a pitcher on her head.)*

JONATHAN (*To her.)* Oh, joyous night. Our Messiah has been born. (SECOND WOMAN *shows momentary disbelief.)* Truly He has been born even as our prophets foretold. (FIRST WOMAN *hesitates on her way.)*

SECOND WOMAN. May God be praised! (*Goes slowly toward the crib. The* SHEPHERDS *begin to move off Left.)*

SAMUEL. Come, we must tell all the town of this! Nay, all the world! (*Off Left.)*

SECOND WOMAN (*Bowing low.)* Thanks, praise, and glory to our God for this wonderful gift. Accept this very humble token of my faith and esteem. (*Rises and moves off Left, leaving the pitcher.* FIRST WOMAN *shrugs and is about to go off at Right when* MAGI *come in from Right. She bows to them.* MAGI *bow shortly to her.)*

BALTHASAR. This must be the place. Look! There. It is really true! *(*MAGI *bow low before the crib.)* Hail to the great new King to whom Thy people have looked with hungry hearts. I bring Thee gold from my country. *(*FIRST WOMAN *scratches her head, shrugs, and leaves.)*

MELCHIOR. And I bring Thee frankincense.

CASPAR. And I bring myrrh. Even in Thy love and power, Thou will have much to suffer.

MARY *(In wonder.)* And how is it that you came here?

BALTHASAR. Oh, most blessed mother, we saw the star in the East, and we knew that the great King had finally come. So we have followed the star to this very stable to worship this new King, even thy Child. *(*MARY *and* JOSEPH *again look at each other wordlessly as the* MAGI *begin to leave from the Left door.)*

CASPAR *(As they leave.)* Now we must go back to King Herod.

BALTHASAR. No, that we cannot do. In a dream an angel of God appeared to me and bade us go another way. *(The* MAGI *leave as this speech is made.* MARY *sings a lullaby.)*

CURTAIN

SCENE IX
FIREPLACE

CURTAIN *pulled back behind the fireplace, showing* TOMMY, SUSAN, *and* STRANGER *in the same position as at the end of Scene I.*

TOMMY. Oh, that was wonderful!

SUSAN. I've heard the Christmas story so often, but never quite like that!

TOMMY. I wish all the boys and girls all over the world could see the Baby Jesus like we saw Him tonight!

STRANGER. They can, and many of them do.

TOMMY and SUSAN. ᴛhey do?

STRANGER. Yes, from far and near, children came tonight to see Him. *(Smiles.)* And He likes children so very much because they believe in Him so simply. Would you like to see some of these children?

TOMMY and SUSAN. Oh, yes.

STRANGER. Very well. *(Curtain opens on MARY, JOSEPH and the BABY. Angel choir hovers near, singing, "Oh Come, Little Children," while tiny tots, any number, come up and kneel around the manger. They sing, "Away In A Manger." The curtain closes.)*

SUSAN. Oh, I'm ever so glad you showed us that.

TOMMY. This much I know. The best Christmas gift *ever* was Jesus! *(STRANGER smiles and places a hand on the arm of TOMMY.)*

SUSAN. Oh! Did you hurt your hand?

TOMMY. Why, there's a scar on each hand.

STRANGER. Yes, I was hurt once. But, you know, I can't feel it now when I see people loving each other and loving the Baby Jesus most of all.

SUSAN. You know, I feel kind of like the shepherds felt —as if Heaven were very, very close.

TOMMY *(Slowly.)* I think it would be nice if we knelt down as the shepherds and wise men did, to say "Thank You" to God. *(Both kneel toward the audience. STRANGER stands behind them and raises his arms as in benediction. Then leaves quietly when the prayer is almost finished.)*

SUSAN. Dear God, we do want to say "Thank You" for the Baby Jesus. Forgive all the people tonight who forgot. Thank you for sending Him into the world where He suffered for us; where He was nailed to the cross, with cruel nails through His hands . . . *(TOMMY and SUSAN look stunned. Look at each other and rise. Rub their eyes. They turn to the STRANGER who is no longer there. Look at each other again.)* He was just here.

TOMMY. Maybe I can call him back. *(Runs out and soon returns. Scratches his head.)* Sis! There aren't any tracks in the snow in front of the door.

SUSAN. Oh . . . Tommy!

TOMMY *(Slowly.)* You know, my leather jacket and my

football don't seem so important anymore. I know what I'll do! If I get my jacket, I'll give it to Billy. His folks are awfully poor and his clothes never seem quite warm enough.

SUSAN. And if I get my pretty blue gloves, I could give them to Helen. Imagine having Christmas when her father is in the hospital!

TOMMY. You know, this is the nicest Christmas I ever had.

SUSAN. The very nicest. It seems as if I can hear all the children in the whole world, singing, "Joy To The World, The Lord Is Come." *(Curtain opens. The children on stage with red candles glowing, see instructions for making candles. All other lights out. Sing "Joy To The World." Curtain slowly closes.)*

END
HOUSE LIGHTS

STAGING

The following sketches are suggested stage settings. These are planned to eliminate any delay in changing scenery. As you will note, the first three scenes can be almost completely set up when the play begins. Then while Scene 4 is progressing in front of the stage curtain, the scenery for Scene 5 can be set up.

During the intermission, Scenes 7 and 8 can be almost completely set up (Scene 6 requiring no special scenery). Scene 9, as you will observe in reading the script, demands no special scenery but includes staging found in Scenes 1 and 8.

This plan is very advantageous to those who have very limited staging facilities.

In order to carry out this plan, it is essential to stretch two wires tightly across the width of the stage, one approximately at center stage and one approximately three-fourths of the way back (high enough to be hidden from the audience). The purpose of these wires is to support the various "backdrops" which can be quickly swished on or off. Use large safety pins, four or five inches apart, to fasten the "backdrops" on the wire.

Scene I

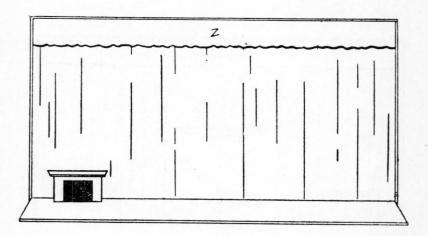

Fireplace is placed immediately behind the curtain. When play is to begin, the curtain man flips the curtain around behind the fireplace (*before* footlights go on). The fire can easily be made by placing a light bulb under red tissue paper crumpled into peaks. Several small pieces of wood criss-cross over the paper complete the effect. A base of cardboard covered with aluminum foil makes an excellent reflector. Also, the rigidity of the cardboard permits the handling of the "fire" without wear and tear (to be used for Scene V also).

When footlights go on, play is to begin.

Scene II

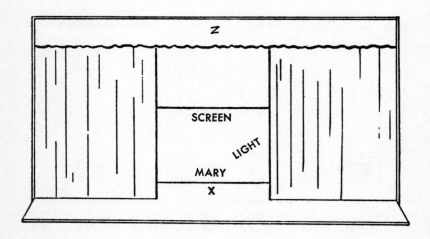

Since Scene III is already set up, it is necessary to use a screen just far enough back to enable Mary to be seated. Pull curtain only as far as indicated.

The angel may actually appear, but a bright light appearing suddenly is more effective. The voice, then, should come from immediately behind the curtain.

Scene III

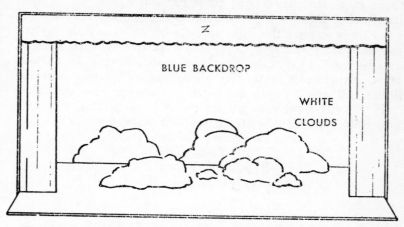

The cloth backdrop of medium blue is to be hung on the wire farthest to the back of the stage. Small silver stars, preferably 1½-inch or 2-inch stars, glued to the curtain are very effective.

Clouds are made of large heavy cardboard boxes (can be obtained most easily from furniture stores). Cut out in shape of clouds, then cover with white crepe paper that has been stretched here and there to give a billowy effect. It is highly desirable to paint the cardboard white with poster paint before covering with crepe paper. (Poster paint is more economical when purchased in powder form). Should the cardboard curl from the dampness after painting, then dampen the unpainted side with water, place the cloud on the floor, painted side down, and weight down with books, etc., until dry. Make triangular standards and fasten securely to the backs of the clouds. This can be done with very heavy cardboard since the clouds are not heavy.

Most effective are two large clouds (approximately 4½ feet high), two somewhat smaller (3½ feet), two still smaller (2½ feet), and two quite small (1½ feet or so). See above for suggested placement.

To give this heavenly scene an ethereal touch, add colored

lighting. If you have no reflectors, make them by cutting three large tin cans (fruit juice cans are perfect) in half, lengthwise. Place a light in each and place behind three of the clouds so that the light reflects on other clouds toward the back of the stage. Cover these reflectors with colored gelatin paper so that the clouds are touched with the various hues. Experiment with the placement of clouds and the lights. All other lights are to be off except the footlights.

If you are unable to obtain the colored gelatin sheets in your city, you may write to the following company:

Brigham Sheet Gelatin, Inc.,
17-19 Weston Street
Randolph, Vermont
(write for samples first)

Scene IV

No scenery is necessary since Scene IV is completely in front of the main curtain. Street lamps give an added touch. They can be made from large tin cans and old lumber, with a flashlight inserted through the bottom of the can. Only other lights are footlights.

Scene V

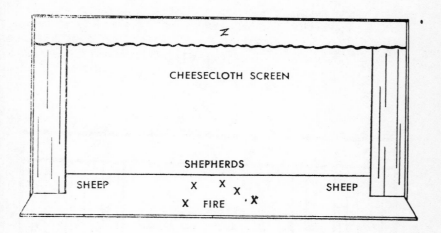

On the wire that is stretched across the stage at about center, hang a netting of cheesecloth, stretched taut. Behind this is the angel choir. These angels may be placed on several step-ladders.

In front of the cheesecloth screen are the shepherds around the fire. To give the effect of night, no lights are on except the fire and several blue lights immediately in front of the cheesecloth screen, shining onto the screen, but not through it. This will also hide the angels behind the screen. Sheep can be made from cardboard with fluffs of cotton pasted on them.

Several bright spotlights behind the cheesecloth screen are necessary. These are switched on simultaneously when the angels are to appear.

Scene VI
No scenery—see script

Scene VII

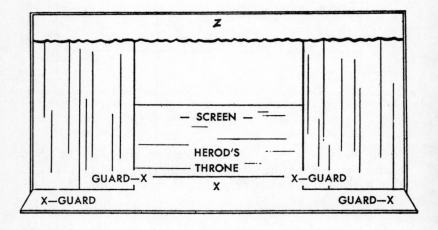

So that the stage may be set for Scene VIII, it is suggested that the screen used in Scene II be used here. Herod's throne is as far front as the main curtain will permit.

The screen can be made from heavy cardboard supported by scraps of lumber, and covered with drapery. Footlights as well as an overhead light will be sufficient lighting.

Scene VIII

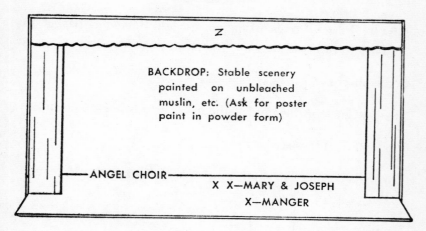

The backdrop should be hung on the wire farthest to the rear of the stage. It is not too difficult to make such a drop, even for the amateur. It is suggested to find a picture of a suitable background, then mark the picture into squares to correspond with the much larger squares marked on the muslin. For convenience, number the squares on all four sides on both picture and muslin. In this manner it is relatively simple to transfer the picture onto the muslin in correct proportions.

Scene IX

Instructions for staging this scene are explained in the play itself.

SPECIAL PROPERTIES

Fireplace (For fire, see staging suggestions in Scene I)

Basket: Fasten strips of paper upright inside a basket to give the impression of a basket in process of weaving.

6 Shepherds' Crooks.

Sheep: Cut from heavy cardboard. Paste tufts of cotton on.

Pitcher or old vase.

Throne: Cover legs and arms of chair with gold paper. Purple or dark green draperies hung over chair.

Manger and stool for Mary.

Gold, frankincense, and myrrh.

Candles for Scene IX. Make from heavy red paper. Make "flame" from yellow crepe paper. Insert lighted Christmas tree light bulbs. (Beautiful effect)

THE LOST STAR

A CHRISTMAS PLAY IN ONE ACT
AND FOUR SCENES

By

MERLO HEICHER and ROBERT ST. CLAIR

PRODUCTION RIGHTS

471

CAST OF CHARACTERS

For thirteen men and six women)

THE NARRATOR, (either male or female)
HEROD, the king
A PRIEST
A ROMAN SOLDIER
A BEGGAR
MELCHIOR ⎫
BALTHAZAR ⎬ the Three Wise Men
CASPER ⎭
AN OLD MAN
AN OLD WOMAN
A MIDDLE-AGED WOMAN
SECOND YOUNG MAN
THIRD YOUNG MAN
SECOND YOUNG WOMAN
SECOND OLD MAN
MARY
JOSEPH
GABRIEL

NOTE: *Where a shorter cast is required, those portraying the characters of the soldier, the beggar spy, the priest, and even Joseph and Mary and Herod may also portray some of the people at "Dry Wells" with a slight change of costume.*

472

SYNOPSIS OF SCENES

SCENE ONE:
A room in Herod's palace.

SCENE TWO:
An oasis outside Jerusalem, called "Dry Wells."

SCENE THREE:
Herod's palace again.

SCENE FOUR:
The stable of an inn at Bethlehem.

PRODUCTION NOTE: The entire play is performed without scenery. All that is needed is a set of masking drapes, a few pieces of furniture, the manger and a fake well. When the play is produced in a church, these things will be used on the chancel, and colored spotlights will be used for the light effects. In this case, the lights will all be turned out at the end of each scene, and will, of course, come on again after the Narrator has finished speaking.

AT THE BEGINNING, *a Narrator, either male or female, appears at the left side of the stage, or platform, dressed in Biblical garments and bathed in a soft, rose-colored light. Appropriate, religious type music fades in softly as a background while the Narrator speaks. The narration may either be committed to memory or read from an ancient-looking scroll.*

NARRATOR. When Jesus first came into the world, and while He was still lying in the manger in Bethlehem, three Wise Men came out of the East to worship Him. The names of the Wise Men, or Magi, as they were called in those days, were Melchior, Balthazar and Casper. Where they first met, no one knows. But each was following the great, new star that was supposed to guide them on their journey and take them to the new-born King. Their arrival in Jerusalem was, of course, reported to Herod, the king, who had already heard that the long-expected Deliverer of the Jews had been born. However, no one seemed to know just where the birth had taken place, and this was something that Herod was trying frantically to discover because he felt that now his throne was in danger. There had been talk of a Jewish rebellion, and now that they had a King, Herod was desperately afraid they would try to overthrow him and the Roman rule and place their own men in power. Since Melchior, Balthazar and Casper told everyone they met why they were taking their long journey, Herod sent for them to come to the palace and have an audience with him. Now, at last, he hoped to find out more about this mysterious child who was destined to become a King, and perhaps he could have the babe assassinated. *(The rose-colored light goes out, the music rises, the* NARRATOR *exits in the darkness, and the stage lights come up.)*

THE LOST STAR

SCENE ONE

LOCALITY: *A room in* HEROD'S *palace. No actual stage setting is required; merely a set of draperies of a cylorama.
However, the curtains my be parted at the back to show
a glimpse of the roof tops of Jerusalem if desired, and a
couple of large hangings may be pinned onto the draperies to give color and atmosphere to the setting. A small
dais, or platform, is halfway down Right Center. This is
discovered with an Oriental rug. A Roman type chair is
on the dais, together with a small taboret, or low pedestal,
on which there is a bowl of fruit. A low, ornate bench
stands halfway down Left. There is no more furniture
required, although the balance of the stage may be
"dressed" according to the wishes of the director. Where
the play is being performed in a church, the dais and
bench may be dispensed with altogether, and instead of
the curtain rising the lights will merely come up for each
scene and go out between them.*

AT THE RISE OF THE CURTAIN: HEROD *is seated in the chair
on the dais, talking to the* PRIEST, *who stands at Center.*
HEROD *is absently munching on a peach as he frowns
and talks. He is a gross, animalistic-looking man, garbed
in a white toga, with Roman sandals on his feet. His dark,
oily hair is tightly curled and he wears a narrow white
band about his head. The elderly priest has a long white
beard and white hair. His costume is typical of the
temple priests of the period. The music dies away as*
HEROD *speaks.*

HEROD *(As if continuing a conversation.)* And you say
they know where the child and his parents are living?

PRIEST. That is what our spies report to us, your majesty.

HEROD. Where did they come from?

PRIEST. The East, they say.

HEROD *(Impatiently.)* Where in the East?

PRIEST *(Shrugging his shoulders.)* I do not know.

HEROD *(Grimly thoughtful. Leaning back in the chair.)* Well, we'll soon find out. They should be here before long. And then . . . *(His voice trails away.)*

PRIEST. They have several camels, sire. One for each of them to ride, and a third heavily laden with gifts, they say.

HEROD *(Looking up. Quickly.)* Gifts?

PRIEST *(Nodding a slow affirmative.)* Gifts for this child they're going to worship. The new born King *they* call Him.

HEROD *(Lowly. Thoughtfully.)* King of the Jews. *(In sudden, angry disgust.)* Pah! What nonsense! I am getting tired of the Jews and their ridiculous superstitions. How do they know that *this* mysterious child is any different from any *other* Jewish baby, hundreds of which are born every day in the *year?*

PRIEST. Because of the prophecies, your Majesty. The ancient Scriptures foretell the coming of the Messiah, and many people believe that at last He is here.

HEROD *(Leaning forward.)* In the form of a baby? What utter stupidity! *(Rises, steps down off the dais and moves Left toward the bench as he continues talking.)* They must have the minds of children. It is small wonder that they have been in captivity and persecuted for so many ages. *(Turning in front of the bench to face the* PRIEST *again.)* Look you here! If there *is* a God such as they believe in, which, of course there isn't, do you not think that He would have the power to appear on the earth as a full *grown man* instead of having to go through all the trouble of being born and waiting to grow up before He could wrest my throne away from me?

PRIEST *(Nodding a quick, obsequious affirmative.)* That seems reasonable, your majesty. *(Moves a step or two closer to* HEROD.*)*

HEROD. To be sure it's reasonable. We Romans are a practical people. That is why we have so many gods. Gods of convenience—one for every occasion. However, we never

take them seriously. To the intelligent, they are merely interesting legends. We would never die for them. If we are
displeased with one we turn to another. That is why we are
so powerful and why we rule the world. Our faith is a material faith, and that is the only way to live. However . . .
*(His voice trails away and he frowns again as he moves
over to the Right.)*

PRIEST. You are very wise, your majesty. *(A soldier
enters briskly down Left and comes to attention with a
quick salute.)*

SOLDIER. The Magi are here, your majesty.

HEROD. Good. I will see them at once. *(Quickly resumes
his seat on the dais.)*

SOLDIER *(Saluting again.)* Yes, your majesty. *(Turns
about in a military fashion and exits.)*

PRIEST. Shall I go, sire? *(Backs away from the dais a
step or two toward the Left.)*

HEROD. No. I want you to remain throughout the interview. You know their beliefs and all the silly prophecies.
The men will be cautious, evasive mayhap. However, they
shall not be allowed to leave the palace until they have told
me all I wish to know. *(Settles himself in his chair and
smiles with false friendliness as the three Wise Men, MEL-
CHIOR, BALTHAZAR and CASPER enter down Left, where they
pause for the greetings. The PRIEST moves up Center, where
he turns to watch the proceedings. The SOLDIER follows the
Wise Men in and remains at attention close to the entrance.)*

MELCHIOR. Hail, Herod ∴ . .

BALTHAZAR. Mighty ruler of Jerusalem . . .

CASPER. Peace be unto you and unto your rule.

HEROD *(Nodding a smiling return.)* And peace be unto
you, my friends. You have journeyed far, I hear? *(Exchanges meaning glances with the PRIEST and waits for the
answer.)*

BALTHAZAR *(Going closer to the dais.)* Far indeed, your
majesty.

MELCHOIR. From Egypt and beyond . . . *(Goes closer to
BALTHAZAR.)*

HEROD *(Leaning forward.)* For what purpose, my I ask?

CASPER *(Calmly. Standing Left, in front of the bench.)* We have come to seek the King . . .

HEROD *(Drawing himself up.)* I am the king . . .

BALTHAZAR. The new-born King . . .

MELCHIOR. King of the Jews.

HEROD *(As if just remembering. With assumed casualness.)* Oh, yes. I *have* heard the tale of the mysterious birth of some infant that is supposed to be the long-awaited Deliverer, or some such nonsense. *(Leaning quickly forward. To* BALTHAZAR, *with a penetrating look.)* What is the name of this child? What is he called?

BALTHAZAR. He is called . . . the Christ.

PRIEST *(Going quickly closer to the upstage end of the dais.)* The Messiah, your majesty.

MELCHIOR *(To* HEROD.*)* And his name is Jesus.

HEROD. Who are his parents? Where do they live?

BALTHAZAR. We do not know, your majesty . . .

MELCHIOR. We each had a dream, and in the dream we were visited by an angel, who told us to rise up and follow the star.

HEROD *(Amazed.)* The star? What star?

CASPER *(Moving closer to* MELCHIOR *and* BALTHAZAR.*)* A new star, your majesty. One that has never been seen before. We follow it every night and it is always before us.

BALTHAZAR. It appears every evening at sunset, and it is larger and more brilliant than all the others in the sky. It seems to move as we move.

HEROD *(His voice silky, his face craftily smiling.)* And it led you here to Jerusalem? The child you seek is here?

MELCHIOR. No, your majesty. The child is in Bethlehem.

HEROD *(Astonished.)* Bethlehem? *(Looks toward the* PRIEST.*)*

PRIEST *(With a sarcastic smile.)* A miserable place for the Savior of a race to be born in.

HEROD *(To the Wise Men again.)* What makes you think that Bethlehem is the end of your journey?

BALTHAZAR. Because it was over Bethlehem that the star was hovering the last time we saw it yesterday at eventide.

HEROD *(Leaning back in his chair. Thoughtfully.)* Over Bethlehem, eh?

PRIEST *(Taking up the interrogation.)* We have been taking a nation-wide census, and thousands of people have been going in and out of Bethlehem for days, even as they are going in and out of Jerusalem. Undoubtedly many children have been born there recently. How will you know which man-child is the great Messiah you seek to worship? *(Smiles at* HEROD, *who nods a slow, smiling approval of the question. The Wise Men look at each other, and this time is is* CASPER *who speaks to* HEROD.)

CASPER. The star will tell us. The star will shine upon the place of His birth, and we . . . shall know. *(There is a short, awkward silence during which* HEROD *frowns and taps his fingers on the arm of his chair. Then he smiles again as he comes to a decision.)*

HEROD. So be it. You are on a wonderful mission and I am sure that you will be rewarded for your pains. *(He rises and steps down off the dais closer to the Wise Men.)* I am grateful to you for accepting my invitation to come to the palace and have this little talk with me. I am greatly impressed by what I have learned. Before you leave, however, I should like to ask a favor of you. *(Lowers his voice a trifle, but emphasizes the words carefully.)* After you have found this miraculous child who is some day to rule the Jews, come back to Jerusalem and tell me where *I* may find Him so that I may give Him recognition and go to worship also. *(Beams at* BALTHAZAR *and lays a friendly hand on his shoulder.)* And now you may depart. *(The Wise Men simply bow a trifle, then start away to the Left. As soon as their backs are turned,* HEROD *turns to give the grinning* PRIEST *a broad wink, and the lights go out. Instantly, the offstage music fades in again, and the* NARRATOR *enters down Left in the darkness.)*

CURTAIN

NARRATOR *(Speaking as soon as the rose-colored light comes on to illuminate him . . . or her . . . again.)* On the road from Jerusalem to Bethlehem there is an old well where it is said that the Three Wise Men paused for a while on their journey to find the new-born King. According to the legend, they started out the morning after their audience with the crafty Herod with high hopes, for their journey was now about over. They had brought many presents: frankincense and myrrh, gold and costly raiment and glittering jewels. Somewhere along the way they got to wondering just what the birth of the Savior was going to mean to them personally. Would they be rewarded? What honors should be theirs for being the first to acknowledge and worship Him? So they stopped alongside the road and made their camp one morning to argue this out. All day they argued back and forth. They were still arguing at sunset, as they prepared to move onward again. This was a great misfortune because, for the first time since they had banded together, greed and jealousy and selfishness became manifest. The Wise Men were wise no longer. *(The music rises, the light goes out, the* NARRATOR *disappears, and another light comes on to illuminate the Wise Men, who are now moving down the aisle from the back of the auditorium, or church, toward the stage, or chancel.)*

SCENE THREE

LOCALITY: *Dry Wells. The curtain does not go up for a while, or—if the play is being produced in a church— the lights on the chancel will not come on immediately. The first part of the scene is supposed to take place on a road leading to Dry Wells, and this is, of course, the center aisle. The Wise Men begin to argue as soon as the light that illuminates them comes on. They walk slowly, and each carries a half-filled water bag.*

CASPER *(As if continuing an argument.)* I have the rarest of frankincense to give Him. So, it is only natural that He shall give especial attention to *me*.

BALTHAZAR. Oh, no, Casper. I have myrrh and gold to lay at His feet. And; for that reason, *I* shall be the favored one.

MELCHIOR. You talk like a stupid man, Balthazar. If any of us are favored it shall be *I*, for I have costly raiments, kingly robes, and a diadem for His head. These things shall show Him that I, Melchior, have great faith and acknowledge Him to be the King of *Kings. (By this time they should be fairly close to the stage, or chancel, and here they stop for a short while.)*

CASPER. *I* acknowledge Him to be the Savior of *mankind.* I shall sit at His feet and worship Him as a God, and for that He shall give me authority and riches.

BALTHAZAR *(Contemptuously.)* Pah! What are riches and authority on this earth compared to the exalted place in heaven that *I* shall win?

MELCHIOR. You are fools, the both of you. I shall have nothing more to do with you. I shall continue on my way *alone. (Moves a step or two ahead of the others, but pauses again as they speak.)*

CASPER *(Suspiciously.)* What do you have in mind, Melchior? Are you going to try and get to the destination before us?

BALTHAZAR *(Nodding an angry affirmative.)* Yea! That

is his intention! He wishes to accept all the credit for our long journey.

CASPER. And reap the rewards alone! *(MELCHIOR looks upwards and stiffens in startled wonder. The other two fail to notice this reaction right away.)*

BALTHAZAR *(He and CASPER go on either side of MEL-CHIOR.)* You cannot take the camels. If you go ahead of us, you go on foot!

CASPER. The star leads *us* as well as *you*.

MELCHIOR *(Without moving. Still looking upwards.)* Peace! Peace, I say!

BALTHAZAR *(To CASPER.)* Suppose we each mount our camels and race?

MELCHIOR. Where is the star?

CASPER *(Puzzledly.)* The . . . star?

MELCHIOR *(Excitedly.)* Yes! Look- upwards! The star is gone!

BALTHAZAR *(He and CASPER jerk their heads up.)* Gone?

CASPER. So it is!

MELCHIOR. And the heavens are dark!

BALTHAZAR *(Awe and fear creeping into his voice.)* It was there a few moments ago!

CASPER. Shining bright and clear!

MELCHIOR. Now there no stars at all!

BALTHAZAR. The sky is like a blank abyss!

CASPER *(Lowly. Fearfully. Shuddering a little.)* I feel a cold wind. It chills me to the bone!

MELCHIOR *(Looking fearfully to the right and left.)* A rushing wind . . .

CASPER *(Also looking slowly around.)* And yet nothing stirs . . .

BALTHAZAR. I feel no wind. All I feel is a great emptiness . . .

MELCHIOR. What is it? What has happened? There is a mystery here!

CASPER. Everything is strange. Which way shall we go? I am fearful . . .

BALTHAZAR. And I! It is as if we had been forsaken! *(Soft music fades in and the curtain rises—or dim amber lights come on—to show the ancient well in the middle of the stage, or platform, with a number of aimless and de-jected-looking men and women slowly moving about. These people are old, middle-aged and young, and are of both sexes. They look miserable and lost. The Wise Men do not notice them at first.)*

MELCHIOR *(Speaking on the cue from* BALTHAZAR *" . . . we had been forsaken.")* Alas! the star is gone and we are lost!

BALTHAZAR. Let us not be frantic. Mayhap the star will come again.

CASPER. We were sinful to quarrel among ourselves, and now we are being punished. Let us cast out the greed and jealousy in our souls and unite ourselves as we were before. *(And now all three of them turn toward the front and react in startled surprise as they see the people around the well.)*

MELCHIOR. Look, yon! An oasis!

BALTHAZAR. With many travelers surrounding a well!

CASPER. Something is wrong with them! Look at their faces. Observe how listless they are!

MELCHIOR. They seem bewildered and lost . . .

BALTHAZAR. My water bag is almost empty.

CASPER *(Shaking his.)* Mine is no more than half full.

MELCHIOR. Mine is about the same. Let us fill them before we go onward to Bethlehem. *(They move closer to the stage or platform. An old man sees them coming and holds up his hand.)*

OLD MAN *(In a hoarse, cracked voice.)* No water here. No water here. *(And now an old woman turns to look at the Wise Men.)*

OLD WOMAN. The well is dry. *(The music fades away.)*

CASPER. Dry?

OLD MAN *(Nodding a sad, dejected affirmative.)* Aye. And we all but die from thirst. *(The rest of the people turn to look at the Wise Men in listless apathy.)*

BALTHAZAR *(To the* OLD MAN.*)* Then why do you stay?

MELCHIOR. Yea. Why do you not go on to another well?

OLD MAN *(Wringing his hands together. In a wailing sort of voice.)* We know not the way! We are lost!

BALTHAZAR *(Amazedly.)* All of you?

OLD WOMAN *(Also wailing.)* Aye! And there is nothing to do but wait for death to overtake us! *(Instantly all the others take up a weird, chanting cry.)*

OMNES. Lost! Forsaken! We have lost the star! *(They start to move about again . . . slowly, from Right to Left and Left to Right, passing each other in front of and back of the well.)*

MELCHIOR *(To BALTHAZAR and CASPER, as he quickly sucks in his breath.)* The . . . star! *(He goes up the steps onto the stage, or platform, addressing the OLD MAN.)* Tell us more. You too have been following a star?

OLD MAN *(Nodding a slow affirmative.)* Every one follows a star. But I turned left when my star told me to turn right. It was a matter of choice. I knew the right way to go, but I was stubborn . . . I thought I knew it all. Nobody could tell me anything. And because I wouldn't listen to good advice I lost the star and ended up here at Dry Wells. *(He sighs deeply and moves away to the Right. CASPER mounts the steps and addresses the OLD WOMAN, who will be on the left side of him as he pauses.)*

CASPER *(To the OLD WOMAN.)* And you, old woman? How did *you* come to Dry Wells?

OLD WOMAN. I was following a star, but I lost my faith and turned back. I just didn't have the courage to go on because the way led over the desert. Desert travel is hard—hot, dusty days—cold nights—meagre food, little water. I got to thinking that back home there was comfort—stew in the pot and water in the well. So I went back. But the star had disappeared and I didn't know the way. So I ended up here. *(She sighs and moves away to the Left.)*

BALTHAZAR *(Going up the steps. Talking to a virile-looking young man who, at that moment, comes through the others and down, to Left Center.)* How do you happen to be here, young man?

YOUNG MAN *(Shrugging his shoulders.)* I tried to take a short cut.

BALTHAZAR. What do you mean?

YOUNG MAN. Well, you see, the star led me into a village

they called Prayer, and there I stayed. I found Prayer a rather stuffy sort of village. People were dull and serious. All they did was kneel or stand around and pray. They didn't seem to be getting any place. There was no fun for me in Prayer. I didn't think I needed what that place had to offer. So I took a short cut and lost the star. I have learned my lesson, but it is too late. Too late. *(His voice trails away, he sighs and moves upstage behind the others.)*

MELCHIOR *(Turning to an attractive young woman who moves downstage beside him.)* Were you following a star?

YOUNG WOMAN. Aye, and I didn't mean to lose it. But, you see, I have a very bad trait.

MELCHIOR. What is that?

YOUNG WOMAN *(Shrugging her shoulders.)* I go around in circles most of the time.

MELCHIOR. Many people do that.

YOUNG WOMAN. I know. But it's the best possible way to lose a star. The star goes forward. The star is one of progress. It takes one to new scenes, new places, new experiences and opportunities, new adventures and new ways of life.

MELCHIOR. Do you really believe that? Many people don't, you know.

YOUNG WOMAN. I know that the star throws a new light on things. So even if it should lead me back home again, it wouldn't be the same place I left. Oh, I wish I could find it again. *(Sighs, twists her fingers together and moves up Right.)*

MIDDLE-AGED WOMAN *(Stepping forward to speak to* CASPER.*)* I got all mixed up. I got the idea that it didn't matter which star a person followed. The sky is full of stars and every one of them, as night progresses, moves on. So—with me—it was one star tonight and another star tomorrow night. I just wandered around following this star and that one until the *real* star of *guidance* was *lost*. *(Nods toward another young man as he comes forward.)* Here is a friend of mine. He has an interesting story to tell. Let him tell you about his star. *(Moves, upstage.)*

SECOND YOUNG MAN *(To each of the Wise Men in turn.)*
Every night the star I had chosen stood over Jericho. That's
where I went and I stayed for many moons. It's a great city,
Jericho—pleasure, palaces, good wine, dancing girls and
races. A man can place a bet in Jericho. But one day when
I looked up at the star I saw that it was red . . . the color
of blood. Then I knew that it was the wrong star for me.
So I left the city in search of the right star and ended up
at Dry Wells. *(A* THIRD YOUNG MAN *steps forward as the*
SECOND YOUNG MAN *turns away.)*   •

THIRD YOUNG MAN *(To the Wise Men, of course.)* My
star took me to Jerusalem. Now there's a city for you! It
isn't dull like Prayer, nor is it debauched like Jericho. A
man has to be up-and-coming in Jericho. He has to be on
his toes. Everything there is business, money, getting on in
the world. You have to shove people aside and step over
them if you want to get along. It's very social too . . . high
society . . . I was lucky enough to be invited to Herod's
palace once. But I lost my shekles in a bad investment and
then people wouldn't have anything to do with me any
more because I was no longer successful. So I realized that
I had been following a wrong star and took the road out
of the city to Dry Wells. Now there is no star . . . no water
. . . no anything, and I am lost. I have nothing to follow
now. *(Sighs, shakes his head and moves away.)*

MELCHIOR *(To the other Wise Men.)* All this makes one
feel that to have a *destination* in life is a great and important thing.

CASPER *(Nodding a slow, thoughtful affirmative.)* And
the star of *guidance* is the only one that can lead you to
your destination . . .

BALTHAZAR. Aye. With no wrong turns, no going back,
no moving around in circles, and no lingering too long
in cities like Jericho or Jerusalem.

MELCHIOR *(Looking upward.)* Look you! There isn't a
cloud in the sky . . .

SECOND YOUNG WOMAN *(Coming forward.)* No. The
cloud is gone that shut out my star.

MELCHIOR. You mean, you lost your star in a cloud?

SECOND YOUNG WOMAN *(Nodding a slow, sad affirmative.)* Aye. In the cloud of my own fear. And there is nothing blacker than a night when the clouds shut out the stars. You see, I was afraid . . . afraid of the dark, afraid of venture, afraid of myself, afraid I was sick, or would get sick, afraid I'd lose something, afraid I'd run out of food or water, afraid I'd die. If there was a little rift in the clouds and the star shone through I'd close the hole up again with my fears. Finally, I was afraid I'd lose the star altogether, and I did. I . . . did. *(Catches her voice in a sob and moves away as another middle-aged woman comes forward.)*

SECOND MIDDLE-AGED WOMAN. I heard my fellow traveler's words. I, too, lost the star in a cloud. But I am not a woman of fear. I raised a cloud of *bitterness*. I was just one of those persons who get sour on life. I was in a ferment all the time. I was bitter against my father and mother because they gave me such a poor start in life. I was a bitter wife and mother. Other people prospered. I worked my hands to the bone, but things never came my way. The blight was always worse on *my* fruit trees. If the epidemic came to the sheep, our flock always lost the greater proportion. All right, I said. I'll stand on my own feet. I can do without friends, and if God's that kind of a God I can do without *Him!* I don't know how I got the wanderlust and started out following a star; restlessness, I guess. But I couldn't shake off my bitterness, so I lost it again. Then I was caught up in this crowd at Dry Wells. *(Moves away.)*

MELCHIOR *(To the other Wise Men.)* Alas, poor deluded people. How tragic that they should all have chosen the wrong stars. *(Moves toward another dejected old man who is sitting on a stool near by.)* Old man, you look ill and tired. Why do you sit alone?

SECOND OLD MAN. I am ashamed to mingle with the others because my cloud was a cloud of *guilt*. I warrant that fear or bitterness or both together cannot raise a blacker cloud than guilt. When you feel that you have hurt life, hurt the universe, hurt God, the stars go out and you are in the blackness of despair. It's not so much like a cloud as like blowing out all the lamps in the world. Life becomes black . . . black as death, black as hell! What's more, you carry a horrible burden around with you. And that gets a man. You feel as if you want to do something and you can't. All you can do .is try to escape. That's what I did, started running away. Caught up with people trying to find a star. I'd try anything. I was a desperate man. I had sinned in many ways. If only I could find a star of forgiveness and peace .'. . (His voice breaks and he bows his head.)

OMNES (All-of-sudden, the entire crowd take up a despairing chant.) Water! We thirst! Water or we die! (They start moving back and forth again.)

BALTHAZAR (To the other Wise Men.) Look you, my friends. These people are dying of thirst. Perhaps, if we were to pass around our water bags . . .

MELCHIOR (Interrupting.) Better still . . . empty them in the well.

CASPER. Then we should die. There is no more than enough for us.

MELCHIOR (To BALTHAZAR.) And the bags are half empty. There would be no more than enough to wet their tongues . . .

CASPER (To BALTHAZAR.) Whereas if we keep it for ourselves, Balthazar, it might last us until we come to another well . . .

BALTHAZAR. Even so, I say we must share it among them.

MELCHIOR (To CASPER.) Balthazar is right, Casper. Even a few drops apiece might give the poor wretches renewed faith and a desire to mend their ways and continue their search for the star of guidance. Let us empty our bags into the well. (The people draw back on either side of the well as he goes behind it and the other two Wise Men go to either side.)

FIRST OLD MAN (Excitedly.) Look you! They have water!

FIRST OLD WOMAN. What are they going to do with it?

FIRST YOUNG MAN. Pour it into the well!

FIRST YOUNG WOMAN. Nay! Don't waste it! Don't waste a single drop!

SECOND YOUNG MAN *(Getting a cup from his girdle and holding it out.)* Measure it out equally among us . . .

MIDDLE-AGED WOMAN. Do it that way and it will seep through the stones and be lost.

THIRD YOUNG MAN *(Desperately.)* For the love of God, give us to drink! *(By this time, the Wise Men have up-ended their water bags. The sound of rushing water is heard, and this grows rapidly louder. Soft music fades in and continues until the end of the scene.)*

CASPER *(To MELCHIOR and BALTHAZAR. Looking surprised.)* There is more water here than I had thought!

MELCHIOR. In my bag too!

BALTHAZAR. Strange! Mine seems *bottomless!*

CASPER. The water is coming out in a veritable torrent.

BALTHAZAR. Enough to give them all!

OMNES *(Chanting again, in unison.)* Water! Water! Enough to quench our thirst! *(The sound of the pouring water suddenly ceases.)*

MELCHIOR *(Putting down his bag.)* It is done.

BALTHAZAR *(Doing likewise.)* And the well is half full!

CASPER. A miracle! *(To the people.)* Come ye. Come and drink. *(The people surge forward, but are brought to a sudden stop as a brilliant white light comes on within the well.)*

MELCHIOR *(Dramatically.)* Look you! *Look!*

BALTHAZAR *(Looking down into the well.)* The *star!* The *star!*

CASPER *(Also looking down into the well. The light is reflected on their faces.)* It is there . . . in the well . . . reflected on the surface of the water! *(The people give vent to a low "Ah-h-h!" of wonder.)*

MELCHIOR. We have found it again!

BALTHAZAR *(Looking upward.)* It is in the heavens . . . visible to all! *(Everyone looks upwards.)*

OMNES. The star! The *true* star! *(The music rises.)*

MELCHIOR *(To the other Wise Men.)* That which we lost by bickering and thinking only of ourselves, we have found again by thinking of others.

CASPER *(To the crowd. Dramatically.)* Gather round,

friends, and drink your fill. Never more allow your hearts to know bitterness, jealousy, greed nor guilt. The star of faith and guidance is there in the sky and we shall follow it together. It shall lead us straight to Bethlehem and the new-born King! *(The music swells to a loud, joyous climax, and the people eagerly surround the well as the curtain comes down, or the lights go out.)*

CURTAIN

NOTE: *(At once, the NARRATOR enters as before and the music dies down and stops as he—or she—begins to speak, while the rose-colored light comes on.)*

NARRATOR. And so, the Three Wise Men became wiser still after their experience at Dry Wells. Of course, this part of their adventure is purely imaginary; just a colorful bit of allegory which makes a very good sermon with its beautiful moral. But their journey following the star is recorded Bible history, and so is their interview with Herod, the evil king. However, the Wise Men did not return to Jerusalem after finding and worshipping the new-born King. They were much too wise for that. Instead, they left Bethlehem in the dead of night and successfully eluded the soldiers that Herod had sent to spy on their movements. When Herod heard about this he was almost wild. *(The music in again, the rose-colored light goes out, the NARRATOR exits, and we are ready for Scene Three.)*

SCENE THREE

SCENE: HEROD'S *palace again, with the same dais, chair, bench, etc.* HEROD *is sitting in the chair, munching on another piece of fruit as the curtain rises and the lights come on. N. B. If the play is being produced in a church, the changes of furniture, etc., will have to' be made in the darkness while the* NARRATOR *is speaking. The music stops playing as the lights come on and the* SOLDIER *enters.*

SOLDIER *(Entering down Left, coming stiffly to attention and saluting with outstretched hand, Roman fashion.)* Hail, Herod, mighty king. There is a man without—dressed in beggar's rags—who will not be turned aside.

HEROD *(Leaning forward.)* He wishes to see me? *(The music stops.)*

SOLDIER. Yes, your Majesty. He says he has come from Bethlehem. He showed me a ring, wrought in the form of a serpent . . .

HEROD *(Eagerly.)* Good. He is one of my spies . . . a soldier I can trust. Bid him enter, then leave us alone. *(Rises.)*

SOLDIER *(Saluting.)* Yes, your Majesty. *(Turns in military fashion and exits.* HEROD *beams like the cat that swallowed the canary, steps down off the dais and dry washes his hands together as the* SOLDIER *returns with a bronzed, bearded man, dressed in the rags of a begger.)*

MAN *(Moving swiftly closer to* HEROD *and saluting. As he does this, the* SOLDIER *exits.)* Hail, Herod.

HEROD. What have you learned? Give me your report. Quickly now. Where is the child?

MAN. I do not know, your Majesty.

HEROD *(Explosively.)* What's that?

MAN. The three Magi you sent me to spy upon left Bethlehem last night . . . secretly. No one knows in what direction. It was as if they had suddenly vanished into thin air.

HEROD *(Narrowing his eyes. His anger mounting.)* And the child . . . the Jewish Deliverer?

MAN *(Throwing out his arms in an expressive apologetic*

gesture.) They found Him. They must have. But no one could tell me when. Those men are magicians, your Majesty, and I have heard it said that the magicians from the East have the power to make themselves *invisible* . . .

HEROD *(Suddenly grasping the man by the throat. Raging.)* You fool! You feeble-minded lout! I'll have your eyes burned out with hot irons! Your superstitious tongue shall be torn out by the roots! You let them get *away!* *(Shrieks the last word and flings the* MAN *away from him to the floor.)*

MAN *(Fearfully.)* Your Majesty . . . *(Lies where he has fallen, afraid to get up.)*

HEROD *(Pacing furiously upstage and down again.)* The Jews are afraid. That's why they will not talk. That's why they're keeping this child hidden. They want to raise Him in secret until He's old enough to ascend a throne. Then they'll rise up in revolt, overthrow *me* and place *Him* in power. *(Pausing at Center. Raising his clenched hands. Practically shouting now.)* But I'll thwart them. I'll put a stop to their mad scheme. *(To the* MAN.*)* Arise! Get to your feet! Stop laying there like a whipped dog. *(The* MAN *scrambles hastily to his feet.)* In spite of everything I'll find this mysterious infant and *kill* Him! He must never live to bring trouble to the Roman Empire! *(Claps his hands smartly together. Almost immediately, the* SOLDIER *enters and stands at attention. The spy backs quickly upstage as* HEROD *hurries closer to the* SOLDIER, *barking his orders.)* Look you, and mark well my words! Somewhere in the village of Bethlehem there is a Jewish child . . . a child I want done away with. You, as trusted Captain of the Guard, will take a detachment with you immediately to carry out this order.

SOLDIER. But, Majesty, how shall we find this child?

HEROD. You will surround the village, search through every house and building, and whenever you come across a new-born Jewish man-child you will kill him without mercy! *(The* SOLDIER *and spy gasp at the almost insane cruelty of the order.)*

492

SOLDIER. Your Majesty!

HEROD *(With a contemptuous leer.)* Hah! Your face blanches with fear?

SOLDIER. No. Not fear, your Majesty. But Bethlehem is crowded. There must be many new-born babies. Surely you would not have us kill them *all?*

HEROD *(His voice rising to a shriek.)* All! *All!* Then there will be no mistake. Spare only the *girl* children. *(Lowly, breathing heavily as he points toward the entrance down Left.)* And now . . . go! The work must be carried out before nightfall! *(The* SOLDIER *hesitates.* HEROD *stamps his foot and screams again.)* Well, what are you waiting for? You heard my orders. See to it that they are obeyed or I shall have your own life in forfeit. *(The* SOLDIER *stiffens, hesitates again, then salutes, turns on his heel and exits. Music fades in again as* HEROD *watches after the man, his lips turned upward in a grotesque, villainous grin. At once the curtain comes down, or the lights go out. The music continues playing for a short interlude and to give people the opportunity to quickly clear away the chair, table and bench, and for the curtains at the back to be lowered together. While this is happening, the manger is brought onstage, together with a small, three-legged stool. A bit of straw is scattered about, and then the curtain rises, or the lights come on for Scene Four.)*

SCENE FOUR

SCENE: *A stable in Bethlehem.* MARY *is sitting quietly behind the manger as* JOSEPH *enters hastily down Right. The music seques into, "O Little Town of Bethlehem," and continues playing this until otherwise indicated.*

JOSEPH *(Speaking as he enters. Smilingly.)* Still awake, Mary?

MARY *(Smiling softly.)* Yes, Joseph. I have been waiting for you to return before lying on my bed of straw to sleep.

JOSEPH *(Going closer to the manger.)* The child . . . ?

MARY: Sleeping peacefully, my husband.

JOSEPH *(Introspectively. Looking down into the manger.)* One has only to gaze upon this infant to know that here indeed is a *miraculous* child. *(Bringing his thoughts back to the present.)* Well, we have registered for the census . . . our work in Bethlehem is done. Soon now we must return to Nazareth and I must get back to the business of earning more shekles. I hope everything has been all right with the shop during our absence. *(Moves slowly to Left Center.)*

MARY *(Rising. Quietly.)* There is something worrying you, Joseph, and it is not fear of thieves entering your shop in Nazareth. What is it, beloved? *(Moves a step or two closer to him.)*

JOSEPH *(Smiling. Tenderly. Placing his hands on her upper arms.)* You read my every thought, don't you? *(Sighs and turns serious.)* Yea, Mary. I am worried. Herod has been trying to find the child.

MARY *(Widening her eyes in sudden fear.)* Herod?

JOSEPH *(Nodding a slow, frowning affirmative.)* Yes. You know, what the three Magi from the East said about their interview with him?

MARY *(Softly.)* Yes . . .

JOSEPH *(Continuing. Dropping his hands to his sides.)* Well, I have just been talking with the owner of the inn and he tells me that one of Herod's soldiers . . . disguised as a beggar from Jerusalem . . . has been going about Bethlehem asking where he could find the babe. The innkeeper recognized the man in spite of his tattered clothing. He had gambled with him for an entire night one time when he was in the city, seeking an audience with the king. But there was something about his manner that made the innkeeper cautious, and he said he did not know.

MARY. What do you think it means?

JOSEPH (*Looking troubled.*) I wish I knew. (*Moves in front of her, going toward the manger again.*)

MARY. It is only natural that he has heard the ancient prophecy, and that he should have been told of the *signs*. Perhaps he is curious to *see* the Son of . . .

JOSEPH (*Interrupting.*) No, Mary. Herod is evil, and the coming of your Son presages the deliverance of our people. The temple priests are in league with him. They will not believe what we *know* to be *true*. Between them they may wish to . . . (*Breaks off suddenly as he sees the sudden look of fear on her face. This is not fear for herself, but for the child. JOSEPH goes closer to place a comforting hand on her shoulder.*) But there, be not afraid, Mary. We are under the protection of God, and God will safeguard His own. You are tired, and so am I. Let us go to our rest and cast all worries aside. (*They turn toward the manger, only to come to a sudden stop as the music swells on a loud note, changing from "O Little Town of Bethlehem" to a more rousing hymn. At the same time, the curtains open at the back to reveal the figure of the angel, Gabriel, who stands with lifted hand.*)

GABRIEL (*The music softens as he speaks, in loud, commanding tones.*) Arise, Joseph. Arise, and take the child and his mother and fly into Egypt; and be there until I shall tell you. For this will come to pass that Herod will *seek the child to destroy Him!* (MARY *and* JOSEPH *stiffen, the music swells . . . the voices of a choir may fade in, singing the praises of God, and it is on this picture that the curtain falls, or the lights go out.*)

CURTAIN

LET NOTHING YE DISMAY

A CHRISTMAS PLAY IN ONE ACT

By

DORA MARY MACDONALD

LET NOTHING YE DISMAY

For two men, two women, and extras

CHARACTERS
(*In the order of their first appearance*)

SALLY DARNELL.............*A lonely Christmas celebrant*
AUNT JENNIE CRAIG....*Caretaker of the Randolph mansion*
SYDNEY RANDOLPH II............*Owner of the mansion*
SYDNEY RANDOLPH IV...................*His grandson*

Any number of carol singers, with only a few brief lines to speak, off stage

TIME—*Christmas Eve*

PLACE—*The long-deserted Randolph mansion.*

TIME OF PLAYING—*Thirty minutes.*

498

COSTUMES AND CHARACTERISTICS

Sally is a typical well-bred, wealthy, intelligent college girl, who has retained the ideals and dreams of childhood. Her hair is very simply dressed, without regard to the latest style. She is well dressed for a long, cold motor trip, in a fur-trimmed coat and hat, with heavy gloves. Later in the play she makes a quick change to a very beautiful old-fashioned evening gown.

Aunt Jennie is a brisk, cheerful, little woman, in her late sixties, whose face and clothes show the results of hard work and economy. She wears a neat house dress and a plain, well-worn coat.

Sydney is a thoughtful young man in his early twenties with a wealth of sympathy and understanding. He is well dressed for a drive, in a business suit with heavy overcoat and hat.

Randolph is a feeble, tired, aristocratic, proud old man, in his middle sixties. His clothes are well-tailored but shabby, wearing a heavy overcoat over his suit, with hat and gloves.

PROPERTIES

For Sally: flashlight; tray, on which are a tarnished silver coffeepot, three cups, three plates, plate of sandwiches and cake, and three napkins; two holly wreaths; small Christmas tree; basket containing Christmas tree ornaments and tinsel, also a phonograph record of the carol, "God Rest Ye, Merry Gentlemen." For Aunt Jennie: box of matches; armload of old-fashioned evening gowns, some of them very elaborate and beautiful.

MUSIC

The Christmas carols mentioned in the play will be found in "Denison's Christmas Songs and Carols," which may be obtained from the publishers of this book for the price of 40 cents, postpaid.

LET NOTHING YE DISMAY

SCENE: *Living room of the old, untenanted Randolph mansion, early Christmas Eve. There are two doors: one up right center opening into the front vestibule, and the other at right leading to the dining room and rear of the house. In the back drop up center are several high, wide casement windows, leaded, with faded shades and silk draperies. In spite of its neglected and dusty appearance and old-fashioned furnishings, it is a luxurious and dignified room. The handsome old furniture is shrouded in slip covers, and the shades are drawn. In the corner up right, near the door, is a small table with a straight-backed chair beside it. At left center is a davenport with pillows, and with a rather large center table at right of it. A fireplace with a mantelshelf is in the wall down left, with a large, upholstered armchair at the up-stage end of it, half facing it. The fireplace is equipped with a few half-charred logs, beneath which are concealed a red electric bulb or two, to simulate fire when turned on. A similar armchair is down right, not far from a phonograph, which stands down extreme right. Candelabra and single candlesticks are distributed about the room—two candelabra on the mantelshelf, two on the two tables respectively, and two candlesticks on the phonograph. On the mantelshelf also stands a large framed photograph of a handsome elderly woman in an old-fashioned evening gown, while on the center table is a smaller framed picture of a small boy. Luxurious rugs in dark colors are on the floor, and some fine old pictures adorn the walls. At the beginning of the play, the stage is in darkness.*

At rise of curtain, a door is heard to open and shut, up right center, as SALLY'S *and* AUNT JENNIE'S *voices are heard off stage. Immediately the two women enter, up right center,* SALLY *carrying a flashlight and* AUNT JENNIE *a box of matches.*

SALLY (*flashing her light around the dark room*). It's spooky in here, Aunt Jennie. (*Turns flashlight on candles on table by davenport.*)

AUNT JENNIE (*bustling around*). I'll light some candles in a jiffy, Sally.

SALLY. Have you matches?

AUNT JENNIE. Yes, I brought a box from home.

(AUNT JENNIE *strikes a match and lights candles on table, then goes to mantelshelf and lights candles there, leaving box of matches on mantelshelf. The stage lights come on, burning dimly throughout the scene.*)

SALLY (*looking around*). What a lot of candles!

AUNT JENNIE. The Randolphs would never have anything but firelight and candlelight in this room. (*Chuckling.*) Young Syd used to say the room would get an awful shock if it ever saw an electric light or modern furniture.

SALLY (*enthusiastically*). Let's light 'em all. I'll help. (*Shuts off flashlight and places it on table by davenport. Picks up lighted candle.*)

AUNT JENNIE (*laughing*). What a child you are! Just like your mother.

(SALLY *and* AUNT JENNIE *light candles, talking as they move about.*)

SALLY. I really am awfully apologetic about putting you to all this trouble, Aunt Jennie. On Christmas Eve, too.

AUNT JENNIE (*cheerfully*). Don't worry about that. I'm glad to have a chance to do something for Caroline Darnell's daughter. You know I took care of your mother till she was fourteen years old. My lands! How she cried and carried on when I left to get married!

SALLY. She used to tell me how good you were to her.

That's the reason I had the nerve to ask about the costumes. Mother said you had shown her just what I'll need for the play, so I thought I'd stop on my way to Chicago to see about the dresses.

AUNT JENNIE (*emphatically*). You did just right, Sally. I'd have been mad if you hadn't. (*After a slight pause.*) So your mother's in Hollywood.

SALLY. Yes. She's been quite a success in pictures out there.

AUNT JENNIE. She's liked to play-act ever since she was a little tyke. I s'pose you'll be followin' in her footsteps, seein' as how you're goin' to be in this play.

SALLY. Oh, this is just a college play. I shall never be so good an actress as mother. To tell the truth, I don't care about her profession. I'd rather read and try to write and do things like that.

AUNT JENNIE. You take after your pa—God rest his soul! The pore man died while he was writin' some sort of a book.

SALLY (*quietly*). I don't remember him.

AUNT JENNIE. It's too bad you can't remember your home.

SALLY. That's just it, Aunt Jennie; I don't remember a home. Mother likes hotels, and people around her all the time. I've rented a little apartment for myself in Chicago. That's why I'm driving all the way there to-night. I've got all the makings of a Christmas dinner in the car, and I'm going to cook it to-morrow.

AUNT JENNIE (*in dismay*). That's no way to spend Christmas. All by yourself! I just wish we wasn't goin' over to Hiram's sister's to-night. I'd like you to spend Christmas with us.

SALLY (*putting her arm around* AUNT JENNIE). That's sweet of you, Aunt Jennie, but I don't know of anything that makes one feel more lonely than trying to celebrate Christmas with some family that doesn't need one. I've tried it a lot of times, going home with the girls from boarding school. But we'd better hurry, or your husband will be here for you.

AUNT JENNIE (*energetically*). That's right. You light that fire, so you won't freeze to death. Hiram laid fires the last time we was over here. I'll run upstairs and get the dresses.

SALLY (*handing* AUNT JENNIE *the flashlight*). You'll need this.

AUNT JENNIE (*taking flashlight*). Thanks. I'll be back in a jiffy. (*Exit, up right center, turning right.*)

(SALLY *takes off her gloves, gets match from box on mantelshelf, strikes it, and lights fire. Then she goes around the room, removing slip covers from furniture and dusting mantelshelf and phonograph with them, and finally standing beside phonograph and surveying room with satisfaction. At last she goes to right door, opens it, and tosses slip covers out the door, then grabs candle from phonograph and exits at right.*)

AUNT JENNIE *enters, up right center, from right, with a load of old-fashioned dresses on her arm, and looks around room in surprise.*

AUNT JENNIE (*calling*). Sally!

SALLY (*off right*). I'll be there in a minute!

AUNT JENNIE (*walking around room, touches furniture lovingly, picks up pictures from table by davenport, dusts it on her coat, and gazes at it*). Pore little Syd! (*Drops dresses on davenport, and walks to mantelshelf, where she stands gazing at photograph.*) It was a sad day for us when you died, Mis' Randolph, but *you* were saved a heap o' grief.

Enter SALLY *at right.*

SALLY (*looking around*). I thought I heard you talking to someone.

AUNT JENNIE (*turning*). I guess I was talkin' out loud. I jus' was feelin' rather glad that pore Elizabeth Randolph didn't have to know the tragedy of this house. (*Picks up dresses.*) Here are the dresses. You can take your pick.

SALLY. I lit a fire in the kitchen range. When the house

gets a little warmer, I'll try the dresses on. In the meantime, let's sit down, and you can tell me about this house till Hiram comes for you. I can lock up the place for you.

AUNT JENNIE (*doubtfully*). Well, I s'pose that'ud be all right. The night latch is on, and you could leave the house without me.

SALLY (*reassuringly*). Of course I can. I promise to put out the candles and shroud the furniture again and leave things just exactly as I found them. (*Coaxingly, pulling* AUNT JENNIE *down on davenport.*) Now, let's sit down and be cozy.

(AUNT JENNIE *sits stiffly on davenport.*)

AUNT JENNIE. Why did you take the covers off the furniture?

SALLY. Oh, the place intrigued me, and I wanted to see what it would look like in its natural clothes.

AUNT JENNIE (*reminiscently*). I wish you could have seen it on Christmas Eve in the old days. A candle in every window, and Christmas greens everywhere! For as long as I can remember, the whole countryside used to gather out on the lawn and sing Christmas carols. (*Sighs.*) It was beautiful, walkin' up that long driveway under the trees, singin'. Mr. Randolph and his family would come to the window there (*motioning up center*), and call, "Merry Christmas," and then they'd all greet us at the door and invite us in. We wouldn't stay long. But how old Mr. Randolph would enjoy givin' us treats!

SALLY. Sort of the lord of the manor?

AUNT JENNIE. Yes, jus' like the squire in those old English stories I used to read to your mother. Those were grand times—all but his last Christmas here. I can't bear to think of that.

SALLY. What happened?

AUNT JENNIE. It's a long story.

SALLY. But I want to know about it.

AUNT JENNIE (*settling herself against back of davenport*).

This house was built four generations ago by the first Sydney Randolph. He owned most of the country around here and built this place on acres and acres of land. There were formal gardens and orchards and conservatories and all that. That was before my time, but I've heard how all the neighbors brought their troubles to him—and their money, too. He'd invest it for them.

SALLY. That doesn't sound like the Middle West.

AUNT JENNIE. All the Randolphs were like squires. Well, his son, Sydney Randolph the second, married a beautiful girl from the East. Elizabeth von Cardwell, her name was. That's her picture over there. (*Nodding to mantelshelf.*) It's her clothes that I brought down to you, knowin' she wouldn't mind. She was always a generous soul. They had a son named Sydney, too—the third—but he wasn't much like his father.

SALLY. What was he like?

AUNT JENNIE. This third Sydney Randolph was a disappointment to his folks. Maybe it was havin' too much money that ruined him. Anyway, he was sort of wild. He went to the World War and married a nurse in France. He was killed soon after that. His folks was heartbroken.

SALLY. Did that end the illustrious family of Randolphs?

AUNT JENNIE. No. The next thing Randolphs heard, their grandson Sydney was sent to them from France at the death of his mother.

SALLY. Sydney Randolph the fourth!

AUNT JENNIE. Yes. Well, the old folks found more happiness in him than they'd had in their own son. Then Mis' Randolph died, and there was the two Sydney Randolphs here with their great crowd of servants. They was inseparable, and the boy had everything he wanted. Mr. Randolph was president of the bank in town—he owned it— and everybody went to him jus' as they had to his father for advice in money matters. I reckon he invested money for everyone for fifty or a hundred miles around here. (*Pauses.*)

SALLY (*questioningly*). Well?

AUNT JENNIE (*slowly*). Then came the year 1929. There

was something wrong with the bank. I never could understand about it. Anyway, everybody's money was gone, and everybody blamed Mr. Randolph for losing it.

SALLY. Was he really crooked?

AUNT JENNIE (*decidedly*). No, indeed! Everybody realizes now, when it's too late, that it was really conditions that was to blame, and it was really not all his fault. He had nothin' left for himself. He sold everything he owned except this house and an acre or two around it, that he'd put in his grandson's name. (*Sighs.*) I don't s'pose there's a person around here that doesn't miss old Mr. Randolph and wish he was back again.

SALLY. What happened to him?

AUNT JENNIE. People who'd had the greatest respect for him, and those that he'd helped the most turned against him with hate. He was brought to trial—and was sentenced to the penitentiary.

SALLY. How awful!

AUNT JENNIE. Unless you understood the pride of the Randolphs, you wouldn't know what an awful thing it was for him.

SALLY. What became of his grandson?

AUNT JENNIE. I don't know. He left to stay with some relatives down south. That was ten years ago. He's a young man by now, but he's never been back. Hiram an' I look after the place. Old Mr. Randolph trusted us an' asked us to keep things all right for the boy.

SALLY. Is Mr. Randolph still in the penitentiary?

AUNT JENNIE. I s'pose so. It's jus' as if he was dead. (*The honking of a car sounds, off up center.* AUNT JENNIE *jumps up.*) There's Hiram now! We'll have to get goin' if we expect to reach Susie's in time to help with the tree.

(SALLY *follows* AUNT JENNIE *to door up right center.*)

SALLY. I hope I haven't made you late.

AUNT JENNIE (*pausing at door*). You'll take good care of the dresses, won't you?

SALLY. Absolutely! I'll send them back to you as soon as the play is over.

AUNT JENNIE. And you'll leave the house in order?

SALLY. Don't you worry about that. Everything will be all right.

AUNT JENNIE (*nervously*). The curtains are drawn, so no one can see if there's a light here. You won't be afraid, will you?

SALLY (*laughing*). Of course not!

AUNT JENNIE (*wistfully*). I imagine the old house is glad to be alive for an hour or so on Christmas Eve.

(*The auto horn honks again off up center.*)

SALLY (*opening door*). Thanks so much for everything, Aunt Jennie. Merry Christmas!

AUNT JENNIE. Merry Christmas, dear. Merry Christmas!

(SALLY *and* AUNT JENNIE *kiss.* SALLY *can be seen in the vestibule, holding door open, waving, as* AUNT JENNIE *exits, turning left. The sound of a closing door is heard, then* SALLY *enters, up right center, and closes door, goes to windows up center, opens curtains, and waves. She then draws curtains closely and moves slowly toward davenport.*)

SALLY (*musing aloud*). The old house is glad to be alive on Christmas Eve! (*Suddenly.*) Why not make it a real Christmas Eve? (*Enthusiastically.*) Why, I could even stay here all night! The house could be alive, and I could have a real home on Christmas Eve! (*Ponders.*) I could even cook my Christmas dinner on a real old wood stove to-morrow! I'd give both the house and myself a treat. (*Decidedly, dancing a bit.*) I'll do it! I'll do it! I'll get the things from the car right now!

SALLY *dashes off at right, and quickly rushes back, carrying two Christmas wreaths and a small tree. Singing "Deck the Halls," she sets the tree on the table by the davenport, fastens a wreath on curtains of windows up center and places another on the mantelshelf. She dashes off again at right and returns with a basket, from which she takes ornaments and tinsel, which she quickly puts on the tree. She pauses, to look around.*

SALLY (*saluting the room*). Now, you look like Christmas! (*Picks up dresses and basket.*) I'll put on the coffee, and change my dress and have me an old-fashioned Christmas Eve! (*Stops at phonograph.*) Oh, I'll set you going, old dear. (*Takes phonograph record, "God Rest Ye, Merry Gentlemen," from basket, puts it on machine, and starts phonograph.*) You may break your ten years' silence with the Christmas records I was taking home. (SALLY *bows to phonograph, picks up basket, and exits at right for a quick change of costume.*)

As the last lines of the carol are played, there are the sounds of voices and a door closing, off up right center. The door up right center opens, and SYDNEY RANDOLPH II *enters, walking feebly and leaning heavily on the arm of young* SYDNEY.

RANDOLPH (*in surprise*). Why, Sydney, the candles are lighted.

SYDNEY. I guess we didn't see the light outside, because the curtains were drawn. Come over and sit down, grandfather, and— (*Breaks off, in surprise.*) Here's a Christmas tree! And the fire is going.

RANDOLPH (*in pleased surprise, stretching out hands to fire*). So it is. So it is. I wonder how that happens.

SYDNEY (*taking off* RANDOLPH'S *overcoat*). I'll make you comfortable and then investigate. (*Gayly.*) It must be spirits!

RANDOLPH (*sadly*). There should be the spirit of Christmas. (*Sinks wearily on davenport near fire.*)

(SYDNEY *removes his own coat, and puts coats and hats on chair in rear right corner, as he talks nervously and very kindly.*)

SYDNEY. I'll run upstairs and look through the rooms to see if I can solve the mystery.

RANDOLPH. Don't leave now, Sydney. Everything seems so natural. It's just as if we'd left this morning, instead of ten years ago. Come here to the fire, boy. You must be cold after that long drive.

SYDNEY (*coming to bench by fire*). I wish I had something hot for you to drink.

RANDOLPH. Never mind. I'm contented just to be here.

SYDNEY (*looking around*). Gee! Everything looks just the same. Doesn't it, grandfather?

RANDOLPH (*slowly*). Yes, just the same. The furniture, the candles, the fire—and Elizabeth's picture. (*Pauses a moment.*) You haven't been back?

SYDNEY. No, not since—since you left. I couldn't bear to be here without you.

RANDOLPH. Poor boy! I know. The disgrace and shame would have been too much.

SYDNEY (*quickly*). You know it wasn't that, grandfather. It was just that I couldn't have stood the loneliness. (*Pauses.*) I hadn't realized how much I've missed home.

RANDOLPH. You have grown up, Sydney, since I've seen you.

SYDNEY. That's because you've never let me visit you.

RANDOLPH. I know. But you understand why I couldn't let you come to see me at the penitentiary!

SYDNEY (*simply*). I understood that you wished to be alone. That was enough.

RANDOLPH. You've been a good boy, Sydney. Your weekly letters were my one touch with the world outside the walls. (*Pauses a moment.*) One of my deepest sorrows is the fact that I couldn't give you the things you should have had—the things the other Randolphs have had as their birthright.

SYDNEY (*firmly*). Now, none of that! To tell the truth, I think I have done very well—worked my way through college with honors—

RANDOLPH (*interrupting*). I had expected to send you to Princeton, as a gentleman.

SYDNEY (*laughing*). I'm no less a gentleman, grandfather, for having worked my way through Tech. I'm a good engineer.

RANDOLPH (*quickly*). Oh, I know that. (*Musing.*) You're twice the man your father was, and he had everything money could give him. It's queer. I gave him everything—and now you have to give to me—even the necessities.

SYDNEY. Rubbish! We're going to live together as in old times.

RANDOLPH. It isn't right that you should give me so much of yourself, Sydney. It's occurred to me several times today that perhaps you have made other attachments. A girl, perhaps?

SYDNEY (*laughing*). No girl!

RANDOLPH. You should have a wife, Sydney. I want you to enjoy such companionship as I had—with Elizabeth.

SYDNEY. All right, grandfather. When I find a girl who will fit into this house as grandmother did, I promise I'll grab her quick and marry her. (*Laughs.*) But that means I shall die a bachelor, because girls in these days prefer the hotels and the bright lights to a real home. (*In a speculative tone.*) It's odd about these candles and the fire.

RANDOLPH. I prefer to enjoy them and not wonder about them.

SYDNEY. I suppose Aunt Jennie must have been here. Maybe she got word we were coming.

RANDOLPH. No, she couldn't have. (*Laughs shakily.*) I didn't know myself till two o'clock this morning, when you came with the Governor's pardon. I—I shall never forget that moment—

SYDNEY (*interrupting*). Don't talk about it, grandfather. Just think how splendid it is to be home for Christmas.

RANDOLPH (*sighing*). I thought I should never see my

home again, Sydney. Every Christmas for ten years, I've sat in my cell and thought of this lonely house that has seen so many happy Christmases.

SYDNEY (*quickly*). Yes, I know, grandfather. (*Decidedly.*) And from now on, we'll have many happy Christmases.

RANDOLPH. Only this one, Sydney. I think that's why the Governor pardoned me. He knew this would be my last Christmas. After this, I shall be with Elizabeth. (*Glances at portrait on mantelshelf.*)

SYDNEY (*heartily, rising*). Now, grandfather, that's enough of that! Dr. Judson is coming down from Chicago in a few days, and he'll fix you up as good as new.

RANDOLPH (*shaking his head*). No, Sydney. Even if he could fix up my heart, he couldn't help me.

SYDNEY. What do you mean?

RANDOLPH. The Randolphs are proud people, boy. I enjoyed life here when I was respected and honored by my neighbors. But I can't live among people who hate and despise me.

SYDNEY (*alarmed*). Why, grandfather! (*Sits on left arm of davenport and flings arm around* RANDOLPH's *shoulders.*) You mustn't lose your nerve like this. But if you feel that way, we'll make our home in some other town.

RANDOLPH. No. This is my home. I came back here to die. (*Brokenly.*) I have to admit it, Sydney. I can't face people. I've lost my courage.

RANDOLPH *stops suddenly.* SYDNEY *sits up straight, and both gaze right, as they hear* SALLY, *off right, singing "God Rest Ye, Merry Gentlemen." She opens right door, so that the line, "Let nothing ye dismay," is heard distinctly.* SALLY *stands a moment silent, with a gesture of astonishment. She wears the old-fashioned gown of the woman in the portrait.* SYDNEY *rises, staring in amazement.* RANDOLPH *rises slowly.*

RANDOLPH (*hoarsely, stretching out his arms*). Elizabeth! My Elizabeth!

(*Overcome by emotion,* RANDOLPH *sinks to davenport again, still staring at* SALLY. SYDNEY, *at his left, steps to his side and leans over him, supporting him with one arm.* SALLY *rushes to the davenport and kneels on floor, taking* RANDOLPH'S *hand in hers.*)

SALLY (*distressed*). Oh, I'm so sorry—so sorry! I didn't know anyone was here. (*Appealing to* SYDNEY.) Oh, what can I do?

SYDNEY (*trying to be reassuring*). He's all right. Aren't you, grandfather? (RANDOLPH *nods weakly.*) We just weren't expecting a young lady to come in, singing Christmas carols. Were we, grandfather? It gave us a sort of a start. (*To* SALLY.) I thought you were a ghost.

RANDOLPH (*in a weak, hushed voice*). So did I. The voice of Elizabeth chiding me, "Let nothing ye dismay. Let nothing ye dismay." I'd said I had lost courage, and I thought you were Elizabeth singing, "Let nothing ye dismay."

SALLY (*brightly*). I thank you for the compliment, sir, if your Elizabeth is the one in the picture. (*Nodding to photograph.*)

RANDOLPH (*almost reverently*). She was my wife.

SALLY. Then you must be the Sydney Randolph Aunt Jennie told me about! (*With a gasp of understanding.*) And this house belongs to you.

RANDOLPH (*indicating* SYDNEY). My grandson, Sydney Randolph the fourth, owns this house.

SALLY. How lovely you're here for Christmas! (*Jumps up.*) And what a trespasser I am! My name is Sally Darnell. Aunt Jennie Craig can vouch for me. (*Energetically.*) I'm going to get you some hot coffee, and then I'll explain how I happen to be here.

SYDNEY (*rising*). Coffee! That's just what we were wishing for. May I help you?

SALLY. No, thank you. It's all perked. (*Exit at right.*)

SYDNEY (*solicitously, to* RANDOLPH). Do you feel better, now?

RANDOLPH. Oh, yes—yes. I'm all right. It was just tne surprise—and her song. She was so like Elizabeth.

SYDNEY (*walking to mantelshelf*). By Jove! She had on a dress just like grandmother's in this picture.

RANDOLPH. Yes, that's what startled me. (*Thoughtfully.*) She's a pretty girl, Sydney. (*Slyly.*) She fits in here.

SYDNEY. I wonder who she is.

RANDOLPH. She said Jennie Craig could vouch for her. That ought to be enough.

SYDNEY (*musing*). But it's odd—this house being ready for Christmas, and then that girl in grandmother's dress— and coffee—and everything.

RANDOLPH (*smiling*). Take your blessings as they come, Sydney. "Let nothing ye dismay.'

SYDNEY *laughs.* SALLY. *enters at right, carrying a tray, on which there are a tarnished silver coffeepot, three cups and three plates, a plate of sandwiches and cake, and napkins.* SYDNEY *steps toward her.*

SYDNEY. Let me carry the tray.

SALLY (*indicating bench by fireplace*). Just put that bench by the davenport, so I can set the things on it.

(SYDNEY *places bench in front of davenport, and* SALLY *places tray on it.*)

RANDOLPH. That coffee smells good. I guess I was more tired than I thought.

SYDNEY. No wonder you're tired! We've been driving since four o'clock this morning, with just a bite now and then.

SALLY. Then you're lucky I have some sandwiches and cake. I didn't want to waste time stopping at a restaurant to-night, so I had a substantial supper with me.

RANDOLPH. We shouldn't allow you to divide it.

SALLY. Nonsense! I'm lucky you let me eat here instead of chucking me out in the cold.

RANDOLPH (*indicating place at his right*). Will you sit here by me and be our hostess?

SALLY (*sitting beside him on davenport*). Thank you, Mr. Randolph. (SYDNEY *sits left of* RANDOLPH, *leaning forward. The conversation continues as* SALLY *gives the men napkins, pours the coffee, and serves.*) As an interloper, I really shouldn't be invited to eat with you, but the pangs of hunger overcome my natural sense of propriety.

SYDNEY. You've practically saved our lives with this coffee.

RANDOLPH (*in a courtly manner*). The Randolph home has always welcomed beautiful ladies.

SALLY (*smiling*). Thank you. But I owe you an explanation. I wanted some old-fashioned dresses for a play I'm to be in at college. Mother wrote me that Aunt Jennie—mother's old nurse—could find just what I needed, so, as I was passing near here on my way home for Christmas, I stopped to ask her. She brought me over here and got the dresses, but had to leave me to shut up the house. (*Anxiously.*) You don't mind my borrowing this dress, Mr. Randolph?

RANDOLPH. On the contrary, I'm happy to see you wearing it.

SALLY. That's most generous of you.

(*There is a slight pause, during which* SALLY *shows nervousness, while the men drink their coffee.*)

SYDNEY (*looking around*). The furniture is in mighty good condition for not having been covered.

SALLY. Oh, it was covered. (*Hesitatingly.*) But it looked so lonesome—and it was Christmas Eve—and—and— Well, this room looked hungry for a bit of Christmas, and all my life I've yearned for a real home—like this, so I— Well (*in a rush*), I just thought we'd get together—the house and I. I brought my things from the car and decorated to make both of us happy.

SYDNEY (*swiftly*). That's a sweet thought.

RANDOLPH (*puzzled*). But you said you were going home

for Christmas. Why, then, were you so interested in this house?

SALLY. I was going to spend Christmas in my one-room apartment in Chicago. It's the nearest thing to a home that I've ever had.

RANDOLPH. You have no family?

SALLY. Mother is a successful motion picture actress— Andrea Darnelli. Perhaps you've seen her. She likes hotels. I've never lived in a house, and I thought no one would ever know if I adopted this one for Christmas and made believe it was mine. I realize, Mr. Randolph, what a liberty I took. I sincerely apologize, and ask you not to think too badly of me.

RANDOLPH. Not at all. Not at all. I can appreciate your feelings about a home.

SYDNEY (*suddenly*). Can you cook?

SALLY. Of course! I've been planning my Christmas dinner for a month.

SYDNEY (*eagerly*). And no one is expecting you in Chicago?

SALLY. No one. I've quit trying to make believe I'm part of somebody else's family at Christmas.

SYDNEY (*enthusiastically*). Good! I'll rustle around for a turkey and the trimmings, and you stay and cook it and help grandfather and me celebrate to-morrow. (*Eagerly.*) Will you?

RANDOLPH. I don't like the idea of Miss Darnell's preparing our feast. Perhaps, Sydney, you can find someone else to do the cooking. (*To* SALLY.) We would be very much pleased, Miss Darnell, if you would spend Christmas with us as—as—well, we'll say as my granddaughter.

SALLY. Oh, thank you, Mr. Randolph, but I'd love to cook. It's lots more fun to get the meal.

SYDNEY. I'll help you. I don't think we could find anyone at this late date, anyhow. (*To* SALLY.) Will you make a list of articles I'm to get? I'll dash into town for them.

SALLY (*laughing*). Everything is in the kitchen— turkey 'n' all! (*Ruefully.*) You see I'd decided that this was my chance to cook my Christmas dinner on a real stove in a real kitchen. But, even at that, the meal would have been a lonely one! It'll be ten times as much fun to be (*with a little bow to* RANDOLPH)—your granddaughter. (*To* SYDNEY.) Shall I be your sister or your cousin?

RANDOLPH (*smiling gently*). Let's say, "cousin."

SYDNEY. That's swell! I'll get the furnace going and warm up the whole house, and we'll light every candle in the place. We'll have a Christmas that is a Christmas! Isn't this splendid, grandfather?

RANDOLPH (*shakily*). It's almost too good. (*To* SALLY.) You don't know what you've done for me, Miss—

SALLY (*interrupting*). Don't you think you should call your favorite granddaughter Sally?

RANDOLPH (*patting her shoulder*). Of course, Sally. (*Looks into space, then speaks suddenly.*) But—a thought just came to me. (*Slowly.*) Perhaps you'd rather not stay —if you knew— (*Hesitates.*)

SALLY. What?

SYDNEY (*sharply*). Grandfather, don't!

RANDOLPH. I must tell her, Sydney. It's only fair. (*To* SALLY, *with difficulty.*) Did Jennie Craig tell you where I've been?

SALLY. Yes.

RANDOLPH (*hopefully*). And it doesn't make any difference?

SALLY (*emphatically*). Of course not! I'm just highly honored to be invited to share your Christmas.

RANDOLPH. Sydney came to—where I was—at two o'clock this morning with a pardon from the Governor. He told me so joyously that he was going to take me home for Christmas. I didn't tell him—he was so pleased with the idea— but I dreaded coming. Nothing is sadder than a cold, neglected house, especially if that house was once the center of laughter, luxury, and hospitality.

SALLY. That's what I thought when I stepped into this room.

SYDNEY. I confess that I had some qualms, too. I tell

you I dreaded entering this room. I was so glad for the warmth and light that I was willing to believe in fairies.

SALLY (*laughing*). I'm afraid I'm a pretty substantial fairy.

RANDOLPH. I thought I must be dreaming. The contrast of this home with the place where I've been—! I was completely unnerved. And then you came, the image of my dear wife, singing "Let nothing ye dismay."

SALLY. That was a coincidence. But I'm glad it happened.

SYDNEY (*heartily*). So am I! Just think, grandfather! To-morrow this house is going to see a turkey dinner for the first time in ten years.

SALLY (*whimsically*). The house is going to be pleased.

RANDOLPH. For the first time in ten years! This may give me courage to face the hatred of my neighbors.

SALLY (*in surprise*). Hatred! (*Quickly.*) Aunt Jennie told me that now all of them realize what a wonderful person you were to them and how you always helped them. They know you weren't to blame for the toppling-over of everything. She says they miss you terribly and wish—

RANDOLPH (*interrupting*). Don't, Sally. I can expect almost anything to happen, after the surprise of my homecoming to-night, but if you could have seen their faces at the trial— No, no. (*Shakes his head.*) I can't expect that.

SYDNEY (*argumentatively*). But Ike Johnson seemed overjoyed to see you in town!

RANDOLPH (*doubtfully*). Yes—Ike, but— (*Stops suddenly, startled.*) What's that?

(*The sound of chorus singing a Christmas carol comes faintly from off up right center. It gradually becomes stronger.*)

SALLY. It's people singing Christmas carols. (*As the others talk, she goes to one of the windows up center and opens curtains.*)

RANDOLPH (*reminiscently*). There was a time when our

neighbors used to sing carols for the Randolphs on Christmas Eve. But my last Christmas here (*shudders*), they sang just long enough to attract me to the window. (*Brokenly.*) Then they threw stones and bricks at me and called me vile names. I had to send for the police.

SYDNEY (*distressed*). Grandfather, don't recall those things. They're all in the past.

SALLY (*turning from window*). There's quite a crowd of people coming up the driveway. There must be twenty-five cars parked out there.

RANDOLPH (*sharply*). Come away from the window, Sally. They might hurt you.

(SALLY *opens the window, and the carol, "Hark! the Herald Angels Sing," is heard from off stage.*)

SALLY. Nobody could sing carols like that without meaning them. They're giving a message of "Peace on earth, good will to men," if anyone ever did.

SYDNEY (*excitedly, jumping up*). Ike must have told them you're here, grandfather, and they're coming to honor you.

RANDOLPH (*bitterly*). Honor!

VOICES (*calling in confused chorus from off up center*). Mr. Randolph. Mr. Randolph.

SALLY (*insistently to* RANDOLPH, *coming to davenport*). Come to the window. They want to see you.

RANDOLPH (*half dazed*). What can it mean? What do they want of me now? My God! Haven't I been punished enough?

SALLY (*softly, helping* RANDOLPH *to rise*). They've come to give you Christmas greetings.

RANDOLPH (*rising feebly and walking hesitatingly to window, assisted by* SALLY *and* SYDNEY). Oh, it can't be! It can't be! (*As he appears at window, he stands center with* SYDNEY *at right of him.* SALLY *gets his coat and throws it around him. He puts an arm around her. Meanwhile, the chorus is singing. He speaks excitedly, looking off up cen-*

ter.) There's Ike—and old Mr. Wade—and Carrie Wessell —and poor Danny Keever!

SYDNEY (*also excited*). Look at the youngsters! They've brought all the children.

RANDOLPH. They always did.

(*The singing stops.*)

VOICES (*off up center, calling in confused chorus*). Merry Christmas, Mr. Randolph! Merry Christmas!

RANDOLPH, SALLY, *and* SYDNEY (*calling in concert*). Merry Christmas!

SYDNEY (*to* SALLY, *behind* RANDOLPH'S *back*). Sally, they always have come in. If they come now, we ought to have refreshments. What shall we do?

SALLY (*laughing excitedly*). Didn't you see? They all have baskets! (*Happily.*) Isn't this thrilling?

RANDOLPH (*calling out of window in a voice shaking with emotion*). My family and I cordially invite you to join us in celebrating this Christmas Eve.

VOICES (*loudly and in confused chorus from off up center*). Sure, we'll come! You bet! Oh, boy! Let's go!

SALLY (*dancing excitedly*). They're coming in! Oh, they're coming in!

RANDOLPH (*turning, straightening, and speaking with great dignity and the poise of a benign aristocrat*). Yes, they're coming in. You know they always do on Christmas Eve. (*To* SYDNEY.) Close the window, Sydney. (SYDNEY *closes the window. Off up center, "God Rest Ye, Merry Gentlemen" is sung very softly till the end of the play, as conversation continues.* RANDOLPH *takes candle from table left, and walks with strong step toward door up right center, speaking in an authoritative tone.*) Come, children. We must welcome our guests. They expect the whole family.

SALLY (*diffidently, moving toward davenport*). I'll clear the lunch things away.

SYDNEY (*grabbing* SALLY'S *arm and speaking decisively*). You'll come with us.

SALLY. No, no! Your grandfather is waiting for you. This is for the Randolphs. It's your home—and your happiness—and—and—it's just for the family. (*Half to herself.*) I don't belong to a family.

SYDNEY (*puzzled*). But—but—Sally!

RANDOLPH (*standing at door, turns, facing front and smiling*). Sally, my dear, you're in the family. You're the hostess. You're the one who saved the pride of the Randolphs to-night.

SALLY (*stubbornly*). It's sweet of you to try to include me, but I'm an outsider. I'm not a Randolph.

SYDNEY (*grimly, taking both* SALLY's *hands*). Well, you're going to be a Randolph just as soon as we can arrange it!

(*A very slight pause, as* SALLY *and* SYDNEY *look at each other in surprise.*)

RANDOLPH (*smiling gently*). Come, children. We must wish our neighbors "Merry Christmas."

(*Hand in hand,* SALLY *and* SYDNEY *start toward the door up right center.*)

CURTAIN

THE CHRISTMAS STAR

A CHRISTMAS PLAY IN FOUR SCENES

By

ETHEL DURNAL POSEGATE

PRODUCTION RIGHTS

CAST OF CHARACTERS

(For Four Men and Five Women)

GEORGE WORDEN .... the father
MARTHA WORDEN .... the mother
CLIF WORDEN .... ⎱
SHERYL WORDEN .... ⎰ 17-year-old twins
NANCY WORDEN .... 8-year-old daughter
DICK MONROE .... 18-year-old neighbor friend of Sheryl
FLO DESSERAY .... a movie star
MRS. CHADWICK .... Flo's grandmother
DR. LARRY SHIELDS .... childhood admirer of Flo's

TIME

SCENE ONE: Late afternoon.

SCENE TWO: Evening of the same day.

SCENE THREE: An extra scene which takes place early in the morning before most of the family has risen.

SCENE THREE: Mid-afternoon of the day before Christmas.

SETTING: *Only one stage setting is required. The living room of a well-to-do, modern rural family. A telephone is required. A decorated Christmas tree with packages at one side of the room, with a brightly lighted Christmas at the top. Several wrapped packages will be needed in the last act and material for wrappings.*

COSTUMES: *An expensive looking fur coat will be required for Flo Desseray in the first act. All her clothes should be of an expensive type, but in good taste and not gaudy. Costumes for the family—just ordinary and neat. Costumes for those who arrive in the plane should be appropriate and in good taste to fit the nature of the characters.*

THE CHRISTMAS STAR

SCENE ONE

AT THE RISE OF THE CURTAIN: *Mrs. Martha Worden is seated, knitting. Nancy is cutting out paper dolls. Sheryl is talking on the telephone.*

SHERYL. It surely is too bad, Dick. I know of course that we can't go tonight. Isn't it a shame? We had planned on such a nice time at the church party. *(Pause. Laughs.)* Yes, I know I said I had been praying for a white Christmas. I think everyone else had been praying too and we over-did it. *(Pause.)* Yes, that's what Daddy said. It looks like it's going to be too white as far as snow goes. He thinks we are in for a regular blizzard. *(Pause.)* Well, the same to you, Dick, if we don't get to see each other before Christmas. *(Pause.)* I will. Thanks. You say "Merry Christmas" to your folks too. Good bye, Dick. *(Replaces the phone.)* That was Dick.

NANCY. *No?* Well, to tell the truth, we had a hunch it must be some boy by that name. I'll bet you said "D-i-c-k" *(Drawls it out in exaggeration.)* twenty-five times at least, didn't she, Mother?

MRS. WORDEN. I wasn't counting "Dicks," honey, I was counting stitches. I did gather it was Dick though.

SHERYL. Well, anyway, he said to say "Merry Christmas" to all of you.

NANCY. That was a clever and original thought on his part.

MRS. WORDEN. Nancy, "Merry Christmas" is *always* a clever and original greeting when it is sincerely spoken. I appreciate his thoughtfulness, Sheryl, and I am truly sorry the storm is going to spoil the church festivities.

SHERYL. Thank you, *Mother.*

NANCY *(Laying aside her dolls and going over to Sheryl,*

putting her arm around her.) Well, I guess Mother put me in my place and I had it coming. I am sorry I was "snippy," Sheryl. To tell the truth I think about as much of Dick as you do and I am glad he said to say "Merry Christmas." Looks like we were going to need a lot of those to make it very merry. I didn't say it to be mean. I am feeling kinda low and disappointed myself, I guess.

SHERYL. That's all right, honey. Don't you get to feeling low. We always depend on you to keep us cheered up. *(Enter Mr. Worden and Clif. They have removed outside wraps before entering but are rubbing their hands and faces as though very cold.)*

MRS. WORDEN. My, I'm glad you finished with the chores early. You must be about frozen.

MR. WORDEN. It's getting colder by the hour. It's going to be a bitter night for man or beast.

CLIF. It's a good thing this came up before the crowd gathered at the church. It'll be a mess of a storm to be caught in.

NANCY. Did you put my pony Gypsy in where he will be nice and warm?

CLIF. That I did, Cricket. Gave him a few extra oats and patted him once for you. He nickered and rubbed my arm with his nose. I think he was sending a message to you.

NANCY *(Laughing.)* I'll bet he was too. I have a package of sugar all wrapped for his Christmas gift.

MR. WORDEN. I thought I heard a car up west on this road. Clif and I both went out to the road and looked and listened but couldn't see anything and we never heard it again, so guess it must have been the wind. It sure is howling.

CLIF. None of the neighbors would start out on this road, unless they were trying to get home. They all know how badly it drifts and blocks.

SHERYL. Dick called, Clif. He said to tell you he saw Susan and she was buying your Christmas gift.

CLIF. Hurray for Susan! I've had hers for over a week. I want you to help me wrap it up pretty, will you please?

SHERYL. Of course.

NANCY. It's a good thing Santa comes through the air or he'd never make it. We'll have to leave some hot coffee or cocoa out for him this time. *(A noise is heard outside. Clif and Mr. Worden both rise at once and go to the window.)*

CLIF. We did hear a car, Dad. One just drove in the yard. I can scarcely see it for the snow, it is blowing and snowing so hard. Come on, let's put on our wraps and see who it is. *(Clif and Mr. Worden exit. Others all look out the window.)*

SHERYL. I can see enough to know that is no neighbor's car.

NANCY *(Wiping off the window.)* Mother, does snow magnify? If it doesn't, that is the longest car I ever saw.

MRS. WORDEN. No, it doesn't magnify and that's no neighbor lady they're helping out of the car.

SHERYL. Do we have any rich relative who might be coming for Christmas?

MRS. WORDEN. None who notified us.

NANCY *(Still looking out the window.)* Well, *that* fur coat never came off a *rabbit.*

MRS. WORDEN. Who ever it is, we will make her welcome. I'm glad she found our place before she got stalled in a drift some place. *(Enter Mr. Worden and Clif, who have removed their wraps, and a young lady in her late twenties, dressed in an expensive fur coat with other clothing corresponding.)*

MR. WORDEN. Martha, this young lady evidently lost her way in the storm and how she ever got her car safely through the rapidly drifting roads I will never know. *(To the young lady.)* I don't know your name, but this is my wife, Mrs. Worden, our daughters, Sheryl and Nancy, and this is Clif, our son.

FLO *(Acknowledging the introduction.)* I am Flo Desseray. I was glad to see your house. I won't trouble you long. I just want to get you men to help me get on to the next town at once. I evidently turned off onto this isolated road, instead of following the highway. The snow was blowing so it was hard to see the signs. May we start now?

MR. WORDEN. *That,* my dear young lady, is an utter impossibility.

FLO. It can't be an impossibility. It is imperative that I

get to Omaha by tomorrow noon at the latest. I know all farmers have *some* kind of machinery to push stalled cars. My car is powerful in itself and won't cause you much trouble. Of course, I'll pay you extremely well for all your time and trouble.

MRS. WORDEN. Miss Desseray, do you seriously believe that my husband and son would allow you to start out on a night like this?

FLO. That is *exactly* what I'm thinking and plan to do. I'm not one to have my plans changed easily. Surely you won't object to make a handsome fee for yourselves. I thought farmers *always* needed money.

MR. WORDEN. Young woman, you are evidently a stranger in this part of the country, and unfamiliar with the treachery of a western plains blizzard. If it were at all possible to assist you on your journey tonight, my son and I would gladly do so and without any thought of "the handsome fee" to which you referred. But within a half hour's time, your *car*, our *tractor* and all of *us* would be hopelessly stalled in three or four-foot drifts of snow which could be twice that depth by morning.

FLO *(Angrily.)* Then what am I to do? I *have* to be in Omaha tomorrow.

NANCY. Just do like we had to do—forget it. We all had to be at a Christmas program at the church tonight too, but we won't be there. Even *I* had sense enough to know we couldn't go—long before the storm got *this* bad.

MRS. WORDEN. No doubt you are deeply disappointed, Miss Desseray, but you're most fortunate to have reached our house safely and you should offer up a prayer of thanks to God for His careful watch over you. You are most welcome to stay in our home as long as it is necessary.

FLO. *"Offer up a prayer of thanks!!"* And for *what* pray tell? I don't call it "careful watch over me" to be forced to give up all my plans and have to stay in a *farm* home. I say *curses* on such luck.

MR. WORDEN. Young lady, my wife told you that you were welcome to stay here but I'm going to add a proviso to the welcome part. You can stay certainly, but I will tell you frankly that no one is welcome in our home who has the effrontery to speak with blasphemy of God and what He sees fit to do, whether it be storm or anything else that interferes with original plans. This is our *home*. It *is* a *farm* home—and a Christian one. God be praised for both. If you wish to adjust yourself to our way of living and cease acting like a spoiled brat, we'll do what we can to make your stay pleasant. I regret extremely the need to speak to you in such a harsh manner, when you think you are already in deep trouble. But the sooner you realize the futility of going farther at this time, the better it will be for all concerned. We can all have a happy time here together. Christmas is a joyous time in this household, and we intend that it shall aways be. *(Goes over and offers Flo his hand.)* Let's be good friends.

FLO *(Breaking into tears and meekly offering her hand.)* Forgive me, please. I *am* a spoiled brat. I feel so helpless.

SHERYL. Would you like to make a phone call to wherever you were going? If so, perhaps you should do so now. Sometimes the telephone lines "go out" during storms of this kind.

FLO *(Wiping her eyes.)* Oh yes, that would be wonderful. Do you have phones in the country?

CLIF. Certainly we have telephones. Who needs them more than farmers? I can see you need to be brought up to date on your knowledge of farming.

FLO. I guess I need to be brought up to date on several things. I seem to have had a very wrong impression all the way around. I would love to place a call to New York.

MRS. WORDEN. There is the phone. *(Indicating it.)* You go right ahead. We must all go out and see about getting some supper started. You can phone in privacy. *(All start to exit and Flo starts toward the phone as the curtain falls.)*

SCENE TWO

The setting remains the same as Scene One. It is evening. All are seated around the living room.

FLO. How right you were, Mrs. Worden, when you said I should "Thank God for His careful watch over me!" If it hadn't been for this delay by the storm, I would have gone on to Omaha as planned and taken a plane on to New York, only to have found I had made the trip for nothing. I shudder at what a fool I would have made of myself.

MRS. WORDEN. Do not feel you have to tell us *anything*, Miss Desseray. I know your call to New York was another disappointment to you and we are sorry.

FLO. You might as well know what a silly fool I was. I was advised by all my friends in Hollywood, not to undertake the trip alone at this time of year. For the first time, here in the peaceful atmosphere of your lovely home, I can see what a willful, obstinate, useless, and vain creature I have become. I became infatuated with this man in New York when he came to Hollywood on business. I've been hearing from him right along. I wanted him to come to Hollywood for Christmas. He phoned me a few days ago that he couldn't come but gave me no logical reason. I decided to go to him. That phone call this evening informed me that he was a married man and had gone back to his wife.

NANCY. He's lucky she would have him back. *(All laugh.)*

FLO. You are so right, honey. I should be a horrible example to you girls. I am so humiliated.

CLIF. I *thought* I recognized you as one of the movie stars when I first saw you. We don't go to too many shows, being in school and all, but we've seen your picture lots of times in magazines.

NANCY. Those are mostly the kind of pictures that Mother and Daddy "sent-sure." Is that the right word, Mother?

MRS. WORDEN. Yes, the word is censure.

NANCY *(Continuing.)* Censure for us. I don't like 'em anyway. Too "squashy." I like fairy story pictures or horse pictures. The kind where it tells the story of a horse's life. It's a good thing I like that kind. That's all I would get to see anyway. *(All laugh.)*

FLO. You're a fortunate little girl to have parents who take the trouble to select the kind of pictures for you to see. You be sure to do as they tell you. Believe me, you'll never be sorry.

MR. WORDEN. Where do your people live?

FLO. I don't have a *real* family. My mother died of a broken heart after my father's tragic death, when I was about five years old. After that I had to go to live with my grandmother. I thought she was too strict and I know I made her life miserable. I won a beauty contest and that was the beginning of a series of events that led me to stardom. I can see now as I look back, that winning a beauty contest is often the worst thing that can happen to a girl. Grandmother could do nothing with me after that.

MRS. WORDEN. I have always felt that when a girl won a contest on physical beauty alone, it was a great misfortune.

NANCY. You'll never have to worry about that with me, will you, Mother? *(All laugh.)*

FLO. You have the kind of beauty that counts, young lady. Beauty of soul, beauty of thought, and a home foundation of common sense and humor. Keep cultivating it all your life. It is priceless.

MR. WORDEN. You have made money and have become a star, but has it made up, I wonder, for what you lost in not leading a normal life?

FLO. In being a star, Mr. Worden, I must confess that all that glitters is not real star-dust. I made good money—yes—lots of it. I am ashamed to say, however, that all I own is that foreign-made car sitting out in your yard, and a horribly extravagant wardrobe and a few hundred dollars in the bank. All has gone for show, or to impress others, and waiting for the next big check to "fritter" away. Now I am ashamed to ever go back. Everyone will know I am a jilted woman.

NANCY. Now what does that mean?

FLO. It simply means that this man from New York turned me down.

NANCY. Humph! I wouldn't worry about him. He wasn't really a man anyway if he treated his wife that way.

FLO. Child, you certainly have a knack for hitting the nail on the head—and hard. You said a true mouthful that time.

SHERYL. Why don't you surprise your grandmother by

calling her and then go on to see her when the roads clear?

MRS. WORDEN. I was going to suggest that, too. You have no idea how much it would please her.

FLO. I think I will. Suddenly I feel the need of her after all these years. I can see I have missed everything worthwhile in life, by not having a real family and by not appreciating what I did have.

SHERYL. Aren't you a singer, Flo? I think it would be nice to sing some Christmas carols this evening.

FLO. Yes—I am a singer. I'm afraid the songs I sing haven't been Christmas carols. I haven't sung any of those since I was a young girl in school. I do love them. Do you play, Sheryl?

CLIF. Oh yes, Sheryl plays fine.

NANCY. You don't do so bad yourself, Clif, on your saxaphone. *(Optional.)* Go get it and let's *do* sing. *(If an instrument is used, Clif goes and gets it.)*

MR. WORDEN. Now you are talking my language. I was just waiting to get in a word edgewise to suggest that we sing carols. That puts cheer into a stormy night. We can sing loud and drown out the howling wind.

NANCY. Bear down hard on those low bass notes, Daddy. I love 'em. Mother, I'll stand over here by you, so you can help me with the alto. Sometimes I don't know whether to go up or down and I sort of scatter all over the place.

CLIF. Nothing wrong with your singing, Cricket. As long as you know when you are off key, you're all right. *(Here as much of a Christmas musical program may be interpolated as desired. Each person suggests carols and special numbers.)*

MR. WORDEN. That was a fine Christmas program. Sort of took the place of the party at the church. *(Rises.)* Well, Mother, I want to take a look outside and see if the storm is subsiding any, and see if all is well with the stock.

MRS. WORDEN. I have a few things I want to do in the kitchen. Tomorrow is the last day before Christmas and will be a busy day for us all. Flo, now will be a good time for you to call your grandmother. I hope you can still get through on the line.

FLO. Yes, that's what I will do. It will probably frighten her half to death. I do call her once every few months though. *(Starts to the phone.)*

MRS. WORDEN. I have an idea it will mean more to her than you will ever know. *(All start to exit and exchange goodnight greetings. The curtain falls.)*

SCENE THREE

After a short lapse of time the curtain is opened revealing an empty stage. The telephone is ringing. It is early morning. Mrs. Worden enters wearing a housecoat and answers the phone, speaking softly as though not to disturb a sleeping household.

MRS. WORDEN *(Picking up the phone.)* Hello—*(Pause.)* Yes, this is the George Worden residence. *(Pause.)* Yes, she is here. She is not up yet. No one is up except my husband and myself. *(Pause.)* You say you wanted to speak to me anyway? *(Pause.)* No, it isn't storming here this morning. The storm blew itself out during the night. The drifts are enormous though. *(Pause.)* Oh yes, I see. *(Pause.)* That would be wonderful. *(Pause.)* Well, I can't tell you that. I haven't looked out that way. Just a minute—I'll ask my husband what *he* thinks. *(Pause.)* Oh, it is that kind. Well, keep the line open just a few minutes. *(Exits and returns in a short time smiling to herself. Picks up the phone and speaks softly.)* Hello. Mr. Worden says he thinks it could be managed at this end of the line. *(Pause.)* Oh, indeed, *yes.* More than welcome. *(Pause.)* No, we won't. Not a word to anyone. My husband said you should check with the weather stations as to the location and the nature of the storm. *(Pause.)* Fine. That will be great. Good luck. Goodbye. *(Exits.)*

CURTAIN

SCENE FOUR

It is mid-afternoon. Flo and Sheryl are busily engaged at a table wrapping some gifts.

FLO. This is going to be my very nicest Christmas after

all. I had lost all the true meaning of Christmas someplace along the line, in the mad scramble of the "make believe" world in which I've been living. Everything there is judged from a monetary standpoint. Every gift had to out-do the other person's and be showy above all else. It has been anything but the calm, peaceful love-filled festivity I see now that it should be.

SHERYL. Yes, we all love Christmas and always have most of our gifts and plans made well ahead of time so we won't be too busy and hurried at the last minute to enjoy the real meaning of the day. We make most of our gifts to each other during the year, keeping it secret of course. That keeps the spirit alive all during the year.

FLO. I went through my things and I believe I have found something for each of you. Of course yours is already wrapped and on the tree. Nancy will like this set of tiny adjustable bracelets, and this autographed picture of Roy Rogers and family, including "Trigger," of course. She loves *her* pony "Gypsy" so much I'm sure she will prize the picture. Otherwise I wouldn't part with it. Roy autographed it for me, but I know how much it will mean to Nancy.

SHERYL. Flo, you shouldn't do it. You know, of course, that Nancy will prize that more than anything, for "Trigger" is by far her favorite movie star. You doing this for her will put you a close second to Trigger. *(Both laugh.)*

FLO. I am wrapping this silk scarf and lace collar and cuff set for your mother. I bought them in Paris last summer, but have never worn them.

SHERYL. They are lovely, Flo. Mother will be so thrilled.

FLO. I have some cash in each of these envelopes, one for your father and one for Clif. I put on the card for your father, "From *The Spoiled Brat* whom you reformed."

SHERYL *(Laughing.)* Father will get a big laugh out of that. *(Enter Mrs. Worden and Nancy with several packages.)*

NANCY. Everybody shut their eyes so you can't see what Mother and I have or where we put them around the tree. It might be something for you. You never can tell. *(Sheryl and Flo quickly cover the things on the table.)*

SHERYL. Say! That goes for you too, young lady.

FLO. Everybody will have to ring a warning bell when they come in here. Santa is busy at work.

NANCY. Flo—Mother, may I say Flo and not Miss Desseray?

FLO. Say yes, Mrs. Worden. I want to be one of the family.

MRS. WORDEN. You may, dear. What did you start to say to Flo?

NANCY. Flo, I just thought of something awhile ago. See that Christmas star on the top of our tree? It always holds top place. This year we have *another* Christmas "Star."

FLO. Oh, have you? Did you get a new one?

NANCY. It *came* to us. I mean *you*, Flo. You are a "Star" and you came to us at Christmas, so you are another Christmas *"Star."*

FLO *(Deeply affected and thoughtful.)* Thank you, honey. That is my highest compliment. You are a most clever little girl. I am afraid I have been a very dim Christmas Star up to now, but thanks to this wonderful family, I'm going to try to "let my light shine" to a much better advantage from now on. Nancy, I'll never forget that you called me a "Christmas Star" and I'm going to try to live up to the compliment. *(A knock is heard. Sheryl goes to the door, speaking as she goes.)*

SHERYL. This is probably Clif trying to fool us. *(Opens the door.)* Dick!! Oh, you dear. Of all people. How in the world did you get here? *(Enter Dick Monroe with several packages. Sheryl continues.)* Dick, this is Flo Desseray. This is my friend, Dick Monroe. *(Natural introductions are acknowledged.)*

DICK. Are you *"The"* Flo Desseray?

FLO. I am afraid I am.

DICK *(To Sheryl.)* I saw that huge, good-looking new car out in your yard and I was afraid I had some competition.

SHERYL *(Laughing.)* I doubt if you were too worried about anything like that. We want to know how you ever got here through all this snow.

DICK. I rode over on horseback. I cut across the fields and by letting "Ginger" pick his way I had very little trouble. I think Ginger knew where I was trying to go and did his best. *(All laugh. Hands the packages to Sheryl.)* Here are some gifts I wanted you to have for your exchange tonight, if possible.

MRS. WORDEN. Can't you stay for our Christmas exchange this evening?

NANCY. Sure you can, Dick. I know you don't have your opening of gifts until Christmas morning, 'cause your brother Max told me.

DICK *(Looking at Sheryl.)* I would love to stay.

SHERYL. Now I really *do* believe in Santa Claus. I just never once dreamed you could get over it, but this just makes everything ideal. *(Enter Clif.)*

CLIF. Hi, Dick. Sure glad to see you. I saw Ginger tied out in the yard just now. Dad and I were busy in the barn and didn't hear you when you came. How were the roads?

DICK. They were well protected. I never saw them at all. I cut across the fields.

NANCY. That Ginger knew where he wanted to come. He knew I would probably have some sugar for him. I'll wrap up some for him like I have fixed for Gypsy.

CLIF. I nearly forgot to tell you. Dad told me to come in and tell you we heard an airplane and it keeps circling around. I am afraid it's in trouble. There! I heard it now. *(All go to the window but Flo.)*

NANCY. My land! It landed right out the other side of our barn. We have more excitement around this place.

SHERYL. I hope no one was hurt.

CLIF. A man and a woman are coming to the house with Dad.

FLO. Do airplanes even get stranded in the air, from blizzards?

MRS. WORDEN *(Going to the door.)* Welcome, folks. Come right in. *(Enter Mr. Worden, an elderly lady and a man about thirty years of age. Mr. Worden has removed his wraps. The others are dressed in appropriate attire for air travel.)*

FLO *(In great surprise.) Grandmother! (They embrace. She looks at the young man a moment, then speaks.) Larry Shields! (Shakes hands.)*

MRS. CHADWICK. Flo dear, it's so good to see you.

FLO *(Looking at Mr. and Mrs. Worden.)* Excuse me, all. I am so overcome by surprise and joy I forgot everything else. This is my grandmother, Mrs. Chadwick, and this is Larry Shields. This is Mr. and Mrs. Worden, Sheryl, Nancy and Cliff and this is Dick Monroe. *(All acknowledge introductions in a natural manner. Do not hurry the scene, make it natural.)*

SHERYL. Mother, you and Daddy didn't seem very surprised.

MRS. WORDEN. All of you find chairs and remove your wraps. Well, we were *not* surprised. In fact, your father and I have been hoping and praying for the plane's safe arrival for the past hour or so. We received a phone call from Mrs. Chadwick early this morning, before anyone else was out of bed, wanting to know if we thought a ski-plane could land any place near here. Now, Mrs. Chadwick, you take it from there.

MRS. CHADWICK. Flo dear, after your call last night I phoned Dr. Larry right away. You don't know what a loyal friend you've had in Larry ever since your school days. He has never forgotten you or ceased to be your ardent "fan" although you never knew it.

FLO. How wonderful, Larry!

LARRY. You're the one who is wonderful. You have gone far and all on your own. I couldn't help but admire your ability to succeed.

MRS. CHADWICK. Well—as I said—I called Larry. He had the idea of making the trip out here in his ski-plane. You know Larry hasn't done badly himself, Flo. He's a wonderful doctor. He has to have this kind of a plane to make emergency calls.

FLO. How wonderful, Larry! Congratulations!

LARRY. Thank you, Flo.

MRS. CHADWICK. The idea really appealed to me. Larry has been almost like a son to me. He has taken me up so many times in his plane, he has made a real air traveler out of me. I called, as Mrs. Worden said, and that is about the whole story.

LARRY. I took the liberty of bringing my chauffeur along to drive your car back to your grandmother's as soon as the roads are cleared. We left him at a small town not too far away from here where he has a sister, with whom he was delighted to spend Christmas.

FLO. How very, very thoughtful of you, Larry! It suddenly seems grand to have someone take an interest in my welfare just because he really likes me.

LARRY. I hope you continue to feel that way.

NANCY. She will. I think she has had enough being a movie star. Right now she is our *Christmas* "Star" and has she made our Christmas *bright*.

FLO. Nancy here has given me the finest title I have ever had and I'm going to do my very best to try to live to be worthy of being called *"A Christmas Star."*

CURTAIN